*Institutions of
Higher Education*

**Recent Titles in
Bibliographies and Indexes in Education**

Integrating Women's Studies into the Curriculum: An Annotated Bibliography
Susan Douglas Franzosa and Karen A. Mazza, compilers

Teacher Evaluation and Merit Pay: An Annotated Bibliography
Elizabeth Lueder Karnes and Donald D. Black, compilers

The Education of Poor and Minority Children: A World Bibliography, Supplement, 1979-1985
Meyer Weinberg, compiler

Comparative Reading: An International Bibliography
John Hladczuk and William Eller, compilers

Higher Education in American Life 1636-1986: A Bibliography of Dissertations and Theses
Arthur P. Young, compiler

Literacy/Illiteracy in the World: A Bibliography
John Hladczuk, William Eller, and Sharon Hladczuk, compilers

Career Index: A Selective Bibliography for Elementary Schools
Gretchen S. Baldauf, compiler

Institutions of Higher Education

AN INTERNATIONAL BIBLIOGRAPHY

Compiled by
LINDA SPARKS

Bibliographies and Indexes in Education,
Number 9

GREENWOOD PRESS
New York • Westport, Connecticut • London

Library of Congress Cataloging-in-Publication Data

Sparks, Linda.
　　Institutions of higher education : an international bibliography / compiled by Linda Sparks.
　　　p.　cm. — (Bibliographies and indexes in education, ISSN 0742-6917 ; no. 9)
　　Includes bibliographical references.
　　ISBN 0-313-26686-7 (alk. paper)
　　1. Universities and colleges—History—Bibliography.　I. Title. II. Series.
Z5814.U7S69　1990
[LA173]
016.378—dc20　　　　89-29355

British Library Cataloguing in Publication Data is available.

Copyright © 1990 by Linda Sparks

All rights reserved. No portion of this book may be reproduced, by any process or technique, without the express written consent of the publisher.

Library of Congress Catalog Card Number: 89-29355
ISBN: 0-313-26686-7
ISSN: 0742-6917

First published in 1990

Greenwood Press, Inc.
88 Post Road West, Westport, Connecticut 06881

Printed in the United States of America

The paper used in this book complies with the Permanent Paper Standard issued by the National Information Standards Organization (Z39.48-1984).

10 9 8 7 6 5 4 3 2 1

Contents

Preface	ix
Afghanistan	1
Antigua and Barbuda	1
Argentina	2
Australia	3
Austria	7
Bangladesh	9
Barbados	9
Belgium	10
Bolivia	11
Brazil	11
Bulgaria	13
Burma	13
Canada	13
Channel Islands	28
Chile	28
China	28
Colombia	30
Costa Rica	31
Cuba	32
Czechoslovakia	32

Denmark	33
Dominican Republic	34
Ecuador	34
Egypt	35
El Salvador	35
Ethiopia	35
Finland	36
France	37
German Democratic Republic	39
Germany, Federal Republic of	41
Ghana	50
Great Britian	
England	51
Northern Ireland	79
Scotland	79
Wales	82
Greece	83
Guatemala	83
Honduras	84
Hong Kong	84
Hungary	85
Iceland	85
India	85
Indonesia	88
Iraq	89
Ireland	89
Israel	91
Italy	91
Ivory Coast	97
Jamaica	97
Japan	97
Kenya	103
Lebanon	103
Liberia	104
Malawi	104
Mexico	104
Netherlands	107
New Zealand	108
Nicaragua	109
Nigeria	110
Norway	112
Pakistan	112
Peru	113
Phillipines	113
Poland	115
Portugal	117
Puerto Rico	118
Romania	119

Saudi Arabia	119
Sierra Leone	120
South Africa	120
Spain	122
Sri Lanka	126
Sweden	126
Switzerland	127
Thailand	129
Taiwan	129
Trinidad and Tobago	130
Turkey	130
Uganda	130
Union of Soviet Socialist Republics	131
United States	
Alabama	132
Alaska	138
Arizona	138
Arkansas	140
California	142
Colorado	158
Connecticut	161
Delaware	166
District of Columbia	166
Florida	170
Georgia	173
Hawaii	180
Idaho	181
Illinois	182
Indiana	194
Iowa	203
Kansas	208
Kentucky	212
Louisiana	218
Maine	221
Maryland	224
Massachusetts	229
Michigan	242
Minnesota	249
Mississippi	254
Missouri	259
Montana	266
Nebraska	267
Nevada	270
New Hampshire	270
New Jersey	273
New Mexico	280
New York	281
North Carolina	304

North Dakota 312
Ohio 314
Oklahoma 327
Oregon 330
Pennsylvania 333
Rhode Island 351
South Carolina 353
South Dakota 358
Tennessee 360
Texas 370
Utah 388
Vermont 390
Virginia 392
Washington 402
West Virginia 406
Wisconsin 409
Wyoming 413
Uruguay 414
Venezuela 415
Viet Nam 416
Yugoslavia 416

Author Index 417
Subject Index 455

Preface

This bibliography is an attempt to bring together in one comprehensive source citations of books, dissertations, theses, and ERIC microfiche relating to the history of specific institutions of higher education worldwide. All types of postsecondary institutions - two year colleges, liberal arts colleges, seminaries, specialized institutions, and universities - have been included.

Entries are by country, dependency, and territory. The United States has been further divided by state. Names of institutions are in English. References are in the language in which they were written. Generally histories of departments and schools within a university are not included. There are exceptions such as the University of Cambridge and the University of Oxford.

When a school has merged or changed name, the citation has been put under the present name. An asterisk (*) after the school name indicates that its status could not be verified. For consistency, names beginning with Saint and St. are alphabetized under Saint.

The references were found in many places. Most were verified and/or found in OCLC, RLIN, *Dictionary Catalog of the Teachers College Library, United*

States Department of Health, Education and Welfare Catalog, National Union Catalog, and *Dissertation Abstracts.* Some master's theses were verified with the schools at which they were written. The majority of the citations should be available in U. S. libraries. Obscure sources that may be difficult to obtain have been included because they are often the only citation. All editions of a title as well as older works are included because of their potential value to a researcher.

Entries include the following elements when available: author/editor, title, place of publication, publisher, date, and number of pages.

Sincere appreciation is extended to the many people who helped with this project, especially Bill Covey and Tom Kinney.

AFGHANISTAN

Kabul University

Zai, Baqui Y. "The Goals of Kabul University: An Historical Approach." Ph.D. diss., Indiana University, 1974. 158 pp. *Dissertation Abstracts International,* vol. 35A, p. 6489.

ANTIGUA AND BARBUDA

University of the West Indies

University of the West Indies (St. John's, Antigua). University Centre. *10th Anniversary, 1967-1977.* St. John's, Antigua: Antigua University Centre, University of the West Indies, 1977. 40 pp.

ARGENTINA

National University of Cordoba

Diaz Castillo, Roberto. *La reforma universitaria de Cordoba.* Guatemala: Universidad de San Carlos de Guatemala, 1971. 79 pp.

Garro, Juan M. *Bosque historico de la Universidad de Cordoba, con un apendice de documentos.* Buenos Aires: Impr. de M. Biedma, 1882. 540 pp.

Pueyrredon, Alfredo. *Algunos aspectos de la ensenanza en la Universidad de Cordoba durante la regencia franciscana.* Cordoba, Republica Argentina: Direccion General de Publicidad de la Universidad Nacional, 1953. 56 pp.

Tunnermann, Bernheim C. *Sesenta y cinco anos de la reforma universitaria de Cordoba, 1918-1983.* Managua, J. R., Nicaragua: Ediciones Distribuidora Cultural, 1983. 103 pp.

--------. *Sesenta anos de la reforma Universitaria de Corboda, 1918-1978.* Ciudad Universitaria Rogrigo Facio: Editorial Universitaria Centroamericana, 1978. 103 pp.

River Plate College*

Wenstell, Egil. H. "River Plate College: An Historical Study of a Missionary Institution, 1898-1951." Ed.D. diss., Andrews University, 1982. 380 pp. *Dissertation Abstracts International,* vol. 43A, p. 1064.

University of Buenos Aires

Amadeo, Jaime. *La universidad condicionada: la Universidad de Buenos Aires y su lugar en el proyecto politico del siglo XIV.* Buenos Aires: C.I.E., 1976. 231 pp.

Halperin Donghi, Tulio. *Historia de la Universidad de Buenos Aires.* Buenos Aires: Editorial Universitaria de Buenos Aires, 1962. 227 pp.

AUSTRALIA

Assumption College

Carroll, Raymond W. *The Fields Are Green: Assumption College, Kilmore: Chronicles of a Country Boarding School.* Kilmore, Vic.: Lowden Publishing, 1976. 192 pp.

Australian National University

The Australian National University: The History of the Site Plan, 1912-1971. Canberra: Australian National University, 1973. 31 pp.

Bendigo College of Advanced Education

Burnett, J. C. *History of Bendigo Teachers' College, 1926-1973.* Bendigo, Victoria: Cambridge Pr., 1973.

Christian Brothers College*

Moore, Peter L. *Pride of the Hills: The Story of Rostrevor House.* Blackwood, S. A.: Lynton Publishers, 1975. 187 pp.

Clarendon College*

Clarke, Jan, and Cochran, Margaret. *The Lamp Burns Brightly; The First Century of Clarendon College, Ballarat, 1868-1968.* Ballarat, Vic.: Clarendon College, 1971. 120 pp.

Cumberland College of Health Sciences

Rodgers, John A. *A Quest for Change: Cumberland College of Health Sciences, 1973-1983.* 2d ed. Lidcombe, N. S. W.: The College, 1986. 284 pp.

Duntroon Royal Military College

Coulthard-Clark, Christopher D. *Duntroon: The Military College of Australia, 1911-1986.* Sydney: Allen & Unwin, 1986. 367 pp.

Gippsland Institute of Advanced Education

Meek, Vincent L. *Brown Coal or Plato?: A Study of the Gippsland Institute of Advanced Education.* Victoria: Australian Council for Educational Research, 1984. 297 pp.

Gordon Technical College*

Long, Gordon. *The Gordon: A Century of Influence.* Greenlong, Vic.: Gordon Technical College, 1987. 304 pp.

Graylands Teachers College*

Reilly, Cam. *The Graylands Story.* Graylands, W. A.: Graylands Teachers College, 1979. 149 pp.

Melbourne College of Advanced Education

Garden, Donald S. *The Melbourne Teacher Training Colleges: From Training Institution to Melbourne State College, 1870-1982.* Melbourne: Heinemann Educational Australia, 1982. 298 pp.

Sweetman, Edward. *History of the Melbourne Teachers' College and Its Predecessors.* Capetown, Melbourne: Melbourne University Pr., 1939. 144 pp.

Mercy Teachers College

Mercy Teachers' College: 75 Years of Catholic Teacher Education, 1908-1984. Ascot Vale, Victoria: Institute of Catholic Education. 1984. 184 pp. ERIC Microfiche ED 251 382.

Monash University

Blackwood, Robert. *Monash University, the First Ten Years.* Melbourne: Hampden Hall, 1968. 262 pp.

Matheson, James A. L. *Still Learning.* South Melbourne, Vic.: Macmillan, 1980. 180 pp.

Murdoch University

Bolton, Geoffrey C. *It Had Better Be a Good One: The Years of Murdoch University.* Perth, W. A.: Murdoch University, 1985. 75 pp.

Ormond College*

Macintyre, Stuart, ed. *Ormond College, Centenary Essays.* Carlton, Vic.: Melbourne University Pr., 1984. 206 pp.

Royal Melbourne Institute of Technology

Murray-Smith, Stephen, and Dare, Anthony J. *The Tech: A Centenary History of the Royal Melbourne Institute of Technology.* South Yarra, Vic.: Hyland House, 1987. 495 pp.

St. Stanislaus College*

Hall, John. *History of St. Stanislaus College, Bathurst, Including St. Charles Seminary (1867 to May 24th, 1944).* Bathurst, N.S.W.: St. Stanislaus College, 1944. 225 pp.

School of Mines and Industry, Ballarat*

Perry, Warren. *The School of Mines and Industries Ballaret: A History of Its First One Hundred and Twelve Years, 1870-1982.* Ballarat: School of Mines and Industry Ballarat, 1984. 635 pp.

University of Adelaide

Duncan, Walter G. K., and Leonard, Roger A. *The University of Adelaide, 1874-1974.* Adelaide: Rigby, 1973. 203 pp.

Price, Archibald G. *A History of St. Mark's College, University of Adelaide and the Foundation of the Residential College Movement.* Adelaide: Council of St. Mark's College, 1968. 112 pp.

University of Adelaide. *Centenary, 1874-1974.* Adelaide: University of Adelaide, 1973. 54 pp.

Woodburn, S. *The Founding of a University: The First Decade.* Adelaide: University of Adelaide, 1983. 15 pp.

University of Melbourne

Bechervaise, John M. *University of Melbourne: An Illustrated Perspective.* Carlton, Vic.: Melbourne University Pr., 1985. 86 pp.

Blainey, Geoffrey. *A Centenary History of the University of Melbourne.* Melbourne: University Pr., 1957. 220 pp.

--------. *The University of Melbourne; A Centenary Portrait.* Carlton: Melbourne University Pr., 1956. 176 pp.

Grant, James. *Perspective of a Century: A Volume for the Centenary of Trinity College, Melbourne, 1872-1972.* Melbourne: Council of Trinity College, 1972. 202 pp.

Scott, Ernest. *A History of the University of Melbourne.* Melbourne: Melbourne University Pr., 1936. 226 pp.

Trinity College, University of Melbourne. *The Foundation Era, 1872-1918: Trinity College Centenary Exhibition.* Parkville, Vic.: Trinity College, 1972. 11 pp.

University of New England

Black, Hermann, D. *Silver Jubilee Oration.* Armindale, N. S. W.: University of New England, 1979. 15 pp.

University of New South Wales

Willis, Albert H. *The University of New South Wales: The Baxter Years.* Kensington, N.S.W.: New South Wales University Pr., 1983. 231 pp.

University of Queensland

Brotherton, Hilda. *A College is Built.* Brisbane: Women's College Old Collegians' Association, 1973. 101 pp.

Queensland. University, Brisbane. *An Account of the* University of *Queensland During Its First Twenty-Five Years, 1910-1935.* Brisbane: Published by the Authority of the Senate. 1935. 96 pp.

--------. *The University of Queensland, 1910-1922.* Brisbane: A. J. Cumming, 1923. 93 pp.

--------. *The University of Queensland Jubilee Celebrations, 25, 26, and*

27 May 1960. Melbourne: University of Queensland Pr., 1966. 72 pp.

Thomis, Malcolm I. *A Place of Light & Learning: The University of Queensland's First Seventy-Five Years.* St. Lucia: University of Queensland Pr., 1985. 429 pp.

University of Queensland: A Portrait. Brisbane: University of Queensland Pr., 1985. 24 pp.

University of Sydney

Barff, Henry E. *Short Historical Account of the University of Sydney.* Sydney: Angus & Robertson, 1902. 162 pp.

Dallen, Robert A. *The University of Sydney; Its History and Progress from Its Foundation in 1852 to 1938, Together with Short Biographical Sketches of Its Ten Chancellors.* Sydney: Angus & Robertson, 1938. 60 pp.

Sydney. University. *The University of Sydney, 1850-1975: Some History in Pictures to Mark the 125th Year of Its Incorporation.* Sydney: University of Sydney, 1975. 132 pp.

Wesley College, Melbourne. *The History of Wesley College.* 2 vols. Melbourne: McCarron, Bird and Co., 1921-1941.

University of Western Australia

Cotter, D. *Farmers Ringmasters and Builders: A History of Kingswood College, Box Hill.* Box Hill, Vic.: Kingswood College, 1985. 198 pp.

Hasluck, Nicholas. *College: Recollections and Images of the University of Western Australia.* Fremantle: Fremantle Arts Center Pr., 1987. 137 pp.

Stewart, Noel. *St. Catherine's College, from Dream to Reality, 1928-1978.* Perth, Western Australia: St. Catherine's College, 1978. 77 pp.

AUSTRIA

University of Graz

Krones, Franz von. *Geschichte der Karl Franzens-Universitat in Graz: Festgabe zur Feier ihres dreihundertjahrigen Bestandes.* Graz: Verlag der Karl Franzens-Universitat, 1886. 684 pp.

Schauenstein, Adolf. *Die ersten drei Jahrhunderte der Karl-Franzens-Universitat in Graz.* Graz: Leuschner & Lubensky, Universitats-buchhandlung, 1886. 23 pp.

Smekal, Ferdinand G. *Alma Universitas: die Geschichte der Grazer Universitat in vier Jahrhunderten.* Wien: Verlag Eine Welt der Vereinten Nationen, 1967. 290 pp.

Die Universitat Graz: Jubilaumsband 1827-1977: ein Funfjahr-Buch. Graz: Akademische Druckund Verlagsanstalt, 1977. 224 pp.

University of Innsbruck

Holbing, Franz. *300 Jahre Universitas Oenipontana. Die Leopold-Franzens- Universitat zu Innsbruck u. ihre Studenten. Zur 300-Jahr-Feier.* Innsbruck: Verl. d. Tiroler Nachrichten, 1970 280 pp.

Innsbruck. Universitat. *Die Leopold-Franzens-Universitat zu Innsbruck in den Jahren 1848-1898.* Innsbruck: Verlag der Wagnerschen Universitats-buchhandlung, 1899. 264 pp.

Probst, Jacob. *Geschichte der Universitat Innsbruck seit ihrer Entstehung zum Jahre 1860.* Innsbruck: n.p., 1869. 412 pp.

University of Salzburg

Muhlbock, Annemarie. *Die Pflege der Geschichte an der alten Universitat Salzburg.* Wein: Geyer, 1973. 148 pp.

Wagner, Hans, and Wicha, Barbara, eds. *Festschrift.* Salzburg: Pustet, 1972. 386 pp.

University of Vienna

Aschbach, Joseph, Ritter von. *Geschichte der Wiener universitat.* 3 vols. Wien: Verlag der K. K. Universitat, 1865-88.

Gall, Franz. *Die Alte Universitat.* Wein: Zsolnay, 1970. 133 pp.

Kink, Rudolf. *Geschichte der Kaiserlichen Universitat zu Wien.* 2 vols. Wein: C. Gerold & Sohn, 1854.

--------. *Geschichte der Kaiserlichen Universitat zu Wien.* 3 vols. Frankfurt: Minerva-Verlag, 1969.

Singer, Walter E. "A Study of the Early History of the University of Vienna from the Foundation Through the Supremacy of Humanistic Thought: 1365-1500." Ed.D. diss., University of Houston, 1971. 291 pp. *Dissertation Abstracts International,* vol. 32A, p. 2453.

Universitat Wien. Katholisch-Theologische Fakultat. *Der Katholische Charakter der Wiener Universitat: eine Denkschrift* der theologischen *Facultat.* Wien: Mechitharisten-Congregations-Buchhandlung, 1863. 163 pp.

Vienna. Universitat. Akademischer Senat. *Geschichte der Wiener Universitat von 1848 bis 1898. Als Hundigungsfestschrift zum funfzigjahrigen Reierungsjubilaum des Kaisers Franz Josef I.* Wien: In Commission be: A. Holder, 1898. 436 pp.

Wolf, G. *Zur geschichte der Wiener universitat.* Wein: A. Holder, 1883. 242 pp.

BANGLADESH

University of Dacca

Rahim, M. A. *The History of the University of Dacca.* Dacca: University of Dacca, 1981. 266 pp.

Stock, Amy G. *Memoirs of Dacca University, 1947-1951.* Dacca: Green Book House, 1973. 202 pp.

BARBADOS

Codrington College

Langley, Nina. *Christopher Codrington and His College.* London: S.P.C.K., 1964. 64 pp.

Simmons, George C. "The History of Codrington College, Barbados, 1710-1875." Ph.D. diss., Harvard University, 1963. 70 pp.

Presentation College*

Recte et Fortiter: Presentation College, Barbados, Silver Jubilee, 1958/59-1983/84. Barbados: Presentation College, 1984. 92 pp.

BELGIUM

Catholic University of Louvain

Denis, Valentin. *Catholic University of Louvain, 1425-1958.* Louvain: n.p., 1958. 247 pp.

Essen, Leon van der. *Une institution d'enseignement superieur, sous l'ancien regime, L'universite de Louvain (1425-1797).* Paris: Vromant & cie, 1921. 156 pp.

--------. *De Universiteit te Leuven: haar instaan, haar geschiedenis, haar organisatie, 1425-1953.* Brussel: Office de Publicite, 1955. 39 pp.

Lousse, Emile. *The University of Louvain during the Second World War.* Burges: Desclee, de Brouwer, 1946. 94 pp.

Louvain. Universite Catholique. *Universite de Louvain, 1425-1834-1905.* Louvain: J. Van Linthout, 1905. 35 pp.

Reusens, Edmond H. J. *Documents relatifs a l'historie de 'Universite de Louvain 1425-1797.* Louvain: Bibliotheque Centrale de l'Universite, 1977. 70 pp.

L'Universite de Louvain; coup d'oeil sur son historie et ses institutions, 1425-1900. Bruxelles: n.p., 1900. 192 pp.

Free University of Brussels

Brussels. Universite libre. *1884-1909. L'Universite de Bruxelles LXXV anniversaire de la fondation; relation des fetes, Novembre 1909.* Bruxelles: M. Weissenbruch, 1910. 126 pp.

Uyttebrouck, Andre, and Despy-Meyer, Andree. *Les Cent cinquante ans de l'Universite libre de Bruxelles, 1834-1984.* Bruxelles: Editions de l'Universite e libre de Bruxelles, 1984. 506 pp.

State University of Ghent

Rijkeuniversiteit te Gent. *Rijksuniversiteit Gent, 1817-1967.* Gent: Rijksuniversiteit, 1967. 117 pp.

Rijksuniversiteit te Gent. Faculteit der Letteren en Wijsbegeerte. *Zestig jaren onderwijs en wetenschap aan de Faculteit van de Wijsbegeerte en Letteren der Rijksuniversiteit te Gent.* Brugge: De Tempel, 1952. 211 pp.

State University of Liege

Hulewicz, Jan. *Studia Polakow w uniwersytecia w Liege w latach 1880-1914.* Krakow: Panstwowe Wydawn. Naukowe, 1969. 49 pp.

BOLIVIA

University of San Andres

Salinas, Jose M. *Historia de la Universidad Mayor de San Andres.* 2 vols. La Paz: Editorial U.M.S.A., 1948.

--------. *Historia de la Universidad Mayor de San Andres.* La Paz: Universidad Mayor de San Andres, 1967-

BRAZIL

Agnes Erskine College*

Sisk, Lorie C. "The History of the Agnes Erskine College in Brazil, 1904-1970." Ph.D. diss., George Peabody College for Teachers, 1973. 307 pp. *Dissertation Abstracts International,* vol. 34A, p. 4816.

Federal University of Minas Gerais

Moraes, Eduardo R. Affonso de. *Historia da Universidade Federal de Minas Gerais.* 2 vols. Belo Horizonte: Universidade Federal de Minas Gerais, 1971.

Federal University of Para

Moreira, Eidorfe. *Para a historia de Universidade Federal do Para: panorama do primeiro decenio.* Belem, Para: GRAFISA, 1977. 170 pp.

Federal University of Parana

Carneiro, David. *Educacao, Universidade e Hitoria da Primeira Universidate do Brasil.* Curitiba: Universidade Federal do Parana, 1972. 204 pp.

Wachowicz, Ruy C. *Universidade do mate: historia da UFPR.* Curitiba: Edicao da APUFPR, 1983. 189 pp.

University of Rio de Janeiro

Paim, Antonio. *Cienciana Universidade do Rio de Janeiro, 1931-1945.* Rio de Janeiro, RJ: Tempo Brasileiro, 1981. 144 pp.

--------. *A UDF e a ideia de Universidade.* Rio de Janeiro, RJ: Tempo Brasileiro, 1981. 144 pp.

University of Sao Paulo

Campos, Ernesto de Souza. *Historia de Universidade de Sao Paulo.* Sao Paulo: n.p., 1954. 582 pp.

Cardoso, Irene de Arruda R. *A Universidade da comunhao paulista: o projeto de criacao da Universidade de Sao Paulo.* Sao Paulo: Authores Associados: Cortez, 1982. 187 pp.

Mendes, Josue C. *Universidade de Sao Paulo: sumula da sua historia.* Sao Paulo: Secretaria da Cultura, Ciencia e Technologia, 1977. 47 pp.

Reale, Miguel. *Quatro anos de reitoria.* Sao Paulo: USP, 1973. 45 pp.

BULGARIA

University of Sofia

Sofiiski universitet "Kliment Okhridski": 9. IX. 1944-9. IX. 1974. Sofiia: SU Kliment Okhridski, 1975. 351 pp.

BURMA

University of Rangoon

Lu Pe Win, U. *History of the 1920 University Boycott.* Rangoon: U Lu Pe Win, 1970. 46 pp.

CANADA

Acadia University

Acadia University, Wolfville, N. S. *Memorials of Acadia College and Horton Academy for the First Half-Century, 1825-1878.* Montreal: Dawson, 1881. 260 pp

Kirkconnell, Watson. *The Fifth Quarter-Century: Acadia University, 1938-1963.* Wolfville, N. S.: Governors of Acadia University, 1968. 141 pp.

Longley, Ronald S. *Acadia University, 1838-1939.* Wolfville, N. S.: Kentville Publishing Co., 1939. 187 pp.

Albert University

Smith, Waldo E. L. *Albert College, 1857-1957.* n.p., 1957. 56 pp.

Athabasca University

Hughes, Laurie J. *The First Athabasca University.* Edmonton, Alta.: Athabasca University, 1980. 155 pp.

Small, Michael W. "A Case Study in Educational Policy-Making: The Establishment of Athabasca University." Ph.D. diss., University of Alberta, 1980.

Bishop's University

Bishop's University, Lennoxville, Que. *Historical Sketch of the University of Bishop's College, Established at Lennoxville, C. E.,* Showing Its Origin, Progress, and Present Condition. *Montreal: n.p.,* 1857. 26 pp.

Giroux, A. *Historie de College Basile-Moreau, 1933-1968.* Montreal: Soeurs de Sainte-Croix, 1976. 268 pp.

Masters, Donald C. *Bishop's University: The First Hundred Years.* Toronto: Clark, Irwin, 1950. 253 pp.

Brandon University

McKenzie, A. E., ed. *History of Brandon College, Inc.* Brandon: Privately Printed, 1962. 48 pp.

Stone, Charles G., and Garnett, F. Joan. *Brandon College: A History, 1899-1967.* Brandon: The University, 1969. 217 pp.

Brescia College

Skidmore, Patricia G. *Brescia College, 1919-1979.* London, Ont.: Brescia College, 1980. 100 pp.

Briercrest Bible College

Budd, Henry H. *Wind in the Wheatfields: A Pictorial History of Briercrest Bible College, 1935-1985.* Caronport, Sask.: The College, 1986. 63 pp.

Calgary College (Closed)

McLeod, Norman L. "Calgary College, 1912-1915: A Study of an Attempt to Establish a Privately Financed University in Alberta." Ph.D. Diss., University of Calgary, 1970.

Centennial College of Applied Arts and Technology

Centennial College of Applied Arts and Technology. *Centennial College: The Early Years.* Scarborough, Ont.: Centennial College of Applied Arts and Technology, 1977. 128 pp.

College Sainte-Marie-de-Monnoir*

Robillard, Jean-Jacques. "Historie du College Sainte-Marie-de-Monnoir, 1853-1912." Master's thesis, University of Ottawa, 1980.

Concordia University

Hall, Henry F. *The Georgian Spirit; The Story of Sir George Williams University.* Montreal: n.p., 1967. 138 pp.

Jones, Ginny, and McCormick, Joel, eds. *The Illustrated Companion History of Sir George Williams University.* Montreal: Concordia University, 1977. 185 pp.

Dalhousie University

Bennet, Jim. *There Stands Dalhousie.* Winnipeg: Josten's/National School Services, 1976. 127 pp.

Dalhousie University. *One Hundred Years of Dalhousie, 1818-1918.* Halifax: Rous & Mann, 1919. 59 pp.

--------. *Years of Growth and Change: Dalhousie University, 1963/64 to 1975/76: The President's Report.* Halifax: Dalhousie University, 1976. 51 pp.

Harvey, Daniel C. *An Introduction to the History of Dalhousie University.* Halifax: McCurdy Printing Co., 1938. 109 pp.

Patterson, George G. *The History of Dalhousie College and University.* Halifax: Morning Herald, 1887. 72 pp.

Lakehead University

Braun, H. S., and Morgan, D. W. *Lakehead College: Origin and Growth.* Port Arthur: Lakehead College of Arts, Science & Technology, 1963. 12 pp.

McGill University

Abbott, Maude E. S. *McGill's Heroic Past, 1821-1921; An Historic Outline of the University from Its Origin to the Present Time.* Montreal: McGill University, 1921. 30 pp.

Collard, Edgar A. *Oldest McGill.* Toronto: Macmillan, 1946. 135 pp.

Dawson, John W. *The Recent History of McGill University.* Montreal: The College, 1883. 19 pp.

Frost, Stanley B. *The History of McGill in Relation to the Social, Economic and Cultural Aspects of Montreal and Quebec.* Montreal: McGill University, 1979. 57 pp.

--------. *McGill University for the Advancement of Learning.* Montreal: McGill-Queen's University Pr., 1980-

Macdonald College. *Macdonald College Semi-Centenary, 1905-1955.* Ste. Anne de Bellevue, Quebec: Macdonald College, 1955. 54 pp.

MacLennan, Hugh. *McGill; The Story of a University.* London: Allen & Unwin, 1960. 135 pp.

Macmillan, Cyrus. *McGill and Its Story, 1821-1921.* London: John Lane, 1921. 304 pp.

Markell, Harold K. *History of the Presbyterian College, Montreal, 1865-1986.* Montreal: Presbyterian College, 1987. 128 pp.

Marling, Francis H. *Congregational College of British North America: The Story of the Fifty Years 1839-1889.* Montreal: n.p., 1889. 34 pp.

Snell, John F. *Macdonald College of McGill University, a History from 1904-1955.* Montreal: McGill University Pr., 159 pp.

McMaster University

Frost, R. W. *Concerning McMaster: The University's Past and Present in Facts and Figures.* Hamilton: The University, 1947. 15 pp.

Hamilton, Robert. "The Founding of McMaster University." Bachelor of Divinity thesis, McMaster University, 1938. 82 pp.

Johnson, Charles M. *McMaster University.* Toronto: University of Toronto Pr., 1976-

McMaster University, Hamilton Ontario. *McMaster University, 1890-1940; The Historical Address and Commemorative Ode, Presented at McMaster University, Hamilton, Ontario, May 10th, 1940.* Hamilton: The University, 1940 20 pp.

Montreal Diocesan Theological College

Howard, Oswald. *The Montreal Diocesan Theological College; A History from 1873 to 1963.* Montreal: McGill University Pr., 1963. 141 pp.

Mount Allison University

Evans, Mary G. "Mount Allison Wesleyan Academy and College, 1843-1886." Master's thesis, Bishop's University, 1978. 131 pp.

Reid, John G. *Mount Allison University: A History, to 1963.* 2 vols. Toronto: University of Toronto Pr., 1984.

Nova Scotia Agricultural College

Cox, Kenneth. *A History of the Nova Scotia Agricultural College.* Truro, N. S.: n.p., 1965. 151 pp.

Queen's Theological College

Rawlyk, George A., and Quinn, Kevin. *The Redeemed of the Lord Say So: A History of Queen's Theological College, 1912-1972.* Kingston, Ont.: The College, 1980. 270 pp.

Queen's University at Kingston

Bindon, Kathryn M. *Queen's Men, Canada's Men: The Military History of Queen's University, Kingston.* Kingston: Queen's University, 1978. 180 pp.

Calvin, Delano D. *Queen's University at Kingston, the First Century of Scottish-Canadian Foundation, 1841-1941.* Kingston: The Trustees of the University, 1941. 321 pp.

Gibson, Frederick W., and Graham, Roger, eds. *Queen's University.* 2 vols. Montreal: McGill-Queen's University Pr., 1978-1983.

Hamilton, Herb. *Queen's! Queen's! Queen's!* Kingston, Ont.: Alumni Association of Queen's University, 1977. 310 pp.

Kingston, Ontario. Queen's University. *Queen's University: An Illustrated Sketch of Its Foundation, Growth and Present Proportions.* Kingston: Queen's Quarterly, 1903. 42 pp.

McNeill, William E. *The Story of Queen's; An Address Delivered on Student and Alumni Day, Queen's University Centenary Celebration, October 16-18.* Kingston: Queen's University, 1941. 16 pp.

Queen's University (Kingston, Ont.). *Queen's, 1841-1911.* Kingston: n.p., 1911. 40 pp.

--------. *Queen's University, a Centenary Volume, 1841-1941.* Toronto: The Ryerson Pr., 1942. 189 pp.

Trotter, B. *Queen's University, 1963-1968: Some Facts and Figures.* Kingston: Queen's University, Office of Academic Planning, 1968. 45 pp.

Royal Military College of Canada

Kingston, Ontario, Royal Military College of Canada. *The Royal Military College, 1876 to 1919.* 2d ed. Kingston: n.p., 1920. 20 pp.

Preston, Richard A. *Canada's RMC; A History of the Royal Military College.* Toronto: University of Toronto Pr., 1969. 415 pp.

Simon Fraser University

Simon Fraser University: The Early Years. Burnby, B. C.: Simon Fraser University, 1980. 39 pp.

Strand, Kenneth. *Simon Fraser University: A Report by the President on Its Early Years.* Burnaby, B. C.: Simon Fraser University, 1974. 44 pp.

Trinity Western University

Wiebe, Jeffrey J. "Trinity Junior College: Its History, Development and Institutional Mission." Ph.D. diss., University of North Dakota, 1970. 176 pp. *Dissertation Abstracts International,* vol. 32A, p. 6787.

Union College*

Stewart, Charles M. *The Story of Union College.* Vancouver: Board of Governors, Union College of British Columbia, 1972. 46 pp.

University of Alberta

Alexander, W. H. *The University of Alberta: A Retrospect, 1908-1929.* Edmonton: The University, 1929.

Johns, Walter H. *A History of the University of Alberta, 1908-1969.* Edmonton: University of Alberta Pr., 1981. 544 pp.

Johnson, Richard D. "Mount Royal College: A Case Study." Master's thesis, University of Alberta, 1977. 118 pp.

MacDonald, John. *History of the University of Alberta, 1908-1958.* Edmonton: University of Alberta, 1958. 102 pp.

Parker, James M., et. al. *The University of Alberta, 1908-1983.* Edmonton: University of Alberta, 1982. 131 pp.

University of British Columbia

British Columbia. University. *The University of British Columbia. Twenty-First Anniversary, 1915-1936.* n.p., 1936. 38 pp.

Logan, Harry S. *Tuum Est; A History of the University of British Columbia.* Vancouver: University of British Columbia, 1958. 268 pp.

Woodcock, George. *The University of British Columbia: A Souvenir.* Toronto: Oxford University Pr., 1986. 92 pp.

University of Calgary

Simon, F. A. "A Brief History of the Alberta Institute of Technology and Art." Master's thesis, University of Alberta, 1962. 364 pp.

University of Guelph

Ontario Agricultural College. *Diamond Jubilee of the College.* Guelph: Ontario Agricultural College, 1934. 17 pp.

Ontario Agricultural College and Experimental Farm, Guelph. *Half Century of the College.* Guelph: Ontario Agricultural College, 1924. 28 pp.

Ontario Agricultural College 1874-1949: Proceedings of the Celebration of the Seventy-Fifth Anniversary June 18, 1949. Guelph: The College, 1949. 27 pp.

Ross, Alexander M. *The College on the Hill: A History of the Ontario Agricultural College, 1874 to 1974.* Toronto: Copp Clark, 1974. 180 pp.

University of Halifax (Closed 1881)

Gillis, Ann A. "The University of Halifax, 1876-1881." Master's thesis, Dalhousie University, 1969. 165 pp.

University of King's College

Akins, Thomas B. *A Brief Account of the Origin, Endowment, and Progress of the University of King's College, Windsor, Nova Scotia.* Halifax: MacNab & Shaffer, 1865. 84 pp.

DeWolf, John M., and Flie, George. *1789: All the King's Men: The Story of a Colonial University.* Halifax: Alumni Association of the University of King's College, 1972. 58 pp.

Hind, Henry Y. *The University of King's College, Windsor, Nova Scotia, 1790-1890.* New York: The Church Review Co., 1890. 119 pp.

Vroom, Fenwick W. *Kings' College: A Chronicle, 1789-1939.* Halifax: Imperial Publishing Co., 1941. 160 pp.

University of Laval

College de L'Assomption. *Les Celebrations de 150e Anniversaire de College de L'Assomption.* L'Assomption, Quebec: Le College, 1982. 31 pp.

Dansereau, Arthur. *Annales Historiques de College de L'Assomption depuis sa Fondation.* L'Assomption, Quebec: College de L'Assomption, Bibliotheque, 1984. 60 pp.

Forget, Anastase. *Historie de College de L'Assomption.* Montreal: Imprimeire Populaire, Limitee, 1933. 800 pp.

Laberge, Paul A. *L'Universite Laval, 1952-1977: vers L'Autonomie.*
Quebec: Presses de l'Universite Laval. 1978. 92 pp.

Lavallee, Andre. *Quebec contre Montreal: la querella Universitaire, 1876-1891.* Montreal: Presses de l'Universite de Montreal, 1974. 259 pp.

Lebon, Wilfrid. *Histoire de College de Sainte-Anne-de-la-Pocatiere, le Premier Demi-Siecle, 1827-1927.* 2 vols. Quebec: Charrier & Dugal, 1948. 573 pp.

--------. *Histoire de College de Sainte-Anne-de-la-Pocatiere; le Second Demi-Siecle, 1877-1927.* Quebec: Charrier & Dugal, 1949. 550 pp.

Richard, Louis. *Histoire de College des Trois-Rivieres, Premiere Periode de a 1860 a 1874.* Trois Rivieres: P. V. Ayotte, 1885. 521 pp.

L'Universite Laval, 1852-1952. Quebec: Presses de l'Universite Laval, 1952. 22 pp.

Vachon, Louis A. *Memorial.* Quebec: Les Presses de l'Universite Laval, 1963. 165 pp.

University of Lethbridge

Holmes, Owen G. *Come Hell or High Water.* Lethbridge: Lethbridge Herald, 1972. 141 pp.

Lethbridge Junior College. *Past, Present and Future of Lethbridge Junior College.* Lethbridge: The College, 1965. 37 pp.

University of Manitoba

Fraser, William J. "A History of St. John's College, Winnipeg." Master's thesis, University of Manitoba, 1966. 142 pp.

From Rural Parkland to Urban Centre: One Hundred Years of Growth at the University of Manitoba, 1877 to 1977. Winnipeg: Hipperion Pr. 1978. 174 pp.

Legal, Roger D. "L'Evolution de College Universitaire de Saint-Boniface Entre 1967 et 1983: Expose Historique et Comparaison de Diverses Interpretations vis-a-vis de Certains Changements Majeurs Survenus." Ph.D. diss., University of Manitoba, 1985. *Dissertation Abstracts International,* vol. 46A, p. 1204.

Mackenzie, Margaret, comp. *The University of Manitoba, Almost One Hundred Years.* Winnipeg: University of Manitoba Libraries, 1972. 26 pp.

Morton, William L. *One University: A History of the University of Manitoba, 1877-1952.* Toronto: McClelland & Stewart, 1957. 200 pp.

Regnier, Paul R. "A History of St. Boniface College." Master's thesis, University of Manitoba, 1964. 157 pp.

Saunderson, Hugh H. *The Saunderson Years.* Winnipeg: University of Manitoba, 1981. 228 pp.

University of Moncton

Cormier, Clement. *L'Universite de Moncton Historique.* Moncton: Universite de Moncton, 1975. 404 pp.

University of Montreal

Dumas-Rousseau, M. "L'Universite de Montreal de 1852 a 1865: tentatives de fondation." Theses, Universite Laval, 1974. 202 pp.

Slattery, T. P. *Loyola and Montreal: A History.* Montreal: Palm Publishers, 1962. 319 pp.

University of New Brunswick

Bailey, Alfred G., ed. *The University of New Brunswick Memorial Volume: Published on the Occasion of the One Hundred and Fiftieth Anniversary of the Granting of the First Charter of Incorporation, February 12th, 1800.* Fredericton, N. B.: The University, 1950. 125 pp.

Fraser, James A. *By Force of Circumstance; A History of St. Thomas University.* Fredericton, N. B.: Students Representative Council, St. Thomas University, 1970. 125 pp.

King's College (Fredericton, N. B.). *King's College, 1829-1859: The University of New Brunswick from 1859: A Celebration of the Sesquicentenary, New Year's Eve, 1978.* Fredericton, N. B.: n.p., 1978. 8 pp.

Raymond, William O. *The Genesis of the University of New Brunswick; With a Sketch of the Life of William Brydone Jack, A. M., D. C. L.,*

President, 1861-1885. Saint John, N. B.: n.p., 1919. 40 pp.

Trueman, Albert W. *Canada's University of New Brunswick: Its History and Its Development.* New York: Newcomen Society in North America, 1952. 32 pp.

University of Ottawa

Carriere, Gaston. *L'Universite d'Ottawa, 1848-1861.* Ottawa: Editions de l'Universite, 1960. 94 pp.

University of Ottawa. *Transition, 1966-1970.* Ottawa: University of Ottawa, 1970. 290 pp.

University of Prince Edward Island

MacDonald, George E. "And Christ Dwelt in the Heart of His House: A History of St. Dunstan's University, 1855-1955." Ph.D. diss., Queen's University at Kingston, 1984. *Dissertation Abstracts International,* vol. 45A, p. 912.

--------. *The History of St. Dunstan's University, 1855-1956.* Charlottetown: Board of Governors of St. Dunstan's University. 1988. In Press.

Moase, Lorne R. "The Development of the University of Prince Edward Island, 1964-1972." Master's thesis, University of New Brunswick, 1972.

University of Quebec

Audet, Louis P. *Historie de L'Enseignement au Quebec.* 2 vols. Montreal: Holt, Rinehart and Winston. 1971.

University of Quebec at Trois-Rivieres

Hamelin, Louis-Edmond. *Les chemins de l'Universite: Trois-Rivieres et sa region, de 1930 a 1985.* Trois-Rivieres: Universite du Quebec a Trois-Rivieres, 1985. 275 pp.

University of Regina

Luther College (Regina, Sask.). *Luther College at the University of Regina.* Regina: Luther College, University of Regina, 1981. 28 pp.

Mitchell, Ken. *Luther: The History of a College.* Regina: Luther College, 1981. 47 pp.

Pitsula, James M. *An Act of Faith: The Early Years of Regina College.* Regina: University of Regina, Canadian Plains Research Centre, 1988. 169 pp.

University of Saskatchewan

Gorman, Jack. *Pere Murray and the Hounds: The Story of Saskatchewan's Notre Dame College.* Sidney, B. C.: Gray's Publishing, 1977. 164 pp.

Hayden, Michael. *Seeking a Balance: The University of Saskatchewan, 1907-1982.* Vancouver: University of British Columbia Pr., 1983. 379 pp.

King, Carlyle. *The First Years: Teaching, Research and Public Service at the University of Saskatchewan, 1909-1959.* Toronto: McClelland & Stewart, 1959. 186 pp.

Morton, Arthur S. *Saskatchewan: The Making of a University.* Rev. and edited by Carlyle King. Toronto: University of Toronto Pr., 1959. 120 pp.

Riddell, W. A. *The First Decade: A History of the University of Saskatchewan, Regina Campus, 1960-1970.* Regina: University of Regina, 1974. 155 pp.

Spinks, J. W. T. *Decade of Change: The University of Saskatchewan, 1959-70.* Saskatoon: University of Saskatchewan, 1972. 169 pp.

Taft, Michael. *Inside These Greystone Walls: An Anecdotal History of the University of Saskatchewan.* Saskatoon: The University, 1984. 230 pp.

Thomas, Lewis H. *The University of Saskatchewan, 1909-1959.* Saskatoon: n.p., 1959. 64 pp.

Thompson, Walter P. *The University of Saskatchewan; A Personal History.* Toronto: University of Toronto Pr., 1970. 233 pp.

Thomson, James S. *Yesteryears at the University of Saskatchewan, 1937-1949.* Saskatoon: University of Saskatchewan, 1969. 91 pp.

University of Sherbrooke

Desilets, Andree; Lavallee, Jean-Guy; and Brunelle-Lavoie, Louise. *Les 25 ans de l'Universite de Sherbrooke, 1954-1979.* Sherbrooke, Quebec: Editions de l'Universite de Sherbrooke, 1982. 148 pp.

University of Sudbury

Universite de Sudbury. *50 ans: le College de Sacre-Couer, Sudbury, 1963.* Sudbury: n.p., 1963. 66 pp.

University of Toronto

Bissell, Claude T. *Halfway Up Parnassus: A Personal Account of the University of Toronto, 1932-1971.* Toronto: University of Toronto Pr., 1974. 197 pp.

--------, ed. *University College, a Portrait, 1853-1953.* Toronto: University of Toronto Pr., 1953. 148 pp.

Blake, Samuel H. *Wycliffe College: An Historical Sketch.* Toronto: n.p., 1910. 43 pp.

Burwash, Nathanael. *The History of Victoria College.* Toronto: Victoria College Pr., 1927. 571 pp.

Dickson, George, ed. *A History of Upper Canada College, 1829-1892.* Toronto: Rowsell & Hutchinson, 1893. 327 pp.

Edinborough, Arnold, ed. *The Enduring Word: A Centennial History of Wycliffe College.* Toronto: University of Toronto Pr., 1978. 129 pp.

Howard, Richard B. *Upper Canada College, 1829-1979: Colborne's Legacy.* Toronto: Macmillan, 1979. 462 pp.

Knox College, Toronto. Centenary Committee. *The Centenary of the Granting of the Charter of Knox College, Toronto, 1858-1958.* Toronto: The College, 1958. 22 pp.

Melville, Henry. *Rise and Progress of Trinity College, Toronto; With a Sketch of the Life of the Bishop of Toronto.* Toronto: n.p., 1852. 95 pp.

Owen, Derwyn R. G. *Trinity College: A History of the Building and Expansion Programme, 1957-1963: A Report.* n.p., 1964. 12 pp.

Reed, Thomas A., ed. *A History of the University of Trinity College, Toronto, 1852-1952.* Toronto: University of Toronto, 1952. 313 pp.

Sheraton, James P. *The History and Principles of Wycliffe College: An Address to the Alumni.* Toronto: J. E. Bryant, 1891. 32 pp.

Sissons, Charles B. *A History of Victoria University.* Toronto: University of Toronto Pr., 1952. 346 pp.

Toronto. Wycliffe College. *The Jubilee Volume of Wycliffe College.* Toronto: Wycliffe College, 1927. 301 pp.

University of Toronto. *A Brief Sketch of Its History and Its Organization.* Toronto: University of Toronto Pr., 1947. 32 pp.

--------. *The Origin, History, and Management of the University of King's College, Toronto.* Toronto: Printed by G. Brown, 1844. 101 pp.

Wallace, William S. *History of the University of Toronto, 1827-1927.* Toronto: Toronto University Pr., 1927.

University of Waterloo

Greene, Maurice. *Reflections of Waterloo: University of Waterloo, Canada.* Waterloo: University of Waterloo Bookstore, 1980. 65 pp.

McLean, Celia, and Redmond, Chris. *University of Waterloo, 1957-1982: The Twenty-Fifth Anniversary Year Begins.* Waterloo: University of Waterloo, 1982. 24 pp.

Scott, James. *Of Mud and Dreams: University of Waterloo, 1957-1967.* Toronto: Ryerson Pr., 1967. 194 pp.

University of Western Ontario

Gwynne-Timothy, John R. W. *Western's First Century.* London, Ont.: University of Western Ontario, 1978. 854 pp.

Lutman, John H. *Heritage Western: A Celebration, 1878-1978: An Illustrated History of the University of Western Ontario in Celebration of Its First Hundred Years.* London, Ont.: University of Western Ontario, 1978. 58 pp.

Talman, James J. *Huron College, 1863-1963.* London, Ont.: Huron College, 1963. 102 pp.

Talman, James J., and Talman, Ruth D. *"Western" 1878-1953, Being the History of the Origins and Development of the University of Western Ontario during Its First Seventy-Five Years.* London, Ont.: University of Western Ontario, 1953. 185 pp.

Tamblyn, William F. *These Sixty Years; An Unconventional Chronicle of the Lives, the Faith, the Labour and the Comradeship That Have Gone Into the Building of "Western's" Household of Learning.* London, Ont.: University of Western Ontario, 1938. 135 pp.

University of Windsor

Assumption University. *Golden Jubilee, Assumption College, 1870-1920.* Windsor: Assumption College, 1920. 158 pp.

Leddy, John F. *An Historical Review of the University of Windsor, 1972-1978: President's Report.* Windsor, Ont.: The University, 1978. 14 pp.

Power, Michael. *Assumption College: The O'Connor Years, 1870-1890.* Windsor, Ont.: Assumption College, 1986-

--------. *A Documentary History of Assumption College.* Leamington, Ont.: M. Power, 1984-

University of Winnipeg

Bedford, Allen G. *The History of Winnipeg: A History of the Founding Colleges.* Toronto: University of Toronto Pr., 1976. 479 pp.

Wilfrid Laurier University

Lyon, B. *The First 60 Years: A History of Waterloo Lutheran University from the Opening of Waterloo Lutheran Seminary in 1911, to the Present Day.* Waterloo: The University, 1971. 68 pp.

York University

York University (Toronto, Ont.). *Those Ten Years, 1960-70; the President's Report on the First Decade of York University.* Toronto: n.p., 1970. 59 pp.

CHANNEL ISLANDS

Victoria College

Cottrill, D. J. *Victoria College, Jersey, 1852-1972.* London: Phillimore, 1977. 123 pp.

CHILE

Southern University of Chile

Baltra Montaner, Lidia. *Nace una universidad: libertas capitur, universidad Austral de Chile.* Santiago de Chile: n.p., 1977. 107 pp.

University of Chile

Avila Martel, Alamiro de. *Resena historica de la Universidad de Chile, 1622-1979.* Santiago: Educiones de la Universidad Chile, 1979. 79 pp.

La Universidad de Chile, 1843-1934. Santiago: n.p., 1934. 201 pp.

CHINA

Beijing University

Pei-Ching ta hsueh. *L'Universite nationale de Pekin: historie et organisation.* Pekin: Universite Nationale, 1920. 34 pp.

Fukien Christian University (Closed)

Scott, Roderick. *Fukien Christian University, a Historical Sketch.* New York: United Board for Christian Colleges in China, 1954. 138 pp.

Hangchow Presbyterian College*

The Hangchow Presbyterian College, Hangchow, China; Introspect, Retrospect, Prospect. Omaha, Neb.: Franklin Publishing Co., 1916. 20 pp.

Hangchow University (Closed)

Day, Clarence B. *Hangchow University, a Brief History.* New York: United Board for Christian Colleges in China, 1955. 183 pp.

Hangzhou University

Day, Clarence B. *Hangchow University, a Brief History.* New York: United Board for Christian Colleges in China, 1955. 183 pp.

Huachung University (Closed)

Coe, John L. *Huachung University.* New York: United Board for Christian Education in Asia, 1962. 215 pp.

Hwa Nan College (Closed)

Wallace, Lydia E. *Hwa Nan College; The Woman's College of South China.* New York: United Board for Christian Colleges of China, 1956. 164 pp.

Lingnan University

Corbett, Charles H. *Lingnan University, a Short History Based Primarily on the Records of the University's American Trustees.* New York: Trustees of Lingnan University, 1963. 216 pp.

National Ginling University*

Thurston, Matilda S., and Chester, Ruth M. *Ginling College.* New York: United Board for Christian Colleges in China, 1955. 171 pp.

St. John's University

Lamberton, Mary. *St. John's University, Shanghai, 1879-1951.* New

York: United Board for Christian Colleges in China, 1955. 261 pp.

St. John's University, Shanghai, China. *St. John's University, 1879-1929.* Shanghai, China: Printed by Kelly and Walsh, Ltd., 1929. 92 pp.

Shantung Christian University (Closed)

Corbett, Charles H. *Sangtung Christian University, (Cheeloo).* New York: United Board for Christian Colleges in China, 1955. 281 pp.

University of Shanghai

Hipps, John B. *History of the University of Shanghai.* n.p.: Board of Founders of the University of Shanghai, 1964. 240 pp.

Yenching University (Closed)

Edwards, Dwight W. *Yenching University.* New York: United Board for Christian Higher Education in Asia, 1959. 408 pp.

Peking, Yenching University. Women's College. *Yenching College, 1905-1921.* Peking: Joint Committee on Women's Union Christian Colleges in the Orient, 1921. 20 pp.

Zhongshan (Sun Yat-sen) University

Canton, China. Sun Yat-sen University. *The National sunyatsen University, a Short History.* Canton: Wai Hing Printing Co., 1935. 160 pp.

COLOMBIA

Bolivar Pontifical University

Lotero Orozco, Gildardo. *La Pontificia Bolivariana: medio siglo de historia universitaria.* Medellin, Colombia: Universidad Pontificia Bolivariana. 1986-

Universidad Pontificia Bolivariana. *La fundacion.* Medellin, Colombia: Universidad Pontificia Bolivariana, 1975. 98 pp.

University of Santo Tomas

Ariza S., Alberto E. *El Colegio-Universidad de Santo Tomas de Aquino de Santa Fe de Bogota, 1580, 13 de junio, 1980.* Bogota: Editorial Kelly, 1980. 148 pp.

Universidad Santo Tomas, 400 Anos. Bogota: Universidad Santo Tomas, Centro de Ensenanza Desescolarizada, Seccion de Publicaciones, 1980. 314 pp.

Xavier Pontificia University

Loftus, Mary M. "Javeriana University: A Private University in Transition Toward Relevancy in Colombian Society." Ph.D. diss., Saint Louis University, 1966. 172 pp. *Dissertation Abstracts,* vol. 27A, p. 884.

COSTA RICA

Autonomous University of Central America

Historia de una decada. San Jose: Universidad Autonoma de Centro America, 1986. 258 pp.

National University of Costa Rica

Leon, Edwin. *Una universidad en una ciudad de maestros: origenes de la Universidad Nacional, 1870-1973.* Heredia: Universidad Nacional, 1982. 232 pp.

University of Costa Rica

Barahona Jimenez, Luis. *La Universidad de Costa Rica, 1940-1973.* San Jose: Editorial Universidad de Costa Rica, 1976. 408 pp.

Tinoco, Luis D. *La Universidad de Costa Rica: trayectoria de su creacion.* San Jose: Editorial Costa Rica, 1983. 502 pp.

Universidad de Costa Rica. *Estatuto organico de la Universidad de Costa Rica.* Ciudad Universitaria Rodrigo Facio, 1971. 55 pp.

CUBA

University of Havana

Le-Roy y Galvez, Luis F. *La Real y Literaria Universidad de la Habana: sintesis historica.* La Habana: n.p., 1966. 69 pp.

--------. *Requisitos para graduarse en la Universidad de la Habana, en su etapa real y pontificia, 1728-1843.* La Habana: Universidad de la Habana, Centro de Informacion Cientificay Tecnica, 1972. 26 pp.

--------. *La Universidad de la Habana: sintesis historica. El escudo de la universidad; su simbolismo.* Habana: Impr. de la Universidad de la Habana, 1960. 26 pp.

University of Las Villas

Universidad Central de las Villas. *Memoria inaugural de la Universidad Central de Santa Clara.* Havana: Editorial Selecta, 1948. 77 pp.

CZECHOSLOVAKIA

Comenius University

Univerzitna Kniznica v Bratislave, 1969-1979: zbornik z prilezitosti 60. vyrocia. Bratislava: Univerzitna Kniznica v Bratislave, 1980. 431 pp.

Varsik, Branislav; Bartl, Julius; and Dolan, Ondrej. *The Fiftieth Anniversary of Comenius University in Bratislava, 1919-1969.* Bratislava: Slovenske Pedagogicke Nakladatelstvo, 1969. 89 pp.

Jana Ev. Purkyne University

Univerzita J. E. Purkyne v Brne. *Rocenka Univerzity Jana Evangelisty Purkyne, 1968-1975.* Brno: Univerzita J. E. Purkyne, 1976. 1061 pp.

Palacky University

Navralil, Jan, ed. *Kapitoly z dejin olomoucke univerzity, 1573-1973.*
Ostrava: Profil, t. Tisk 4. Prerov, 1973. 371 pp.

Santavy, Frantisek. *Organizace, peceti a insignie olomoucke univerzity v letech, 1573-1973.* Olomouc: Univerzita Palackeho, 1980. 191 pp.

Univerzita Palackeho: 1946-1976: 30 let socialisticke vysokeskoly.
Olomouc: Univerzita Palackeho, 1976. 310 pp.

DENMARK

University of Aarhus

Aarhus Universitet 1928-1978. Aarhus: Universitetsforlaget: Aarhus, 1987. 648 pp.

Blinkenberg, Andreas P. D. *Aarhus universitet, 1928-1953.* Aarhus: Universitetsforlaget, 1953. 221 pp.

University of Copenhagen

Bodelsen, Carl A. G. *The University of Copenhagen; A Brief Survey of Its Organization and Activities.* Copenhagen: S. L. Mollers Bogtrykkeri, 1938. 63 pp.

Branth, Ellen. *The University of Copenhagen: A Brief Survey of Its Organization and Activities.* Copenhagen: University of Copenhagen, 1965. 28 pp.

Festskrift udgivet; anledning at universitetsbibiltekets 500 ars jubilaum 28. juni 1982. Kobenhaven: Lageforeningens forlag, 1982. 232 pp.

Matzen, Henning. *Kjobenhavns universitets retshistorie, 1479-1879.*
2 vols. Kjobenhaven: trykt hos J. H. Schultz, 1879.

Rordam, Holger F. *Kjobenhavns universitets historie fra 1537 til 1621.*
4 vols. Kjobenhaven: B. Lunos bogtrykkeri, 1868-1877.

--------. *Fra universitetets fortid.* Kjobenhaven: G. E. C. Gad, 1879.
207 pp.

Stybe, Svend E. *Copenhagen University: 500 Years of Science and*

Scholarship. Kobenhavn: The Royal Danish Ministry of Foreign Affairs, 1979. 219 pp.

DOMINICAN REPUBLIC

Universidad Nacional Pedro Henriquez Urena

Universidad Nacional Pedro Henriquez Urena. *Estatuto organico de la Universidad Nacional Pedro Henriquez Urena.* Santo Domingo: UNPHU, 1979. 24 pp.

University of Santo Domingo

Batista del Villar, Guarocuya. *Universidad critica y patria soberana: dos anos de gestion universitaria, 1976-1978.* Santo Domingo: Editora "Alfa y Omega", 1978. 619 pp.

Kasse Acta, Rafael. *Temas del movimiento renovador.* Santo Domingo: Editora de la UASD, 1979. 239 pp.

Rosario, Antonio. *La palabra del rector.* Santo Domingo: Editora de la UASD, 1980. 198 pp.

Sanchez Hernandez, Antonio. *Problematica universitaria, 1977-1978.* Santo Domingo: Editora de la Universidad Autonoma de Santo Domingo, 1979. 177 pp.

ECUADOR

University of Cuenca

Llore Mosquera, Victor. *La Universidad de Cuenca; apuntes para su historia.* Cuenca: Publicaciones de la Universidad de Cuenca, 1968. 163 pp.

Universidad de Cuenca. *Estatuto organico de la Universidad de Cuenca.* Cuenca: La Universidad, 1961. 35 pp.

EGYPT

American University in Cairo

Murphy, Lawrence R. *The American University in Cairo: 1919-1987.* Cairo: American University in Cairo Pr., 1987. 288 pp.

Riyadh University*

Jammaz, Saud I. "Riyadh University: Historical Foundations, Current Status, Critical Problems, and Suggested Solutions." Ph.D. diss., University of Southern California, 1973. 205 pp. *Dissertation Abstracts International,* vol. 34A, p. 3910.

EL SALVADOR

University of El Salvador

Duran, Miguel A. *Historia de la Universidad de El Salvador.* San Salvador: Talleres graficos Ariel, 1941. 236 pp.

--------. *Historia de la Universidad de El Salvador, 1841-1930.* 2d ed. San Salvador: Editorial Universitaria, 1975. 237 pp.

Universidad de El Salvador. *Guion historico de la Universidad Autonoma de El Salvador.* San Salvador: Editorial Universitaria, 1949. 84 pp.

ETHIOPIA

Addis Ababa University

Addis Ababa University. *Addis Ababa University, Major Events, 1974-1984, with Directory of Principal Units.* Addis Ababa: The University, 1984. 26 pp.

Haile, Fisseha. "A Study of Institutionality: Addis Ababa University, 1961-1981." Ed.D. diss., Indiana University, 1984. 189 pp. *Dissertation Abstracts International,* vol. 45A, p. 2772.

Three Decades of University Education (1950-1980). Addis Ababa: Addis Ababa University, 1980. 56 pp.

FINLAND

University of Helsinki

Heikel, Ivar A. *Helsingfors Universitet, 1640-1940.* Helsingfors: Soderstrom, 1940. 796 pp.

Jorgensen, Arne. *Universitetsbiblioteket: Helsingfors, 1827-1848.* Helsingfors: Helsingin yliopisto, 1980. 298 pp.

Kaila, Eino. *Les trois siecles de l'Universite de Finlande, 1640-1940.* Helsinki: Otava, 1940. 81 pp.

University of Jyvaskyla

Kuusi, Sakari. *Miten Jyvaskylan yliopisto syntyi. Jyvasklan yliopistokysymyksen ja Yliopistoyhdistyksen historia.* Jakaja: Jyvaskylan yliopisto, Julkaisuvarasto, 1967. 213 pp.

University of Oulu

Julku, Liisa. *Oulun yliopiston perustamisen historia.* Rovaniemi: Pohjois-Suomen Historiallinen Yhdistys, 1983. 306 pp.

Saarela, Ahti. *Oulun yliopiston synty ja Kehitys.* Joensuu: Joensuun Korkeakoulu, 1974. 62 pp.

Varjo, Uuno, and Huttunen, Marja-Leena. *The Founding of the University of Oulu and Its Effect Upon Regional Development.* Oulu: University of Oulu, 1977. 46 pp.

University of Turku

Perala, Tauno. *Turun yliopisto, 1939-1974.* Turku: Turun yliopisto, 1977. 521 pp.

Somerkoski, Pirjo, and Nurmi, Matti, eds. *The University of Turka.* Turka: Serioffset, 1982. 158 pp.

FRANCE

Catholic Institute of Paris

Institut catholique de Paris. *Le livre du centenaire: 1875-1975.* Paris: Beauchesne, 1975. 404 pp.

Ecole Polytechnique

Langins, Janis. "The Ecole Polytechnique (1794-1804): From Encyclopaedic School to Military Institution." Ph.D. diss., University of Toronto, 1979. *Dissertation Abstracts International,* vol. 40A, p. 6396.

University of Aix-Marsielles

Belin, Ferdinand. *Historie de l'ancienne Universite de Provence, ou Historie de la fameuse universite d'Aix.* Paris: A. Picard, 1896-

University of Caen

L'Universite de Caen: son passe, son present. Caen: Imprimerie artistique Malherbe, 1932. 296 pp.

University of Grenoble

Berriat-Saint-Prix, Jacques. *Historie de l'ancienne University de Grenbole.* 2. ed. Valence: L. Borel, 1839. 60 pp.

University of Paris

Bonnerot, Jean. *L'Universite de Paris du Moyen Age a nos Jours.* Paris: Larousse, 1933. 222 pp.

Budinszky, Alexander. *Die Universitat Paris and Die Fremden an Dersclben im Mittelalten.* Berlin: W. Hertz, 1876. 234 pp.

Crevier, Jean B. L. *Historie de l'Universite de Paris, Dupuis son Origine Jusquen l'annee 1600.* 7 vols. Paris: Desaint and Saillant, 1761.

Delegue, Rene. *L'Universite de Paris, 1224-1244.* Paris: A. Chevalier-Marescq, 1902. 48 pp.

Desmaze, Charles A. *L'Universite de Paris, 1200-1875, la Nation de Picardie, les Colleges de Laon et de Presles, la loi sur* l'enseignement superieur. Paris: Charpentier, 1876. 343 pp.

Dubarle, Eugene. *Historie de l'Universite de Paris.* 2 vols. Paris: Typ. de Firmin Didot Freres, 1844.

Ferruolo, Stephen C. *The Origins of the University: The Schools of Paris and Their Critics, 1100-1215.* Stanford, Calif.: Stanford University Pr., 1985. 380 pp.

Garcia Robles, Alfonso. *La Sorbone ayer y hoy, sinopsis historica de la Universidad de Paris desde sus origenes hasta nuestros dias.* Mexico: Universidad Nacional Autonoma, 1943. 167 pp.

Glorieux, Palemon. *Les origines du College de Sorbonne.* Notre Dame, Ind.: Mediaeval Institute, University of Notre Dame, 1959. 24 pp.

Halmagrand, Charles N. *Origine de l'Universite.* Paris: Au Comptoir des Imprimeurs-Unis, 1845. 384 pp.

Hoyt, John W. *The University of Paris during the Middle Ages.* Washington: n.p., 1905.

Jourdain, Charles. *Historie de l'Universite de Paris an XVII et au XVIII Siecle.* Paris: L. Hachette, 1862-1866. 293 pp.

North Carolina. University of North Carolina. *The Septicentennial Celebration of the Founding of the Sorbonne College in the University of Paris.* Chapel Hill: n.p., 1953. 49 pp.

Paris. Universite. *La vie universitaire a Paris.* Paris: A. Colin, 1918. 231 pp.

Raleigh, Thomas. *The University of Paris, from Its Foundation to the Council of Constance.* n.p.: Thos. Shrimpton & Son, 1873. 39 pp.

Thourot, Charles. *De l'organisation de l'enseignement dans l'universite de Paris, au Moyen-age.* Paris: E. Magdeleine, 1850. 213 pp.

Ziegler, Gilette G. *Le Defi de la Sorbonne (sept siecles de contestation).* Paris: Julliard, 1969. 191 pp.

University of Poitiers

L'Universite de Poitiers, 1431-1981: exposition du 500e anniversaire.
Poitiers: L'Universite: Musee de la Ville: Societe des Antiquaires de l'Quest, 1981. 127 pp.

University of Toulouse

Smith, Cyril E. *The University of Toulouse in the Middle Ages: Its Origins and Growth to 1500 A.D.* Milwaukee: Marquette University Pr., 1958. 244 pp.

GERMAN DEMOCRATIC REPUBLIC

Ernst Moritz Arndt University of Greifswald

Kosegarten, Johann G. L. *Geschichte der Universitat Greifswald mit urkundlichen Beilagen.* 2 vols. Greifswald: n.p., 1856-1857.

Friedrich Schiller University of Jena

Muller, Wilhelm. *Jena in den Letzten Hundert Jahren.* Jena, Universitatsbuchdr: G. Neuenhahn, 1896. 17 pp.

Humboldt University of Berlin

Berlin. Universitat. *Die Humboldt-Universitat gestern, heute, morgen.* Berlin: Deutscher Verlag der Wissenschaften, 1960. 250 pp.

Klein, Helmut, ed. *Humboldt-Universitat zu Berlin. Dokumente 1810-1985.* 2 vols. Berlin: VLG.D. Wissensch, 1985.

Lenz, Max. *Geschichte der Koniglichen Friedrich-Wilhelms-Universitat zu Berlin.* 4 vols. Halle: Buchhandlung des Waisenhauses, 1910-1918.

Wissenschaftliche Zeitschrift der Humboldt-Universitat zu Berlin. Berlin: Selbstverlag der Humboldt-Universitat zu Berlin, 1961. 319 pp.

Karl Marx University of Leipzig

Bruchmuller, Wilhelm. *Beitrage zur geschichte der universitaten Leipzig und Wittenberg.* Leipzig: n.p., 1898. 60 pp.

Engelberg, Ernst, ed. *Karl-Marx-Universitat Leipzig, 1409-1959.* 2 vols. Leipzig: Verlag Enzyklopedie, 1959.

Friedberg, Emil A. *Die Universitat Leipzig in Vergangenheit und Gegenwart.* Leipzig: Veit & Co., 1898. 157 pp.

Gretschel, Carl C. C. *Die Universitat Leipzig in der Vergangenheit und Gegenwart.* Dresden: n.p., 1830. 292 pp.

Kreussler, Heinrich G. *Geschichte der Universitat Leipzig von ihrem Ursprunge bis auf unsre Zeiten.* Dresden: n.p., 1810. 248 pp.

Leipzig. Universitat. *Beitrage zur Geschichte der Universitat Leipzig im Funfzehnten Jahrhundert. Zur Feier des 500 Jahrigen Jubilaums der Universitat, Gewidmet von der Universitats-Bibliothek.* Leipzig: O. Harrassowitz, 1909. 93 pp.

--------. *Die Universitat Leipzig, 1409-1909. Gedenkblatter zum 30.Juli 1909.* Leipzig: Press-Ausschuss der Jubilaums-Kommission, 1909. 86 pp.

Schulze, Johann D. *Abriss Einer Geschichte der Leipziger Universitat im Laufe des Schtzenhenten Jahrhunderts Nebst Ruckblicken auf die Fruhern zeiten.* Leipzig: A. L. Reinicke, 1802. 461 pp.

Martin Luther University of Halle-Wittenberg

Bruchmuller, Wilhelm. *Beitrage zur Geschichte der Universitaten Leipzig und Wittenberg.* Leipzig: n.p., 1898. 60 pp.

Grohmann, Johann C. A. *Annalen der Universatat zu Wittenberg.* 2 vols. Meissen: C. F. W. Erbstein, 1801-1802.

Hoffbauer, Johann C. *Geschichte der Universitat zu Halle; bis zum Jahre 1805.* Halle: Schimmelpfenning, 1805. 542 pp.

Schrader, Wilhelm. *Geschichte der Friedrich-Universitat zu Halle.* 2 vols. Berlin: F. Dummler, 1894.

Technical University of Dresden

Aus der Geschichte der Technischen Universitat Dresden. Dresden: Der Arbeitskreis, 1975. 77 pp.

Chronik der TU Dresden von 1971-1979. Dresden: Technische Universitat Dresden, Sektion Philosophie und Kulturwissenschaften, 1981. 246 pp.

Dresden. Technische Universitat. *125 Jahre Technische Hochschule, Dresden: Festschrift.* Berlin: Deutscher Verlag der Wissenschaften, 1953. 270 pp.

Geschichte der Technischen Universitat Dresden: 1828-1978. Berlin: Deutscher Verlag der Wissenschaften, 1978. 468 pp.

Kaemmel, Otto. *Geschichte des Leipziger Schulwesens vom Anfange des 13. bis Gegen die Mitte des 19, Jahrhunderts (1214-1846).* Leipzig: B. G. Teubner, 1909. 634 pp.

Technische Universitat Dresden. *Ein Jahrhundert. Sachsische Technische Hochschule, 1828-1928. Festschrift zur Jahrundertfeier, 4. bis 6. Juni 1928.* Dresden: W. Limpert, 1928. 222 pp.

University of Rostock

Ammer, Thomas. *Universitat zwischen Demokratie und Diktatur; ein Beitrag zur Nachkreigsgeschichte der Universitat Rostock.* Koln: Verlag Wissenschaft und Politik, 1969. 174 pp.

Geschichte der Universitat Rostock, 1419-1969: Festschrift zur Funfhundertfunfzig Jahr-Feier der Universitat. 2 vols. Berlin: Deutscher Verlag der Wissenschaften, 1969.

Krabbe, Otto C. *Die Universitat Rostock im 15. und 16. Jahrhundert.* 2 vols. 1854. Reprint. Aalen: Scientia, 1970.

Lorenz, Adolf F. *Die Universitats gebaude zu Rostock und ihre Geschichte.* Rostock: G. B. Leopold's Universitats Buchhandlung, 1919. 80 pp.

Schnitzler, Elisabeth. *Beitrage zur Geschichte der Universitat Rostock im 15.* Leipzig: St. Benno-Verlag, 1979. 134 pp.

--------. *Die Grundung der Universitat Rostock, 1419.* Wein: Bohlau, 1974. 105 pp.

GERMANY, FEDERAL REPUBLIC OF

Christian Albrecht University of Kiel

Bargmann, Wolfgang. *Die Christiana Albertina in Vergangenheit, Gegenwart und Zukunft.* Kiel: F. Hirt, 1965. 24 pp.

Jordan, Karl. *Die Christian-Albrechts-Universitet, Kiel, im Wandel der Jahrhunderte.* Kiel: F. Hirt, 1953. 32 pp.

Ratjen, Henning. *Beitrag zur geschichte der Kieler Universitat.* Kiel: Akademische buchandlung, 1859. 76 pp.

Scharff, Alexander. *Verfall und Wiederaufstieg der Christian-Albrechts-Universitat im 18. Jahrundert.* Kiel: Hirt, 1967. 28 pp.

Eberhard Karl University of Tubingen

Angerbauer, Wolfram. *Das Kanzeleramt an der Universitat Tubingen und sein Inhaber, 1590-1817.* Tubingen: Mohr, 1972. 166 pp.

Emberger, Gudrun. *"In alten Vigor undt quten Standt zu bringen": Studien zum Wiederaufbau der Universitat Tubingen nach dem Drieeigjahrigen Krieg.* Tubingen: Aus dem Institut fur geschichtliche Landeskunde und historiche Hilfswissenschaften der Universitat Tubingen, 1977. 71 pp.

500 Jahre Universitat Tubingen: die Kehrseite der Medaille: Universitat Heute: Schwarzheft zur Asstellung. Tubingen: The Universitat, 1977. 119 pp.

Haller, Johannes. *Die anfanger der Universitat Tubingen, 1477-1537.* 2 vols. Stuttgart: W. Kohlhammer, 1927-1929.

Jens, Walter. *Eine deutsche Universitat: 500 Jahre Tubinger Gelehrtenrepublik.* Munchen: Kindler, 1977. 417 pp.

Klupfel, Karl, and Eifert, Max. *Geschichte und Beschreibung der Stadt und Universitat Tubingen.* 2 vols. 1849. Reprint. Aalen: Scientia Verlag, 1977.

Sieber, Eberhard. *Stadt und Universitat Tubingen in der Revolution von 1848-49.* Tubingen: Laupp, 1975. 436 pp.

Teufel, Waldemar. *Universitas studii Tuwingensis: die Tubinger Universitatsverfassung in vorreformatorischer Zeit (1477-1534).* Tubingen: Mohr, 1977. 299 pp.

Free University of Berlin

Funfzehn Jahre Freir Universitat Berlin, 1948-1963. Berlin: FU-Spiegel, 1963. 87 pp.

Tent, James F. *The Free University of Berlin: A Political History.*
Bloomington: Indiana University Pr., 1988. 512 pp.

Friedrich Alexander University of Erlangen-Nuremberg

Kolde, Theodor von. *Die Universitat Erlangen unter dem hause Wittelsbach, 1810-1910: Festschrift zur Jahrhundertfeier der verbindung der Friderico-Alexandrina mit der Krone Bayern.* Leipzig: A. Deichert, 1910. 587 pp.

Universitat Erlangen. *Geschichte der Universitat Erlangen in Zeitlicher Vebersicht: auf Veranlassung der Direkton der Universitat atsbibiothek.* Erlangen: Palm & Enke, 1927. 101 pp.

Die Universitat Erlangen von 1743 bis 1843: zum Jubilaum der Universitat 1843. Erlangen: F. F. Barfus, 1943? 255 pp.

Georg August University of Gottingen

Ebel, Wilhelm. *Gottingen Universitatsreden aus zwe: Jahrhunderten, 1737-1934.* Gottingen: Vandenhoeck und Ruprecht, 1978. 650 pp.

--------. *Memorabilia Gottingensia. Elf Studien zur Sozailgeschichte der Universitat.* Gottingen: Vandenhoeck u. Ruprecht, 1969. 192 pp.

Meinhardt, Gunther. *Die Universitat Gottingen: ihre Entwicklung u. Geschichte von, 1734-1974.* Gottingen: Musterschmidt, 1977. 123 pp.

Oesterley, Georg H. *Geschichte der Universitat Gottengen in dem Zeitraume von Jahre 1820 bis zu ihre ersten Sacularfier im. Jahre 1837.* Gottingen: Vanderhoeck and Ruprecht, 1838. 521 pp.

Rossler, Emil F. *Die Grundung der Universitat Gottingen: Entwurfe, Berichte und Briefe der Zeitgenossen.* Gottingen: Vandenhoeck & Ruprecht, 1855. 503 pp.

Saalfeld, Friedrich. *Geschichte der Universitat Gottingen in-dem Zeitraume von 1788 bis 1820.* Hannover: n.p., 1820. 644 pp.

Selle, Gotz von. *Die Georg-August-Universitat zu Gottingen, 1737-1937.* Gottingen: Vandenhoeck & Ruprecht, 1937. 398 pp.

200 Jahre Universitat Gottingen, 1737-1937. Gottingen: Verlagsabteilung vor Gottinger Studentenschaft, 1937. 76 pp.

Johannes Gutenberg University of Mainz

Just, Leo. *Die alte Universitat Mainz von 1477 bis 1798; ein Uberblick. Mit einem Anhand: Quellen zur Geschichte der Universitat in der Zeit nach der Restauration von 1784.* Wiesbaden: F. Steiner, 1957. 81 pp.

Just, Leo, and Mathy, Helmut. *Die Universitat Mainz. Grundzuge ihrer Geschichte.* (Trautheim ub. Darmstadt u Mainz a Rh.). Mushake, 1965. 167 pp.

Justus Liebig University of Giessen

Giessen. Universitat. *Die Universitat Giessen von 1607 bis 1907; Beitrage zu ihrer Geschichte.* 2 vols. Giessen: A. Topelmann, 1907.

Justus-Liebig-Universitat Giessen. *Ludwigs-Universitat, Justus-Liebig-Hochschule, 1607-1957.* Giessen: n.p., 1957. 543 pp.

Moraw, Peter. *Kleine Geschichte der Universitat Giessen, 1607-1982.* Giessen: Verlag der Ferber schen Universitats-Buchandlung, 1982. 271 pp.

Werner, Norbert, and Pfeifer, Hans-Georg. *375 Jahre Universitat Giessen, 1607-1982: Geschichte und Gegenwart.* Geissen: Feber schen Universitatsbuchhandlung, 1982. 327 pp.

Rhenish Fredrich Wilhelm University of Bonn

Bezold, Friedrich. *Geschichte der Rheinischen Freidrich-Wilhelms-Universitat von der Grundung bis zum Jahr 1870.* Bonn: A. Marcus & E. Weber, 1920. 535 pp.

Braubach, Max. *Die erste Bonner Universitat und ihre Professoren; ein Beitrag zur rheinischen Heistegeschichte im Zeitalter der Aufklaurung.* Bonn: Universitats-Verlag, 1947. 199 pp.

--------. *Kleine Geschichte der Universitat Bonn.* Bonn: Rohrscheid, 1968. 70 pp.

Dreyfus-Brisac, Edmond. *The University of Bonn.* Washington: Government Printing Office, 1882. 67 pp.

Horoldt, Dietrich. *Stadt und Universitat; Ruckblick aus Anlass der 150 Jahr-Feier der Universitat Bonn.* Bonn: L. Rohrscheid, 1969. 410 pp.

Lutzeler, Heinrich. *Die Bonner Universitat. Bauten und Bildwerke.*
Bonn: Bouvier; Rohrscheid, 1968. 365 pp.

Renger, Christian. "Die Grundung und Einrichtung der Universitat Bonn und die Berufengspolitik des Dulturministers Altenstein." Doctoral Thesis, University of Bonn, 1981. 309 pp.

Schafer, Karl T. *Verfassungsgeschichte der Universitat Bonn, 1818 bis 1960.* Bonn: H. Bouvier, 1968. 569 pp.

University of Bonn: Its Rise, Progress and Present State. London: n.p., 1845. 242 pp.

Varrentrapp, Conrad. *Beitrage zur Geschichte der Kurkolnischen Universitat Bonn.* Bonn: Gedr. auf Kosten des Vereins bei A. Marcus, 1868. 53 pp.

Rupert Charles University of Heidelberg

Buhl, Heinrich. *Zur Geschichte der Universitat Heidelberg Unter Grossherzog Fredrich.* Heidelberg: Universitatsbuchdr. von J. Horning, 1902. 17 pp.

Buselmeier, Karin; Harth, Dietrich; and Jansen, Christian. *Auch eine Geschichte der Universitat Heidelberg.* Mannheim: Edition Quadrat, 1985. 512 pp.

Classen, Peter, and Wolgast, Eike. *Kleine Geschichte der Universitat Heidelberg.* Berlin: Springer-Verlag, 1983. 119 pp.

Die Geschichte der Universitat Heidelberg: Vortrage im Wintersemester 1985/86. Heidelberg: Heidelberger Verlagsanstalt, 1986. 247 pp.

Hautz, Johann F. *Geschichte der Universitat Heidelberg.* 2 vols. Mannheim: J. Schneider, 1862-1864.

Heidelberg. Universitat. *Urkundenbuch der Universitaet Heidelberg.* 2 vols. Heidelberg: C. Winter, 1886.

Helm, Gustav. *Heidelberg und seine Universitat.* Freiburg im Breisgau: Herder, 1886. 172 pp.

Hins, Gerhard, ed. *Aus der Geschichte der Universitat Heidelberg und ihre Fakultaten.* Heidelberg: n.p., 1961. 455 pp.

--------. *The History of Heidelberg University.* Translated into English by Robin Crompton. Heidelberg: Association of Friends of the Heidelberg University Students, 1967. 64 pp.

Keller, Richard A. *Geschichte der Universitat Heidelberg im Ersten jahrzehnt nach der Reorganisation durch Karl Friedrich (1803-1813).* Heidelberg: C. Winter, 1913. 346 pp.

Raff, Diether. *Die Ruprecht-Karls-Universitat in Vergangenheit und Gegenwart.* Heidelberg: Heidelberger Verlagsanstalt und Druckerei, 1983. 183 pp.

Ritter, Gerhard. *Die Heidelberger Universitat, ein Stuk Deutscher Geschichte.* Heidelberg: C. Winter, 1936-

--------. *Geschichte der Universitat Heidelberg im ersten jahrzehnt nach der Reorganisation durch Karl Friedrich (1803-1813).* Heidelberg: C. Winter, 1913. 356 pp.

Schneider, Franz. *Die Universitat Heidelberg im Jahre 1803.* Heidelberg: C. Winter, 1913. 34 pp.

Thorbecke, August. *Geschichte der Universitat Heidelberg im Auftrage der Universitat Dargestellt.* Heidelberg: G. Koester, 1886-

Universitat Heidelberg; Geschichte und Gegenwart, 1386-1961. 1 vol. n.p., 1961.

Vezina, Birgit. *"Die Gleichschaltung" der Universitat Heidelberg im Zuge der Nationalsozialistischen Machtergreifung.* Heidelberg: C. Winter, 1982. 181 pp.

Weisert, Hermann. *Geschichte der Universitat Heidelberg: Kurzer Uberblick, 1386-1980.* Heidelberg: C. Winter, 1983. 136 pp.

Wolgast, Eike. *Die Universitat Heidelberg, 1386-1986.* Berlin: Springer, 1986. 219 pp.

Technical University of Berlin

Berlin. Technische Hochschule. *Die Technische Hochschule zu Berlin, 1799-1924.* Berlin: G. Stike, 1925. 136 pp.

University of Augsburg

Universitat Augsburg, 1970-1980: zum zehnjahrigen Bestehen der Universitat Augsburg. Augsburg: Die Universitat, 1980. 222 pp.

University of Cologne

Bianco, Franz Joseph von. *Die alte Universitat Koln administrierten Studien-Stiftungen.* 2 vol. Aalen: Scientia-Verlag, 1974.

Cologne. Universitat. *Universitat Koln, 1919-1929.* Koln: Druck, M. DuMont Schauberg, 1929. 305 pp.

Festschrift zur Erinnerung an die Grundung der alten Universitat Koln im Jahre 1388. Koln: K. Schroder, 1938. 671 pp.

University of Constance

Hess, Gerhard. *Sieben Jahre Universitat Konstanz, 1966-1972.* Konstanz: Druckerei und Verlagsanstalt Konstanz, Universitatsverlag, 1973. 91 pp.

Hess, Gerhard, and Jauss, Hans R. *Gebremste Reform: ein Kapitel deutscher Hochschulgeschichte: Universitat Konstanz,1966-1976.* Konstanz: Universitatsverlag, 1977. 347 pp.

University of Duisburg

Schrey, Helmut. *Die Universitat Duisburg: Geschichte und Gegenwart: Traditionen, Personen, Probleme.* Duisburg: W. Braun, 1982. 162 pp.

University of Hamburg

Festschrift zum 150 jahrigen Bestehen der Universitat Hannover. 2 vols. Stuttgart: W. Kohlhammer, 1981.

Hamburg. Universitat. *Universitat Hamburg, 1919-1969.* Hamburg: n.p., 1969. 382 pp.

University of Hannover

Festschrift zum 150 Jahrigen Bestehen der Universitat Hannover. 2 vols. Stuttgart: W. Kohlhammer, 1981.

University of Hoenheim

Universitat Hohenheim. *Universitat Hohenheim, Landwirtschaftliche Hochschule 1818-1968.* Stuttgart: E. Ulmer, 1968. 331 pp.

University of Karlsruhe

Bauernfeind, Ulf, and Herlitzka, Adolf, eds. *Dokumentation 150 [i.e. hundertf-unfzig] Jahre Universitat Karlsruhe: as Jubilaumsjahr in Wort und Bild.* Karlsruhe: Pressestelle der Universitat Karlsruhe, 1976. 210 pp.

Hotz, Joachim. *Kleine Geschichte der Universitat Fridericiana Karlsruhe (Technische Hochschule).* Karlsruhe: Muller, 1975. 64 pp.

University of Mannheim

Cloer, Bruno, and Jentsch, Christoph, eds. *75 Jahre Universitat Mannheim: Gesellschaft und Universitat, Probleme und Perspektiven: Festschrift zur 75 Jahr Feier der Universitat.* Mannheim: Das Rektorat der Universitat Mannheim, 1982. 287 pp.

University of Marburg

450 Jahre Philipps-Universitat Marburg: d. Grundungs jubilaum 1977. Marburg: Elwert, 1979. 152 pp.

Die Philipps-Universitat zu Marburg, 1527-1927. Marburg: Elwert, 1927. 865 pp.

University of Munich

Boehm, Laetitia, and Sporl, Johannes. *Die Ludwig Maximilians Universitat in ihren Fakultaten.* Berlin: Duncker & Humblot, 1972-

Bruch, Rudiger vom, and Muller, Rainer A., eds. *Erlebte und Gelebte Universitat: die Universitat Munchen im 19. und 20. Jahrhundert.* Pfaffenhofen: W. Ludwig, 1986. 400 pp.

--------. *Ludwig-Maximilians-Universitat: Ingolstadt, Landshut, Munchen; 1472-1972.* Berlin: Duncker und Humblot. 1972. 404 pp.

Mayr-Wallenreiter, Clara. *Die Vermogensverwaltung der Universitat Landshut-Munchen: ein Beitr. z. Geschichte d. bayer. Hochschultyps vom 18. z. 20. Jahrhundert.* Berlin: Duncker und Humblot, 1971. 267 pp.

Muller, Rainer A. *Universitat und Adel: eine soziostrukturelle Studie z. Geschichte d. bayer. Landesuniv. Ingolstadt, 1472-1648.* Berlin: Duncker und Humblot, 1974. 246 pp.

Polnitz, Gotz, Freiherr von. *Denkmale und Dokumente zur Geschichte der Ludwig-Maximilians-Universitat, Ingolstadt, Landshut, Munchen.* Munchen: G. D. W. Callwey, 1942. 83 pp.

Prantl, Carl. *Geschichte der Ludwig-Maximiliams-Universitat in Ingolstadt, Landshut, Munchen.* 2 vols. Munich: C. Kaiser, 1872.

University of Munster

Pieper, Anton. *Die alte Universitat Munster, 1773-1818: ein geschichtlicher Uberblick.* Munster: Regensbergsche Buchhandlung und Buchdruckerei, 1902. 98 pp.

Ribhegge, Wilhelm. *Geschichte der Universitat Munster.* Munster: Verlag Regensberg, 1985. 251 pp.

200 Jahre zwischen Dom und Schloss: ein Lesebuch zu Vergangenheit und Gegenwart der Westfalischen Wilhelms-Universitat Munster. Munster: L. Kurz, 1980. 250 pp.

Die Universitat Munster: 1780-1989. Munster: Aschendorff, 1980. 520 pp.

University of Oldenburg

Helmers, Hermann. *Geschichte der Universitat Oldenburg.* Oldenburg: H. Holzberg, 1983. 490 pp.

Luthje, Jurgen. *Universitat Oldenburg: Entwicklung und Profil.* Oldenburg: H. Holzberg, 1984. 445 pp.

University of Osnabruck

Wetterling, Horst. *Die Grundung der Universitat Osnabruck, 1960-1970.* Osnabruck: Fromm, 1972. 139 pp.

University of Stuttgart

Borst, Otto. *Schule des Schwabenlands: Geschichte d. Univ. Stuttgart.* Stuttgart: Deutsche Verlags-Anstalt, 1979. 510 pp.

Festschrift zum 150 jahrigen [i.e. hundertfunfzigjahrigen] Bestehen der Universitat Stuttgart: Beitr. zur Geschichte d. Univ. Stuttgart: Deutsche Verlags-Anstalt, 1979. 463 pp.

Voigt, Johannes H. *Universitat Stuttgart: Phasen ihrer Geschichte.*
Stuttgart: Wittwer, 1981. 96 pp.

University of Trier

Zenz, Emil. *Die Trierer Universitat, 1473 bis 1798; ein Beitrag zur abendlandischen Universitatsgeschichte.* Trier: Paulinus-Verlag, 1949. 221 pp.

University of Ulm

10 [i.e. Zehn] Jahre Universitat Ulm: Ansprachen, Referate und Ludwig-Heilmeyer-Gedachtnisvorlesung aus Anlass des 10 jahrigen Bestehens der Universitat Ulm im Februar 1977. Ulm: Pressestelle der Universitat im Auftrag des Rektors der Universitat, 1979. 109 pp.

University of Wurzburg

Baumbart, Peter, ed. *Vierhundert Jahre Universitat at Wurzburg: eine Festschrift.* Neustadt an der Aisch: Degener & Co., 1982. 1081 pp.

Bonicke, Christian. *Grundriss einer Geschichte von der Universitat zu Wirzburg.* 2 vols. Wurzburg: n.p., 1782-1788.

Schubert, Ernst. *Materielle und organisatorische Grundlagen der Wurzburger Universitatsentwicklung, 1582-1821.* Neustadt (an der Aisch): Degener & Co., 1973. 238 pp.

Wegele, Franz X. *Geschichte der Universitat Wurzburg.* 2 vols. 1882. Reprint. Aalen: Scientia, 1969.

GHANA

University of Ghana

Williams, Charles K. *Achimota; The Early Years, 1924-1948.* Accra: Longmans, 1962. 158 pp.

GREAT BRITIAN
ENGLAND

Battersea College of Technology

Arrowsmith, H. *Pioneering in Education for the Technologies: the Story of Battersea College of Technology, 1891-1962.* London: University of Surrey, 1966. 136 pp.

Bedford College of Higher Education

Smart, Richard. *Bedford Training College, 1881-1982: A History of a Froebel College and Its Schools.* Bedford: Bedford Training College Publications Committee, 1982. 178 pp.

Borough Road College*

Bartle, G. F. *A History of Borough Road College.* Isleworth: The College, 1976. 114 pp.

Brighton College of Technology

Jones, Martin D. W. *A History of Brighton College.* Brighton: Brighton College Development Fund, 1986. 56 pp.

Brunel University

Faherty, Janette. "From Technical College to University: A Case Study of Brunel College." Thesis, M. Phil. Brunel University, 1976. 214 pp.

Topping, James. *The Beginnings of Brunel University, from Technical College to University.* London: Oxford University Pr., 1981. 449 pp.

Camborne School of Mines

Piper, L. P. S. *A Short History of the Camborne School of Mines.* Truro: Trevithick Society, 1975. 40 pp.

Charlotte Mason College*

Inman, J. P. *Charlotte Mason College.* Wincester: Cormorant, 1985. 88 pp.

Chester College

Bradbury, John L. *Chester College and the Training of Teachers, 1839-1975.* Chester: Chester College, 1975. 255 pp.

Clifton College

Christie, Octavius F. *A History of Clifton College, 1860-1934.* Bristol: J. W. Arrowsmith, Ltd., 1935. 384 pp.

Coventry Technical College

Temple, Hilary. *Life Begins at Forty: A Look at the History of Coventry Technical College in the Fortieth Year of Its Existence in the Present Building.* Coventry: Coventry Technical College, 1975. 32 pp.

Culham College (Closed 1979)

Naylor, Leonard. *Culham: Church of England Training College for Schoolmasters, 1853-1953: Centenary History.* Abingdon-on-Thames: Abby Pr., 1953. 149 pp.

Naylor, Leonard, and Howat, Gerald. *Culham College History.* 2d ed. Oxfordshire: Culham Educational Foundation, 1982. 139 pp.

Didsburg College of Education*

Body, Alfred H., and Frangopulo, Nicholas J. *Silver Jubilee: The Story of Didsburg College of Education, Manchester, 1946-1971.* Manchester: E. J. Morten, 1970. 108 pp.

Eastbourne College of Education*

Allom, Vincent M. *Ex Oriente Salus: A Centenary History of Eastbourne College.* Eastbourne, Sx.: Eastbourne College, 1967. 184 pp.

Hertfordshire College of Agriculture and Horticulture

Pelham, Eric C. *The Oaklands Story, 1921-1971.* St. Albans: Hertfordshire College of Agriculture and Horticulture, 1971. 136 pp.

Hillcroft College

Cockerill, Janet. *Second Chance: The Story of Hillcroft, the Residential Working Women's College, and Its Contribution to the Development of Women's Adult Education.* Surbiton, Surrey: Hillcroft College, 1986. 78 pp.

Holly Royde College

Waller, Ross D. *Residential College: Origins of the Lamb Guildhouse and Holly Royde.* Manchester: Manchester University Pr., 1954. 59 pp.

King Alfred's College, Winchester

Rose, Martial. *A History of King Alfred's College, Winchester, 1840-1980.* London: Phillimore, 1981. 152 pp.

Kingston Upon Hull Training College

Bibby, Harold C., ed. *The First Fifty Years; A Brief History of Kingston Upon Hull Training College, 1913-1963.* Hull, Eng.: Kingston Upon Hull Trining College, 1964. 84 pp.

Loughborough University

Cantor, Leonard M., and Matthews, Geoffrey F. *Loughborough from College to University: A History of Higher Education at Loughborough, 1909-1966.* Loughborough: Loughborough University of Technology, 1977. 199 pp.

Open University

Eurich, Nell, and Schwenkmeyer, Barry. *Great Britian's Open University; First Chance, Second Chance, or Last Chance?* New York: Academy for Educational Development, 1971. 31 pp.

Horlock, John H. *The Open University After 15 Years: Presented 17th January 1984.* Manchester: Manchester Statistical Society, 1984. 23 pp.

Preston Polytechnic

Timmins, Geoffrey; Foster, David; and Law, Harry. *Preston Polytechnic: The Emergence of an Institution, 1828-1978.* Preston: Preston Polytechnic, 1979. 55 pp.

Royal College of Art

Frayling, Christopher. *The Royal College of Art: 150 Years of Art and Design.* London: Barrie and Jenkins, 1987. 192 pp.

Royal College of Music

Colles, Henry C., and Cruft, John. *The Royal College of Music: A Centenary Record, 1883-1983.* London: Royal College of Music, 1982. 113 pp.

Royal College of Surgeons of England

Cope, Zachary. *The Royal College of Surgeons of England; A History.* Springfield: C. C. Thomas, 1959. 360 pp.

Ruskin College

Pollins, Harold. *The History of Ruskin College.* Oxford: Ruskin College Library, 1984. 71 pp.

Yorke, Paul. *Education and the Working Class: Ruskin College, 1899-1909.* Oxford: Ruskin College, 1977. 41 pp.

St. Mary's College*

St. Mary's College (Fenham). *St. Mary's College, Fenham, 1905-1985.* London: Society of the Sacred Heart, 1984. 90 pp.

St. Peter's College*

Seaman, Robert D. H. *St. Peter's College, Saltley, 1944-1978.*
  Birmingham: The College, 1978. 215 pp.

Sandhurst Royal Military College

Mockler-Ferryman, Augustus F. *Annals of Sandhurst; A Chronicle of the
  Royal Military College from Its Foundation to the Present Day, with
  a Sketch of the History of the Staff College.* London: W. Heinemann,
  1900. 318 pp.

Shepperd, Gilbert A. *Sandhurst; The Royal Military Academy Sandhurst
  and Its Predecessors.* Feltham, Middlesex: Country Life Books, 1980.
  224 pp.

Smyth, John G. *Sandhurst, the History of the Royal Military Academy,
  Woolwich, the Royal Military College, Sandhurst, and the Royal
  Military Academy Sandhurst, 1741-1961.* London: Weidenfeld and
  Nicolson, 1961. 301 pp.

Thomas, Hugh. *The Story of Sandhurst.* London: Hutchinson, 1961.
  244 pp.

Yardley, Michael. *Sandhurst; A Documentary.* London: Harrap, 1987.
  256 pp.

Trinity College of Music

Rutland, Harold. *Trinity College of Music, the First Hundred Years.*
  London: Trinity College of Music, 1972. 72 pp.

Twickenham College of Technology*

Pearce, Brian L. *Twickenham College of Technology; The First Thirty-Five
  Years, 1937 to 1972.* Twickenham: Twickenham College of Technology,
  1974. 64 pp.

University of Bath

Moore, George H. *The University of Bath: The Formative Years, 1949-1969:
  A Short History of the Circumstances and the Planning Which Led to the
  Foundation of the University of Bath.* Bath: Bath University Pr.,
  1982. 110 pp.

University of Birmingham

Burstall, Frederic W., and Burton, Cecil G. *Souvenir History of the Foundation and Development of the Mason Science College and of the University of Birmingham, 1880-1930.* Birmingham: n.p., 1930. 83 pp.

Cheeesewright, Maurice. *Mirror to a Mermaid: Pictorial Reminiscences of Mason College and the University of Birmingham, 1875-1975.* Birmingham: University of Birmingham, 1975. 144 pp.

Vincent, Eric W., and Hinton, Percival. *The University of Birmingham, Its History and Significance.* Birmingham: Cornish Brothers Ltd., 1947. 240 pp.

University of Bristol

Carleton, Don. *A University for Bristol: An Informal History in Text and Pictures.* Bristol: University of Bristol Pr., 1984. 152 pp.

Sherborne, J. W. *University College, Bristol, 1876-1909.* Bristol: Bristol Branch of the Historical Association, 1977. 26 pp.

University of Cambridge

Atkinson, Thomas D. *Cambridge Described & Illustrated: Being a History of the Town and University.* London: Macmillan, 1897. 528 pp.

Attwater, Aubrey L. *Pembroke College, Cambridge; A Short History.* Cambridge: The University Pr., 1936. 129 pp.

Austen-Leigh, Augustus. *King's College.* London: F. E. Robinson and Co., 1899. 302 pp.

Baker, Thomas. *History of the College of St. John the Evangelist, Cambridge.* 2 vols. Cambridge: The University Pr., 1869.

Ball, Walter W. R. *Cambridge Papers.* London: Macmillan and Co., 1918. 326 pp.

--------. *Notes on the History of Trinity College, Cambridge.* London: Macmillan and Co., 1899. 183 pp.

--------. *Trinity College, Cambridge.* London: J. M. Dent and Co., 1906. 106 pp.

Benson, Arthur C. *Magdalene College, Cambridge; A Little View of Its Buildings and History.* Cambridge: Bowes & Bowes, 1923. 51 pp.

Benstead, Charles R. *Portrait of Cambridge.* London: Hale, 1968. 221 pp.

Bradbrook, Muriel C. *'That Infidel Place': A Short History of Girton College, 1869-1969, with an Essay on the Collegiate University in the Modern World.* London: Chatto & Windus, 1969. 168 pp.

Brooke, Christopher N. L. *The History of Gonville and Caius College.* Woodbridge, Suffolk: Boydell, 1986. 354 pp.

Brooke, Christopher N. L., ed. *A History of the University of Cambridge.* 4 vols. Cambridge: Cambridge University Pr., 1988-

Brooke, Christopher N. L., and Highfield, Roger. *Oxford and Cambridge.* Cambridge: Cambridge University Pr., 1988. 367 pp.

Brown, Algernon L. *Selwyn College, Cambridge.* London: Hutchinson & Co., 1906. 207 pp.

Browne, Archibald D., and Seltman, Charles T. *A Pictorial History of the Queen's College of St. Margaret and St. Bernard, Commonly Called Queen's College, 1448-1948.* Cambridge: Printed for the College, 1951. 23 pp.

Browne, George F. *St. Catharine's College.* London: F. E. Robinson and Co., 1902. 267 pp.

Bury, John P. T. *The College of Corpus Christi and of the Blessed Virgin Mary; A History from 1822 to 1952.* Cambridge: Printed for the College, 1952. 362 pp.

Caius, John. *The Annals of Gonville and Caius College.* Cambridge: Deighton, Bell & Co., 1904. 431 pp.

Cambridge in the Seventeenth Century. 3 vols. Cambridge: University Pr., 1856-1871.

Carter, Edmund. *The History of the University of Cambridge, from Its Original, to the Year 1753.* London: Printed for the Author, 1753. 471 pp.

Clark, John W. *Cambridge: Brief History and Descriptive Notes.* London: n.p., 1890. 325 pp.

Cobban, Alan B. *The King's Hall Within the University of Cambridge in the Later Middle Ages.* London: Cambridge University Pr., 1969. 355 pp.

--------. *The Medieval English Universities: Oxford and Cambridge to c.1500.* Berkeley: University of California Pr., 1988. 465 pp.

Cooper, Charles H. *Annals of Cambridge.* 4 vols. Cambridge: n.p., 1842-1852.

Crawley, Charles. *Trinity Hall: The History of a Cambridge College, 1350-1975.* Cambridge: The College, 1976. 289 pp.

Documents Relating to the University and Colleges of Cambridge. 3 vols. London: Printed by G. Eyre and W. Spottiswoode for H. M. S. O., 1852.

Downs, B. W. *Cambridge Past and Present.* London: Methuen, 1926. 257 pp.

Dyer, George. *History of the University and Colleges of Cambridge; Including Notices Relating to the Founders and Eminent Men.* 2 vols. London: Longman, 1814.

Edwards, Gerald M. *Sidney Sussex College.* London: F. E. Robinson and Co., 1899. 234 pp.

Fay, Charles R. *King's College, Cambridge.* London: J. M. Dent and Co., 1907. 127 pp.

Forbes, Mansfield D., ed. *Clare College, 1326-1926; University Hall, 1326-1346, Clare Hall, 1346-1856.* 2 vols. Cambridge: Cambridge University Pr., 1928-1930.

Fowler, Laurence, and Fowler, Helen, eds. *Cambridge Commemorated: An Anthology of University Life.* New York: Cambridge University Pr., 1984. 384 pp.

French, Stanley. *The History of Downing College, Cambridge.* Cambridge: Downing College Association, 1978. 145 pp.

Fuller, Thomas. *The History of the University of Cambridge, and of Waltham Abbey.* London: Printed for T. Tegg, 1840. 688 pp.

--------. *The History of the University of Cambridge from the Conquest to the Year 1634.* Cambridge: J. & J. J. Deighton, and T. Stevenson, 1840. 335 pp.

Gardner, Alice. *Short History of Newnhan College, Cambridge.* Cambridge: Bowes & Bowes, 1921. 144 pp.

Garland, Martha M. *Cambridge Before Darwin: The Ideal of a Liberal Education, 1800-1860.* New York: Cambridge University Pr., 1980. 196 pp.

Grave, W. W. *Fitzwilliam College Cambridge, 1869-1969: Its History as the Non-Collegiate Institution of the University and Its Beginnings as an Independent College.* Cambridge: Fitzwilliam Society, 1983. 564 pp.

Gray, Arthur. *Cambridge University, an Episodical History.* Cambridge: W. Heffer & Sons Ltd., 1926. 310 pp.

--------. *Jesus College.* London: F. E. Robinson and Co., 1902. 245 pp.

Gray, Arthur, and Brittain, Frederick. *A History of Jesus College, Cambridge.* Rev. ed. London: Heinemann, 1979. 226 pp.

Gray, Joseph H. *The Queen's College of St. Margaret and St. Bernard in the University of Cambridge.* London: F. E. Robinson and Co. 1899. 308 pp.

Hackett, M. B. *The Original Statutes of Cambridge University; The Text and Its History.* Cambridge: Cambridge University Pr., 1970. 398 pp.

Hamilton, Mary A. *Newnham; An Informal Biography.* London: Faber and Faber, 1936. 199 pp.

Heywood, James, and Wright, Thomas. *Cambridge University Transactions during the Puritan Controversies of the Sixteenth and Seventeenth Centuries.* 2 vols. London: H. G. Bohn, 1854.

The History and Antiquites of the University of Cambridge. London: T. Warner, 1721. 265 pp.

Howarth, Thomas E. B. *Cambridge Between Two Wars.* London: Collins, 1978. 258 pp.

Jones, William H. S. *A History of St. Catharine's College, Once Catharine Hall, Cambridge.* Cambridge: The University Pr., 1936. 413 pp.

--------. *The Story of St. Catharines College, Cambridge.* Cambridge: W. Heffer, 1951. 174 pp.

Karp, Alan. "The Academic Corporations of England in the Middle Ages: Oxford and Cambridge, 1150-1509." Ed.D. diss., Columbia University, Teachers College, 1977. 409 pp. *Dissertation Abstracts International,* vol. 38A, p. 668.

Keynes, Margaret E. *A House by the River: Newnham Grange to Darwin College.* Cambridge: Darwin College, 1976. 259 pp.

Lamb, Robert. *Masters' History of the College of Corpus Christi and the Blessed Virgin Mary in the University of Cambridge.* Cambridge: John Smith, 1831. 504 pp.

Leigh, A. A. *King's College.* London: n.p., 1899. 307 pp.

Little, Bryan D. G. *The Colleges of Cambridge, 1286-1973.* Bath: Adams and Dart, 1973. 192 pp.

Lloyd, Albert H. *The Early History of Christ's College.* Cambridge: The University Pr., 1934. 477 pp.

Loggan, David. *Cantabrigia Illustrata; A Series of Views of the University and Colleges and of Eton College.* Cambridge: Macmillan and Bowes, 1905. 43 pp.

Masters, Robert. *The History of the College of Corpus Christi and the b. Virgin Mary (Commonly Called Benet) in the University of Cambridge, from Its Foundation to the Present Time.* 2 vols. Cambridge: J. Bentham, 1753.

Mayor, John E. B., ed. *Cambridge under Queen Anne.* Cambridge: Deighton, Bell & Co., 1911. 545 pp.

--------. *Early Statutes of the College of St. John the Evangelist in the University of Cambridge.* Cambridge: Macmillan and Co., 1859. 408 pp.

Megson, Barbara, and Lindsay, Jean O. *Girton College, 1869-1959, an Informal History.* Cambridge: W. Heffer, 1961. 69 pp.

Miller, Edward. *Portrait of a College; A History of the College of Saint John the Evangelist, Cambridge.* Cambridge: Cambridge University Pr., 1961. 149 pp.

Mullinger, James B. *St. John's College.* London: F. E. Robinson and Co., 1901. 333 pp.

--------. *The University of Cambridge.* 2 vols. 1873. Reprint. New York: Johnson Reprint Corp., 1969.

Parker, Richard. *The History and Antiquities of the University of Cambridge.* London: T. Warner, 1721. 265 pp.

Peile, John. *Christ's College.* London: F. E. Robinson and Co., 1900. 300 pp.

Purnell, Edward K. *Magdalene College.* London: F. E. Robinson and Co., 1904. 215 pp.

Rackham, H., ed. *The Early Statutes of Christ's College, Cambridge: With the Statutes of the Prior Foundation of God's House.* Cambridge: Fabb & Tyler, 1927. 152 pp.

Rich, Edwin E., ed. *St. Catharine's College, Cambridge, 1473-1973: A Volume of Essays to Commemorate the Quincentenary of the Foundation of the College.* Cambridge: St. Catharine's College, 1973. 314 pp.

Roberts, Sydney C. *Introduction to Cambridge: A Brief Guide to the University from Within.* 2d ed. Cambridge: University Pr., 1938. 103 pp.

Rolph, Rebecca S. "Emmanuel College, Cambridge and the Puritan Movements of Old and New England." Ph.D. diss., University of Southern California, 1979. *Dissertation Abstracts International,* vol. 40A, p. 2202.

St. Catharine's College (University of Cambridge). *Documents Relating to St. Catharines College in the University of Cambridge.* Cambridge: University Pr., 1861. 192 pp.

Scott, Robert F. *St. John's College, Cambridge.* London: J. M. Dent and Co., 1907. 110 pp.

Scott-Giles, Charles W. *Sidney Sussex College: A Short History.* Cambridge University Pr., 1951. 125 pp.

--------. *Sidney Sussex College: A Short History.* Cambridge: Sydney Sussex College, 1975. 144 pp.

Searle, William G. *The History of the Queen's College of St. Margaret and St. Bernard in the University of Cambridge.* 2 vols. Cambridge: Deighton Bell & Co., 1867-1871.

Sherman, John. *Historia Collegii Jesu Cantabrigiensis.* London: T. Rodd, 1840. 43 pp.

Shuckburgh, Evelyn S. *Emmanuel College.* London: F. E. Robinson and Co., 1904. 259 pp.

Sicca, Cinzia M. *Committed to Classicism: The Building of Downing College, Cambridge.* Cambridge: Downing College, 1987. 226 pp.

Simms, T. H. *Homerton College, 1695-1978: From Dissenting Academy to Approved Society in the University of Cambridge.* Cambridge: Trustees of Homerton College, 1979. 109 pp.

Steegman, John. *Cambridge As It Was and As It Is To-day.* London: Batsford, 1941. 120 pp.

--------. *Cambridge As It Was and As It Is To-day.* 2d ed. London: Batsford, 1941. 120 pp.

--------. *Cambridge As It Was and As It Is To-day.* 3d ed. London: Batsford, 1945. 120 pp.

--------. *Cambridge As It Was and As It Is To-day.* 4th ed. London: Batsford, 1949. 120 pp.

--------. *Cambridge As It Was and As It Is To-day.* 5th ed. London: Batsford, 1954. 120 pp.

Stephen, Barbara N. *Girton College, 1869-1932.* Cambridge: The University Pr., 1933. 202 pp.

Stephen, Leslie. *Sketches from Cambridge.* London: Macmillan, 1865. 144 pp.

Stevens, Horace W. P. *Downing Dollege.* London: F. E. Robinson and Co., 1899. 285 pp.

Stokes, Henry P. *Corpus Christi.* London: F. E. Robinson and Co., 1898. 251 pp.

Stubbs, Charles W. *Cambridge and Its Story.* London: J. M. Dent and Co., 1903. 290 pp.

--------. *Cambridge and Its Story.* 2d ed. London: J. M. Dent and Co., 1904. 300 pp.

Thompson, Alexander H. *Cambridge and Its Colleges.* London: Methuen, 1897. 330 pp.

--------. *Cambridge and Its Colleges.* 2d ed. London: Methuen, 1898. 330 pp.

--------. *Cambridge and Its Colleges.* 3d ed. London: Methuen, 1899. 330 pp.

--------. *Cambridge and Its Colleges.* 4th ed. London: Methuen, 1901. 330 pp.

--------. *Cambridge and Its Colleges.* 5th ed. London: Methuen, 1903. 330 pp.

--------. *Cambridge and Its Colleges.* 6th ed. London: Methuen, 1904. 329 pp.

--------. *Cambridge and Its Colleges.* 7th ed. London: Methuen, 1906. 337 pp.

--------. *Cambridge and Its Colleges.* 8th ed. London: n.p., 1908.

--------. *Cambridge and Its Colleges.* 9th ed. London: Methuen, 1910. 337 pp.

--------. *Cambridge and Its Colleges.* 11th ed. London: Methuen, 1919. 337 pp.

--------. *Cambridge and Its Colleges.* 12th ed. London: Methuen, 1923. 353 pp.

--------. *Cambridge and Its Colleges.* 13th ed. London: Methuen, 1926. 353 pp.

Trevelyan, George M. *Trinity College; An Historical Sketch.* Cambridge: Cambridge University Pr., 1943. 320 pp.

Twigg, John. *A History of Queen's College, Cambridge, 1448-1986.* Woodbridge, Suffolk: Boydell & Brewer, 1987. 533 pp.

Venn, John. *Biographical History of Gonville and Caius College, 1349-1847.* 4 vols. Cambridge: Cambridge University Pr., 1897-1912.

--------. *Caius College.* London: F. E. Robinson and Co., 1901. 271 pp.

--------. *Early Collegiate Life.* Cambridge: W. Heffer and Sons Ltd., 1913. 286 pp.

Walker, Thomas A. *Peterhouse.* London: Hutchinson & Co., 1906. 248 pp.

--------. *Peterhouse.* Cambridge: W. Heffer, 1935. 157 pp.

Walsh, Benjamin D. *A Historical Account of the University of Cambridge, and Its Colleges.* London: J. Ridgway, 1837. 162 pp.

Wardale, John R. *Clare College.* London: F. E. Robinson and Co., 1899. 218 pp.

Wardale, John R., ed. *Clare College: Letters and Documents.* Cambridge: Macmillan, 1903. 152 pp.

Wilkinson, L. P. *A Century of King's: 1873-1972.* Cambridge: King's College, 1980. 182 pp.

--------. *Kingsmen of a Century, 1873-1972.* Reprinted with Corrections. Cambridge: King's College, 1981. 394 pp.

Willis, Robert. *The Architectural History of the University of Cambridge and of the Colleges of Cambridge and Eton.* 4 vols. Cambridge: University Pr., 1886.

Wilson, Joseph. *Memorabilia Cantabrigiae, or an Account of the Different Colleges in Cambridge.* London: E. Harding, 1803. 341 pp.

Winstanley, Denys A. *Early Victorian Cambridge.* Cambridge: The University Pr., 1940. 460 pp.

--------. *Later Victorian Cambridge.* Cambridge: University Pr., 1947. 367 pp.

--------. *The University of Cambridge in the Eighteenth Century.* Cambridge: The University Pr., 1922. 349 pp.

--------. *Unreformed Cambridge: A Study of Certain Aspects of the University in the Eighteenth Century.* Cambridge: The University Pr., 1935. 411 pp.

Young, Frank G. *Darwin College, 1963-1966, and the University of Cambridge.* Cambridge: Printed for Darwin College, 1967. 30 pp.

University of Durham

Fowler, Joseph T. *Durham University; Earlier Foundations and Present Colleges.* London: F. E. Robinson and Co., 1904. 312 pp.

Heesom, Alan. *The Founding of the University of Durham: Lecture Delivered in Elvet Riverside, Durham, 11 March 1982.* Durham: Dean and Chapter of Durham, 1982. 32 pp.

Hird, Marilyn, ed. *St. Mary's College, 1899-1974: An Account of the Woman's Hostel, 1899-1920, and Some Impressions of Later College Life.* Durham: St. Mary's College Society, 1974. 95 pp.

Whiting, Charles E. *The University of Durham, 1832-1932.* London: Sheldon Pr., 1932. 345 pp.

Whitworth, Thomas A. *Fellow Sandstone and Mellow Brick: An Account of Hatfield College, Durham, 1846-1971.* Durham: University of Durham, Hatfield College, 1971. 104 pp.

University of Essex

Sloman, Albert E. *A University in the Making.* New York: Oxford University Pr., 1963. 90 pp.

University of Exeter

Clapp, Brian W. *The University of Exeter: A History.* Exeter, Devon.: University of Exeter, 1982. 208 pp.

University of Hull

Bamford, T. W. *The University of Hull: The First Fifty Years.* Oxford: Oxford University Pr., 1978. 290 pp.

University of Keele

Mountford, James F. *Keele: An Historical Critique.* London: Routledge, 1972. 332 pp.

University of Lancaster

McClintock, Marion E. *University of Lancaster: Quest for Innovation; A History of the First Ten Years, 1964-1974.* Lancaster: University of Lancaster, 1974. 464 pp.

University of Leeds

Gosden, P. H. J. H., and Taylor, A. J., eds. *Studies in the History of a University, 1874-1974: To Commemorate the Century of the University of Leeds.* Leeds: E. J. Arnold, 1975. 318 pp.

Leeds. University. *A Short Account of the Growth of the University of Leeds.* Leeds: Jowett & Sowry Ltd. Printers, 1924. 31 pp.

Shimmin, Arnold N. *The University of Leeds, the First Half-Century.* Cambridge: University Pr., 1954. 229 pp.

University of Liverpool

Kelly, Thomas. *For Advancement of Learning: The University of Liverpool, 1881-1981.* Liverpool: Liverpool University Pr., 1981. 560 pp.

University of Liverpool. *The University of Liverpool, 1903-1953.* Liverpool: n.p., 1954. 63 pp.

University of London

Allchin, William H. *An Account of the Reconstruction of the University of London.* 3 vols. n.p.: H. K. Lewis.

Bellot, Hugh H. *University College London, 1826-1926.* London: University of London Pr., 1929. 464 pp.

--------. *The University of London: A History.* London: London University, 1969. 54 pp.

Bingham, Caroline. *The History of Royal Holloway College, 1886-1986.* London: Constable, 1987. 313 pp.

Burns, Cecil D. *A Short History of Birkbeck College (University of London).* London: University of London Pr., 1924. 169 pp.

Carus-Wilson, Eleanora, ed. *Westfield College, University of London, 1882-1932.* London: Favil Pr., 1932. 81 pp.

Cumbers, Frank H., ed. *Richmond College, 1843-1943.* London: Epworth Pr., 1944. 190 pp.

Davies, John L., ed. *The Working Men's College, 1854-1904; Records of Its History and Its Work for Fifty Years, by Members of the College.* London: Macmillan, 1904. 296 pp.

Dymon, Dorothy, ed. *The Forge; The History of Goldsmiths' College, 1905-1955.* London: Methuen, 1955. 158 pp.

Ellis, John. *LHMC, 1785-1985: The Story of the London Hospital Medical College, England's First Medical School.* London: London Hospital Medical Club, 1986. 200 pp.

Foster, Gregory. *The University of London: History, Present Resources and Future Possibilities.* London: University Pr., 1922. 48 pp.

Godwin, George S. *Queen Mary College: An Adventure in Education.* London: Queen Mary College and The Acorn Pr., 1939. 209 pp.

Gollancz, Hermann. *A Contribution to the History of University College, London.* Oxford: n.p., 1930. 46 pp.

Harris, Isidore. *History of Jews' College: November 11th 1855-November 10th 1905.* London: Luzac, 1906. 202 pp.

Harrison, John F. C. *A History of the Working Men's College, 1854-1954.* London: Routledge, 1954. 215 pp.

Harte, Negley B. *The University of London, 1836-1986: An Illustrated History.* London: Athlone Pr., 1986. 303 pp.

Harte, Neagley B., and North, John. *The World of University College, London, 1828-1978.* London: University College, 1978. 216 pp.

Hearnshaw, Fossey J. C. *The Centenary History of King's College, London, 1828-1928.* London: Harrap & Company Ltd., 1929. 542 pp.

Heulin, Gordon. *King's College London, 1828-1978.* London: King's College, 1978. 248 pp.

Hyamson, Albert M. *Jews' College, London, 1855-1955.* London: Jews' College, 1955. 142 pp.

Jews' College. *Jews' College Jubilee Volume, Comprising a History of the College by the Rev. Isidore Harris, M. A. and Essays by Teachers and Former Students of the Institution.* London: Luzac and Co., 1906. 274 pp.

Kaye, Elaine. *A History of Queen's College London, 1848-1972.* London: Chatto and Windus, 1972. 190 pp.

London. University. *The University of London. A Sketch of Its Work and History from Its Foundation in 1837 to the Present Time.* London: Darling & Son, Ltd., 1900. 45 pp.

--------. *University of London, 1836-1936.* London: Chiswick Pr., 1936. 79 pp.

--------. *University of London, the Historical Record (1836-1912), Being a Supplement to the Calendar, Completed to September 1912.* London: University of London Pr., 1912. 572 pp.

Marsh, Neville. *The History of Queen Elizabeth College: One Hundred Years of University Education in Kensington.* London: King's College London, 1986. 336 pp.

Merrington, W. R. *University College Hospital and Its Medical School: A*

History. London: Heinemann, 1976. 301 pp.

Moss, Gerard P., and Saville M. V. *From Palace to College: An Illustrated Account of Queen Mary College. (University of London).* London: The College, 1985. 152 pp.

Pearson, Karl. *The New University for London; A Guide to Its History and a Criticism of Its Defects.* London: T. F. Unwin, 1892. 139 pp.

Silver, Harold, and Teague, Sydney J., eds. *Chelsea College, a History.* London: Chelsea College, 1977. 96 pp.

Sondheimer, Janet. *Castle Adamant in Hampstead: A History of Westfield College, 1882-1982.* London: Westfield College, University of London, 1983. 189 pp.

Teague, Sydney J. *The City University, a History.* London: City University, 1980. 270 pp.

Thomson, Herbert C. *The Story of the Middlesex Hospital Medical School, 1835-1935.* London: John Murray, 1935. 182 pp.

Tuke, Margaret J. *A History of Bedford College for Women, 1849-1937.* London: Oxford University Pr., 1939. 364 pp.

University of London. *The Federal University of London.* London: University of London, 1983. 16 pp.

Warmington, Eric H. *A History of Birkbeck College, University of London, during the Second World War, 1939-1945.* London: Birkbeck College, 1954. 206 pp.

Wilson, Stanley G. *The University of London and Its Colleges.* London: University Tutorial Pr., 1923. 150 pp.

University of Newcastle Upon Tyne

Bettenson, Ernest M. *University of Newcastle-Upon-Tyne: A Historical Introduction, 1834-1971.* Newcastle Upon Tyne: University of Newcastle Upon Tyne, 1971. 108 pp.

University of Nottingham

Wood, Alfred C. *A History of the University College, Nottingham, 1881-1948.* Oxford: Blackwell, 1953. 181 pp.

University of Oxford

Amhurst, Nicholas. *Terra-Filius: or, The Secret History of the University of Oxford: In Several Essays.* 2d ed. 2 vols. London: R. Francklin, 1726.

-------. *Terra-Filius: or, The Secret History of the University of Oxford: In Several Essays.* 3d ed. London: R. Francklin, 1754. 369 pp.

Aston, T. H. *The History of the University of Oxford.* 3 vols. New York: Oxford University Pr., 1984-

Ayliffe, John. *The Ancient and Present State of the University of Oxford.* 2 vols. London: Printed for W. Mears and J. Hooke, 1723.

Bailey, Gemma C., ed. *Lady Margaret Hall; A Short History Issued on Behalf of the Lady Margaret Hall Appeal Fund.* London: H. Milford, 1923. 144 pp.

Baker, John N. L. *Jesus College, Oxford, 1571-1971.* Oxford: Jesus College, Oxford, 1971. 153 pp.

Balliol College. *Balliol College Oxford: A Brief History and Guide.* Oxford: Balliol College, 1982. 40 pp.

Balsdon, John P. V. D. *Oxford Now and Then.* London: Duckworth, 1970. 267 pp.

Baxter, Dudley. *The Story of an Oxford College.* Oxford: J. Vincent, 1907. 12 pp.

Bill, Edward G. W. *Education at Christ Church, Oxford, 1660-1800.* Oxford: Clarendon Pr., 1987. 256 pp.

Bill, Edward G. W., and Mason, John F. A. *Christ Church and Reform, 1850-1867.* Oxford: Clarendon Pr., 1970. 269 pp.

Blakiston, Herbert E. D. *Trinity College.* London: F. E. Robinson and Co., 1898. 248 pp.

Bowra, C. M., and Jewell, Derek, eds. *The Wadham Miscellany.* Oxford: Wadham College, 1948. 120 pp.

Brodrick, George C. *A History of the University of Oxford.* London: Longmans, 1900. 235 pp.

Brooke, Christopher N. L., and Highfield, Roger. *Oxford and Cambridge.* Cambridge: Cambridge University Pr., 1988. 367 pp.

Buchan, John. *Brasenose College.* London: F. E. Robinson and Co., 1898. 202 pp.

Burnett, Richard G. *Oxford and Cambridge in Pictures.* London: Phoenix House, 1950. 181 pp.

Burney, Lester. *Cross Street Chapel Manchester and Its College.* Manchester: L. Burney, 1983. 84 pp.

Buxton, John, and Williams, Penry, eds. *New College, Oxford, 1379-1979.* Oxford: Warden and Fellows of New College, Oxford, 1979. 380 pp.

Byrne, Muriel S., and Mansfield, Catherine H. *Sommerville College, 1879-1921.* Oxford: Printed by F. Hall, 1922. 99 pp.

The Canterbury Quadrangle, 1636-1986: An Anthology. Cowley: Bocardo, 1986. 44 pp.

Carr, William. *University College.* London: F. E. Robinson and Co., 1902. 242 pp.

Catto, J. I., ed. *The Early Oxford Schools.* Oxford: Oxford University Pr., 1984. 684 pp.

Chalmers, Alexander. *A History of the Colleges, Halls, and Public Buildings, Attached to the University of Oxford, Including the Lives of the Founders.* 2 vols. Oxford: Printed by Collingwood and Co., 1810.

Clark, Andrew. *The Colleges of Oxford: Their History and Traditions.* London: Methuen, 1891. 480 pp.

--------. *Lincoln.* London: F. E. Robinson and Co., 1898. 220 pp.

Cobban, Alan B. *The Medieval English Universities: Oxford and Cambridge to c.1500.* Berkeley: University of California Pr., 1988. 465 pp.

Colvin, Havard M., and Simmons, John S. G. *All Souls: An Oxford College and Its Buildings: Three Lectures.* New York: Oxford University Pr., 1988. 104 pp.

Combe, William. *A History of the University of Oxford, Its Colleges,Halls, and Public Buildings.* 2 vols. London: R. Ackermann, 1814.

Costin, William C. *The History of St. John's College, Oxford, 1598-1860.* Oxford: Clarendon Pr., 1958. 297 pp.

Daniel, Charles H. O., and Barker, W. R. *Worcester College.* London: F. E. Robinson and Co., 1900. 268 pp.

Davis, Henry W. C. *Balliol College.* London: F. E. Robinson and Co., 1899. 237 pp.

--------. *A History of Balliol College.* Oxford: Basil Blackwell, 1963. 329 pp.

Davis, Valentine D. *A History of Manchester College from Its Foundation in Manchester to Its Establishment in Oxford.* London: Allen & Unwin, 1932. 216 pp.

Durand, Ralph A. *Oxford, Its Buildings and Gardens.* London: Grant Richards, 1909. 238 pp.

Emden, Alfred B. *An Oxford Hall in Medieval Times, Being the Early History of St. Edmund Hall.* Oxford: Clarendon Pr., 1927. 320 pp.

Evans, Robert J. W., and Richards, Bernard A. *Brasenose College: A Short Guide.* Oxford: The College, 1977. 16 pp.

Fowler, Thomas. *The History of Corpus Christi College, with Lists of Its Members.* Oxford: Oxford Historical Society, 1893. 482 pp.

Fyfe, Dorthea H. *Oxford.* New York: F. A. Stokes Co., 1917. 287 pp.

Gaunt, William. *Oxford.* London: B. T. Batsford, 1965. 191 pp.

George, Hereford B. *New College, 1856-1906.* London: Oxford University Pr., 1906. 102 pp.

Glasgow, Edwin. *Sketches of Magdalen College, Oxford.* London: J. M. Dent and Co., 1901. 11 pp.

--------. *Sketches of Wadham College, Oxford.* London: Methuen, 1900. 20 pp.

Gloucester, Richard, and Hobhouse, Herminie. *Oxford and Cambridge.* New York: Thames and Hudson, 1980. 184 pp.

Godley, Alfred D. *Oxford in the Eighteenth Century.* London: Methuen, 1908. 291 pp.

Green, Vivian H. H. *The Commonwealth of Lincoln College, 1427-1977.* Oxford: University of Oxford Pr., 1979. 726 pp.

--------. *A History of Oxford University.* B. T. Batsford, 1974. 214 pp.

--------. *Oxford Common Room; A Study of Lincoln College and Mark Pattison.* London: E. Arnold, 1957. 336 pp.

Griffin, Penny, ed. *St. Hugh's: One Hundred Years of Women's Education in Oxford.* Basingstoke: Macmillian, 1986. 339 pp.

Hamilton, Sidney G. *Hertford College.* London: F. E. Robinson and Co., 1903. 175 pp.

Hardy, Ernest G. *Jesus College.* London: F. E. Robinson and Co., 1899. 252 pp.

Headlam, Cecil. *Oxford and Its Story.* London: J. M. Dent and Co., 1904. 365 pp.

Henderson, Bernard W. *Merton College.* London: F. E. Robinson and Co., 1899. 294 pp.

Hobhouse, Christopher. *Oxford As It Was and As It Is Today.* London: B. T. Batsford, 1939. 120 pp.

--------. *Oxford As It Was and As It Is Today.* Oxford: Oxford University Pr., 1946. 120 pp.

--------. *Oxford As It Was and As It Is Today.* 3d ed. London: B. T. Batsford, 1945. 120 pp.

--------. *Oxford As It Was and As It Is Today.* 4th ed. London: B. T. Batsford, 1948. 120 pp.

--------. *Oxford As It Was and As It Is Today.* 5th ed. London: B. T. Batsford, 1952. 120 pp.

Hodgkin, Robert H. *Six Centuries of an Oxford College: A History of the Queen's College, 1340-1940.* Oxford: Blackwell, 1949. 224 pp.

Hollis, Christopher. *Oxford in the Twenties: Recollections of Five Friends.* London: Heinemann, 1976. 136 pp.

Hussey, Christopher. *Oxford; The College and University Buildings.* London: Country Life, 1932. 48 pp.

Hutton, William H. *St. John Baptist College.* London: F. E. Robinson and Co., 1898. 274 pp.

Ingram, James. *Memorials of the Colleges and Halls in the University of Oxford.* 2d ed. 3 vols. Oxford: J. H. Parker, 1847.

Ingram, James, ed. *Memorials of Oxford.* 3 vols. Oxford: J. H. Parker, H. Slatter, and W. Graham, 1834-1837.

Jackson, Thomas G. *Wadham College, Oxford, Its Foundation, Architecture and History, with an Account of the Family of Wadham and Their Seats in Somerset and Devon.* Oxford: Clarendon Pr., 1893. 228 pp.

Jessup, Frank. *Wolfson College, Oxford: The Early Years.* Oxford: Wolfson College, 1979. 32 pp.

Jones, John. *Balliol College: A History, 1263-1939.* Oxford: Oxford University Pr., 1988. 323 pp.

Karp, Alan. "The Academic Corporations of England in the Middle Ages: Oxford and Cambridge, 1150-1509." Ed.D. diss., Columbia University, Teachers College, 1977. 409 pp. *Dissertation Abstracts International,* vol. 38A, p.668.

Keble College. *Keble College.* Derby: English Life, 1987. 16 pp.

Lang, Andrew. *Oxford.* London: Seeley, Jackson and Halliday, 1882. 56 pp.

--------. *Oxford, Brief Historical and Descriptive Notes.* New ed. London: Seeley and Co. Limited, 1906. 282 pp.

Lyte, Henry C. M. *A History of the University of Oxford from the Earliest Times to the Year 1530.* London: Macmillan, 1886. 504 pp.

McConica, James, ed. *The Collegiate University.* Oxford: Clarendon Pr., 1986. 775 pp.

Macleane, Douglas. *A History of Pembroke College, Oxford, Anciently Broadgates Hall.* Oxford: Clarendon Pr., 1897. 544 pp.

Maden, Falconer, ed. *Brasenose College Quatercentenary Monographs.* 2 vols. Oxford: Clarendon Pr., 1909.

Magrath, John R. *The Queen's College, Oxford.* 2 vols. Oxford: Clarendon Pr., 1921.

Mais, Stuart P. B. *The Story of Oxford.* London: Staples Pr., 1951. 87 pp.

Mallet, Charles E. *A History of the University of Oxford.* 3 vols. London: Methuen, 1924-1927.

Mansbridge, Albert. *The Older Universities of England: Oxford and Cambridge.* London: Longmans, 1923. 296 pp.

Milne, Joseph G. *The Early History of Corpus Christi College, Oxford.*

Oxford: Basil Blackwell, 1946. 72 pp.

Morris, Jan, ed. *The Oxford Book of Oxford.* Oxford: Oxford University Pr., 1978. 402 pp.

Oxford. University. Bodleian Library. *The History of the University of Oxford: Guide to an Exhibition Held in 1953.* Oxford: n.p., 1953. 36 pp.

Paravicini, Frances de. *Early History of Balliol College.* London: K. Paul, Trench, Trubner and Co., Ltd., 1891. 370 pp.

Parker, James B., and Oxon, M. A. *The Early History of Oxford, 727-1100, Preceded by a Sketch of the Mythical Origin of the City and University.* Oxford: Clarendon Pr., 1885. 420 pp.

Pechell, John. *The History of the University of Oxford.* 2 vols. Oxford: J. and F. Rivington, 1772-1773.

Plummer, Charles. *Elizabethan Oxford.* Oxford: Clarendon Pr., 1887. 316 pp.

Prickard, Arthur O. *New College, Oxford.* London: J. M. Dent and Co., 1906. 98 pp.

Rannie, David W. *Oriel College.* London: F. E. Robinson and Co., 1900. 244 pp.

Rashdall, Hastings, and Rait, Robert S. *New College.* London: F. E. Robinson and Co., 1901. 256 pp.

Robertson, Charles G. *All Souls College.* London: F. E. Robinson and Co., 1899. 234 pp.

Rowse, Alfred L. *Oxford in the History of England.* New York: Putnam, 1975. 256 pp.

Smith, Alic H. *New College, Oxford, and Its Buildings.* London: Oxford University Pr., 1952. 192 pp.

Smith, Barbara, ed. *Truth, Liberty, Religion: Essays Celebrating Two Hundred Years of Manchester College.* Oxford: Manchester College, 1986. 325 pp.

Smith, Eric H. F. *St. Peter's, the Founding of an Oxford College.* Gerrards Cross, Eng.: C. Smythe, 1978. 301 pp.

Smith, Goldwin. *Oxford and Her Colleges: A View from the Radcliffe Library.* New York: Macmillan, 1893. 170 pp.

Stevenson, William H. *The Early History of St. John's College.* Oxford: Clarendon Pr., 1939. 548 pp.

Stride, William K. *Exeter College.* London: F. E. Robinson and Co., 1900. 262 pp.

Sutherland, Lucy S. *University of Oxford in the Eighteenth Century: A Reconsideration.* Oxford: Blackwell, 1973. 29 pp.

Sutherland, Lucy S., and Mitchell, L. G. *The Eighteenth Century.* Oxford: Clarendon Pr., 1986. 949 pp.

Taylor, George R. S. *Oxford: A Guide to Its History and Buildings: With Twenty-Five Illustrations and a Map.* London: Longmans, Green and Co., 1923. 125 pp.

Thackrah, John R. *The University and Colleges of Oxford.* Lavenham, Suff.: Dalton, 1981. 152 pp.

Thompson, Henry L. *Christ Church.* London: F. E. Robinson and Co., 1900. 288 pp.

Trevor-Roper, Hugh R. *Christ Church, Oxford; Official Guidebook to the College.* Oxford: Published by Authority of the Governing Body of Christ Church, 1950. 28 pp.

--------. *Christ Church, Oxford: The Portrait of a College.* 2d ed. Oxford: n.p., 1973. 36 pp.

Vallance, Aymer. *The Old Colleges of Oxford; Their Architectural History.* London: B. T. Batsford, 1912. 134 pp.

Ward, Bernard N. *History of St. Edmund's College, Old Hall.* London: K. Paul, Trench, Trubner & Co. Ltd., 1893. 344 pp.

Warner, Stephen A. *Lincoln College, Oxford.* London: Sidgwick and Jackson, 1908. 107 pp.

Warren, Thomas H. *Magdalen College, Oxford.* London: J. M. Dent and Co., 1907. 134 pp.

Wells, Joseph. *Oxford and Its Colleges.* London: Methuen, 1897. 330 pp.

--------. *Oxford and Its Colleges.* 2d ed. London: Methuen, 1898. 330 pp.

––––––––. *Oxford and Its Colleges.* 3d ed. Boston: L. C. Page, 1899. 330 pp.

––––––––. *Oxford and Its Colleges.* 4th ed. London: Methuen, 1901. 330 pp.

––––––––. *Oxford and Its Colleges.* 5th ed. London: Methuen, 1903. 330 pp.

––––––––. *Oxford and Its Colleges.* 6th ed. London: Methuen, 1904. 329 pp.

––––––––. *Oxford and Its Colleges.* 7th ed. London: Methuen, 1906. 342 pp.

––––––––. *Oxford and Its Colleges.* 8th ed. London: Methuen, 1908. 337 pp.

––––––––. *Oxford and Its Colleges.* 9th ed. London: Methuen, 1910. 337 pp.

––––––––. *Oxford and Its Colleges.* London: Methuen, 1913. 337 pp.

––––––––. *Oxford and Its Colleges.* 11th ed. London: Methuen, 1919. 337 pp.

––––––––. *Oxford and Its Colleges.* 12th ed. London: Methuen, 1923. 353 pp.

––––––––. *Oxford and Its Colleges.* 13th ed. London: Methuen, 1926. 354 pp.

––––––––. *Oxford and Its Colleges.* 14th ed. London: Methuen, 1931. 353 pp.

––––––––. *Wadham College.* London: F. E. Robinson and Co., 1898. 222 pp.

White, Henry J. *Merton College, Oxford.* London: J. M. Dent and Co., 1906. 103 pp.

Wilkinson, Carlton B. "The Reform of Oxford University in the Nineteenth Century." Master's thesis, Wisconsin State University, Platteville, 1969. 82 pp.

Wilson, Henry A. *Magdalen College.* London: F. E. Robinson and Co., 1899. 281 pp.

Wood, Anthony A. *History and Antiquities of the Colleges and Halls in the University of Oxford.* Oxford: n.p., 1786. 692 pp.

University of Reading

Holt, James C. *The University of Reading: The First Fifty Years.* Reading: Reading University Pr., 1977. 371 pp.

University of Salford

Gordon, Colin. *The Foundations of the University of Salford.* Altrincham: Sherratt, 1975. 219 pp.

University of Sheffield

Boylan, Maureen. *The University of Sheffield: A Pictorial History.* Sheffield: The University, 1985. 64 pp.

Chapman, Arthur W. *The Story of a Modern University: A History of the University of Sheffield.* Oxford: Oxford University Pr., 1955. 551 pp.

Smith, George C. M. *The Story of the People's College, Sheffield, 1842-1878.* Sheffield: Printed by J. W. Northend, 1912. 73 pp.

University of Southampton

Patterson, Alfred. *The University of Southampton; 1862-1962.* Southampton: University of Southampton, 1962. 245 pp.

University of Surrey

Arrowsmith, H. *Pioneering in Education for the Technologies: The Story of Battersea College of Technology, 1891-1962.* London: University of Surrey, 1966. 136 pp.

University of Sussex

Blin-Stoyle, Roger J., ed. *The Sussex Opportunity: A New University and the Future.* Brighton, Suss.: Harvester Pr., 1986. 222 pp.

Ushaw College*

Milburn, David. *A History of Ushaw College; A Study of the Origin, Foundation, and Development of an English Catholic Seminary, with an Epilogue, 1908-1962.* Durham, Eng.: Ushaw Bookshop, 1964. 384 pp.

Victoria University of Manchester

Burney, Lester. *Cross Street Chapel Manchester and Its College.* Manchester: L. Burney, 1983. 84 pp.

Charlton, Henry B. *Portrait of a University, 1851-1951, to Commemorate the Centenary of Manchester University.* Manchester: Manchester University Pr., 1951. 185 pp.

Fiddes, Edward. *Chapters in the History of Owens College and of Manchester University, 1851-1914.* Manchester: Manchester University Pr., 1937. 239 pp.

Hartog, Philippe J. *The Owens College Manchester: Founded 1851, a Brief History of the College and Description of Its Various Departments.* Manchester: J. E. Cornish, 1900. 260 pp.

Thompson, Joseph. *The Owens College: Its Foundation and Growth, and Its Connection with the Victoria University.* Manchester: n.p., 1886. 671 pp.

Tout, Thomas F., and Tait, James, eds. *Historical Essays.* Manchester: The University Pr., 1907. 572 pp.

Westminster College

Pritchard, Frank C. *The Story of Westminister College, 1851-1951.* London: Epworth Pr., 1951. 213 pp.

Working Men's College

Davies, John L., ed. *Working Men's College, 1854-1904; Records of Its History and Its Work for Fifty Years, by Members of the College.* London: Macmillan, 1904. 296 pp.

Harrison, John F. C. *A History of the Working Men's College, 1854-1954.* London: Routledge, 1954. 215 pp.

Working Men's College. *The Working Men's College, 1954-1979: An Interim Impression.* London: The College, 1983. 84 pp.

NORTHERN IRELAND

Methodist College*

Marshall, Ronald. *Methodist College, Belfast: The First Hundred Years.* Belfast: Methodist College, 1968. 220 pp.

Queen's University of Belfast

Kane, Robert J. *The Queen's University in Ireland and the Queen's Colleges, Their Progress and Present State.* Dublin: Hodges, Smith, and Co., 1856. 59 pp.

Moody, Theodore W., and Beckett, James C. *Queen's Belfast, 1845-1949; The History of a University.* 2 vols. London: Faber & Faber, 1959.

SCOTLAND

University of Aberdeen

Bulloch, John M. *A History of the University of Aberdeen, 1495-1895.* London: Hodder and Stroughton, 1895. 220 pp.

Henderson, George D. *The Founding of Marischal College, Aberdeen.* Aberdeen: University Pr., 1947. 100 pp.

University of Dundee

Shafe, Michael, comp. *University Education in Dundee, 1881-1981.* Dundee: University of Dundee, 1982. 214 pp.

Southgate, Donald. *University Education in Dundee: A Centenary History.* Edinburgh: Edinburgh University Pr., 1982. 417 pp.

University of Edinburgh

Bower, Alexander. *The History of the University of Edinburgh.* 3 vols. Edinburgh: Oliphant, Waugh and Innes, 1817-1830.

Dalzel, Andrew. *History of the University of Edinburgh from Its Foundation.* 2 vols. Edinburgh: Edmonston and Douglas, 1862.

Donaldson, Gordon, ed. *Four Centuries: Edinburgh University Life, 1583-1983.* Edinburgh: University of Edinburgh, 1983. 185 pp.

Grant, Alexander. *The Story of the University of Edinburgh during Its First Three Hundred Years.* 2 vols. London: Longmans, 1884.

Harrison, John. *Oure Tounis Colledge; Sketches of the History of the Old College of Edinburgh, with an Appendix of Historical Documents.* Edinburgh: W. Blackwood, 1884. 166 pp.

Horn, David B. *A Short History of the University of Edinburgh, 1556-1889.* Edinburgh: University Pr., 1967. 228 pp.

Lee, John. *The University of Edinburgh: From Its Foundation in 1583 to the Year 1839: A Historical Sketch.* Edinburgh: David Douglas, 1884. 124 pp.

Marsden, Robert S., ed. *A Short Account of the Tercentenary Festival of the University of Edinburgh: Including the Speeches and Addresses Delivered on the Occasion.* Edinburgh: W. Blackwood, 1884. 217 pp.

Morgan, Alexander, ed. *University of Edinburgh; Charters, Statutes, and Acts of the Town Council and the Sentus, 1583-1858.* Edinburgh: Oliver and Boyd, 1937. 294 pp.

Tomaszewski, Wiktor, ed. *University of Edinburgh and Poland: An Historical Review.* Edinburgh: The Author, 1968. 95 pp.

Turner, Arthur L., ed. *History of the University of Edinburgh, 1883-1933.* Edinburgh: Oliver and Boyd, 1938. 452 pp.

University of Glasgow

Coutts, James. *An Account of the University of Glasgow.* Glasgow: J. Maclehose and Sons, 1901. 65 pp.

-------. *A History of the University of Glasgow, from Its Foundation in*

1451 to 1909. Glasgow: J. Maclehose and Sons, 1909. 615 pp.

Durkam, John, and Kirk, James. *The University of Glasgow, 1451-1577.* Glasgow: University of Glasgow Pr., 1977. 498 pp.

Glasgow. University. *Gilmorehill Centenary, 1870-1970.* Glasgow: University of Glasgow, 1970. 72 pp.

--------. *The University of Glasgow through Five Centuries.* Glasgow: n.p., 1951. 94 pp.

Glasgow. University. Centenary Committee. *The Curious Diversity: Glasgow University on Gilmorehill: The First Hundred Years.* Glasgow: University of Glasgow, 1970. 119 pp.

Mackie, John D. *The University of Glasgow, 1451-1951; A Short History.* Glasgow: Jackson, 1954. 341 pp.

Memorials of the Old College of Glasgow. Glasgow: J. Maclehose, 1871. 124 pp.

University of St. Andrews

Adamson, Peter G. *St. Andrews by the Northern Sea: A Selection of Photographic Studies.* St. Andrews: Peter G. Adamson, 1978. 79 pp.

Baxter, James H. *St. Andrews University before the Reformation.* St. Andrews: W. C. Henderson and Son, 1927. 14 pp.

Blair, J. S. G. *University of St. Andrews O.T.C.: A History.* Edinburgh: Scottish Academic Pr., 1982. 153 pp.

Boyd, Andrew K. H. *Twenty-Five Years of St. Andrews, September 1865 to September 1890.* 3d ed. 2 vols. London: Longmans, 1892.

Cant, Ronald G. *The University of St. Andrews: A Short History.* Edinburgh: Oliver and Boyd, 1946. 156 pp.

--------. *The University of St. Andrews: A Short History.* New and Rev. ed. Edinburgh: Scottish Academic Pr., 1970. 164 pp.

University of Strathclyde

Glasgow. University of Strathclyde. *A Decade of Progress, 1964-1974.* Glasgow: University of Strathclyde, 1974. 55 pp.

WALES

Coleg Harlech

Stead, Peter. *Coleg Harlech: The First Fifty Years.* Cardiff: University of Wales Pr., 1977. 135 pp.

Saint David's University College

Price, David T. W. *A History of Saint David's University College Lampeter.* Cardiff: University of Wales Pr., 1977. 222 pp.

University College, Cardiff

Jones, Gwyn, and Quinn, Michael, eds. *Fountains of Praise: University College, Cardiff, 1883-1983.* Cardiff: University College, Cardiff Pr., 1983. 207 pp.

University College of Aberystwyth

Ellis, Edward L. *The University College of Wales, Aberystwyth, 1872-1972.* Cardiff: University of Wales Pr., 1972. 353 pp.

Thomas, Ben B. *"Aber", 1872-1972.* Cardiff: Gwasg Prifysgol Cymru, 1972. 105 pp.

University College of North Wales, Bangor

Williams, J. Gwynn. *Centenary Lecture: The Founding of the University College of North Wales, Bangor.* Newtown, Powys.: Gwasg Gregynogg, 1985. 31 pp.

--------. *The University College of North Wales: Foundations, 1884-1927.* Cardiff: University of Wales Pr., 1985. 499 pp.

University of Wales

Davies, William, and Jones, W. Lewis. *The University of Wales and Its Constituent Colleges.* London: F. E. Robinson and Co., 1905. 226 pp.

Evans, David E. *The University of Wales; A Historical Sketch.* Cardiff: University of Wales Pr., 1953. 175 pp.

GREECE

Anatolia College*

Stephens, Everett, and Stephens, Mary. *Survival Against All Odds: The First 100 Years of Anatolia College.* New Rochelle, N.Y.: Aristide D. Caratzas, 1986. 205 pp.

Athens College*

Athens College, Athens, Greece. *Athens College, 1925-1975: Fiftieth Anniversiary.* Athens, Greece: Athens College, 1976. 255 pp.

GUATEMALA

University of San Carlos of Guatemala

Casteneda Paganini, Ricardo. *Historia de la Real y Pontifcia Universidad de San Carlos de Guatamala.* Guatamala: n.p., 1947-

Ferrus Roig, Francisco. *General mayor de la Universidad de San Carlos en Guatemala de la Asuncion; resena historica.* Guatemala: Universidad de San Carlos, 1962. 92 pp.

Lanning, John T. *The Eighteenth - Century Enlightment in the University of San Carlos de Guatemala.* Ithaca: Cornell University Pr., 1956. 372 pp.

Mata Gavidia, Jose. *Fundacion de la Universidad en Guatemala (1548-1688).* Guatemala: Editorial Universitaria, 1976. 388 pp.

Rodriguez Cabal, Juan. *Universidad de Guatemala: su origen, fundacion, organizacion.* Guatemala: Editorial Universitaria, 1976. 522 pp.

Universidad de San Carlos de Guatemala. *Ley organica y estatutos de la Universidad de San Carlos, 1947.* Guatemala: USC, 1947. 48 pp.

--------. *Publicacion commemorativa, tricentenario, Universidad de San*

Carlos de Guatemala, 1676-1976. Guatemala: La Universidad, 1976. 341 pp.

HONDURAS

National Autonomous University of Honduras

Cerrato Valenzuela, Armando. *Centenario de la Universidad (sintesis historica) 19 de septiembre de 1847 - 19 de septiembre de 1947.* Tegucigalpa: n.p., 1947. 54 pp.

Guardiola, Esteban. *Historia de la Universidad de Honduras; centenario del Padre Reyes.* Tegucigalpa: Tip. Nacionales, 1955. 163 pp.

--------. *Historia de Universidad de Honduras en la primera centuria de su fundacion: seguida de un estudio critico de las pastorelas del doctor Jose Trinidad Reyes.* Tegucigalpa: Talleres Tipograficas Nacionales, 1952. 207 pp.

HONG KONG

Hong Kong Baptist College

Tharpe, Gertrude A. "The History of Hong Kong Baptist College." Master's thesis, Furman University, 1965. 175 pp.

University of Hong Kong

Harrison, Brian, ed. *University of Hong Kong: The First 50 Years, 1911-1961.* Hong Kong: Hong Kong University Pr., 1962. 247 pp.

Hong Kong University. *The University of Hong Kong; Its Origin and Growth.* Hong Kong: n.p., 1926. 58 pp.

Hornell, William W. *The University of Hong Kong, 1912-1933.* Hong Kong: The Newspaper Enterprise Ltd., 1933. 36 pp.

Mellor, Bernard. *The University of Hong Kong, an Informal History.* 2 vols. Hong Kong: Hong Kong University Pr., 1980.

HUNGARY

Eotvos Lorand University

Paulovits, Julius G. "Foundation of the Eotvos Lorand University and Its History Under Jesuit Administration, 1635-1773." Ph.D. diss., Iowa State University, 1977. 242 pp. *Dissertation Abstracts International,* vol. 38A, p. 3334.

Keszthely Agricultural University

Kolozsvari, Ivan B. "The Organizational Development of the Keszthely Agricultural University, 1797-1982." Ed.D. diss., University of San Francisco, 1986. 232 pp. *Dissertation Abstracts International,* vol. 47A, p. 3335.

ICELAND

University of Iceland

GuDni, Jonsson. *Saga Haskola Islands: Yfirlit um halfrar alder starf.* Reykjavik: Haskoli Islands, 1961. 306 pp.

INDIA

Aligarh Muslim University

Bhatnagar, Shyam K. *History of the M.A.O. College, Aligarh.* Bombay: Asia Publishing House, 1969. 373 pp.

Lelyveld, David. *Aligarh's First Generation: Muslim Solidarity in British India.* Princeton, N. J.: Princeton University Pr., 1978. 380 pp.

Annamalai University

Nagaraja, K. *The Annamalai University, 1929-1979: A Short History.* Annamalainagar: Annamalai University, 1979. 195 pp.

Bhopal University

Regional College of Education, Bhopal. *Retrospects and Prospects, 1964-1968.* New Delhi: National Council of Educational Research and Training, 1968. 49 pp.

Maharaja Sayajirao University of Baroda

Desai, Dhanwant M., and Saraswati, S. Pandit. *Growth and Development of the Maharaja Sayajirao University of Baroda, 1949-1967.* Baroda: Dept. of Educational Administration, Maharaja Sayajirao University of Baroda, 1968. 126 pp.

Mayo College*

McGreal, Shirley P. "A History of Mayo College, Ajmer, India, 1875-1971." Ed.D. diss., University of Cincinnati, 1971. 301 pp. *Dissertation Abstracts International,* vol. 33A, p. 2745.

Osmania University

Abdul, Ali. *Seventeen Years in Osmania University.* Madras: Printed at the Diocesan Pr., 1968. 126 pp.

Panjab University

Bruce, J. F. *A History of the University of the Panjab.* Lahore: Ishwar Das, 1933. 221 pp.

Sethi, R. R., and Mehta, J. L. *A History of the Panjab University, Chandigarh, 1947-1967.* Chandigarh: Panjab University Publication Bureau, 1968. 441 pp.

Patna University

Jha, Hetukar. *Colonial Context of Higher Education in India: Patna University from 1917 to 1951: A Sociological Appraisal.* New Delhi: Usha, 1985. 152 pp.

University of Bombay

Dongerkery, Sunderkery R. *A History of the University of Bombay, 1857-*

1957. Bombay: University of Bombay, 1957. 313 pp.

Tikekara, Aruna. *The Cloisters Pale: A Biography of the University of Bombay*. Bombay: Somaiya, 1984. 292 pp.

University of Bombay. *University of Bombay, 1857-1957: Centenary Souvenir*. Bombay: T. V. Chididambaran, Registrar, University of Bombay, 1957. 301 pp.

University of Calcutta

Hundred Years of the University of Calcutta, a History of the University Issued in Commemoration of the Centenary Celebration. Calcutta: University of Calcutta, 1957. 539 pp.

University of Delhi

Monk, Francis F. *A History of St. Stephen's College, Delhi*. Calcutta: Y.M.C.A. Publishing House, 1935. 262 pp.

University of Madras

Adiseshiah, Malcolm S. *The Quinquennial of the University's 165 Colleges, 1971-1976*. Madras: University of Madras, 1977. 40 pp.

--------. *The University in 1975*. Madras: University of Madras, 1976. 36 pp.

--------. *The University in 1976*. Madras: University of Madras, 1977. 44 pp.

Pillay, Koppappa K. *History of Higher Education in South India*. Madras: Associated Printers, 1957-

University of Madras Centenary Celebrations: An Account. Madras: The University, 1959. 202 pp.

Vaidyanathan, P. S. *University of Madras: A Record of Twenty-Five Years, 1942-1967*. Madras: Higginbothams, 1967(?). 71 pp.

University of Patna

Sarkar, Jagadish N., and Jha, Jagdish C. *A History of the Patna College, 1863-1963*. Patna: Patna College, 1963. 170 pp.

University of Poona

Golay, Wasant H. *The University of Poona, 1949-1974.* Poona: University of Poona, 1974. 448 pp.

INDONESIA

Airlangga University

Universitas Airlangga. *20 [i. e. Duapuluh] tahun Universitas Airlangga, 10 Nopember, 1954-1974.* Surabaya: Universitas Airlangga, 1975. 253 pp.

Diponegora University

Abdullah, Hamid. *Dari Universitas Semarang Ke Universitas Diponegoro: studi kasas tentang sejarah Kelahiran sebuah universitas.* Semarang: Badan Penerbit Universitas Diponegoro, 1984. 205 pp.

Gadjah Mada University

Universitas Gadjah Mada. *Buku Kenangan seperempat abad Universitas Gadjah Mada, 19 Desember 1949-19 Desember 1974.* Yogyakarta: Panitia Dies Natalis Seperempat Abad Universitas Gadjah Mada, 1974. 149 pp.

National University

Universitas Nasional. *Universitas Nasional, sekolah-sekolah tinggi nasional, akedemi-adademi nasional 1981/82: petunjuk singkat.* Jakarta: Universitas, 1981. 89 pp.

Satya Wacana Christian University

Dalam Tuhan jerih payahmu tidak sia-sia: buku peringatan 25 tahun Universitas Kristen Satya Wacana, Salatiga. Salatiga: Panitia Dies Natalis Ke-XXV, Universitas Kristen Satya Wacana, 1981. 298 pp.

Syiah Kuala University

Darussalam dan hari pendidikan. Kutaradka: Pemerintah Daerah/Panitia Persiapan Pendirian Universitas Negeri Sijah Kuala, 1961. 60 pp.

Universitas Syiah Kuala menjelang 20 tahun. Darussalam: Universitas, 1980. 469 pp.

Udayana State University

Universitas Udayana. *Dwi dasa warsa Universitas Udayana, 1962-1974.* Denpasar: Bagian Publikasi, Universitas Udayana, 1975. 349 pp.

IRAQ

University of Baghdad

Al-Arif, Shoala I. "An Historical Analysis of Events and Issues Which Have Led to the Growth and Development of the University of Baghdad." Ed.D. diss., George Washington University, 1986. 133 pp. *Dissertation Abstracts International,* vol. 47A, p. 2809.

IRELAND

College of St. Patrick

Healy, John. *Maynooth College: Its Centenary History.* Dublin: Browne and Nolan, 1895. 774 pp.

Newman, Jeremiah. *Maynooth and Georgian Ireland.* Galway: Kenny's Bookshops and Art Galleries, 1979. 267 pp.

--------. *Maynooth and Victorian Ireland.* Galway: KG, 1983. 268 pp.

National University of Ireland

Morrissey, Thomas J. *Towards a National University: William Delany, SJ (1835-1924): An Era of Initiative in Irish Education.* Dublin: Wolfhound Pr., 1983. 425 pp.

Royal College of Surgeons in Ireland

Cameron, Charles A. *History of the Royal College of Surgeons in Ireland and of the Irish Schools of Medicine.* Dublin: Fannin and Co., 1886. 759 pp.

--------. *History of the Royal College of Surgeons in Ireland and of the Irish Schools of Medicine.* 2d ed. Dublin: Fannin and Co., 1916. 882 pp.

University College, Cork

O'Rahilly, Ronan. *A History of the Cork Medical School, 1849-1949.* Cork: Cork University Pr., 1949. 69 pp.

University College, Dublin

Jesuits. Ireland. *A Page of Irish History: Story of University College, Dublin, 1883-1909.* Dublin: Talbot Pr., 1930. 640 pp.

University College, Dublin. *University College Dublin: The Past, the Present, the Plans.* Dublin: The University College, 1976. 81 pp.

University of Dublin

Bailey, Kenneth C. *A History of Trinity College, Dublin, 1892-1945.* Dublin: University Pr., 1947. 274 pp.

Dixon, William M. *Trinity College, Dublin.* London: F. E. Robinson and Co., 1902. 298 pp.

Dublin. University. *The Book of Trinity College, Dublin, 1591-1891.* Belfast: M. Ward and Co., 1892. 316 pp.

Heron, Denis C. *The Constitutional History of the University of Dublin.* Dublin: J. McGlashan, 1847. 256 pp.

Jones, T. Mason. *Old Trinity: A Story of Real Life.* 3 vols. New York: Garland, 1979.

McDowell, Robert B., and Webb, D. A. *Trinity College, Dublin, 1592-1952: An Academic History.* London: Cambridge University Pr., 1982. 580 pp.

Mahaffy, John P. *An Epoch in Irish History: Trinity College, Dublin, Its*

Foundation and Early Fortunes, 1591-1660. London: T. Fisher Unwin, 1903. 389 pp.

Maxwell, Constantia E. *A History of Trinity College, Dublin, 1591-1892.* Dublin: The University Press, Trinity College, 1946. 299 pp.

Murphy, Harold L. *A History of Trinity College, Dublin, from Its Foundation to 1702.* Dublin: Hodges, Figgis, 1951. 212 pp.

Stubbs, John W. *The History of the University of Dublin from Its Foundation to the End of the Eighteenth Century.* Dublin: Dublin University Pr., 1889. 429 pp.

Taylor, William B. S. *History of the University of Dublin.* London: T. Cadell, 1845. 540 pp.

Urwick, William. *The Early History of Trinity College, Dublin, 1591-1660.* London: T. F. Unwin, 99 pp.

ISRAEL

Hebrew University of Jerusalem

Bentwich, Norman D. *The Hebrew University of Jerusalem, 1918-60.* London: Weidenfeld and Nicholson, 1961. 167 pp.

Jerusalem. Hebrew University. *The Hebrew University of Jerusalem, 1925-1950.* Jerusalem: n.p., 1950. 207 pp.

Levensohn, Lotta. *Vision and Fulfillment; The First Twenty-Five Years of the Hebrew University, 1925-1950.* New York: Greystone Pr., 1950. 190 pp.

Parzen, Herbert. *The Hebrew University, 1925-1935.* New York: Ktav Publishing House, 1974. 121 pp.

ITALY

Catholic University of the Sacred Heart

Schianchi, Francesco. *L'Universita Cattolica del Sacro Cuero.* Milano: G. Mazzotta, 1974. 207 pp.

University of Bari

Pedio, Tommaso. *Lotte e contrasti per l'istituzione dell'Universita degli studi di Bari.* Galatine: Congedo, 1977. 154 pp.

University of Bologna

Bezzetti, Dino, et. al., eds. *Le Lotte Universitarie a Bologna.* Bologna: Cooperativa libraria universitaria, 1969. 139 pp.

Encinas, Jose A. *Historia de las universidades de Bolonia y de Padua.* Santiago de Chile: Editorial Ercilla, 1935. 72 pp.

Fasoli, Gina. *Per la storia dell'Universita di Bologna nel Medio Evo. Dalle lezioni tenute alla Facolta de magistero nellanno accademico 1969-70.* Bologna: R. Patron, 1970. 197 pp.

Favaro, Antonio. *Lo Studio di Bologna nel 1610 secondo un carteggio del tempo.* n.p., 1892. 209 pp.

Malagola, Carlo. *Monografie storiche sullo studio bolognese.* 1888. Reprint. Bologna: A. Forni, 1979. 467 pp.

Piana, Celestino. *Ricerche su le Universite di Bologna e di Parma nel secolo XV.* Quaracchi, Florentiae: Typ. Collegii S. Bonaventurae, 1963. 562 pp.

Ricci, Corrado. *I primordi dello studio bolognese: nota storica.* Bologna: Monto, 1877. 100 pp.

--------. *I primordi dello studio di Bologna.* 2. ed. Bologna: Romagnoli dall'Acqua, 1888. 373 pp.

Universita di Bologna. *Statuti delle Universite e dei collegi dello studio bolognese.* 1888. Reprint. Torino: Bottega d'Erasmo, 1966. 524 pp.

--------. *Storia della Universita di Bologna.* 2 vols. Bologna: N. Zanichelli, 1944-1947.

Vianelli, Athos. *L'antica Universita di Bologna: origini, fatti e vicende.* Bologna: Tamari, 1978. 140 pp.

University of Ferrara

Borsett Ferranti Bolani, Ferrante. *Historia almi Ferrariae Gymnasii.*

1735. Reprint. 2 vols. Bologna: Forni, 1970.

Pardi, Giuseppe. *Lo studio di Ferrara nei secoli XV e XVI: con documenti inediti.* Ferrara: G. Zuffi, 1903. 274 pp.

University of Florence

Gherardi, Alessandro. *Statuti della Universita e studio fiorentino dell'anno MCCCLXXXVII.* 1881. Reprint. Bologna: Forni, 1973. 582 pp.

Spagnesi, Enrico. *Utiliter edoceri: atti inediti degli ufficiali dello studio fiorentino (1391-96).* Milano: A. Giuffre, 1979. 288 pp.

Verde, Armando F. *Lo Studio fiorentino, 1473-1503.* 3 vols. Firenze: Istituto nazionale di studi sul Rinascimento, 1973-

University of Genoa

Boudard, Rene. *L'organisation de l'Universite et de l'enseignement secondaire dans l'Academie imperiale de Genesentre 1805 et 1814.* Paris: Mouton, 1962. 153 pp.

Isnardi, Lorenzo. *Storia della Universita di Genova.* 1861. Reprint. 2 vols. Bologna: Forni, 1975.

University of Macerata

Corsi, Michele. *L'Universita di Macerata nel periodo della Restaurazione, 1816-1824.* Fermo: Tipografia La Rapida, 1978. 186 pp.

University of Modena

Mor, Carlo G. *Storia della Universita di Modena.* Modena: Societa tip. modenese, editrice, 1952. 343 pp.

--------. *Storia della Universita di Modena.* 2. ed. Aggiornata Modena: Societa tip. editrice Modenesse-Mucchi, 1963. 352 pp.

Mor, Carlo G., and Di Pietro, Pericle. *Storia dell'Universita di Modena.* 2 vols. Firenze: L. S. Olschki, 1975.

University of Naples

Naples. Universita. *Notizie intorno alla origine, formazione e stato presente della R. Universita di Napoli per l'Esposizione nazionale di Torino nel 1884, rettore Luigi Capano.* Napoli: Tip. dell'Accademia reale delle scienze, 1884. 268 pp.

Torraca, Francesco, and Monti, Gennaro M., ed altri. *Storia della Universita di Napoli.* Napoli: R. Ricciardi, 1924. 757 pp.

Universita di Napoli. *Settimo centenario della Regia Universita di Napoli, 1224-1924.* Napoli: Tipografia Napoletana, 1924. 198 pp.

University of Padua

Encinas, Jose A. *Historia de las universidades de Bolonia y de Padua.* Santiago de Chile: Editorial Ercilla, 1935. 172 pp.

Facciolati, Jacopo. *Fasti Gymnasii Patavini.* 1757. Reprint. 3 vols. Sala Bolognese: Forni, 1978.

Favaro, Antonio. *Gli storiografi ufficiali dello Studio di Padova.* Venezia: C. Ferrari, 1922. 169 pp.

--------. *Lo Studio di Padova e la Compagnia di Gesu sul finire del secolo decimosesto; narrazione documentata.* Venezia: n.p., 1878. 535 pp.

Gloria, Andrea. *Monumenti della Universita di Padova, 1318-1405.* 1888. Reprint. 2 vols. Bologna: Forni, 1972.

Ohl, Ronald E. "The University of Padua, 1405-1509: An International Community of Students and Professors." Ph.D. diss., University of Pennsylvania, 1980. 244 pp. *Dissertation Abstracts International,* vol. 41A, p. 2970.

Riccoboni, Antonio. *De Gymnasio Patavino.* Sala Bolognese: Forni, 1980. 148 pp.

University of Palermo

Sampolo, Luigi. *La R. Accademia degli studi di Palermo: narrazione storica.* 1888. Reprint. Paleermo: Edizioni e ristampe Siciliane, 1976. 210 pp.

ITALY / 95

University of Parma

Berti, Giuseppe. *Lo Studio Universitario Parmense Alla Fine del Seicento.* Parma: Presso la Deputazione di Storia Patria per le Provincie Parmensi, 1967. 107 pp.

Piana, Celestino. *Ricerche su le Universita di Bologna e di Parma nel secolo XV.* Quaracchi, Florentiae: Typ. Collegii S. Bonaventurae, 1963. 562 pp.

Universita di Parma. *Corpus statutorum almi studii Parmensis (saec. XV): con introduzione su la storia della Universita di Parma dalle origini al secolo XV.* 2. ed. Milano: A. Giuffre, 1978. 200 pp.

University of Pavia

Universita di Pavia. *Statuti e ordinamenti della Universita di Pavia dall anno 1361 all anno 1859.* Pavia: Tip. Cooperativa, 1925. 394 pp.

Vaccari, Pietro. *Storia della Universita di Pavia.* Pavia: Il Portale, 1948. 212 pp.

--------. *Storia della Universita di Pavia.* 2a ed. Pavia: Universita di Pavia, 1957. 374 pp.

University of Perugia

Bini, Vincenzo. *Memorie istoriche della perugina Universita degli studi.* 1816. Reprint. Bologna: Forni, 1977. 671 pp.

Ermini, Giuseppe. *Storia dell'Universita di Perugia.* 2 vols. Firenze: L. Olschki, 1971.

Padelletti, Guido. *Contributo alla storia dello studio di Perugia nei secoli XIV e XV.* 1872. Reprint. Bologna: Forni, 1976. 134 pp.

Perugia. Universita. *Cenno storico della Libera Universita di Perugia.* Perugia: Tip. di V. Santucci, 1873. 59 pp.

Universita di Perugia. *Documenti per la storia dell'Universita di Perugia. con l'albo dei professori ad ogni quarto di secolo.* 3 parts in 1 vol. Perugia: G. Boncompagni, 1875-1878.

University of Pisa

Carranza, Niccola. *Monsignor Gaspare Certi provveditore dell'Universita di Pisa nel settecento delle riforme.* Pisa: Pacini, 1974. 390 pp.

--------. *L'Universita di Pisa nei secoli XVII e XVIII.* Pisa: Liberia Scientifica G. Pellegrini, 1971. 82 pp.

Fabroni, Angelo. *Historia academiae Pisanae.* 1791. Reprint. 3 vols. Bologna: Forni, 1971.

Marrara, Danilo. *L'Universita di Pisa come Universita statale nel granducato mediceo.* Milano: A. Girffre, 1965. 59 pp.

Pisa. Universita. *L'Ateneo di Pisa.* Pisa: Tipografia P. Mariotti, 1929. 334 pp.

University of Sassari

Tola, Pasquale. *Notizie Storiche della Universita degli studi di Sassari.* Genova: Tip. del R. I. de'Sordomuti, 1866. 134 pp.

University of Siena

Marrara, Danilo. *Lo Studio di Siena nelle riforma del Granduca Ferdinando I (1589 e 1591).* Milano: A. Giuffre, 1970. 346 pp.

Zdekauer, Lodovico. *Lo studio di Siena nel Rinascimento.* Sala Bolognese: Forni, 1977. 204 pp.

University of Turin

Bellone, Ernesto. *Il primo secolo di vita della Universita di Torino (sec. XV-XVI): ricerche ed ipotesi sulla cultura nel Piemonte Quattrocentesco.* Torino: Centro studi piemontesi, 1986. 256 pp.

Bongiovanni, Bruno. *L'Universita di Torino durante il fascismo: le facolta umanistiche e il Politecnico.* Torino: G. Giappichelli, 1976. 238 pp.

Turin. Universita. *Cenni storici sulla R. Universita di Torino; origini, vicende e condizioni attuali dell Universita, notizie sommarie sugli istituti scientifici, pubblicazioni degli attuali membri del corpo accademico.* Roma-Torino-Firenze: Presso i Fratelli Bocca, 1873. 119 pp.

L'Universita di Torino nei sec. XVI e XVII. Universita di Torino: Memori dell'Istituto giuridico, 1972. 487 pp.

University of Urbino

Marra, Filippo. *Chartularium: per una storia dell'Universita di Urbino, 1563-1799.* 2 vols. Urbino: Argalia, 1975.

IVORY COAST

National University of the Ivory Coast

Hamilton, Karen E. "The Ivoirienization of the National University of the Ivory Coast, 1958-77." Ph.D. diss., University of Pennsylvania, 1979. 376 pp. *Dissertation Abstracts International,* vol. 40A, p. 5333.

JAMAICA

University of the West Indies

Parker, Paul C. "Change and Challenge in Caribbean Higher Education: The Development of the University of the West Indies and the University of Puerto Rico." Ph.D. diss., Florida State University, 1971. 548 pp. *Dissertation Abstracts International,* vol. 33A, p. 4129.

University of the West Indies, Mona Campus: An Historical Guide. Kingston: Valbees Printers Limited, 1976. 16 pp.

JAPAN

Chuo University

Korekara dosuru: Chuo Daigaku no dai 2-seiki: Chuo Daigaku soritsu 100-shunen Kinen shuppan. Tokyo: Chuo Daigaku Shuppanbu, 1985. 324 pp.

Doshisha University

Doshisha hyakunenshi tsushihen. 2 vols. Kyoto: Doshisha, 1979.

Hitotsubashi University

Hitosubashi Daiguku gakumonshi: Hitotsubashi Daigaku soritsu hyakunen kinen. Tokyoto Kunitachishi: Hitotsubashi Daigaku, Showa 61, 1986. 1417 pp.

Hokkaido University

Hokkaido Daigaku. *The Semi-Centennial of the Hokkaido Imperial University, Japan, 1876-1926.* Sapporo: Kokkaido Imperial University, 1927. 210 pp.

Hosei University

Hosei Daigaku hachijunenshi. Tokyo: Do Daigaku, Showa 36, 1961. 773 pp.

Hosei Daigaku hyakunenshi. Tokyo: Do Daigaku, 1980. 986 pp.

Hosei Daigaku no 100-nen: 1880-1980. Tokyo: Hosei Daigaku, 1980. 212 pp.

Japan Women's University

Nihon Joshi Daigaku. *Japan Women's University; Its Past, Present, and Future.* Tokyo: n.p., 1912. 74 pp.

Kansai University

Kansai Daigaku hyakunenshi. Osaka-fu Suitashi: Kansai Daigaku, Showa 61, 1986. 900 pp.

Keio University

Keio Gijuku Daigaku. *A Pictorial History of Keio University, 1858-1958.* Toyko: Keiogijuku University, 1959. 96 pp.

Keio Gijuku hyakunenshi. Bekkan daigakuhen. Tokyo: Keio Gijuku, Showa

37, 1962. 911 pp.

Keio Gijuku hyakunenshi. furoku. Tokyo: Keio Gijuku, Showa 44, 1969. 548 pp.

Keiogijuku University, Tokyo. *The Keiogijuku University. A Brief Account of Its Foundation, Character, and Equipment.* Tokyo: The Keiogijuku University, 1909. 49 pp.

--------. *The Keiogijuku University. A Brief Account of Its History, Aims, and Equipment.* Tokyo: Keiogijuku University, 1936. 104 pp.

--------. *The Keiogijuku University. A Brief Account of Its History, Aims, and Equipment.* Tokyo: n.p., 1940. 107 pp.

Kiyooka, Eiichi. *A History of Keio Gijuku Through the Writings of Fukuzawa.* Tokyo: Hokuseido Pr., 1979-

Kiyooka, Eiichi, ed. *Keio Gijuku Daigakubu no tanjo: Habado Daigaku yori no shin shiryo. (Birth of the University Section in Keio Gijuku: From New Materials Found in Harvard University.* Tokyo: Keio Gijuku, 1983. 142 pp.

Kobe College

DeForest, Charlotte B. *The History of Kobe College: Compiled on the Occasion of the Seventy-Fifth Anniversary of Kobe College, Nishinomiya,* Japan, 1875-1950. *n.p., 1950. 222 pp.*

Kobe Jogakuin hyakunenshi. *Kobe Jogakuin hyakunenshi.* 2 vols. Nishinomiya: Do Jogakuin, Showa 51-56, 1976-1981.

Okadayama no gojunen. Nishinomiyashi: Kobe Jogakuin, Showa 59, 1984. 245 pp.

Kobe University

Sakuko Yosio, Eto T. *Kobe Daigaku rysos shichijunenshi.* Toyko: Zaikai Hyoron Shinsha, Showa 51, 1976. 1440 pp.

Kogakkan University

Kogakkan Daigaku. *Kogakkan Daigaku hyakunen shoshi.* Mieken Iseshi: Kogakkan Daigaku, Showa 57, 1982. 124 pp.

Kokushikan University

Shashin de miru Kokushikan no rekishi: Kunan to eiko no Kiroku. Tokyo: Kokusho Kankokai, Showa 59, 1984. 316 pp.

Konan University

Konan Daigaku no 30-nen: Kenkyu Kyoiku no ayumi. Kobeshi: Konan Daigaku, 1984. 638 pp.

Kumamoto University

Kumamoto Daigaku sanjunenshi. Kumamoto: Do Daigaku, 1980. 1263 pp.

Kurume University

Kurume Daigaku gojunenshi: senkyuhyaku shichijuhachinen. Kurume: Kurume Daigaku Soritsu Gojisshunen Kinen Kiseikai, 1978. 857 pp.

Kyoto University

Sasaki, Soichi. *Kyodia jiken.* Tokyo: Iwanami Shoten, 1933. 400 pp.

Matsuyama University

Matsuyama Shoka Daiguku rokujunenshi. Shashinhen. Matsuyamashi: Matsuyama Shoka Daigaku, Showa 59, 1984. 267 pp.

Nagasaki University

Nagasaki Daigaku sanjugonenshi. Nagasaki Daigaku, Showa 59, 1984. 678 pp.

Nihon University

Nihon Daigaku no Kyujunen. Tokyo: Nihon Daigaku Kohobu, Showa 54, 1979. 155 pp.

Niigata University

Niigata Daiguku. 25-nenshi Henshu Iinkai. *Niigata Daigaku nijugonenshi.* 2 vols. Niigata: Niigata Daigaku Nijugonenshi Kanko Iinkai, Showa 49-55, 1974-1980.

Ochanomizu University

Ochanomizu Joshi Daigaku hyakunenshi. Tokyo: Ochanomizu Joshi Daiguku Hyakunenshi Kanko Iinkai, Showa 59, 1984. 873 pp.

Osaka University

Osaka Daigaku gojunenshi. 3 vols. Osaka: Osaka Daigaku, 198?-

Osaka Daigaku nijugonenshi. Osakashi: Osaka Daigaku, Showa 31, 1956. 641 pp.

Seinan Gakuin University

Seinan Gakuin shichijunenshi. 2 vols. Fukuokashi: Seinan Gakuin, 1986.

Seisen Women's College

Seisen Joshi Daiguku sanjunen no ayumi. Tokyo: Seisen Joshi Daiguku, 1979. 80 pp.

Senshu University

Senshu Daigaku hyakunen shoshi. Tokyo: Senshu Daigaku, Showa 54, 1979. 120 pp.

Senshu Daigaku hyakunenshi. 2 vols. Tokyo: Senshu Daigaku Shuppankyoku, Showa 56, 1981.

Senshu Daigaku 105-nen. Tokyo: Senshu Daigaku Shuppankyoku, Showa 59, 1984. 184 pp.

Tokyo to Kobunshokan shozo senshu Gakko senshu Daigaku Kankei Kobunsho shusei. Tokyo: Senshu Daigaku Nenshi Hensanshitsu, Showa 50, 1975. 304 pp.

Tokai University

Zenshinsuru Tokai Daigaku. Tokyo: Tokai Daigaku, Showa 58, 1983. 278 pp.

Tokyo Women's Christian University

Aoyama, Nao. *Yasui Tetsu to Tokyo Joshi Daigaku.* Tokyo: Deio Tsushin, Showa 57, 1982. 450 pp.

United Nations University

Altomare, George. "The United Nations University: Origins, Founding, and Future." 2 vols. Thesis, Columbia University, 1977.

University of the Ryukyus

Ryukyu Daigaku sanjunen: 1980. Nahashi: Do Daigaku, Showa 56, 1981. 1241 pp.

University of Tottori

Tottori Daigaku sanjunenshi. Tottori: Do Daigaku, Showa 58, 1983. 874 pp.

University of Tsukuba

Tsukuba Daigaku sonojunen: kaigaku jisshunen kinen. Ibarakiken Niiharigun Sakuramura: Do Daigaku, Showa 58, 1983. 154 pp.

Waseda University

Tokyo. Waseda University. *Waseda University; Its History, Aims and Regulations.* Tokyo: n.p., 1936. 88 pp.

Waseda Daogku, Tokyo. Daigakushi Henshujo. *Waseda Daigaku hyakunenshi.* Tokyo: Waseda Daigaku Shuppanbu, Showa 53-. 1978-

Waseda 365-nichi/Waseda gakuhohen. Tokyo: Waseda Daigaku Shuppanbu, 1985. 223 pp.

Yamaguchi University

Yamaguchi Daigaku sanjunenshi. Yamaguchiken Yamaguchishi: Do Daigaku, Showa 57, 1982. 1475 pp.

KENYA

University of Nairobi

Kirubi, Gichuhi M. M. "Turmoil in a University: An Analytical Study of the Conflicts, Confrontations and Strikes in the University of Nairobi and Kenyatta University College in the Republic of Kenya, 1960-1978." Ph.D. diss., Ohio University, 1983. 281 pp. *Dissertation Abstracts International,* vol. 44A, p. 936.

LEBANON

American University of Beirut

American University of Beirut. *Description of Its Organization and Work.* n.p., 1934. 1 vol.

Dodge, Bayard. *The American University of Beirut; A Brief History of* the University and the Lands Which It Serves. Beirut: Khayst's, 1958. 127 pp.

Munro, John M. *A Mutual Concern: The Story of the American University of Beirut.* Delmar, N. Y.: Caravan Books, 1977. 198 pp.

Penrose, Stephen B. L. *That They May Have Life: The Story of the American University of Beirut, 1866-1941.* New York: The Trustees of the American University of Beirut, 1941. 347 pp.

Sayah, Edward N. "The American University of Beirut and Its Educational Activities in Lebanon, 1920-1967." Ph.D. diss., University of North Texas, 1988. 277 pp. *Dissertation Abstracts International,* vol. 49A, p. 1390.

Beirut College for Women

Sabri, Marie A. "Beirut College for Women and Ten of Its Distinguished Pioneering Alumnae." Ed.D. diss., Columbia University, 1965. 451 pp. *Dissertation Abstracts,* vol. 26, p. 6454.

--------. *Pioneering Profiles; Beirut College for Women.* Beirut: Printed by Khayat Book & Publishing Co., 1967. 314 pp.

LIBERIA

University of Liberia

Hoff, Advertus A. *A Short History of Liberia College and the University of Liberia.* Monrovia, Liberia: Consolidated Publications, 1962. 128 pp.

MALAWI

University of Malawi

Kimble, David. *Growth and Change in the University.* Zamba, Malawi: Government Printer, 1981. 21 pp.

MEXICO

Autonomous University of Ciudad Juarez

Canizales de Urrutia, Dolores. *Asi empezo: la verdadera historia de la Universidad Femenina de Ciudad Juarez, Chih., y sus transiciones a Universidad Mixta, Universidad de Ciudad Juarez, A. C. y Universidad Autonoma.* Ciudad Juarez: Universidad Autonoma de Ciudad Juarez, 1982. 172 pp.

Autonomous University of Hidalgo

Menes Llaguno, Juan M. *Universidad Autonoma de Hidalgo: pasado y presente.* Pachuca, Mexico: CEHINHAC, 1978. 75 pp.

Autonomous University of Nuevo Leon

Capilla "Alfonsia" Biblioteca Universitaria. *Resena historica de la Universidad Autonoma de Nuevo Leon.* Monterrey, Mex.: Universidad Autonoma de Nuevo Leon, Capilla Alfonsia/Biblioteca Universitaria, 1983. 345 pp.

Autonomous University of Puebla

Silva Andraca, Hector. *Puebla y su universidad.* Puebla, Pue.: Editorial Universidad Autonoma de Puebla, 1980. 98 pp.

Autonomous University of San Luis Potosi

Pedraza Montes, Jose F. *Apuntes historicos de la Universidad Autonoma de San Luis Potosi.* San Luis Potosi: Editorial Universitari Potosina, 1986. 38 pp.

Autonomous University of Sinaloa

Meza, Luis A., and Lopez Cervantes, Gerardo. *Sinaloa, lucha en el ABC: los poderosos, la educacion y la UAS.* Culiacan Rosales, Sinaola, *Mexico: Universidad Autonoma de Sinaloa, Instituto de* Investigaciones Economicas y Sociales, 1983. 115 pp.

Autonomous University of the State of Mexico

Anales de la U.A.E.M. Segun Acuerdos del H. Consejo Universitario (1956-1980). Toluca, Edo. de Mexico: Universidad Autonoma del Estado de Mexico, 1981. 269 pp.

Fundacion del Instituto Literario del Estado de Mexico: testimonios historicos. Toluca: Universidad Autonoma del Estado de Mexico, 1978. 190 pp.

Autonomous University of the State of Morelos

Vega Flores, Hector. *Historia de la Universidad Autonoma del Estado de Morelos.* 2 vols. Cuernavaca, Mor.: Impr. Universitaria, 1980-

Juarez Autonomous University of Tabasco

Universidad Juarez Autonoma de Tabasco. *1958-1983: perfil historico.* Villahermosa, Mexico: Universidad Juarez Autonoma de Tabasco, 1984. 121 pp.

Michoacan University of Saint Nicholas of Hidalgo

Arreola Cortes, Raul. *Historia de la Universidad Michoacana.* Morelia: Universidad Michoacana de San Nicolas de Hidalgo, Coordinacion de la Investigacion Cientifica, 1984. 431 pp.

--------. *Historia del Colegio de San Nicolas.* Morelia, Mich., Mexico: Universidad de San Nicolas de Hidalgo, Coordinacion de la Investigacion Cientifica, 1982. 483 pp.

National Autonomous University of Mexico

Appendini, Guadalupe. *Historia de la Universidad Nacional Autonoma de Mexico.* Mexico: Editorial Porrua, 1981. 446 pp.

La Autonomia Universitaria en Mexico. Mexico: Universidad Nacional Autonoma de Mexico, 1979. 423 pp.

Carranca y Rivas, Raul. *La Universidad Mexicana.* Mexico: Fondo de Cultura Economica, 1969. 141 pp.

Carreno, Alberto M. *Efemerieds de la Real y Pontificia Universidad de Mexico, segun sus libos de claustros.* 2 vols. Mexico: n.p., 1963.

Gonzalez Cosia Diaz, Arturo. *Historia estadistica de la Universidad, 1910-1967.* Mexico: Universidad Nacional Autonoma de Mexico, Instituto de Investigaciones Sociales, 1968. 107 pp.

Myers, Minnie M. P. "The Origin and Beginning of the University of Mexico, 1553-1580." Master's thesis, University of Texas, 1929. 108 pp.

Rojas, Pedro. *La Ciudad Universitaria a la epoca de su construccion.* Mexico: Universidad Nacional Autonoma de Mexico, 1979. 112 pp.

Silva Herzog, Jesus. *Una historia de la Universidad de Mexico y sus problemas.* Mexico: Siglo Veintiuno Editores, 1974. 213 pp.

Universidad Nacional Autonoma de Mexico. *Memoria de la Exposicion Sobre la Universidad.* Mexico: Universidad Nacianal Autonoma de

Mexico, 1979. 494 pp.

--------. *La Universidad Nacional de Mexico, 1910.* 2d ed. Mexico, D. F.: Coordinacion de Humanidades, Centro de Estudios Sobre la Universidad, Universidad Nacional Autonoma de Mexico, 1985. 183 pp.

Valades, Diego. *La Universidad Nacional Autonoma de Mexico: Formacion, Estructura y Funciones.* Mexico: Universidad Nacional Autonoma de Mexico, Comision Tecnica de Legislacion Universitaria, 1974. 129 pp.

University of Guadalajara

Aldana Rendon, Mario A. *Breve historia de la Universidad de Guadalajara.* Guadalajara, Jalisco, Mexico: Universidad de Guadalajara, Instituto de Estudios Sociales, 1979. 31 pp.

Iguiniz, Juan B. *La antigua Universidad de Guadalajara.* Mexico: Universidad Nacional Autonoma de Mexico, Direccion General de Publicaciones, 1959. 162 pp.

University of Guanajuato

Universidad de Guanajuato. *Universidad de Guanajuato, 1961-1967.* Guanajuato: La Universidad, 1967. 54 pp.

NETHERLANDS

State University of Leiden

Athenae Batavae. De Leidse Universiteit-the University of Leiden, 1575-1975. Leiden: Universitaire Pers Leiden, 1975. 111 pp.

Geurts, Pieter A. M. *Voorgeschiedenis van het statencollege to Leiden, 1575-1593.* Leiden: E. J. Brill, 1984. 107 pp.

Jurriannse, Maria W. *The Founding of Leyden University.* Leiden: E. J. Brill, 1965. 24 pp.

Schotel, Gilles D. J. *De Academie te Leiden in de 16e, 17e en 18e eeuw.* Haarlem: Druseman & Tjeenk Willink, 1875. 410 pp.

Siegenbeek, Matthijs. *Geschiednis der Leidsche Hoogeschool, van hare oprigting in den jare 1575, tot het jaar 1825.* 2 vols. Leiden: S. en J. Luchtmans, 1829-1832.

State University of Utrecht

Berkel, A. van. *Utrechts hoogeschool veertien jaren na het begin, en veertien jaren voor het einde der negentiende eeus, 1814 en 1886: historische bijdragen.* Amsterdam: A. Rossing, 1886. 113 pp.

University of Amsterdam

Universitat van Amsterdam. *Gedendboek van het Athenaeum en de Universiteit van Amsterdam, 1632-1932.* Amsterdam: Stadsdrukkerij, 1932. 720 pp.

NEW ZEALAND

Queen Margaret College

Gambrill, Mollie D. *A History of Queen Margaret College.* Wellington: Board of Governors, Queen Margaret College, 1969. 228 pp.

St. Andrew's Presbyterian College*

Livingstone, Rex D. *St. Andrew's College: A Photographic Essay: Diamond Jubilee, 1916-1976.* Christchurch: St. Andrew's College, 1976. 70 pp.

St. Andrew's Presbyterian College. Board of Governors. *St. Andrew's College, 1916-1966; History and School List.* Christchurch: n.p., 1969. 297 pp.

University of Auckland

Sinclair, Keith. *A History of the University of Auckland, 1883-1983.* Auckland: Auckland Univeristy Pr., 1983. 364 pp.

University of Canterbury

Blair, Ian D. *Life and Work at Canterbury Agricultural College; The First Seventy-Five Years of the Agricultural College at Lincoln, New*

Zealand. *Christchurch: Caxton Pr., 1956. 448 pp.*

--------. *The Seed They Sowed: Centennial Story of Lincoln College.* Lincoln: Lincoln College University of Agriculture, 1978. 360 pp.

Gardner, W. J.; Beardsley, E. T.; and Carter, T. E. *A History of the University of Canterbury, 1873-1973.* Christchurch: University of Canterbury, 1973. 530 pp.

University of Otago

Beaglehole, John C. *The University of New Zealand, an Historical Study.* Wellington: Council for Educational Research, 1937. 431 pp.

Lindsay, William L. *The University of Otago, New Zealand: As a College for the People.* Perth: n.p., 1875. 32 pp.

Morrell, William P. *The University of Otago; A Centennial History.* Dunedin: University of Otago Pr., 1969. 261 pp.

New Zealand. University, Wellington. *The University of New Zealand. Its History and Its System.* Wellington: n.p., 1897. 12 pp.

Parton, Hugh N. *The University of New Zealand.* Auckland: University Pr., 1979. 277 pp.

Thompson, George E. *A History of the University of Otago, (1869-1919).* Dunedin: J. Wilkie & Co., 1919. 287 pp.

Victoria University of Wellington

Beaglehole, John C. *Victoria University College; An Essay Towards a History.* Wellington: New Zealand University Pr., 1949. 319 pp.

NICARAGUA

National University of Nicaragua

Alverez Alvarado, Jesus. *Evolucion y desarrollo de la Universidad Nacional Autonoma de Nicaragua: los obstaculos al desarrollo universitario. seminario. 25 anos de actividades universitarias centroamericanas, Tegucigalpa, Honduras, 17-10 octubre 1973.* Leon: n.p., 1973. 58 pp.

Arellano, Jorge E. *Historia de la Universidad de Leon.* 2 vols. Leon: Editorial Universitaria UNAN. 1973-1974.

Castilla Urbina, Miguel de. *Universidad y Sociedad en Nicaragua.* 2 vols. Nicaragua: Editorial Universitaria de la UNAN, 1979.

Universidad Nacional Autonoma de Nicaragua. *Sesqicentenario, 1812-1962.* Leon: Editorial Hospicio, 1962. 171 pp.

NIGERIA

Ahmadu Bello University

Aliu, Y. O., comp. *Silver Jubilee: Ahmadu Bello University, Zaria.* Zaria: Ahmadu Bello University, 1987. 76 pp.

10 Years: The First Decade of Ahmadu Bello University, Zaria, October 1962-October 1972. Zaria: Ahmadu Bello University Pr., 1972. 64 pp.

Anambra State University of Technology

Anamaleze, John, ed. *UNITECH, Anambra State University of Technology: History, Development, Matriculation.* Enuga, Nigeria: Information Division, Governor's Office, 1981. 60 pp.

Katsina College*

Hubbard, James P. "Education under Colonial Rule: A Short History of Katsina College, 1921-1942." Ph.D. diss., University of Wisconsin, 1973. 422 pp. *Dissertation Abstracts International,* vol. 34A, p. 4158.

Obafemi Awolowo University

Akintoye, Stephen A. *Ten Years of the University of Ife, 1962-1972.* Ile-Ife, Nigeria: University of Ife Pr., 1973. 50 pp.

St. Andrew's College*

Ogunkoya, T. O. *St. Andrew's College, Oyo (1896-1978): History of the*

Premier Institution in Nigeria. Ibadan: University Pr., 1979. 193 pp.

St. Andrew's College, Oyo: A Draft History and Register, 1896-1966. Ibadan: Abiodun Printing Works, 1966. 87 pp.

University of Ibadan

Ajayi, J. F. Ade, and Tamuno, Tekena N., eds. *The University of Ibadan, 1948-73; A History of the First Twenty-Five Years.* Ibadan, Nigeria: Ibadan University Pr., 1973. 436 pp.

Mellanby, Kenneth. *The Birth of Nigeria's University.* London: Methuen, 1958. 263 pp.

University of Ilorin

University of Ilorin. *University of Ilorin.* Ilorin, Nigeria: The University, 1985. 130 pp.

University of Lagos

Aderibigbe, A. B., and Gbadamosi, T. G. O., eds. *A History of the University of Lagos, 1962-1987.* Lagos, Nigeria: University of Lagos Pr., 1987. 600 pp.

University of Nigeria

Azikiwe, Nnamdi. *Origins of the University of Nigeria.* Aba: International Pr., 1963. 87 pp.

Obiechina, Emmanuel; Ike, Chukwuemeka; and Umeh, John A., eds. *The University of Nigeria, 1960-1985: An Experiment in Higher Education.* Nsukka, Nigeria: University of Nigeria Pr., 1986. 657 pp.

Ukariwe, Ukariwe K. "The Establishment and Development of the University of Nigeria, Nsukka, 1960-1970." Ph.D. diss., Southern Illinois University at Carbondale, 1984. 185 pp. *Dissertation Abstracts International,* vol. 46A, p. 629.

Zerby, Lewis, and Zerby, Margaret. *If I Should Die Before I Wake: The Nsukka Dream: A History of the University of Nigeria.* East Lansing: Michigan State University, 1971. 295 pp.

Wesley College*

Olbubummo, Adegoke. *In a Christian College.* Ibadan: University Pr., 1980. 198 pp.

Wesley College Ibadan: 80th Anniversary Publication, 1905-1985. Ibadan: Wesley College Old Students Association, 1985. 226 pp.

NORWAY

University of Oslo

Oslo. Universitet. *Universitetet i Oslo, 1911-1961.* 2 vols. Oslo: Universitetsforlaget, 1961.

University of Tromso

Bie, Karen N. *Creating a New University: The Establishment and Development of the University of Tromso.* Oslo: NAVF's Utredningsinstitutt, Norges Almenvilenskapelige forskningsrad, 1981. 169 pp.

PAKISTAN

Government College*

Garrett, Herbert L. O. *A History of Government College, Lahore, 1864-1964.* Lahore: Government College, 1964. 309 pp.

University of Peshawar

University of Peshawar, 1950-83. Peshawar: University Pr., 1983. 120 pp.

PERU

Jesuit College of San Pablo*

Martin, Luis. *The Intellectual Conquest of Peru; The Jesuit College of San Pablo, 1568-1767.* New York: Fordham University Pr., 1968. 194 pp.

National University of San Marcos

Buford, Nick. *The University of San Marcos of Lima in the Eighteenth Century.* Baton Rouge: Louisiana State University, Latin American Studies Institute. 1969. 44 pp.

Davila Condemarin, Jose. *Bosquejo historico de la fundacion de la insigne Universidad Mayor de San Marcos de Lima.* Lima: Eusebio Arando, 1854. 95 pp.

Eguiguren, Luis A. *Historia de la Universidad.* Santa Maria: n.p., 1951-

Temple, Ella D. *La Universidad de San Marcos en el proceso de la emancipacion peruana.* Lima: Universidad Nacional Mayor de San Marcos, 1974. n.p.

Valcarcel, Carlos D. *Historia de la Universidad de San Marcos (1551-1980).* Caracus: Academia Nacional de la Historia, 1981. 159 pp.

--------. *San Marcos, universidad decana de America.* Lima: n.p., 1968. 138 pp.

Valcarcel Esparza, Carlos D. *Reformas virreinales en San Marcos.* Lima: Impr. de la Universidad Nacional Mayor de San Marcos, 1960. 94 pp.

PHILLIPINES

Central Philippine University

Nelson, Linnea A., and Herradura, Elma S. *Scientia et fides: The Story of Central Philippine University.* Iloilo City: The University, 1981. 417 pp.

De La Salle University

Quirino, Carlos. *La Salle, 1911-1986.* Manila: Filipinas Foundation for De La Salle University, 1986. 288 pp.

Holy Cross College of Calinan

Angel, Filemon J. *The Historical Development of the Holy Cross College of Calinan, City of Davao, 1948-1971.* Thesis, Ateneo de Davao Graduate School, 1972. 322 pp.

Philippine Women's University

Benitez, Helena Z. *Story of a University.* Manila: PWU, 1966. 8 pp.

Saint Joseph College

Navarrosa, Optacia I. "Historical Development of St. Joseph College, 1928-1965, Maasin, Southern Leyte." Master's thesis, University of San Carlos, 1966. 148 pp.

Silliman University

Carson, Arthur L. *Silliman University, 1901-1959.* New York: United Board for Christian Higher Education in Asia, 1965. 477 pp.

Tumbagahan, Tiburcio J. "The First Forty Years: A History of Silliman University from 1901-1941." Ph.D. diss., Stanford University. 1949.

University of San Carlos

Bajarias, Dolores O. "A History of the University of San Carlos from 1595 to 1951." Master's thesis, University of San Carlos, 1951. 215 pp.

University of Santo Tomas

Gomez, Fausto, ed. *University of Santo Tomas, Yesterday, Today and Tomorrow.* Manila: Office of the Secretary General, University of Santo Tomas, 1973. 24 pp.

Manila. University of Santo Tomas. *The Manila University of Santo*

Tomas. *A Brief Sketch of Its Origin and Development with a Directory of Its Departments, Officers, and Professors.* Manila: The University Pr., 1908. 39 pp.

Pe, Josefina L. *The University of Santo Tomas in the Twentieth Century.* Manila: University of Santo Tomas Pr., 1973. 221 pp.

Sanchez y Garcia, Juan. *Historical Documentary Synopsis of the University of Santo Tomas of Manila from Its Foundation to Our Day.* Manila: Santo Tomas University Pr., 1929. 181 pp.

University of the Philippines

Alfonso, Oscar M., ed. *University of the Philippines: The First 75 Years (1908-1983).* Quezon City: University of the Philippines Pr., 1985. 726 pp.

Lopez, Salvador P. *Growth and Development Through the Years of Turmoil: The President's Report, 1969-1974.* Diliman, Quezon City: University of the Philippines, 1974. 49 pp.

POLAND

Adam Mickiewicz University

Banasiewicz, Maria. *Zrodla do dziejow Uniwersytetu im. Adama Mickiewicza w Poznania.* Poznan: Wydawn Uniwersytetu im. A. Mickiewicza, 1973-

Miskiewicz, Benon. *University of Poznan, the Past, the Present, the Future.* Poznan: Wydawnictow Naukowe Uniwersytetu im. Adama Mickiewicza w Poznaniu, 1979. 216 pp.

Posen. Uniwersytet. *University of Poznan, 1919-1969.* Poznan, 1971. 435 pp.

Jagiellonian University

Barycz, Henryk. *Uniwersytet Jagiellonski wzyciu narodu polskiego.* Wroclaw: Zaklad Narodowy im. Ossolinskich, 1964. 138 pp.

Hajdukiewicz, Leszek, and Karas, Mieczyslaw. *Jagiellonian University: Traditions, the Present, the Future.* Cracow: Uniwersytetu

Jagiellonskiego, 1975. 107 pp.

Michalewicz, Jerzy, and Michalewiczowa, Marie. *Liber beneficiorum et benefactorum Universitatis Iagellonicae in saeculis XV-XVIII.* Cracoviae: Sumptibus Universitas Iagellonica, 1978-1979.

Morawski, Kazimierz. *Historie de l'Universite de Cracovie: moyenage et renaissance.* 3 vols. Paris: Alphonse Picard, 1900-1905.

Universytet Jagiellonski, 1364-1964. Krakow: Biuro Jubileuszowe 600-Lecia, Uniwersytetu Jagiellonskiego, 1963. 39 pp.

Zareba, Maria Z., and Zareba, Alfred. *Ne cedat Academia: Kartki z dziejow tajnego nauczania w Uniwersytecie Jagiellonskim: 1939-1945.* Krakow: Wydawn. Literackie, 1975. 651 pp.

Technical University of Cracow

Politechnika Krakowska, 1946-1976. Krakow: Politechnika Krakowska, 1976. 490 pp.

Technical University of Poznan

Politechnika Poznanska. *Politechnika Poznanska i wczesniejsze uczelnie techniczne w Poznaniu.* Poznan: n.p., 1976. 480 pp.

Technical University of Szczecin

Politechnika Szczecinska. *Politechnika Szcaecinska w latach, 1946-1976: wydano w roku XXX-lecia Politechnika Szczecinskiej.* Szczecin: PSz, 1976. 138 pp.

Szczecin, Poland. Politechnika. *Politechnika Szczecinska w latch, 1946-1971.* Poznan: Panstwowe Wydawn, 1974. 310 pp.

Technical University of Warsaw

Politechnika Warszawska. *W 150 (i.e. sto piecdziesiata) rocznice utworzenia Politechniki w Warszawie.* Warszawa: PW, 1976. 28 pp.

University of Gdansk

Uniwersytet Gdanski jego poprzediczki. Gdanski: Uniwersytet Gdanski,

1980. 116 pp.

University of Warsaw

Dzieje Uniwersytetu Warszawskiego, 1807-1915. Warszawa: Panstwowe Wydawn. Nauk., 1981. 605 pp.

Dzieje Uniwersytetu Warszawskiego, 1915-1939. Warszawa: Panstwowe Wydawn. Naukowe, 1982. 359 pp.

Gieysztor, Aleksander, ed. *The University of Warsaw.* Warszawa: Warsaw University Pr., 1967. 105 pp.

Gieysztor, Aleksander, and Strzemienski, Marian. *The University of Warsaw, 1808-1818, 1958.* Warsaw: Arkady, 1958. 95 pp.

Warsaw. Uniwersytet. *Przeglad prac naukowo-badawczych w Uniwersytecie Warszawskin w latch, 1971-1974.* Warszawa: Wydawnictwa Uniwersytetu Warszawskiego, 1976. 372 pp.

University of Wroclaw

Uniwersytet Wroclawski im. Boleslawa Bieruta. *Uniwersytet Wroclawski w sluzbie nauki, Kultury i gospodarki narodowej: 1945-1975.* Wroclaw: Wydawn. Uniwersytetu Wroclawskiego, 1975. 160 pp.

PORTUGAL

Lisbon College*

Croft, William. *Historical Account of Lisbon College.* Barnet: St. Andrew's Pr., 1902. 275 pp.

Technical University of Lisbon

O Patrimonio historico de Universidade Tecnica de Lisboa: [exposicao] Fundacao Calouste Gulbenkian, Lisboa, dezembro, 1980. Lisboa: A. Fundacao, 1980. 76 pp.

Serrao, Joaquim V. *A Universidade Tecnica de Lisboa.* Lisboa: Editorial Verbo, 1980-

University of Coimbra

Banderia, Jose R. *Universidade de Coimbra: edificios do corpo central e Casa dos Melos.* 2 vols. Coimbra: Casa do Castelo Editora, 1943-1947.

Brando, Mario. *A Universidade de Coimbra, esboca da sua historia.* Coimbra: Por ordem da Universidade, 1937. 134 pp.

Compendio historico do estado da Universidade de Coimbra, 1771. Coimbra: Por ordem da Universidade, 1972. 348 pp.

Costa, Mario A. N. *Doculmentos para a historia da Universidade de Combra, 1750-1772: introducao, leiture e indices.* Coimbra: Por ordem da Universidade de Coimbra, 1959.

University of Lisbon

Auctarium Chartularii Universitatis Portugalensis: documentos. 3 vols. Lisboa: Instituto de Alta Cultura, 1973-1979.

University of the Azores

Alves, Mariano T. "The Creation of the University of the Azores: A Policy Study." Ph.D. diss., University of Alberta, 1985. 306 pp.

PUERTO RICO

University of Puerto Rico

Aponte-Hernandez, Rafael. "The University of Puerto Rico: Foundations of the 1942 Reform." Ph.D. diss., University of Texas, 1966. 267 pp. *Dissertation Abstracts,* vol. 27A, p. 2054.

Benitez, Jaime. *Special Report on the Development of Puerto Rico University from September 1942 to January 1945.* Rio Piedras: The University, 1945. 139 pp.

Benner, Thomas E. *The Years of Foundation Building; The University of Puerto Rico, 1924-1929.* Rio Piedras: University of Puerto Rico, 1965. 157 pp.

Parker, Paul C. "Change and Challenge in Caribbean Higher Education:

The Development of the University of the West Indies and the University of Puerto Rico." Ph.D. diss., Florida State University, 1971. 548 pp. *Dissertation Abstracts International,* vol. 33A, p. 4129.

Saenz, Mercedes. *Universidad de Puerto Rico: Historia y recuerdos.* Manti, Puerto Rico: Imprenta Rodriguez, 1978. 74 pp.

World University

Ohrnberger, June E. "A History of World University." Ed.D. diss., Columbia University, Teachers College, 1985. 225 pp. *Dissertation Abstracts International,* vol. 46A, p. 2592.

ROMANIA

Al. I. Cuza University

Universitatea "Al. I. Cuza" dis Iasi. *The "Al. I. Cuza" University of Jassy, 1860-1960.* Bucharest: Editura Stiintifica, 1960. 146 pp.

University of Bucharest

Istoria universitatii din Bucuresti. Bucuresti: Universitatea din Bucuresti, 1977-

Universitatea din Bucuresti. *Bucharest University, 1864-1964.* Bucharest: n.p., 1964. 82 pp.

SAUDI ARABIA

Umm Al-Qura University

Karimi, Khalid A. M. "University in Transition, a Study in Institutional Development: A Case Study of Umm Al-Qura University, Mecca, Saudi Arabia." Ed.D. diss., Indiana University, 1983. 208 pp. *Dissertation Abstracts International,* vol. 44A, pp. 2991-2992.

SIERRA LEONE

Fourah Bay College

Foray, Cyril P. *An Outline of Fourah Bay College History (1827-1977).*
  Freetown: Foray, 1979. 35 pp.

One Hundred Years of University Education in Sierra Leone, 1876-1976.
  Freetown: Celebrations Committee, Centenary of University Education,
  1977. 82 pp.

University of Sierra Leone

One Hundred Years of University Education in Sierra Leone, 1876-1976.
  Freetown: Celebration Committee, Centenary of University Education,
  1977. 82 pp.

SOUTH AFRICA

Diocesan College*

McIntyre, Donald G. *The Diocesan College, Rondebosch, South Africa; A Century of "Bishops." Cape Town.* Juta: n.p., 1950. 136 pp.

Rhodes University

Currey, Ronald F. *Rhodes University, 1904-1970; A Grahamstown (South Africa) Chronicle.* n.p., 1970. 186 pp.

St. Aidan's College*

Coleman, Francis L. *St. Aidan's College, Grahamstown: A History.*
  Grahamstown: Institute of Social and Economic Research, Rhodes
  University, 1980. 138 pp.

St. John's College*

Lawson, K. C. *Venture of Faith; The Story of St. John's College, Johannesburg, 1989-1968.* Johannesburg: Council of St. John's
  College, 1968. 426 pp.

University of Cape Town

Boucher, Maurice. *The University of the Cape of Good Hope and the University of South Africa, 1873-1946: A study in National and Imperial Perspective.* Pretoria: Govt. Printer, 1974. 332 pp.

Lennox-Short, Alan, and Welsh, David, eds. *UCT at 150: Reflections.* Cape Town: D. Philip, 1979. 175 pp.

Ritchie, W. *The History of the South African College, 1829-1918.* 2 vols. Cape Town: T. M. Miller, 1918.

Walker, Eric A. *The South African College and the University of Cape Town.* Cape Town: University of Cape Town, 1929. 126 pp.

University of Fort Hare

Kerr, Alenander. *Fort Hare, 1915-48; The Evolution of an African College.* New York: Humanities, 1968. 290 pp.

University of Natal

Brookes, Edgar H. *A History of the University of Natal.* Pietermaritzburg: University of Natal Pr., 1966. 194 pp.

University of South Africa

Boucher, Maurice. *Spes in Arduis: A History of the University of South Africa.* Pretoria: University of South Africa, 1973. 407 pp.

--------. *The University of the Cape of Good Hope and the University of South Africa, 1873-1946: A Study in National and Imperial Perspective.* Pretoria: Govt. Printer, 1974. 332 pp.

University of Stellenbosch

Stellenbosch, 1866-1966. Kaapstad: Nasionale Boekhandel, 1966. 599 pp.

University of Witwatersrand

Murray, Bruce K. *Wits, the Early Years: A History of the University of the Witwatersrand, Johannesburg, and Its Precursors, 1896-1939.*

Johannesburg: Witwatersrand University Pr., 1982. 389 pp.

University of the Witwatersrand. *The Golden Jubilee of the University of the Witwatersrand, Johannesburg, 1972.* Johannesburg: Jubilee Committee, University of the Witwatersrand, 1972. 120 pp.

SPAIN

St. Alban's College*

Williams, Michael C. *St. Alban's College, Valladolid: Four Centuries of English Catholic Presence in Spain.* New York: St. Martin's Pr., 1986. 288 pp.

Universidad International Menendez Pelayo

Madariaga de la Campa, Benito. *La Universidad Internacional de Verano en Santander, 1933-1936.* Ministerio de Universidades e Investigacion, 1981. 338 pp.

University of Alcala de Hernares

Uribe, Angel. *Colegio y colegiales de San Pedro y San Pablo de Alcala (Siglos XVI-XIX).* Madrid: Editorial Cisneros, 1981. 524 pp.

University of Barcelona

Arques, Josep. *Cinc estudies historics sobre la Universitat de Barcelona (1875-1895).* Barcelona: Colomna, 1985. 239 pp.

Palomeque Torres, Antonio. *La Universidad de Barcelona desde el Plan Pidal de 1845 a la ley Moyano de 1857.* Barcelona: Universidad, 1979. 857 pp.

Ribas i Massana, Albert, and Ribas, Frederic. *La Universitat Autonoma de Barcelona (1933-1939).* Barcelona: Edicions 62, 1976. 267 pp.

Torre y del Cerro, Antonio de la. *Documentos para la historia de la Universidad de Barcelona.* Barcelona: Barcelona Universidad, Facultad de Filosofia y Letras, 1971. 1 vol.

SPAIN / 123

University of Cordoba

Aranda Doncel, Juan. *La Universidad Libre de Cordoba: 1870-1874.*
    Cordoba: Servicio de Publicaciones de la Universidad de Cordoba,
    1974. 185 pp.

Tunnermann Bernheim, Carlos. *Sesenta anos de la reforma universitaria
    de Cordoba, 1918-1978.* Ciudad Universitaria Rodrigo Facio: Editorial
    Universitaria Centroamericana, 1978. 103 pp.

University of Deusto

Saenz de Santa Maria, Carmelo. *Historia de la Universidad de Deusto.*
    Bilbao: La Gran Enciclopedia Vasca, 1978. 255 pp.

University of Granada

IV centenario de la Universidad de Granada, 1532-1932. Granada:
    Universidad de Granada, 1932.

Lopez Rodriguez, Miguel. *El Colegio Real de Santa Cruz de la Fe de
    Granada.* Salamanca: Ediciones Universidad de Salamanca, 1979.
    37 pp.

University of Madrid

Entrambasaguas y Pena, Joaquin de. *La Universidad Central.* Madrid:
    Artes Graficas Municipales, 1972. 57 pp.

Martinez Albiach, Alfredo. *La Universidad Complutense segun el Cardenal
    Cisneros: (1508-1543).* Burgos: Facultad de Teologia del Norte de
    Espana, 1975. 129 pp.

University of Murcia

Libro blanco sobre la Universidad de Murcia: analisis y perspectivas.
    Mucia: Secretariado de Publicaciones, Universidad de Murcia, 1979.
    468 pp.

Sanchez Jara, Diego. *Como y por que nacio la Universidad Murciana?*
    Murcia: Sucesores de Nogues, 1967. 222 pp.

University of Oviedo

Alvarez, Lluis X. *La Universidad de Asturias.* Salinas: Ayalga, D. L., 1978. 295 pp.

Canella y Secades, Fermin. *Historia de la Universidad de Oviedo y noticias de los establecimientos de ensenanza de su distrito.* 2. ed. 1904. Reprint. Oviedo: Universidad de Oviedo, 1985. 791 pp.

University of Salamanca

Addy, George M. *The Englightment in the University of Salamanca.* Durham, N. C.: Duke University Pr., 1966. 410 pp.

Beltran de Heredia, Vicente. *Los origenes de la Universidad de Salamanca.* Salamanca: Universidad de Salamanca, 1983-

Esperabe Arteaga, Enrique. *Historia de la Universidad de Salamanca.* 2 vols. Salamanca: F. Nunez Izquierdo, 1914-1917.

Real de la Riva, Cesar. *La Universidad de Salamanca: apunte historico.* Salamanca: Universidad, 1980. 35 pp.

Rodriguez Cruz, Agueda M. *Coleccion documental: seleccion de algunos de los documentos mas importantes de la historia de la Universidad de Salamanca y de su proyeccion en Hispanoamerica.* Salamanca: Universidad de Salamanca, 1977. 64 pp.

--------. *Salmantica Docet: la proyeccion de la Universidad en Hispanoamerica.* 1 vol. Salamanca: Universidad, 1977-

Rodriguez-San Pedro Bezares, Luis E. *La Universidad Salmantina del barroco, periodo 1598-1625.* 3 vols. Salamanca: Ediciones Universidad de Salamanca, 1986.

Sala Balust, Luis. "Vistas y reforma de los colegios mayores de Salamanca en el reinado de Carlos III." Thesis, Valladolid, 1958. 453 pp.

Salamanca. Universidad. *Constituciones, estatutos y ceremonias de los antiguos colegios seculares de la Universidad de Salamanca.* 4 vols. Madrid: Consejo Superior de Investigaciones Cientificas, Patronato Menendez Pelayo, 1962-1966.

University of Santiago de Compostela

Cabeza de Leon, Salvador. *Historia de la Universidad de Compostela.* 2 vols. Santiago de Compostela, Instituto Padre Sarmiento de Estudios Gallegos, Consejo Superior de Investigaciones Cientificas, 1946-1947.

Fraguas Fraguas, Antonio. *Historia del Colegio de Fonseca.* Santiago de Compostela, Spain: Instituto P. Sarmiento de Estudios Gallegos, 1956. 343 pp.

Martinez Rodriguez, Enrique. *La Universidad de Santiago de Compostela al final de la epoca autonomica.* Santiago de Compostela: Universidad de Santiago de Compostela, 1981. 133 pp.

Perez Bustamante, Ciriaco. *La Universidad de Santiago: el pasado y el presente.* Santiago: Universidad de Santiago de Compostela, Publicaciones del Institutude Estudios Regionales, 1934. 138 pp.

University of Saragossa

Fraylla, Diego. *Lucidario de la Universidad y estudio general de la Ciudad de Zaragoza.* Zaragoza: Institucion Fernando el Catolico, 1983. 116 pp.

Garcia Lasaosa, Jose. *Planes de reforma de estudios de la Universidad de Zaragoza en la segunda mitad del siglo XVIII.* Zaragoza: Excmo. Ayuntamiento, D. L., 1978. 184 pp.

Historia de la Universidad de Zaragoza. Madrid: Nacional, 1983. 481 pp.

Jimenez Catalan, Manuel. *Historia de la Real y pontificia Universidad de Zaragoza.* 2 vols. Zaragoza: La Academica, 1922-1923.

University of Seville

Aguilar Pinal, Francisco. *La Universidad de Sevilla en el siglo SVII; estudio sobre la primera reforma universitaria moderna.* Sevilla: Universidad de Sevilla, 1969. 562 pp.

Villa, Antonio M. *Resena historica de la Universidad de Sevilla y descripcion de su Iglesia.* Sevilla: E. Rasco, 1886. 157 pp.

University of Valencia

Baldoi Lacomba, Marc. *La Universitat de Valencia.* Valencia: Institucio Alfons el Magnanim: Institucio Valenciana d'Estudis i Investigacio, 1986. 189 pp.

University of Valladolid

Alcocer y Martinez, Mariano. *Historia de la Universidad de Valladolid.* 7 vols. Valladolid: Imprenta Castellana, 1918-1931.

Almuina Fernandez, Celso. *La Universidad de Valladolid: historia y patrimonio.* Valladolid: Rectorado de la Universidad de Valladolid, 1980. 172 pp.

--------. *La Universidad de Valladolid: historia y patrimonio.* 2a ed. Valladolid: Rectorado de la Universidad de Valladolid, 1986. 208 pp.

Sanz Diaz, Federico. *El alumnado de la Universidad de Valladolid en el siglo XIX: (1837-1886).* Valladolid: Universidad, Secretariado de Publicaciones, 1978. 211 pp.

SRI LANKA

Wesley College*

The Wesley College Centenary Souvenir, 1874-1974. Colombo: The College, 1975. 156 pp.

SWEDEN

Lund University

Lunds universitets historia: utgiven av Universitetet till dess 300 arsjubileum. 4 vols. Lund: Glcerup, 1968-1982.

Ortengren, Per I. *Historiska notiser Krimg Lunds universitets byggnads och markfragor.* Lund: C. W. K. Gleerup. 1951. 156 pp.

Tegner, Elof K. *Lunds universitet, 1872-1897.* Lund: C. W. K. Gleerup,

1897. 346 pp.

University of Stockholm

Bedoire, Fredric; Thullberg, Per; and Adelskold, Elsie. *Stockholms universitet, 1878-1978.* Stockholm: Stockholms Kommunalforvaltning, 1978. 239 pp.

Uppsala University

Annerstedt, Claes. *Upsala Universitets Historia.* 5 vols. Upsala: W. Schultz, 1877-1910.

Lindroth, Sten. *A History of Uppsala University, 1477-1977.* Stockholm: Almqvist & Wiksell, 1976. 260 pp.

--------. *Uppsala universitet 1477.* Stockholm: Almqvist & Wiksell, 1976. 251 pp.

Sallander, Hans, ed. *Uppsala universited. Akademiska Konsistoriets protokoll.* 22 vols. Uppsala: Universitetet. 1968-1977.

SWITZERLAND

Swiss Federal Institute of Technology

Eidgenossische Technische Hochschule Zurich. *Eidgenossische Technische Hochschule, 1855-1955. Ecole Polytechnique Federale.* Zurich: Buchverlag der Neue Zurcher Zeitung, 1955. 723 pp.

--------. *Eidgenossische Technische Hochschule Zurich, 1955-1980: Festschrift zum 125 jahrigen Bestehen.* Zurich: Verlagheue Zurcher Zeitung, 1980. 683 pp.

University of Basel

Basel. Universitat. *Die Universitat Basel in der funfzig jahren seit ihrer reorganisation im jahre 1835.* Basel: Schulzesche Universitatsbuchdr., 1885. 119 pp.

Kreis, Georg. *Die Universitat Basel, 1960-1985.* Basel: Helbing & Lichtenhahn, 1986. 365 pp.

Sieber, Marc. *Die Universitat Basel und die Eidgenossenschaft 1460 bis 1529; eidghossische Studenten in Basel.* Basel: Helbing & Lichtenhahn, 1960. 166 pp.

Staehelin, Andreas. *Geschichte der Universitat Basel, 1632-1818.* 2 vols. Basel: Helbing & Lichtenhahn, 1957.

--------. *Die Universitat Basel en der Jahren 1884-1913, im auftrage der regenz mit unterstutzung des erziehungsdepartements aus anlass der Schweizerischen landesausstellung in Bern.* Basel: F. Reinhardt, Universitatsbuchdr., 1914. 200 pp.

Thomen, Rudolf. *Geschichte der Universitat Basel, 1532-1632.* Basel: Detloffs buchhandlung, 1889. 383 pp.

Universitat Basel. *Gestalten und Probleme aus der Geschichte der Universitaet Basel: Funf akademische Vortrage gehalten zur Fuenfhunderjahrfeier der Universitaet Basel.* Basel: Helbling & Lichtenhahn, 1960.

Vischer, Wilhelm. *Geschichte der Universitat Basel von der Grundung 1460 bis zur Reformation 1529.* Basel: H. Georg, 1860. 328 pp.

University of Berne

Bern. Universitat. *Die Hochschule Bern in den jahren, 1834-1884.* Bern: K. J. Wyss, 1884. 227 pp.

Hochschulgeschichte Berns, 1528-1984: zur 150-Jahr-Feier der Universitat Bern 1984. Bern: Universitat Bern, 1984. 800 pp.

Marti, Hugo. *Die Universitat Bern.* Dussnacht am Rigi: F. Linder, 1932. 95 pp.

Die Universitat Bern, Geschichte und Entwicklung. Bern: P. Haupt, 1984. 136 pp.

University of Geneva

Borgeaud, Charles. *Historie de l'Universite de Geneve.* 4 vols. Geneve: Georg & Co., 1900-1959.

Geisendorf, Paul F. *L'Universite de Geneve, 1559-1959; quatre siecles d'histoire.* Geneve: A. Jullien, 1959. 300 pp.

University of Zurich

Kuhn-Schnyder, Emil. *Lorenz Oken, 1779-1851: erster Rektor der Universitat Zurich: Festvortra zur Feier seines 200. Geburtstages.* Zurich: H. Rohr, 1980. 71 pp.

Die Universitat Zurich, 1933-1983: Festschrift zur 150-Jahr-Feier der Universitat Zurich. Zurich: Universitat, 1983. 808 pp.

Wyss, Georg V. *Die Hochschule Zurich in den jahren 1833-1883.* Zurich: Druck von Zurcher und Furrer, 1883. 111 pp.

THAILAND

Bangkok College

Kanthawongs, Charoen. "Bangkok College: History, Evaluation, and Projection." Ph.D. diss., Syracuse University, 1978. 285 pp. *Dissertation Abstracts International,* vol. 39A, p. 3402.

TAIWAN

Soochow University

Nance, W. B. *Soochow University.* New York: United Board of Christian Colleges in China, 1956. 163 pp.

Tunghai University

Chang, Chung-Ping. "The United Board for Christian Higher Education in Asia in the Development of Tunghai University in Taiwan, 1955-1980." Ph.D. diss., Southern Illinois University at Carbondale, 1982. 211 pp. *Dissertation Abstracts International,* vol. 43A, p. 2248.

TRINIDAD AND TOBAGO

University of the West Indies

Retout, Marie T. *A Light Rising from the West.* Trinidad: Inprint Caribbean, 1985. 186 pp.

St. Augustine Campus, the University of the West Indies: 25 Years, 1985-6. St. Augustine, Trinidad and Tobago: University of West Indies, 1985. 18 pp.

TURKEY

Istanbul Woman's College*

Patrick, Mary M. *A Bosporus Adventure; Istanbul (Constantinople) Woman's College, 1871-1924.* Stanford University, Calif.: Stanford University Pr., 1934. 284 pp.

University of Istanbul

Bilsel, Cemil. *Istanbul Universitesi tarihi.* Istanbul: Kenan Matbaasi, 1943. 168 pp.

Istanbul. Universite. *Universite de Stamboul. Historique, organisation et administration actuelles.* Stamboul: Publications de l'Universite de Stamboul, 1925. 42 pp.

UGANDA

King's College*

McGregor, Gordon P. "The History of King's College, Budo, Uganda, in Relation to the Development of Education in Uganda." Master's thesis, University of East Africa. 1965. 279 pp.

UNION OF SOVIET SOCIALIST REPUBLICS

Leningrad State University

Istoriia Leningradskogo universiteta, 1819-1969: ocherki. Leningrad: Izdvo Leningrad Unta, 1969. 663 pp.

Leningrad. Universitat. *Leningradskii universitet za gody sovetskoi vlasti: kratkii bibliograficheskii ukazalel.* Leningrad: Izdvo Leningr. unta, 1967. 59 pp.

Mavrodin, Vladimir V. *Leningradskii universitet; kratkiiocherk.* Leningrad: n.p., 1957. 126 pp.

Shilov, Lev A. *The University of Leningrad, 1819-1969.* Leningrad: Publishing House of Leningrad University, 1969. 29 pp.

Moscow State University

Moscow. Universitet. *Dokumenty i materialy po istorii Moskovskogo universiteta.* 3 vols. n.p., 1960-1963.

Peoples' Friendship University*

Rosen, Seymour M. *The Development of Peoples' Friendship University in Moscow.* Washington: U. S. Office of Education, Institute of International Studies, 1973. 17 pp.

--------. *The Development of Peoples' Friendship University in Moscow.* Washington: Institute of International Studies, 1973. 23 pp. ERIC Microfiche ED 076 163.

Tartu State University

Sulivask, Karl, ed. *History of Tartu University, 1632-1982.* Astra Books, 1986. 293 pp.

University of Moscow

Koshman, Lidiia V., and Sakharov, Anatolii M. *Moskovskii universitet v sovetskoe vremia.* Moskva: Izdvo Mosk. unta, 1967. 151 pp.

Moscow. Universitet. *Istoriia Moskovskago universiteta.* 2 vols. n.p., 1955.

Shevyrev, Stepan P. *Istoriia Imperatorskago Moskovskago universiteta, napisannaiak stolietnemuegoiubileiu, 1755-1855.* Moskva: V Univ. tip., 1855. 581 pp.

University of Vilnius

Rabikauskas, Paulus. *The Foundation of the University of Vilnius (1579): Royal and Papal Grants.* Roma: Lietuviu Kataliku Mokslo akademija, 1979. 75 pp.

UNITED STATES
ALABAMA

Air University

Shelburne, James C. "Factors Leading to the Establishment of the Air University." Ph.D. diss., University of Chicago, 1953. 289 pp.

Tolson, Billy J. "A History of Air University." Ph.D. diss., University of Oklahoma, 1983. 317 pp. *Dissertation Abstracts International,* vol. 44A, p. 3303.

Alabama State University

Caver, Joseph D. "Marion to Montgomery: A Twenty Year History of Alabama State University, 1867-1887." Master's thesis, Alabama State University, 1982. 128 pp.

Alexander City State Junior College

Hall, Reginald W. "The History of Alexander City State Junior College: Its Beginning, Foundation, and Progress, 1963-80." Ed.D. diss., Auburn University, 1980. 175 pp. *Dissertation Abstracts International,* vol. 41A, p. 4311.

Auburn University

Auburn University. *Auburn's First 100 Years, 1856-1956.* Auburn: The Institute, 1956. 16 pp.

Draughon, Ralph B. *Alabama Polytechnic Institute.* New York: Newcomen Society in North America, 1954. 28 pp.

Edwards, Charles W. *Auburn Starts a Second Century.* Auburn: Alabama Polytechnic Institute, 1958. 32 pp.

Smith, Earle R. "History of the East Alabama Male College Located at Auburn, Alabama." Master's thesis, Alabama Polytechnic Institute, 1932. 15 pp.

Sparks, Robbie S. "A Survey of the Development of Auburn College, 1870-1935." Master's thesis, Alabama Polytechnic Institute, 1935. 400 pp.

Birmingham-Southern College

Berte, Neal R. *Birmingham-Southern College; The Renewal of a Mission.* New York: Newcomen Society of the United States, 1986. 23 pp.

Christenberry, Daniel P. *The Semi-Centennial History of the Southern University, 1856-1906.* Greensboro, Ala.: D. P. Christenberry, 1908. 155 pp.

Corley, Robert G., and Stayer, Samuel N. *View from the Hilltop: The First 125 Years of Birmingham-Southern College.* Birmingham: Birmingham-Southern College, 1981. 150 pp.

Parks, Joseph H., and Weaver, Oliver C., Jr. *Birmingham-Southern College, 1856-1956.* Nashville, Tenn.: Parthenon Pr., 1957. 224 pp.

Perry, Wilbur D. *A History of Birmingham-Southern College, 1856-1931.* Nashville, Tenn.: Methodist Publishing House, 1931. 80 pp.

Community College of the Air Force

O'Connor, Thomas J. "The Community College of the Air Force: A History and a Comparative Organizational Analysis." Ph.D. diss. University of Denver, 1974. 284 pp. *Dissertation Abstracts International,* vol. 35A, p. 4215.

Huntingdon College

Brasfield, Elizabeth B. "History of Alabama Female College." Master's thesis, University of Alabama, 1944. 153 pp.

Ellison, Rhoda C. *History of Huntingdon College, 1854-1954.* University: University of Alabama Pr., 1954. 305 pp.

Jacksonville State University

Sawyer, Effie W. *The First Hundred Years: The History of Jacksonville State University, 1883-1983.* Jacksonville: Centennial Committee, Jacksonville State University, 1983. 206 pp.

Judson College

Epting, James B. "A Chronological Review of the Development of Judson College, Marion, Alabama, 1838-1978." Ed.D. diss., University of Alabama, 1978. 159 pp. *Dissertation Abstracts International,* vol. 39A, p. 5348.

Manly, Louise. *History of Judson College.* Atlanta, Ga.: Foote and Davies Co., 1913. 202 pp.

Views of Judson College. Marion, Ala.: Judson College, 1926.

Livingston University

Lyon, Ralph M. *A History of Livingston University, 1835-1963.* Livingston, Ala.: The Author, 1976. 126 pp.

Oxford College (Closed)

Little, Frank J. "The History of Oxford College." Master's thesis, University of Alabama, 1937. 125 pp.

--------. *The History of Oxford College, Oxford, Alabama.* Alexandria, Ala.: Little, 1937. 124 pp.

Samford University

Garrett, Mitchell B. *Sixty Years of Howard College, 1842-1902.* Birmingham, Ala.: Howard College, 1927. 167 pp.

Wright, Leslie S. *Samford University from Farm Belt to Space Age.* New York: Newcomen Society in North America, 1969. 32 pp.

Snead State Junior College

Millican, Alta. "A History of Snead Junior College Prior to 1940." Master's thesis, University of Alabama, 1936. 289 pp.

Southern Union State Junior College

Phi Theta Kappa. Iota Iota Chapter, Southern Union State Junior College, Wadley, Alabama. *Tap Roots: A Historical Account of Southern Union State Junior College and Areas in Randolph County.* Roanoke, Ala.: The Roanoke Leader, 1976. 48 pp.

Spring Hill College

Kenny, Michael. *Catholic Culture in Alabama; Centenary Story of Spring Hill College, 1830-1930.* New York: The America Pr., 1931. 400 pp.

Smith, Andrew C. *The Phoenix and the Turtle: Some Highlights on the History of Spring Hill College.* Mobile: Spring Hill College Pr., 1957. 13 pp.

Stillman College

Sikes, William M. "The Historical Development of Stillman Institute." Master's thesis, University of Alabama, 1930. 136 pp.

Terry, Paul W., and Lee, L. Tennent. *A Study of Stillman Institute-A Junior College for Negroes.* University of Alabama: University of Alabama Pr., 1946. 304 pp.

Talladega College

Butler, Addie L. J. *The Distinctive Black College: Talladega, Tuskegee and Morehouse.* Metuchen, N. J.: Scarecrow, 1977. 169 pp.

Jones, Maxine D., and Richardson, Joe M. *Talladega College: The First Century.* Tuscaloosa: University of Alabama Pr., 1990. In Press.

Troy State University

Bannon, Michael F. "A History of State Teachers College, Troy, Alabama." Ph.D. diss., George Peabody College for Teachers, 1955. 105 pp.

Shackelford, Edward M. *The First Fifty Years of the State Teachers College at Troy, Alabama, 1887 to 1937.* Montgomery, Ala.: Paragon Pr., 1937. 301 pp.

Smith, Charles B. *Troy State University, 1937-1970, Troy, Alabama: A Continuation of the First Fifty Years by Edward M. Shackelford.* Troy: TSU Pr., 1970. 366 pp.

Tuskegee University

Alverson, Roy T. "A History of Tuskegee." Master's thesis, Alabama Polytechnic Institute, 1929. 20 pp.

Bell, Sallie M. B. "A Study of the Development of Tuskegee Institute under the Administration of Washington, Moton, and Patterson." Master's thesis, Atlanta University, 1950. 73 pp.

Blackwell, Velma L. "A Black Institution Pioneering Adult Education: Tuskegee Institute Past and Present (1881-1973)" Ph.D. diss., Florida State University, 1973. 235 pp. *Dissertation Abstracts International,* vol. 35A, p. 783.

Butler, Addie L. J. *The Distinctive Black College: Talladega, Tuskegee and Morehouse.* Metuchen, N. J.: Scarecrow, 1977. 169 pp.

Citro, Joseph F. "Booker T. Washington's Tuskegee Institute: Black School-Community, 1900-1915." Ed.D. diss., University of Rochester, 1973. 573 pp. *Dissertation Abstracts International,* vol. 34A, p. 153.

DeLoney, Willie L. "A History of Tuskegee Institute." Master's thesis, University of Michigan, 1937. 89 pp.

Dryer, Edmund H. *Origin of Tuskegee Normal and Industrial Institute.* Birmingham, Ala.: Roberts and Sons, 1938. 13 pp.

Ludlow, Helen W., ed. *Tuskegee Normal and Industrial School, for Training Colored Teachers. Its Story and Its Songs.* Hampton, Va.: Normal School Steam Pr., 1884. 21 pp.

McArthur, Jackson. "A Historical Study of the Founding and Development of Tuskegee Institute." Ph.D. diss., University of North Carolina at Greensboro, 1983. 117 pp. *Dissertation Abstracts International,* vol. 44A, p. 1170.

Scipio, L. Albert. *Pre-War Days at Tuskegee: Historical Essay on Tuskegee Institute (1881-1943).* Silver Springs, Md.: Roman Publications, 1987. 541 pp.

Stokes, Anson P. *Tuskegee Institute the First Fifty Years.* Tuskegee: Tuskegee Institute Pr., 1931. 99 pp.

Thrasher, Max B. *Tuskegee, Its Story and Its Work.* New York: Negro Universities Pr., 1969. 215 pp.

University of Alabama

Alabama. University. *Centennial Celebration, 1831-1931.* University, Ala.: n.p., 1931. 114 pp.

Gallalee, John M. *The University of Alabama; A Short History.* New York: Newcomen Society in North America, 1953. 24 pp.

Mellown, Robert O. *The University of Alabama: A Guide to the Campus.* Tuscaloosa: University of Alabama Pr., 1988. 118 pp.

Sellers, James B. *History of the University of Alabama.* University, Ala.: University of Alabama Pr., 1953- 580 pp.

Volker, Joseph F. *The University and the City.* New York: Newcomen Society in North America, 1971. 32 pp.

Wolfe, Suzanne R. *The University of Alabama, a Pictorial History.* University, Ala.: University of Alabama Pr., 1983. 251 pp.

University of Alabama in Huntsville

Ferguson, James E. *The University of Alabama in Huntsville: The Birth and Growth of a Modern University.* Huntsville: The University of Alabama in Huntsville, 1975. 80 pp.

University of Montevello

Griffith, Lucille B. *Alabama College, 1896-1969.* Montevello, Ala.: n.p., 1969. 197 pp.

University of North Alabama

Posey, Walter B. *LaGrange, Alabama's Earliest College.* Birmingham: Birmingham-Southern College, 1933. 23 pp.

Vaughn, Susan K. *The History of the State Teachers College, Florence, Alabama.* Florence, Ala.: n.p., 1930. 47 pp.

ALASKA

Alaska Pacific University

Goldberg, Barbara L. S. "University in Crisis: A Case History of Alaska Methodist University." Ed.D. diss., Harvard University, 1978. 387 pp.

Sheldon Jackson College

Armstrong, Neal A. "Sheldon Jackson Scenes: A Documentary History of Sheldon Jackson Junior College, Sitka, Alaska, 1878-1967." Ed.D. diss., George Peabody College for Teachers, 1967. 105 pp.

ARIZONA

Arizona State University

Barry, John H., Jr. "The History of the Arizona State Teachers College at Tempe, 1885-1935." Master's thesis, Stanford University, 1943. 222 pp.

Hopkins, Ernest J., and Thomas, Alfred, Jr. *The Arizona State University Story.* Phoenix: Southwest Publishing Co., 1960. 305 pp.

Nelson, J. Russell. *Arizona State University: A Centennial Commitment to Excellence for a New Century.* New York: Newcomen Society of the United States, 1985. 24 pp.

Richardson, Harold D. *Arizona State University: Dynamic Educational Leadership in the Great Southwest.* New York: Newcomen Society in North America, 1964. 28 pp.

Arizona Western College

The First 3 Years of Arizona Western College, Yuma, Arizona, 1963-1966. Yuma, Ariz.: Arizona Western College, 19 ?. 47 pp.

Eastern Arizona College

Scott, Thomas A. "Eastern Arizona College: A Comprehensive History of the Early Years." Ed.D. diss., Brigham Young University, 1985. 724 pp. *Dissertation Abstracts International,* vol. 47A, p. 2920.

Grand Canyon College

Jenke, James M. "The Growth and Development of Grand Canyon College." Ph.D. diss., Arizona State Univesity, 1983. 451 pp. *Dissertation Abstracts International,* vol. 45A, p. 427.

Navajo Community College

House, Lloyd L. "The Historical Development of Navajo Community College." Ph.D. diss., Arizona State University, 1974. 169 pp. *Dissertation Abstracts International,* vol. 35A, p. 2024.

Northern Arizona University

Cline, Platt. *Mountain Campus: The Story of Northern Arizona University.* Flagstaff: Northland Pr., 1983. 394 pp.

Hutchinson, Melvin T. "History of Arizona State College at Flagstaff from Its Origin through a Quarter of a Century." Master's thesis, Arizona State College, 1952. 300 pp.

--------. *The Making of Northern Arizona University: A Chronicle.* Flagstaff: Northern Arizona University Pr., 1972. 326 pp.

Walkup, J. Lawrence. *Pride, Promise, and Progress: The Development of Northern Arizona University.* Flagstaff: Author Universal Pub., 1984. 711 pp.

Northland Pioneer College

Albright, Penny, and Westover, Janet Y. *Northland Pioneer College: A Decade of Service: 1974-75 to 1984-85.* Holbrook, Ariz.: n.p., 1985. 66 pp.

University of Arizona

Ball, Phyllis. *A Photographic History of the University of Arizona, 1885-*

1985. Tucson: University of Arizona Pr., 1986. 469 pp.

Fitz-Gerald, John D. *Historia de la Universidad de Arizona.* Ciudad Trujillo, n.p., 1942. 15 pp.

Harvill, Richard A. *Arizona, Its University's Contributions to the Southwest.* New York: Newcomen Society in North America, 1953. 32 pp.

Martin, Douglas D. *Lamp in the Desert; The Story of the University of Arizona.* Tucson: University of Arizona Pr., 1960. 304 pp.

ARKANSAS

Arkansas State University

Ball, Larry D., and Clements, William M. *Voices from State: An Oral History of Arkansas State University.* State University, Ark.: Arkansas State University, 1984. 180 pp.

Dew, Lee A. *The ASU Story; A History of Arkansas State University, 1909-1967.* Jonesboro: Arkansas State University Pr., 1968. 224 pp.

Harding University

Atteberry, James L. *The Story of Harding College.* Searcy, Ark.: J. L. Atteberry, 1966. 56 pp.

Croom, Adlai S. *The Early History of Harding College.* Searcy, Ark.: A. S. Croom, 1954. 131 pp.

Nichols, James D. "A History of Harding College, 1924 to 1984." Ed.D. diss., University of Arkansas, 1985. 231 pp. *Dissertation Abstracts International,* vol. 47A, p. 1631.

Henderson State University

Bledsoe, Bennie G. *Henderson State University: Education Since 1890.* 2 vols. Houston, Tex.: D. Armstrong Co., 1986.

Hall, John G. *Henderson State College, the Methodist Years, 1890-1929.* Arkadelphia, Ark.: Henderson State College Alumni Association, 1974. 171 pp.

Hendrix College

Lester, James E. *Hendrix College: A Centennial History.* Conway, Ark.: Hendrix College Centennial Committee, 1984. 322 pp.

John Brown University

Williams, Earl R. "John Brown University; Its Founder and Its Founding, 1919-1957." Ed.D. diss., University of Arkansas, 1971. 284 pp. *Dissertation Abstracts International,* vol. 32A, p. 2448.

Ouachita Baptist University

Arrington, Michael E. "A History of Ouachita Baptist College: 1886-1933." Ph.D. diss., University of Arkansas, 1982. 253 pp. *Dissertation Abstracts International,* vol. 43A, p. 3396.

--------. *Ouachita Baptist University: The First 100 Years.* Little Rock, Ark.: August House, 1985. 222 pp.

Philander Smith College

Gibson, De Lois. "Philander Smith College, 1877-1969." Ed.D. diss., University of Arkansas, 1972. 200 pp. *Dissertation Abstracts International,* vol. 33A, p. 2140.

Southern Arkansas University

Skelton, Philip D. "A History of Southern Arkansas University from 1909 to 1976." Ed.D. diss., University of Mississippi, 1979. 230 pp. *Dissertation Abstracts International,* vol. 40A, p. 1914.

University of Arkansas

Harrison, Hale. *University of Arkansas, 1871-1948.* Fayetteville: University of Arkansas Alumni Association, 1948. 289 pp.

Leflar, Robert A. *The First 100 Years; Centennial History of the University of Arkansas.* Fayetteville: University of Arkansas Foundation, 1972. 403 pp.

Reynolds, John H. *History of the University of Arkansas.* Fayetteville: University of Arkansas, 1910. 555 pp.

University of Arkansas at Little Rock

Atkinson, James H. *Little Rock Junior College, Now Little Rock University; The First Ten Years, 1927-1937.* Little Rock: Pulaski County Historical Society, 1959. 26 pp.

Lester, James E. *The People's College: Little Rock Junior College and Little Rock University, 1927-1969.* Little Rock: August House, 1987. 239 pp.

University of Arkansas at Pine Bluff

Chambers, Frederick. "Historical Study of Arkansas Agricultural, Mechanical, and Normal College, 1873-1943." Ed.D. diss., Ball State University, 1970. 442 pp. *Dissertation Abstracts International,* vol. 31A, p. 5158.

University of the Ozarks

Basham, Robert H. "A History of Cane Hill College in Arkansas." Ed.D. diss., University of Arkansas, 1969. 408 pp. *Dissertation Abstracts, International* vol. 30A, p. 2816.

Clarksville, Ark. College of the Ozarks. Alumni Association. *The Semi-Centennial Edition of the History-Directory of the College of the Ozarks.* Clarksville: The Alumni Association of the College of the Ozarks, Inc., 1940. 67 pp.

CALIFORNIA

Azusa Pacific University

Brackett, Charles H. "The History of Azusa College and the Friends, 1900-1965." Master's thesis, University of Southern California, 1967. 157 pp.

Goodhew, Edna F. *Echos from Half a Century.* Los Angeles: Los Angeles Pacific College Pr., 1960. 322 pp.

Miller, Melvin J. "The Torch Held High: A History of Pacific Bible College, Azusa, California." Master's thesis, Azusa College, 1957. 79 pp.

Biola University

Williams, Robert, and Miller, Marilyn. *Chartered for His Glory: Biola University, 1908-1983.* La Mirada, Calif.: Associated Students of Biola University, 1983. 110 pp.

California Baptist College

Brown, Olie T., and Nelson, Lawrence E. *It's a Great Day; A History of California Baptist College, Its First Twenty Years.* Riverside: California Baptist College Pr., 1970. 102 pp.

California College of Arts and Crafts

California College of Arts and Crafts (Oakland, Calif.) *California College of Arts and Crafts: Seventy-Five Years, 1907-1982.* Oakland, Calif.: The College, 1982. 12 pp.

Dhaemers, Margaret P. "California College of Arts and Crafts, 1907-1944." Master's thesis, Mills College, 1967. 230 pp.

California Institute of Technology

DuBridge, Lee A. *Frontiers of Knowledge: Seventy-Five Years at the California Institute of Technology.* New York: Newcomen Society in North America, 1967. 24 pp.

Gates, Charlynne. "The History and Development of the California Institute of Technology." Master's thesis, University of Southern California, 1935. 67 pp.

Shirley, Lawrence. *Two Decades of Caltech Development; Sources for Institute Growth, 1920-1940.* Mesa, Ariz.: SPC, 1969. 150 pp.

California Polytechnic State University, San Luis Obispo

Riddell, Steven G. "A History of California Polytechnic State University: 1952-1979." Ed.D. diss., Brigham Young University, 1985. 171 pp. *Dissertation Abstracts International,* vol. 46A, p. 631.

Smith, Morris E. "A History of California State Polytechnic College, the First Fifty Years, 1901-1951." Ed.D. diss., University of Oregon, 1958. 299 pp. *Dissertation Abstracts,* vol. 19, p. 992.

California State University, Chico

Hutchinson, William H. *When Chico Stole the College.* Chico, Calif.: Butte Savings and Loan Association, 1983. 24 pp.

McIntosh, Clarence F. *Chico State College: The First 75 Years.* Oroville, Calif.: Butte County Historical Society, 1962. 23 pp.

Moore, Gail E. "History of Chico State College." Master's thesis, Oregon State University, 1939. 141 pp.

Pihl, Cedric H. "A Dramatized History of Chico State College." Master's thesis, Chico State College, 1953. 67 pp.

California State University, Fresno

Hogan, Fred P. "The History of Fresno State Teachers College." Master's thesis, Stanford University, 1929. 149 pp.

Rowland, Eugenia. "Origin and Development of Fresno State College." Ph.D. diss., University of California at Berkeley, 1949. 229 pp.

Seib, Kenneth A. *The Slow Death of Fresno State: A California Campus Under Regan and Brown.* Palo Alto, Calif.: Ramparts Pr., 1979. 223 pp.

California State University, Hayward

Laird, Johanna, and Romick, Ann. *The Twenty-Fifth Year, 1957-1982; California State University, Hayward.* Hayward: Office of Public Affairs, California State University, Hayward. 1982(?). 20 pp.

Williams, John A. "A History of the Early Development of California State University, Hayward, with Emphasis on the Selection of the Site." Master's thesis, California State University at Hayward, 1973. 77 pp.

California State University, Northridge

Schneider, Lydia E. "The Growth and Development of a California State College." Master's thesis, California State University at Northridge, 1976. 192 pp.

California State University, Sacramento

Craft, George S. *California State University, Sacramento: The First Forty Years, 1947-1987.* Sacramento: Hornet Foundation, 1987. 280 pp.

Moore, Dwain E. *Sacramento State College: The First Eighteen Years.* Sacramento: n.p., 1965. 142 pp.

--------. *Twenty Years of Higher Education: The History of Sacramento State College (1947-1967).* 2d ed. Sacramento: Association of Students of Sacramento State College, 1967. 108 pp.

California State University, San Bernardino

Urata, James H. "The Development of the California State College at San Bernardino." Master's thesis, San Diego State College, 1967. 225 pp.

Chabot College

Staniford, Edward F. *Chabot College, the First Twenty Years: An Informal History.* Hayward: South College Community College District, 1981. 144 pp.

Chapman College

Clover, Haworth A. *Hesperian College, 1861-1896; Pioneer Sacramento Valley Collegiate Institution, Antecedent to Chapman College.* Burlingame, Calif.: Hesperia Pr., 1974. 136 pp.

--------. "An Historical Study of Hesperian College, Woodland, California from 1861 to 1896." Master's thesis, College of the Pacific, 1960. 246 pp.

Christ College

Halm, D. Ray, and Hiatt, Diana B. *The Creation of a Private Religious College, 1955-1985.* Washington, D. C.: Paper Presented at the Annual Meeting of the American Educational Research Association, April 20-24, 1987, 1987. 21 pp. ERIC Microfiche ED 285 454.

Halm, Dennis R. "A History of Christ College Irvine - The First Thirty Years." Ed.D. diss., Pepperdine University, 1986. 289 pp. *Dissertation Abstracts International,* vol. 47A, p. 1215.

Claremont Colleges

Benson, Mabel G., ed. *An Idea Becomes a College: Claremont Men's College, the First Ten Years.* Claremont: Claremont Men's College, 1957. 85 pp.

Clary, William W. *The Claremont Colleges; A History of the Development of the Claremont Group Plan.* Claremont: Claremont University Center, 1970. 314 pp.

Coastline Community College

Martinez, Samuel A. "The Formative Years of Coastline Community College: The Problem of Developing Non-Traditional Education in a Traditional Age." Ed.D. diss., University of Southern California, 1988. *Dissertation Abstracts International,* vol. 49A, pp. 3636-3637.

College of Notre Dame

McNamee, Mary D. *Light in the Valley; The Story of California's College of Notre Dame.* Berkeley: Howell-North Books, 1967. 338 pp.

College of the Desert

Cheeves, Lyndell D. "The Founding of College of the Desert, 1958-1963." Ed.D. diss., University of California, Los Angeles, 1971. 228 pp. *Dissertation Abstracts International,* vol. 32A, p. 6028.

El Camino College

Muck, Steven J. "The History of El Camino College, 1946-1966." Ed.D. diss., University of California, Los Angeles, 1971. 358 pp. *Dissertation Abstracts International,* vol. 32A, p. 3728.

Foothill College

Foothill College: 25 Years. Los Altos Hills, Calif.: Foothill College, 198?. 179 pp.

Golden Gate Baptist Theological Seminary

Graves, Harold K. *Into the Wind: Personal Reflections on the Early Years of Golden Gate Baptist Theological Seminary.* Nashville, Tenn.: Broadman Pr., 1983. 382 pp.

Golden Gate University

Miner, Nagel T. *The Golden Gate University Story.* San Francisco: Golden Gate University Pr., 1982-

Graduate Theological Union

The First Twenty Years: The Graduate Theological Union, 1962-1982. Berkeley, Calif.: Graduate Theological Union, 1982. 27 pp.

Humboldt State University

Davies, Sarah M. "A History of Humboldt State College." Master's thesis, Stanford University, 1947. 200 pp.

Loma Linda University

Utt, Richard H. *From Vision to Reality, 1905-1980: Loma Linda University.* Loma Linda, Calif.: Loma Linda University, 1980. 208 pp.

Los Angeles City College

Lillard, Richard G. *A History of Los Angeles City College; Twenty-Five Years of Community Service.* Los Angeles: Associated Students of Los Angeles City College, 1954. 26 pp.

Los Angeles Pierce College

McHargue, Robert M. "The Early History of Los Angeles Pierce College: Its Genesis, Foundation and Tradition, 1943-1956." Ed.D. diss., University of California, Los Angeles, 1965. 320 pp. *Dissertation Abstracts,* vol. 25, p. 6343

Los Angeles Southwest College

Wainwright, Frank N. "A History of the Early Development of an Urban Community College: The Story of Los Angeles Southwest College: 1967-74." Ed.D. diss., University of Southern California, 1978. *Dissertation Abstracts International,* vol. 39A, p. 2680.

Los Angeles Trade-Technical College

Lawson, Allen L. "Los Angeles Trade-Technical College: 1925-1950." Ed.D. diss., University of California, Los Angeles, 1976. 311 pp. *Dissertation Abstracts International,* vol. 37A, p. 3581.

Menlo College

Curtis, F. Phillar. *Menlo School and College: A History.* Atherton, Calif.: Menlo School and College, 1984. 75 pp.

Howard, Lowry S. *The Story of Menlo, Past, Present, Future.* Menlo Park, Calif.: The School, 1931. 22 pp.

Mills College

Keep, Rosalind A. *Fourscore and Ten Years, a History of Mills College.* Mills College, Calif.: n.p., 1946. 203 pp.

--------. *Fourscore Years, a History of Mills College.* Mills College, Calif.: n.p., 1931. 143 pp.

Mira Costa College

Jorgensen, Sharalee C. "Miracosta College: The First Fifty Years." Ed.D. diss., University of San Diego, 1985. 373 pp. *Dissertation Abstracts International,* vol. 45A, p. 3524.

Occidental College

Cleland, Robert G. *The History of Occidental College, 1887-1937.* Los Angeles: Ward Ritchie Pr., 1937. 115 pp.

Gilman, Richard C. *The College and the City.* New York: Newcomen Society in North America, 1974. 24 pp.

Rolle, Andrew. *Occidental College: A Centennial History.* Los Angeles: Occidental College Bookstore, 1986. 240 pp.

--------. *Occidental College, the First Seventy-Five Years, 1887-1962.* Los Angeles: Occidental College, 1962. 191 pp.

Orange Coast College

Orange Coast College. *Tumbleweeds to Roses; A History of Orange Coast College.* Costa Mesa, Calif.: Pirate Bookstore, 1965. 259 pp.

Pacific Christian College

Tiffen, Gerald C.; Stranlund, Kathy; and Warner, Mike, eds. *Framing the Future: The First Twenty-Five Years of Pacific Christian College, 1928-1953.* Fullerton, Calif.: Pacific Christian College, 1979. 41 pp.

Pacific School of Religion

Hogue, Harland E. *Christian Seed in Western Soil: Pacific School of Religion Through a Century.* Berkeley: Pacific School of Religion, 1965. 276 pp.

Pacific Union College

Hoffman, Philip G. "History of Pacific Union College." Master's thesis, University of Southern California, 1941. 98 pp.

Utt, Walter, C. *A Mountain, a Pickax, a College.* Angwin: Pacific Union College, 1968. 160 pp.

Pasadena City College

Knott, James P. *History of Pasadena College.* Pasadena: Pasadena College, 1960. 124 pp.

Pfeiffer, Clyde E. "A History of Pasadena Junior College." Master's thesis, Occidental College, 1941. 215 pp.

Pepperdine University

Rushford, Jerry, ed. *Crest of a Golden Wave: Pepperdine University, 1937-1987: A 50th Anniversary Pictorial History.* Malibu: Pepperdine University Pr., 1987. 310 pp.

Young, M. Norvel. *Pepperdine University, a Place, a People, a Purpose.* New York: Newcomen Society of the United States, 1982. 27 pp.

Pomona College

Brackett, Frank P. *Granite and Sagebrush; Reminiscences of the First Fifty Years of Pomona College.* Los Angeles: Ward Ritchie Pr., 1944. 251 pp.

Lyon, Elijah W. *The History of Pomona College, 1887-1969.* Claremont, Calif.: The College, 1977.

Sumner, Charles B. *The Story of Pomona College.* Boston: Pilgrim Pr., 1914. 417 pp.

Rio Hondo College

Huffman, Harold T., Jr. "The Early History of Rio Hondo College." Ed.D. diss., Pepperdine University, 1981. 203 pp. *Dissertation Abstracts International,* vol 42A, p. 4744.

Sacramento Junior College

Evans, James M. "The Organization and Promotion of Sacramento Junior College, 1916-1940." Ph.D. diss., University of Southern California, 1974. 432 pp. *Dissertation Abstracts International,* vol. 35A, p. 2716.

Saint Mary's College of California

McDevitt, Matthew. *The History of Saint Mary's College.* Morago: The College, 1970 163 pp.

White, Raymond J. "The Effects of Internal Goals and External Pressures on the Development of a Catholic Liberal Arts College." Ph.D. diss., University of California, Berkeley, 1981. 228 pp. *Dissertation Abstracts International,* vol. 42A, p. 3035.

San Francisco State University

Smith, Robert; Axen, Richard; and Pentony, DeVere. *By Any Means Necessary; The Revolutionary Struggle at San Francisco State.* San Francisco: Jossey Bass, 1970. 370 pp.

San Francisco Theological Seminary

Baird, Jesse H. *The San Anselmo Story: A Personalized History of San Francisco Theological Seminary.* Stockton, Calif.: California Lantern Pr., 1963. 124 pp.

San Jose State University

Gilbert, Benjamin F. *Pioneers for One Hundred Years: San Jose State College, 1857-1957.* San Jose: San Jose State College, 1957. 243 pp.

Gilbert, Benjamin F., and Burdick, Charles B. *Washington Square, 1857-1979; The History of San Jose State University.* San Jose: San Jose State University, 1980. 223 pp.

Greathead, Sarah E. H. *The Story of an Inspiring Past; Historical Sketch of the San Jose State Teachers College from 1862 to 1928.* San Jose: San Jose State Teachers College, 1928. 506 pp.

San Jose State College. *Historical Sketch of the State Normal School at San Jose, California, with a Catalogue of Its Graduates and a Record of Their Work for Twenty-Seven Years.* Sacramento: J. D. Young, 1889. 283 pp.

San Luis Obispo Junior College (Closed 1959)

Jones, Ivan L., Jr. "San Juis Obispo Junior College: Demise and Rebirth." Ed.D. diss., University of California at Los Angeles, 1967. 194 pp. *Dissertation Abstracts,* vol. 28A, p. 2527.

Santa Clara University

Donohoe, Patrick A. *The University of Santa Clara.* New York: Newcomen Society in North America, 1966. 24 pp.

McKevitt, Gerald. "History of Santa Clara College; A Study of Jesuit Education in California, 1851-1912." Ph.D. diss., University of California at Los Angeles, 1972. 372 pp. *Dissertation Abstracts International,* vol. 33A, p. 1654.

--------. *The University of Santa Clara; A History, 1851-1977.* Stanford, Calif.: Stanford University Pr., 1979. 385 pp.

Santa Clara, Calif. University. *University of Santa Clara: A History:*

From the Founding of Santa Clara Mission in 1777 to the Beginning of the University in 1912. Santa Clara: University Pr., 1912. 122 pp.

University of Santa Clara. *University of Santa Clara, Diamond Jubilee Volume, 1851-1926.* n.p., The University of Santa Clara, 1926. 100 pp.

Southern California College of Optometry

Gregg, James R. *Origin and Development of the Southern California College of Optometry, 1904-1984.* Fullerton, Calif.: The College, 1984. 564 pp.

Stanford University

Allen, Peter C. *Stanford: From the Foothills to the Bay.* Stanford: Stanford Alumni Association & Stanford Historical Society, 1980. 228 pp.

Crothers, George E. *Founding of the Leland Stanford University.* San Francisco: A. M. Robertson, 1932. 44 pp.

Elliott, Orrin L. *Stanford University: The First Twenty-Five Years.* Stanford: Stanford University Pr., 1937. 624 pp.

The First Year at Stanford: Sketches of Pioneer Days at Leland Stanford Junior University. Stanford University, Calif.: English Club, 1905. 159 pp.

The First Year at Stanford: Sketches of Pioneer Days at Leland Stanford Junior University. 2d ed. Stanford University, Calif.: English Club, 1910. 159 pp.

James, Norris E., ed. *Fifty Years on the Quad: A Pictorial Record of Stanford University and the 35,000 Men and Women Who Have Spent a Part of Their Lives on the Campus, 1887-1937.* Stanford: The Stanford Alumni Association, 1938. 248 pp.

McDonald, Emanuel B. *Sam McDonald's Farm; Stanford Reminiscences by Emanuel B. "Sam" McDonald.* Stanford: Stanford University Pr., 1954. 422 pp.

Mirrielees, Edith R., ed. *Stanford Mosaic; Reminiscences of the First Seventy Years at Stanford University.* Stanford: Stanford University Pr., 1962. 248 pp.

--------. *Stanford; The Story of a University.* New York: Putnam, 1959. 255 pp.

Mitchell, John P. *Stanford University, 1916-1941.* Stanford: Stanford University Pr., 1958. 167 pp.

Taylor, Katherine A. *The Story of Stanford.* San Francisco: H. S. Crocker Co., 1935. 69 pp.

University of California, Berkeley

Adams, Ansel, and Newhall, Nancy. *Fait Lux: The University of California.* New York: McGraw-Hill, 1967. 192 pp.

California University. Office of University Relations. *A Brief History of the University of California.* Berkeley: University of California, 1966. 61 pp.

Ferrier, William W. *Origin and Development of the University of California.* Berkeley: The Satergate Bookshop, 1930. 710 pp.

Foley, Patrick J. "The Antecedents and Early Development of the University of California, 1849-1875." Ph.D. diss., University of California, Berkeley, 1970. 224 pp.

Heirich, Max. *The Beginning: Berkeley, 1964.* New York: Columbia University Pr., 1971. 317 pp.

Horn, Thayer, S. *A Century of Service: University of California, 1874-1974.* n.p., 1974?. 127 pp.

Jones, William C. *Illustrated History of the University of California.* San Francisco: F. H. Dukesmith, 1895. 413 pp.

--------. *Illustrated History of the University of California.* Rev. ed. Berkeley: Students' Cooperative Society, 1901. 430 pp.

Ouellette, Vernon A. "Daniel Coit Gilman's Administration of the University of California." Ph.D. diss., Stanford University, 1952.

Pickerell, Albert G., and Dornin, May. *The University of California: A Pictorial History.* Berkeley: University of California Pr., 1968. 326 pp.

Sibley, Robert. *The Romance of the University of California.* Berkeley: The California Alumni Association, 1932. 62 pp.

Sibley, Robert, and Sibley, Carol. *University of California Pilgrimage: A Treasury of Tradition, Lore and Laughter.* n.p.: Lederer, Street & Zeus Co., 1952. 201 pp.

Stadtman, Verne A. *The University of California, 1868-1968.* New York: McGraw-Hill, 1970. 594 pp.

Stone, Irving, ed. *There Was Light: Autobiography of a University: Berkeley, 1868-1968.* Garden City, N. Y.: Doubleday, 1970. 454 pp.

Sutliff, Albert. *A Description of the Town of Berkeley: With a History of the University of California.* San Francisco: Bacon, 1881. 24 pp.

University of California, Berkeley. *The University of California Centennial.* Berkeley: n.p., 1968. 48 pp.

Willey, Samuel H. *A History of the College of California.* San Francisco: S. Carson & Co., 1887. 432 pp.

University of California, Davis

Jewett. Alyce W. *Saga of UDC.* Davis, Calif.: The Printer, 1982. 109 pp.

UC Davis: Its Development and Environment. Davis, Calif.: University Farm Circle, 1980. 37 pp.

Windows on the Past: A Personal History of Campus Buildings, University of California, Davis. Davis: The Society, Student Activities, 1984. 27 pp.

University of California, Irvine

Boothby, Neil. *The Irvine Story: History and Development of the University of California, Irvine.* Irvine: N. Boothby, 1972. 47 pp.

University of California, Irvine. *The First Decade: 1965-1975.* Irvine: The University, 1975. 16 pp.

University of California, Los Angeles

Dickson, Edward A. *University of California at Los Angeles: Its Origin and Formative Years.* Los Angeles: Friends of the UCLA Library, 1955. 61 pp.

Hamilton, Andrew, and Jackson, John B. *UCLA on the Move, during Fifty*

Golden Years, 1919-1969. Los Angeles: Ward Ritchie, 1969. 230 pp.

Martin, James R. *The University of California (in Los Angeles): A Resume of the Selection and Acquisition of the Westwood Site.* Los Angeles: n.p., 1925. 317 pp.

Moore, Ernest C. *I Helped Make a University.* Los Angeles: Dawson's Book Shop, 1952. 175 pp.

University of California, Los Angeles. Alumni Association. *California of the Southland, a History of the University of California at Los Angeles.* Los Angeles: University of California at Los Angeles Alumni Association, 1937. 95 pp.

University of California, Santa Barbara

Kelley, Robert L. *Transformation: UC Santa Barbara, 1909-1979.* Santa Barbara: Associated Students, University of California, Santa Barbara, 1981. 148 pp.

O'Reilly, Edmund P. "A History of Santa Barbara State Teacher's College." Master's thesis, Stanford University, 1928. 115 pp.

University of California, Santa Cruz

The First 20 Years: Two Decades of Building at UCSC. Santa Cruz, Calif.: University of California at Santa Cruz, 1988. 12 pp.

University of La Verne

Muir, Gladdys E. *La Verne College, Seventy-Five Years of Service.* La Verne, Calif.: La Verne College, 1967. 115 pp.

University of Redlands

Armacost, George H.; Hone, Ralph E.; and Mertins, Esther N. *"Whose Emblem Shines Afar": A Commemorative Account of the University of Redlands for the Years, 1945-1982.* Redlands, Calif.: The University, 1983. 237 pp.

Nelson, Lawrence E. *Redlands: Biography of a College; The First Fifty Years of the University of Redlands.* Redlands, Calif.: University of Redlands, 1958. 310 pp.

University of San Francisco

Connolly, John F. X. *The University of San Francisco; "A Credo--and a Commitment to Excellence".* New York: Newcomen Society in North America, 1960. 24 pp.

Riordan, Joseph W. *The First Half Century of Saint Ignatius Church and College.* San Francisco: H. S. Crocker, 1905. 389 pp.

University of Southern California

Gates, Samuel E. "History of the University of Southern California, 1900 to 1928." Master's thesis, University of Southern California, 1930.

Henley, William B., and Neelley, Arthur E., eds. *Cardinal and Gold: A Pictorial and Factual Record of the Highlights of Sixty Years of Progress on the Southern California Campus, 1880-1940.* Los Angeles: The General Alumni Association, The University of Southern California, 1939.

Hill, H. W., ed. *The Semicentennial Celebration of the Founding of the University of Southern California.* Los Angeles: University of Southern California, 1930. 211 pp.

Hunt, Rockwell D. *The First Half-Century; University of Southern California.* Los Angeles: University of Southern California Pr., 1930. 109 pp.

Servin, Manual P., and Engstrand, Iris W. *Southern California and Its University: A History of USC, 1880-1964.* Los Angeles: Ward Ritchie, 1969. 319 pp.

Topping, Norman H. *The University of Southern California: An Institution and a Community.* New York: Newcomen Society in North America, 1966. 28 pp.

Zumberge, James H. *The University of Southern California: A Centennial Retrospective.* New York: Newcomen Society in North America, 1981. 24 pp.

University of the Pacific

Brewer, Kara P. *Pioneer or Perish: A History of the University of the Pacific during the Administration of Dr. Robert E. Burns, 1946-1971.* Fresno, Calif.: Pioneer Publishing, 1977. 263 pp.

Burns, Robert E. "The First Half-Century of the College of the Pacific, Stockton, California." Master's thesis, College of the Pacific, 1946. 105 pp.

Hunt, Rockwell D. *History of the College of the Pacific, 1851-1951*. Stockton: College of the Pacific, 1951. 226 pp.

Ventura College

Howe, Catherine P. "A History of Ventura College, 1925-1958." Master's thesis, University of Southern California, 1958. 186 pp.

West Coast Christian College

Smith, Henry J. "A History of West Coast Bible College, Fresno, California, 1949-1970." Master's thesis, Fresno State College, 1970. 73 pp.

West Los Angeles College

Horn, Larry. "History of West Los Angeles College." Ph.D. diss., University of Southern California, 1971. 722 pp. *Dissertation Abstracts International,* vol. 32A, p. 211.

Westmont College

Hillegas, Lyle C. "A History of Westmont College." Ph.D. diss., Dallas Theological Seminary, 1964. 196 pp.

Whittier College

Cooper, Charles W. *Whittier: Independent College in California, Founded by Quakers, 1887.* Los Angeles: Ward Ritchie, 1967. 405 pp.

Elliott, Charles, Jr. *Whittier College: The First Century on the Poet Campus: A Pictorial Remembrance.* Redondo Beach, Calif.: Legends Pr., 1986. 240 pp.

Feeler, William. "History of Whittier College." Master's thesis, University of Southern California, 1919. 78 pp.

Harris, Herbert E. *The Quaker and the West: The First Sixty Years of Whittier College.* n.p., 1948. 175 pp.

Yampa Valley College

Bogue, Lucile. *Miracle on a Mountain: The Story of a College.* San Francisco: Strawberry Hill Pr., 1987. 166 pp.

COLORADO

Colorado College

Buckley, Louise. "The History of Colorado College, 1874-1904." Master's thesis, Colorado College, 1935. 155 pp.

Hershey, Charlie B. *Colorado College, 1874-1949.* Colorado Springs: Colorado College, 1952. 306 pp.

Reid, J. Juan. *Colorado College: The First Century, 1874-1974.* Colorado Springs: Colorado College, 1979. 319 pp.

Riley, Gresham. *Colorado College, an Informal History.* New York: Newcomen Society of the United States, 1982. 20 pp.

Colorado School of Mines

Crain, Harry M., ed. *Seventy-Fifth Anniversary of the Colorado School of Mines, Golden, Colorado: A Record of the Proceedings; September 29 and 30 and October 1, 1949.* Golden: Colorado School of Mines, 1950. 90 pp.

McBride, Guy T. *"Wealth of Good Learning;" The Story of Colorado School of Mines.* New York: Newcomen Society in North America, 1974. 20 pp.

Colorado State University

Hansen, James E. *Democracy's College in the Centennial State: A History of Colorado State University.* Fort Collins: Colorado State University, 1977. 494 pp.

--------. *A History of Colorado State University, 1870-1974.* Fort Collins: Printing and Publications Service, Colorado State University, 1974. 33 pp.

COLORADO / 159

Colorado Women's College

Turner, Wallace B. *Colorado Woman's College, the First Seventy-Five Years.* Boulder, Colo.: Johnson Publishing Co., 1962. 262 pp.

Fort Lewis College

Delaney, Robert W. *Blue Coats, Red Skins and Black Gowns: 100 Years of Fort Lewis.* Durango, Colo.: Durango Herald, 1977. 179 pp.

Loretto Heights College

Casey, Celestine, and Fern, M. Edmond. *Loretto in the Rockies.* Denver: n.p., 1943. 314 pp.

Regis College

Stansell, Harold L. *Regis: On the Crest of the West.* Denver: Regis Educational Corp., 1977. 238 pp.

Trinidad State Junior College

Denbo, Philip G. "The History of Trinidad State Junior College, 1925-1948." Master's thesis, Western State College of Colorado, 1948. 125 pp.

Ross, William R. "The History of the Trinidad State Junior College from 1869 to 1939." Ph.D. diss., University of Northern Colorado, 1940. 243 pp.

United State Air Force Academy

Miller, Ed M. *Wild Blue U.* New York: Macmillan, 1972. 161 pp.

Miller, Edward A., Jr. "The Founding of the Air Force Academy: An Administrative and Legislative History." Ph.D. diss., University of Denver, 1969. 482 pp. *Dissertation Abstracts International,* vol. 31A, p. 1203.

Sands, Gene C. "An Administrative History of the U. S. Air Force Academy, 1954-1979." Ed.D. diss., Catholic University of America, 1982. 137 pp. *Dissertation Abstracts International,* vol. 43A, p. 1002.

Scott, Winfield W. *The United States Air Force Academy: A Commitment to Excellence.* New York: Newcomen Society of the United States, 1986. 24 pp.

United States Air Force Academy. *The United States Air Force Academy's First Twenty-Five Years: Some Perspectives.* Colorado Springs: The Academy, 1979. 415 pp.

University of Colorado

Allen, Frederick S., et. al. *The University of Colorado, 1876-1976: A Centennial Publication of the University of Colorado.* New York: Harcourt Brace Jovanovich, 1976. 319 pp.

Darley, Ward. *The University of Colorado, Eighty Years Young!, 1876-1956.* New York: Newcomen Society in North America, 1956. 24 pp.

Davis, William E. *Glory Colorado!: A History of the University of Colorado, 1858-1963.* Boulder: Pruett Pr., 1965. 798 pp.

--------. "A History of the University of Colorado, 1861-1963." Ed.D. diss., University of Colorado, 1963. 1889 pp. *Dissertation Abstracts,* vol. 28A, p. 2995.

University of Denver

Angel, Donald E. "A History of the University of Denver, 1880-1900." Master's thesis, University of Denver, 1961. 187 pp.

Beasley, Joan H. "The University of Denver Defines Its Purpose: A History of the Junior College and the Community College, 1940 to 1961." Ph.D. diss., University of Denver, 1985. 262 pp. *Dissertation Abstracts International,* vol. 47A, p. 94.

Connor, Donald B. "The University of Denver: The Buchtel Chancellorship, 1900-1920." Master's thesis, University of Denver, 1961. 115 pp.

Dunleavy, Jeannette J. "Early History of Colorado Seminary and the University of Denver." Master's thesis, University of Denver, 1935. 345 pp.

Mayer, Gerard E. "A History of the University of Denver: 1920-1940." Master's thesis, University of Denver, 1963. 134 pp.

Norland, Jim. *The Summit of a Century: A Pictorial History of the*

University of Denver, 1864-1964. Denver: University of Denver, 1963. 127 pp.

Porter, R. Russell. *The University of Denver Centennial; Its Philosophy, Preparation, Presentation.* Denver: Big Mountain Pr., 1965. 156 pp.

University of Northern Colorado

Carter, Albert F. *Forty Years of Colorado State Teachers College, Formerly the State Normal School of Colorado, 1890-1930.* Greeley: Colorado Teachers College, 1930. 395 pp.

Hartman, William F. "The History of Colorado State College of Education - The Normal School Period - 1890-1911." Ed.D. diss., Colorado State College of Education, 1951. 213 pp.

--------. "The History of Colorado State College of Education - The Teachers College Period - 1911-1935." Ed.D. diss., Colorado State College of Education, 1952. 160 pp.

Larson, Robert W. *Shaping Educational Change: The First Century of the University of Northern Colorado at Greeley.* Boulder, Colo.: Colorado Associated University Pr., 1989. 486 pp. In Press.

Pierce, Morris A. "A Century of Campus Planning and Construction at the University of Northern Colorado." Master's thesis, University of Northern Colorado, 1988. 205 pp.

Western State College of Colorado

Fay, Abbott. *Mountain Academia; A History of Western State College of Colorado.* Boulder: Pruett Pr., 1968. 154 pp.

CONNECTICUT

Central Connecticut State University

Fowler, Herbert E. *A Century of Teacher Education in Connecticut; The Story of New Britian Normal School and Teachers College of Connecticut, 1849-1949.* New Britain: n.p., 1949. 125 pp.

Connecticut College

Ames, Oakes. *Connecticut College: Contributing to a Changing Society.* New York: Newcomen Society of the United States, 1987. 24 pp.

Connecticut College. *Fiftieth Anniversary Celebration Publication, Connecticut College, 1911-1961.* New London: Connecticut College, 1961. 69 pp.

Noyes, Gertrude E. *History of Connecticut College.* New London: Connecticut College, 1982. 224 pp.

Nye. Irene. *Chapters in the History of Connecticut College during the First Three Administrations, 1911-1942.* New London: n.p., 1943. 90 pp.

Eastern Connecticut State University

Forst, Arthur C. "From Normal School to State College: The Growth and Development of Eastern Connecticut State College from 1889 to 1959." Ph.D. diss., University of Connecticut, 1980. 259 pp. *Dissertation Abstracts International,* vol. 41A, p. 3453.

Fairfield University

Kelley, Aloysius P. *Fairfield University: "Knowledge with a Moral Dimension".* New York: Newcomen Society of the United States, 1984. 28 pp.

Preville, Joseph R. "Fairfield University: The Emergence of a Modern Catholic Institution." Ph.D. diss., Boston College, 1985. 272 pp. *Dissertation Abstracts International,* vol. 46A, p. 2208.

Hartford Seminary

Geer, Curtis M. *The Hartford Theological Seminary, 1834-1934.* Hartford: Case, Lockwood and Brainard Co., 1934. 296 pp.

Hartford Theological Seminary. *A Memorial of the Semi-Centenary Celebration of the Founding of the Theological Institute of Connecticut.* Hartford: Case, Lockwood and Brainard Co., 1884. 146 pp.

Mitchell College

Roueche, John E.; McFarlane, William H.; and Herrscher, Barton R. *The Private Junior College: Prospects for the 70's; the Mitchell College Story.* Durham, N. C.: National Laboratory for Higher Education, 1971. 50 pp.

Trinity College

Lockwood, Theodore D. *Trinity College: 150 Years of Quality Education.* New York: Newcomen Society in North America, 1974. 19 pp.

Trinity College, Hartford. *Trinity College, Historical and Descriptive.* Hartford: Printed for the College, 1916. 30 pp.

Weaver, Glenn. *The History of Trinity College.* 1 vol. Hartford: Trinity College Pr., 1967-

United States Coast Guard Academy

Hughes, Riley. *Our Coast Guard Academy, a History and Guide.* New York: Devin-Adair, 1944. 213 pp.

University of Bridgeport

Littlefield, Henry W. *The University of Bridgeport, Building for Tomorrow on Values of Yesterday.* New York: Newcomen Society in North America, 1970. 24 pp.

University of Connecticut

Stemmons, Walter. *The Connecticut Agricultural College, a History.* Storrs: n.p., 1931. 258 pp.

Wyllie, Robert H. "Historical Development of Branches of the University of Connecticut." Ph.D. diss., University of Connecticut, 1963. 126 pp. *Dissertation Abstracts,* vol. 24, p. 4529.

Wesleyan University

Price, Carl F. *Wesleyan's First Century, with an Account of the Centennial Celebration.* Middletown: Wesleyan University, 1932. 384 pp.

Wesleyan. University, Middletown, Conn. *1831-1906. Celebration of the Seventy-Fifth Anniversary of the Founding of Wesleyan University.* Middletown: Wesleyan University, 1907. 216 pp.

--------. *Semi-Centennial of Wesleyan University, Wednesday, June 29th, 1881.* Middletown: n.p., 1881. 48 pp.

--------. *Sesquicentennial Papers.* Middletown: Wesleyan University, 1981. 9 nos.

Western Connecticut State University

Isham, Charlotte H. *A History of Western Connecticut State College, Danbury, Connecticut, 1903-1978.* Danbury: The College, 1978. 36 pp.

Yale University

Baldwin, Ebenezer. *Annals of Yale College from Its Foundation to 1831.* New Haven: n.p., 1831. 324 pp.

--------. *Annals of Yale College, from Its Foundation, to the Year 1831.* 2d ed. New Haven: B. & W. Noyes, 1838. 343 pp.

Belden, Ezekiel P. *Sketches of Yale College, with Numerous Anecdotes and Embellished with More than Thirty Engravings.* New York: Saxton & Miles, 1843, 192 pp.

Chamberlain, Joshua L., ed. *Yale University; Its History, Influence, Equipment and Characteristics, with Biographical Sketches and Portraits of Founders, Benefactors, Officers and Alumni.* Boston: R. Herndon Co., 1900.

Clap, Thomas. *The Annals or History of Yale College, in New Haven, in the Colony of Connecticut, from the First Founding Thereof, in the Year 1700, to the Year 1766.* New Haven: J. Hotchkiss and B. Mecom, 1766. 122 pp.

Dexter, Franklin B., ed. *Documentary History of Yale University.* New Haven: Yale University Pr., 1916. 382 pp.

--------. *Founding of Yale College.* New Haven: n.p., 1882. 31 pp.

--------. *Sketch of the History of Yale University.* New York: Holt, 1887. 108 pp.

French, Robert D., comp. *The Memorial Quadrangle; A Book About Yale.*

New Haven: Yale University Pr., 1929. 459 pp.

Holden, Reuben A. *Yale; A Pictorial History*. New Haven: Yale University Pr., 1967.

Kelley, Brooks M. *Yale: A History*. London: Yale University Pr., 1974. 588 pp.

Kingsley, James L. *A Sketch of the History of Yale College, in Connecticut*. Boston: Printed by Perkins, Marvin & Co., 1835. 48 pp.

Kingsley, William L. *Yale College: A Sketch of Its History*. 2 vols. New York: Holt, 1879.

Lord, Jerome E. "Yale or Storrs? The Land-Grant College Controversy in Connecticut, 1885-1896." Ph.D. diss., Columbia University, 1969. 250 pp.

Oviatt, Edwin. *The Beginnings of Yale, 1701-1726*. New Haven: Yale University Pr., 1916. 456 pp.

Pierson, George W. *The Founding of Yale: The Legend of the Forty Folios*. New Haven: Yale University Pr., 1988. 275 pp.

--------. *Yale: A Short History*. New Haven: Office of the Secretary, Yale University, 1976. 95 pp.

--------. *Yale: A Short History*. 2d ed. New Haven: Office of the Secretary, Yale University, 1979. 102 pp.

--------. *A Yale Book of Numbers: Historical Statistics of the College and University, 1701-1976*. New Haven: Yale University, 1983. 633 pp.

--------. *Yale: College and University, 1871-1937*. 2 vols. New Haven: Yale University Pr., 1952-1955.

Walker, Williston. *The Coming of Yale College to New Haven*. New Haven: Yale University Pr., 1917. 11 pp.

Warch, Richard. *School of the Prophets: Yale College, 1701-1740*. New Haven: Yale University Pr., 1973. 339 pp.

--------. "Yale College: 1701-1740." Ph.D. diss., Yale University, 1968. 414 pp. *Dissertation Abstracts International,* vol. 30A, p. 563.

Woolsey, Theodore D. *An Historical Discourse, Pronounced before the Graduates of Yale College, August 14, 1850; One Hundred and Fifty*

Years after the Founding of that Institution. New Haven: B. L. Hamlen, 1850. 128 pp.

DELAWARE

Delaware State College

Satneck, Walter J. "The History of the Origins and Development of the Delaware State College and Its Role in Higher Education for Negroes in Delaware." Ed.D. diss., New York University, 1962. 290 pp. *Disseration Abstracts,* vol. 24, p. 1473.

University of Delaware

Lewis, William D. *University of Delaware: Ancestors, Friends and Neighbors.* Newark: University of Delaware, 1961. 260 pp.

Munroe, John A. *The University of Delaware: A History.* Newark: The University, 1986. 516 pp.

Vallandigham, Edward N. *Fifty Years of Delaware College, 1870-1920.* Newark: Dells, 1920. 147 pp.

Wesley College

Breuckelman, Fred N. *The College that Refused to Die: Wesley College, 1873-1973.* Dover: Dover Graphica, 1973. 52 pp.

DISTRICT OF COLUMBIA

American University

Reynolds, John R., and King, Joanne E. *Highlights in the History of the American University, 1889-1976.* Washington: Hennage Creative Printers, 1976. 91 pp.

Catholic University of America

Ahern, Patrick H. *The Catholic University of America, 1887-1896.* Washington: Catholic University of America Pr., 1949. 220 pp.

Barry, Colman J. *The Catholic University of America, 1903-1909: The Rectorship of Denis J. O'Connell.* Washington: Catholic University of America Pr., 1950 296 pp.

Defferrari, Roy J. *Memoirs of the Catholic University of America, 1918-1960.* Boston: St. Paul Editions, 1962. 455 pp.

Dixon, Blase R. "The Catholic University of America, 1901-1928: The Rectorship of Thomas Joseph Shahan." Ph.D. diss., Catholic University of America, 1972. 403 pp. *Dissertation Abstracts International,* vol. 33A, p. 681.

Ellis, John T. *The Formative Years of the Catholic University of America.* Washington: American Catholic Historical Association, 1946. 415 pp.

Hogan, Peter E. *The Catholic University of America, 1896-1903; The Rectorship of Thomas J. Conaty.* Washington: Catholic University of America Pr., 1949. 212 pp.

Kuntz, Frank A. *Undergraduate Days, 1904-1908; The Catholic University of America.* Washington: Catholic University of America Pr., 1958. 139 pp.

Willis, H. Warren. "The Reorganization of the Catholic University of America during the Rectorship of James H. Ryan, 1928-1935." Ph.D. diss., Catholic University of America, 1971. 359 pp. *Dissertation Abstracts International,* vol. 32A, p. 6162.

Corcoran School of Art

Marsh, Alan T. "Washington's First Art Academy, the Corcoran School of Art, 1875-1925." 2 vols. Ph.D. diss., University of Maryland, 1983. 345 pp.

Gallaudet University

Atwood, Albert W. *Gallaudet College, Its First One Hundred Years.* Lancaster, Pa.: Intelligencer, 1964. 183 pp.

Baughman, Robert T. "A History of Gallaudet College and Its Service to the Deaf." Master's thesis, Gallaudet College, 1934. 52 pp.

Gallaudet, Edward M. *History of the College for the Deaf, 1857-1907.* Washington: Gallaudet College Pr., 1983. 265 pp.

Gallaudet College. Alumni Association. *Our Heritage: Gallaudet College*

Centennial (1864-1964). Washington: Graphic Arts Pr., 1964. 176 pp.

Sturtevant, Charles C. "Gallaudet College, Some Aspects of Its Formation and Development." Master's thesis, Gallaudet College, 1943. 38 pp.

George Washington University

Cobb, Richard. *George Washington University, Its Growth and Individuality*. Washington: The University, 1916. 15 pp.

Kayser, Elmer L. *Bricks Without Straw; The Evolution of George Washington University*. New York: Appleton, 1970. 352 pp.

--------. *The George Washington University, 1821-1966*. Washington: George Washington University, 1966. 31 pp.

Stockton, Charles H. *A Historical Sketch of George Washington University, Delivered before the Columbia Historical Society*. Washington: The University, 1915. 25 pp.

Georgetown University

Bunn, Edward B. *"Georgetown", First College Charter from the U. S. Congress, 1789-1954*. New York: Newcomen Society in North America, 1954. 28 pp.

Daley, John M. *Georgetown University: Origin and Early Years*. Washington: Georgetown University Pr., 1957. 324 pp.

Durkin, Joseph T. *Georgetown University; First in the Nation's Capital*. Garden City: Doubleday, 1964. 143 pp.

--------. *Georgetown University: The Middle Years, 1840-1900*. Washington: Georgetown University Pr., 1963. 333 pp.

Easby-Smith, James S. *Georgetown University in the District of Columbia, 1789-1907, Its Founder, Benefactors, Officers, Instructors and Alumni*. 2 vols. New York: Lewis, 1907.

Friant, John R.; Rover, Thomas; and Dahill, Edwin M. *Glimpses of Old Georgetown*. Washington: Undergraduate History Department of Georgetown University, 1939. 52 pp.

Shea, John D. G. *Memorial of the First Centenary of Georgetown College, D. C., Comprising a History of Georgetown University*. New York: Collier, 1891. 480 pp.

Howard University

Dyson, Walter. *The Founding of Howard University.* Washington: Howard University Pr., 1921. 24 pp.

--------. *Howard University, the Capstone of Negro Education, a History: 1867-1940.* Washington: The Graduate School, Howard University, 1941. 553 pp.

Logan, Rayford W. *Howard University: The First One Hundred Years, 1867-1967.* New York: New York University Pr., 1969. 658 pp.

Patton, William W. *The History of Howard University, Washington, D. C.* Washington, D. C.: Printed at the Industrial Department of Howard University, 1896. 48 pp.

Miner Teachers College (Closed)

Hatter, Henrietta R. "History of Miner Teachers' College." Master's thesis, Howard University, 1939. 76 pp.

Nelson, Bernard H. *Miner Teachers College: The First Century, 1851-1951; The Biography of a School.* Washington: The Author, 1973. 194 pp.

Trinity College

Hilliard, Annie P. "An Investigation of Selected Events and Forces that Contributed to the Growth and Development of Trinity College, Washington, D.C. from 1897 to 1982." Ed.D. diss., George Washington University, 1948. 276 pp. *Dissertation Abstracts International,* vol. 45A, p. 2773.

Mullaly, Columba. *Trinity College, Washington, D. C.: The First Eighty Years, 1897-1977.* Westminster, Md.: Christian Classics, 1987. 581 pp.

University of the District of Columbia

Miller, Stephen S. "The Emergence of Comprehensive Public Higher Education in the District of Columbia: The Establishment of Federal City College." Ph.D. diss., Catholic University of America, 1970. 137 pp. *Dissertation Abstracts International,* vol. 31A, p. 2131.

Wesley Theological Seminary

Chandler, Douglas R. *Pilgrimage of Faith: A Centennial History of Wesley Theological Seminary, 1882-1982.* Cabin John, Md.: Seven Locks Pr., 1984. 296 pp.

FLORIDA

Edward Waters College

Tucker, Samuel J. *Phoenix from the Ashes: EWC's Past, Present and Future.* Jacksonville, Fla.: Convention Pr., 1976. 37 pp.

Embry-Riddle Aeronautical University

McCollister, John, and Ramsden, Diann. *The Sky is Home: The Story of Embry-Riddle Aeronautical University, 1926-1986.* Middle Village, N. Y.: J. David, 1986. 127 pp.

Florida Agricultural and Mechanical University

Neyland, Leedell W., and Riley, John W. *The History of Florida Agricultural and Mechanical University.* Gainesville: University of Florida Pr., 1963. 303 pp.

Florida International University

The Birth of a University-and Plans for Its Development; Florida International University. Miami: n.p., 1970. 137 pp.

Gibbs, Rafe. *Visibility Unlimited: From a Deserted Airport of Yesterday to an Urban University of Tomorrow.* Miami: Florida International University, 1976. 127 pp.

Florida Southern College

Haggard, Theodore M. *Florida Southern College, Lakeland, Florida: The First 100 Years: An Illustrated History, 1985.* Lakeland: The College, 1985. 232 pp.

Thrift, Charles T. *Through Three Decades at Florida Southern College,*

FLORIDA / 171

Lakeland, Florida. Lakeland: Florida Southern College Pr., 1955. 47 pp.

Florida State University

Campbell, Doak S. *A University in Transition.* Tallahassee: Florida State University, 1964. 132 pp.

Dodd, William G. *Florida State College for Women: Notes on the Formative Years.* n.p., 1958-1959. 120 pp.

--------. *West Florida Seminary, 1857-1901; Florida State College, 1901-1905.* Tallahassee: n.p., 1952. 128 pp.

Wills, Martee, and Norris, Joan. *Seminole History: A Pictorial History of Florida State University.* Gainesville, Fla.: South Star Publishing Co., 1987. 240 pp.

Indian River Community College

Lunceford, Charles R. "The Historical Development of Indian River Junior Community College, 1960-1978." Ed.D. diss., Florida Atlantic University, 1980. 264 pp. *Dissertation Abstracts International,* vol. 41A, p. 915.

Jacksonville University

Bald, Ralph D., Jr. *A History of Jacksonville University: The First Twenty-Five Years, 1934-1959.* Jacksonville: Jacksonville University, 1959. 91 pp.

Rollins College

Campen, Richard N. *Winter Park Portrait: The Story of Winter Park and Rollins College.* Beachwood, Ohio: West Summit Pr., 1987. 112 pp.

Hanna, Alfred J. *The Founding of Rollins College.* Winter Park: Rollins Press, Inc., 1936. 69 pp.

Rider, Manning C. "A Brief History of Rollins College with Special Reference to the Curriculum." Master's thesis, Stetson University, 1937. 121 pp.

Rollins 1885, Founded in the Tradition of America's Great Liberal Arts Colleges. Winter Park: Rollins College, 1982. 40 pp.

Wagner, Paul A. *Rollins College and Dr. Hamilton Holt; Pioneering Higher Education in Florida.* New York: Newcomen Society in North America, 1951. 32 pp.

Stetson University

Lycan, Gilbert L. *Stetson University: The First 100 Years.* DeLand, Fla.: Stetson University Pr., 1983. 502 pp.

Tallahassee Community College

Tallahassee Community College Our Ten-Year Report, 1966-1976. Tallahassee: The College, 1977. 17 pp.

University of Florida

Crow, Charles L. *The Florida Agricultural College.* n.p., 1932. 37 pp.

--------. *Florida University, 1883.* n.p., 1932. 22 pp.

--------. *History of the University of Florida through 1908/09.* 2 vols. n.p., 1937.

--------. *St. Petersburg Normal and Industrial School.* n.p., 1932. 2 pp.

--------. *The University of Florida.* n.p., 1932. 13 pp.

Kreher, R. H. *We Are the Boys from Old Florida.* Gainesville, Fla.: R. H. Kreher, 198?. 60 pp.

Proctor, Samuel. *Gator History: The University of Florida-a Pictorial History.* Gainesville, Fla.: South Star Publishing Co., 1986. 272 pp.

--------. "The University of Florida: Its Early Years, 1853-1906." Ph.D. diss., University of Florida, 1958. 574 pp. *Dissertation Abstracts,* vol.18, p. 1779.

Sledd, Andrew. *The University of State of Florida.* n.p., 1905. 16 pp.

Tigert, John J. *The University of Florida in Retrospect: Delivered at Twenty-Fifth Anniversary Program, Auditorium.* Gainesville: The University, 1931. 14 pp.

University of Miami

Pearson, Jay F. W. *Florida and Its University of Miami.* New York: Newcomen Society in North America, 1958. 28 pp.

Tebeau, Charlton W. *The University of Miami: a Golden Anniversary History.* Coral Gables: University of Miami Pr., 1976. 418 pp.

University of North Florida

Schafer, Daniel L. *From Scratch Pads and Dreams: A Ten Year History of the University of North Florida.* Jacksonville: University of North Florida, 1982. 164 pp.

University of South Florida

Cooper, Russell M., and Fisher, Margaret B. *The Vision of a Contemporary University: A Case Study of Expansion and Development in American Higher Education, 1950-1975.* Gainesville, Fla.: University Presses of Florida, 1982. 318 pp.

University of Tampa

Covington, James W. *Under the Minarets: The University of Tampa Celebrates Fifty Years of Progress, 1931-1981.* Tampa: University of Tampa, 1981. 94 pp.

Covington, James W., and Laub, C. Herbert. *The Story of the University of Tampa; A Quarter Century of Progress from 1930 to 1955.* Tampa: University of Tampa Pr., 1955. 137 pp.

GEORGIA

Agnes Scott College

Agnes Scott College, Decatur, Ga. *Agnes Scott College, Yesterday--Today --Tomorrow.* Atlanta: Foote and Davies Co., Printers, 1912. 14 pp.

--------. *Quarto-Centennial Celebration.* 3 vols. Decatur: Agnes Scott College, 1914.

McNair, Walter E. *Lest We Forget: An Account of Agnes Scott College.*
    Decatur: Agnes Scott College, 1983. 392 pp.

Albany State College

Harper, Hoyt H. "A History of Albany State College." Master's thesis,
    Atlanta University, 1951. 62 pp.

Ramsey, Berkley C. "The Public Black College in Georgia: A History of
    Albany State College, 1903-1965." Ph.D. diss., Florida State
    University, 1973. 303 pp. *Dissertation Abstracts International,*
    vol. 34A, p. 4167.

Andrew College

Engram, Irbi D. "A History of Andrew College." Master's thesis, Emory
    University, 1939. 120 pp.

O'Brien, Andrew L. *The Journal of Andrew Leary O'Brien; Including an
    Account of the Origin of Andrew College, Cuthbert, Georgia.* Athens:
    University of Georgia Pr., 1946. 76 pp.

Smith, Boyce O. "A History of the Andrew Female College." Master's
    thesis, University of Texas, 1930. 94 pp.

Atlanta Junior College

Hopkins, Lillie A. "A Descriptive Analysis of the Initial Development of
    Atlanta Junior College." Ed.D. diss., Atlanta University, 1975.

Atlanta University

Adams, Myron W. *A History of Atlanta University.* Atlanta: Atlanta
    University Pr., 1930. 120 pp.

Bacote, Clarence A. *The Story of Atlanta University: A Century of Service,
    1865-1965.* Atlanta: Atlanta University, 1969. 449 pp.

Augusta College

Cashin, Edward J., and Callahan, Helen. *A History of Augusta College.*
    Augusta: Augusta College Pr., 1976. 189 pp.

Berry College

Shatto, Gloria M. *Berry College: Moving Vigorously into the Future.* New York: Newcomen Society of the United States, 1984. 24 pp.

Bowdon College (Closed 1936)

Caswell, Render R. "The History of Bowdon College." Master's thesis, University of Georgia, 1952. 225 pp.

---------. *The History of Bowdon College.* Bowdon, Ga.: Warren P. Sewell Library, 1978. 161 pp.

Clark College

Brawley, James P. *The Clark College Legacy: An Interpretive History of Relevant Education, 1869-1975.* Atlanta: Clark College, 1977. 347 pp.

McPheeters, Alphonso A. "The Origin and Development of Clark University and Gammon Theological Seminary, 1869-1944." Ph.D. diss., University of Cincinnati, 1944. 67 pp.

Taylor, Prince A., Jr. "A History of Gammon Theological Seminary." Ed.D. diss., New York University, 1948. 169 pp. *Dissertation Abstracts,* vol. 9, p. 95.

Columbia Theological Seminary

LaMotte, Louis C. *Colored Light: The Story of the Influence of Columbia Theological Seminary, 1828-1936.* Richmond: Published for the Author, Presbyterian Committee of Publications, 1937. 356 pp.

Emmanuel College

Synan, Vinson. *Emmanuel College: The First Fifty Years, 1919-1969.* Franklin Springs, Ga.: Emmanuel College Library, 1968. 159 pp.

Emory University

Bullock, Henry M. "A History of Emory College, 1834-1915." Ph.D. diss., Yale University, 1932.

--------. *A History of Emory University.* Nashville: Parthenon Pr., 1936. 391 pp.

Emory University. *In This Brief Span: Emory College, 1836-1965. Emory University, 1915-1965, 50th Year.* Atlanta: n.p., 1965. 24 pp.

English, Thomas H. *Emory University, 1915-1965; A Semicentennial History.* Atlanta: Emory University, 1966. 269 pp.

Georgia College

Curl, Lottie M. "History of the Georgia State College for Women." Master's thesis, George Peabody College for Teachers, 1931. 104 pp.

Hair, William I.; Bonner, James C.; and Dawson, Edward B. *History of Georgia College.* Milledgeville: Georgia College, 1979. 282 pp.

Georgia Institute of Technology

Brittain, Marion L. *The Story of Georgia Tech.* Chapel Hill: University of North Carolina Pr., 1948. 385 pp.

Griessman, B. Eugene; Jackson, Sarah E.; and Jenkins, Annibel. *Images and Memories: Georgia Tech, 1885-1985.* Atlanta: Georgia Tech Foundation, 1985. 288 pp.

McMath, Robert C., Jr., et. al. *Engineering the New South: Georgia Tech, 1885-1985.* Athens: University of Georgia Pr., 1985. 560 pp.

Wallace, Robert B. *Dress Her in White and Gold; A Biography of Georgia Tech.* Atlanta: Georgia Tech Foundation, 1963. 426 pp.

Georgia Southern College

Christie, Dudley B. "A History of Georgia Teachers College." Master's thesis, University of Georgia, 1943. 42 pp.

Shurbutt, Thomas R. *Georgia Southern: Seventy-Five Years of Progress and Service.* Statesboro: Georgia Southern College Foundation, 1982. 149 pp.

Georgia State University

Flanders, Bertram H. *A New Frontier in Education: The Story of the*

Atlanta Division, University of Georgia. Atlanta: Atlanta Division, University of Georgia, 1955. 169 pp.

Gordon Military College

Morgan, Charles C. "History of Gordon Military College." Master's thesis, Birmingham-Southern College, 1958. 85 pp.

LaGrange College

Birdsong, Irene B. "The History of LaGrange College." Master's thesis, University of Georgia, 1955. 213 pp.

Murphy, Walter Y. *LaGrange College; Georgia's Oldest Independent School Founded 1831.* New York: Newcomen Society of the United States, 1985. 20 pp.

Medical College of Georgia

Spalding, Phinizy. *The History of the Medical College of Georgia.* Athens: University of Georgia Pr., 1987. 290 pp.

Mercer University

Dowell, Spright. *A History of Mercer University, 1833-1953.* Macon: Mercer University, 1958. 420 pp.

Morehouse College

Brawley, Benjamin G. *History of Morehouse College.* Atlanta: Morehouse College, 1917. 218 pp.

Butler, Addie L. J. *The Distinctive Black College: Talladega, Tuskegee and Morehouse.* Metuchen, N. J.: Scarecrow, 1977. 169 pp.

Jones, Edward A. *A Candle in the Dark; A History of Morehouse College.* Valley Forge, Pa.: Judson Pr., 1967. 380 pp.

Morris Brown College

Sewell, George A., and Troup, Cornelius V. *Morris Brown College, the*

First Hundred Years, 1881-1981. Atlanta: The College, 1981. 275 pp.

Oglethorpe University

Tankersley, Allen P. *College Life at Old Oglethorpe.* Athens: University of Georgia Pr., 1951. 184 pp.

Paine College

Clary, George E., Jr. "The Founding of Paine College-a Unique Venture in Inter-racial Cooperation in the New South, 1882-1903." Ed.D. diss., University of Georgia, 1965. 152 pp. *Dissertation Abstracts,* vol. 26, p. 2575.

--------. *Paine College, Augusta, Georgia: An Account of Its Beginnings (1882-1903).* Brunswick, Ga.: Lemmond Letter Shop, 1975. 19 pp.

Johnson, Alandus C. "The Growth of Paine College, a Successful Interracial Venture." Ph.D. diss., University of Georgia, 1970. 423 pp. *Dissertation Abstracts International,* vol. 31A, p. 5321.

Piedmont College

Lovett, Warren P. "A History of Piedmont College." Master's thesis, University of Georgia, 1943. 64 pp.

Rountree, George W. "Piedmont College: Its History, Resources, and Programs." Ed.D. diss., University of Georgia, 1965. 170 pp. *Dissertation Abstracts,* vol. 26, p. 6498.

Reinhardt College

Yates, Bowling C. *History of Reinhardt College, Waleska, Georgia.* Marietta, Ga.: n.p., 1969. 79 pp.

Shorter College

Gardner, Robert G. *On the Hill: The Story of Shorter College.* Rome, Ga.: Shorter College, 1972. 476 pp.

Sheppard, Lydia D. "The History of Shorter College." Master's thesis, Emory University, 1941. 160 pp.

Spelman College

Guy-Sheftall, Beverly, and Stewart, Jo M. *Spelman, a Centennial Celebration, 1881-1981.* Atlanta: Spelman College, 1981. 120 pp.

Read, Florence M. *The Story of Spelman College.* Atlanta: n.p., 1961. 399 pp.

Tift College (Closed 1986)

Stone, Eugenia W. *Yesterday at Tift.* Doraville: Foote & Davies, 1969. 292 pp.

Truett McConnell College

Holcomb, Jack B. "A History of Truett-McConnell Junior College." Master's thesis, University of Georgia, 1958. 92 pp.

University of Georgia

Boney, F. N. *A Pictorial History of the University of Georgia.* Athens: University of Georgia Pr., 1984. 262 pp.

Brooks, Robert P. *The University of Georgia under Sixteen Administrations, 1785-1955.* Athens: University of Georgia Pr., 1956. 260 pp.

Coulter, Ellis M. *College Life in the Old South.* New York: Macmillan, 1928. 381 pp.

--------. *College Life in the Old South: As Seen at the University of Georgia.* 2d ed. Athens: University of Georgia Pr., 1951. 320 pp.

Dyer, Thomas G. *The University of Georgia: A Bicentennial History, 1785-1985.* Athens: University of Georgia Pr., 1985. 435 pp.

Hammond, Nathaniel J. *The University of Georgia.* Athens: Franklin Printing and Publishing Co., 1893. 173 pp.

Hull, Augustus L. *A Historical Sketch of the University of Georgia.* Atlanta: Foote & Davies, 1894. 147 pp.

Sell, Edward S. *History of the State Normal School, Athens, Georgia.* Athens: n.p., 1923. 108 pp.

Valdosta State College

Hambrick, Thera O. *Valdosta State College, the First Half Century.* n.p., 1961. 132 pp.

Wesleyan College

Akers, Samuel L. *The First One Hundred Years of Wesleyan College: 1836-1936.* Savannah, Ga.: Beehive Pr., 1976. 160 pp.

Curry, Betty L. "Wesleyan College, 1836-1886: The First Half Century of America's Oldest College for Women." Master's thesis, Emory University, 1962. 171 pp.

Miller, Margaret. "The Founding and Early History of Wesleyan College." Master's thesis, University of Georgia, 1935. 78 pp.

Rees, Frances. "A History of Wesleyan Female College from 1836 to 1874." Master's thesis, Emory University, 1936. 145 pp.

Young Harris College

Andress, Robert P. "Young Harris College, Its Development, Resources, and Program." Ph.D. diss., Columbia University, 1960.

Brogdon, Joseph M. "A History of Young L. G. Harris College." Master's thesis, University of Georgia, 1938. 41 pp.

HAWAII

Brigham Young University-Hawaii Campus

Olson, Ralph D. "History of the Church College of Hawaii, 1955-1960." Master's thesis, Utah State University, 1961. 139 pp.

University of Hawaii

Dean, Arthur L. *Historical Sketch of the University of Hawaii.* Honolulu: University of Hawaii, 1927. 19 pp.

Hamilton, Thomas H. *University of Hawaii, Land-Grant College for the Pacific.* New York: Newcomen Society in North America, 1964. 28 pp.

Kittelson, David J. "The History of the College of Hawaii." Master's thesis, University of Hawaii, 1966. 154 pp.

Nickerson, Thomas. *The University of Hawaii, 1907-1957; Higher Education in the Pacific, a Foundation for Freedom.* Honolulu: Office of Publications and Information, University of Hawaii, 1957. 56 pp.

Yap, William K. *The Birth and History of the University of Hawaii.* Shanghai: Printed by Kwang Hseuh Publishing House, 1933?. 53 pp.

University of Hawaii at Manoa

Mehnert, Klaus. *Ein Deutscher auf Hawaii, 1936-1941.* Stuttgart: Firma Benz-Drucke, 1983. 463 pp.

IDAHO

Boise State University

Chaffee, Eugene B. *Boise College: An Idea Grows.* Boise: Syms-York, 1970. 273 pp.

Oliver, Henry L. "Boise State University, the First Fifty Years: 1932-1982." Ph.D. diss., Washington State University, 1983. 164 pp. *Dissertation Abstracts International,* vol. 44A, p. 684.

College of Idaho

Hayman, Herbert H. *That Man Boone: Frontiers Man of Idaho.* Caldwell, Id.: College of Idaho, 1948. 228 pp.

Idaho State University

Beal, Merrill D. *History of Idaho State College.* Pocatello: The Author, 1952. 216 pp.

Northwest Nazarene College

Riley, John E. *From Sagebrush to Ivy: The Story of Northwest Nazarene College, 1913-1988.* Nampa, Idaho: Northwest Nazarene College, 1988. 300 pp.

Ricks College

Manwaring, Hyrum. *Ricks College: History of Fifty-Six Years, 1888-1944.* Rexburg, Id.: Ricks College, 1952. 265 pp.

Roundy, Jerry C. "Ricks College: A Struggle for Survival." Ph.D. diss., Brigham Young University, 1975. 364 pp. *Dissertation Abstracts International,* vol. 36A, p. 8258.

University of Idaho

Gibbs, Rafe. *Beacon for Mountain and Plain.* Moscow: University of Idaho, 1962. 420 pp.

Petersen, Keith C. *This Crested Hill: An Illustrated History of the University of Idaho.* Moscow: University of Idaho Pr., 1987. 240 pp.

Rhodes, Jess D. "The Transition of the University of Idaho from a Pre-University to a University Organization; A Preliminary Survey of the First Quarter Century, 1889-1913." Master's thesis, University of Idaho, 1952. 122 pp.

Ryan, Michael G. "The Historic Origins of the University of Idaho; With Special Reference to More Remote Origins as the Morrill Act, the Educational Philosophy Underlying It, the Land Grant Ordinances, and the Existence of Public Domain." Master's thesis, University of Idaho, 1939. 108 pp.

ILLINOIS

Augustana College

Augustana Evangelical Lutheran Church. *After Seventy-Five Years, 1860-1935; A Jubilee Publication, Seventy-Fifth Anniversary of the Augustana Synod and Augustana College and Theological Seminary.* Rock Island, Ill.: Augustana Book Concern, 1935. 288 pp.

Bergendoff, Conrad J. I. *Augustana, a Profession of Faith; A History of Augustana College, 1860-1935. Rock Island, Ill.: Augustana College,* 1985. 102 pp.

Brolander, Glen E. *An Historical Survey of the Augustana College Campus.* Rock Island, Ill.: Augustana Historical Society, Augustana College, 1985. 102 pp.

ILLINOIS / 183

Belleville Area College

Cox, Marvin L. "A Study of the Development and History of Belleville Junior College, 1946-1966." Ph.D. diss., Saint Louis University, 1980. 112 pp. *Dissertation Abstracts International,* vol. 41A, p. 2954.

Blackburn College

McConagha, Glenn L. *Blackburn College: An Anecdotal and Analytical History of the Private College.* Carlinville, Ill.: Blackburn College, 1988. 555 pp.

Bradley University

Bradley Polytechnic Institute, Peoria, Ill. *Bradley Polytechnic Institute. The First Decade, 1897-1907.* Peoria, Ill.: n.p., 1908. 180 pp.

Yates, Louis A. R. *A Proud Heritage: Bradley's History, 1897-1972.* Peoria, Ill.: Bradley University, 1974. 204 pp.

Carl Sandburg College

Bonner, Harold G. "The Founding of Carl Sandburg College." Master's thesis, Illinois State University, 1971. 85 pp.

Chicago College of Osteopathic Medicine

Berchtold, Theodore A. *To Teach, to Heal, to Serve!: The Story of the Chicago College of Osteopathic Medicine: The First 75 Years (1900-1975).* Chicago: Chicago College of Osteopathic Medicine, 1975. 239 pp.

Chicago State University

Kearney, Edmund. *A History, Chicago State University, 1867-1979.* Chicago: Chicago State University Foundation, 1979. 137 pp.

Chicago Theological Seminary

McGiffert, Arthur C. *No Ivory Tower: The Story of the Chicago Theological Seminary.* Chicago: Chicago Theological Seminary, 1965. 323 pp.

Concordia College

Freitag, Alfred J. *College with a Cause; A History of Concordia Teachers College.* River Forest, Ill.: Concordia Teachers College, 1964. 301 pp.

--------. "A History of Concordia Teachers College: 1864-1964." Ed.D. diss., University of Southern California, 1965. 561 pp. *Dissertation Abstracts,* vol. 26, p. 849.

Concordia Theological Seminary

Concordia Theological Seminary. *Concordia Theological Seminary, Springfield, Illinois, 1846-1946.* Springfield: n.p., 1946. 75 pp.

Eastern Illinois University

Coleman, Charles H. *Eastern Illinois State College; Fifty Years of Public Service.* Charleston, Ill.: Eastern Illinois State College, 1950. 384 pp.

Tingley, Donald F., ed. *The Emerging University: A History of Eastern Illinois University, 1949-74.* Charleston, Ill.: Eastern Illinois University, 1974. 229 pp.

Elmhurst College

Denman, William F. "Elmhurst: Developmental Study of a Church-Related College." Ph.D. diss., Syracuse University, 1966. 768 pp. *Dissertation Abstracts,* vol. 27, p. 4106.

Eureka College

Adams, Harold. *History of Eureka College.* Eureka, Ill.: Board of Trustees of Eureka College, 1982. 312 pp.

Dickinson, Elmira J., ed. *A History of Eureka College with Biographical Sketches and Reminiscences.* St. Louis: Christian Publishing Co., 1894. 359 pp.

Garrett-Evangelical Theological Seminary

Norwood, Frederick A. *Dawn to Midday at Garrett.* Evanston: Garrett-

Evangelical Theological Seminary, 1978. 251 pp.

Greenville College

Jordahl, Donald C. "Greenville College--The Antecedents: A History of Almira College." Ph.D. diss., Southern Illinois University, 1974. 259 pp. *Dissertation Abstracts International,* vol. 35A, p. 4214.

Miller, Donald G. "A Historical Sketch of Greenville College with Special Reference to the Curriculum." Master's thesis, New York University, 1934. 126 pp.

Illinois College

Baldwin, Theron. *Historical Sketch of the Origin, Progress, and Wants, of Illinois College.* New York: John T. West, 1832. 16 pp.

Barton, C. B. *The Founders and Founding of Illinois College.* Jacksonville, Ill.: John K. Long, 1902. 31 pp.

Cain, L. Vernon. *To Heights Beyond: The Story of Illinois College, 1955-1973.* Carbondale: Southern Illinois University Pr., 1986. 198 pp.

Frank, Charles E. *Pioneer's Progress: Illinois College, 1829-1979.* Carbondale: Southern Illinois University Pr., 1979. 409 pp.

Illinois College. *Quarter Century Celebration at Illinois College.* New York: J. F. Trow, Printer, 1855. 52 pp.

Rammelkamp, Charles H. *Illinois College: A Centennial History, 1829-1929.* New Haven: Yale University Pr., 1928. 605 pp.

Yeager, Iver F. *Church and College on the Illinois Frontier: The Beginnings of Illinois College and the United Chruch of Christ in Central Illinois, 1829 to 1867.* Jacksonville, Ill.: Illinois College, 1980. 124 pp.

--------. *Sesquicentennial Papers, Illinois College.* Carbondale: Southern Illinois University Pr., 1982. 400 pp.

Illinois Institute of Technology

Macauley, Irene. *The Heritage of Illinois Institute of Technology.* Chicago: Illinois Institute of Technology, IIT Center, 1978. 98 pp.

Peebles, James C. *A History of Armour Institute of Technology;*

Describing the Circumstances of Its Founding in 1896 and Providing a Chronological Narration of Events until Its Merger in 1940 with Lewis Institute to Form Illinois Institute of Technology. Chicago: n.p., 1954. 147 pp.

Illinois State University

Champagne, Roger J. *A Place of Education: Illinois State University, 1967-1977.* Normal: Illinois State University Foundation, 1978. 134 pp.

Cook, John W., and McHugh, James V. *A History of the Illinois State Normal University.* Bloomington, Ill.: Pantagraph Printing and Binding Establishment, 1882. 255 pp.

Illinois State University (Normal). *Semi-Centennial History of the Illinois State Normal University, 1857-1907.* n.p., 1907. 384 pp.

Marshall, Helen E. *The Eleventh Decade; Illinois State University, 1957-1967.* Normal: Illinois State University, 1967. 114 pp.

--------. *Grandest of Enterprises; Illinois State Normal University, 1857-1957.* Normal: Illinois State University, 1956. 355 pp.

Illinois Wesleyan University

Watson, Elmo S. *The Illinois Wesleyan Story, 1850-1950.* Bloomington: Illinois Wesleyan University Pr., 1950. 276 pp.

John A. Logan College

Hill, Jack D. "Critical Decisions in the Organization and Development of John A. Logan College: A Historical Analysis of the Years 1965 through 1972." Ph.D. diss., Southern Illinois University, 1978. 379 pp. *Dissertation Abstracts International,* vol. 39A, p. 2100

Joliet Junior College

Wood, Susan H. *The People's Legacy: The History of Joliet Junior College.* Joliet, Ill.: Joliet Junior College Foundation, 1987. 264 pp.

Jubilee College (Closed 1862)

Shively, Roma L. *Jubilee--a Pioneer College.* Elmwood: Elmwood Gazette,

1935. 79 pp.

Kaskaskia College

Pedtke, Dorothy A. H. "A History of Kaskaskia College." Ph.D. diss., Southern Illinois University, 1979. 154 pp. *Dissertation Abstracts International*, vol. 40A, p. 4444.

Knox College

Bailey, John W. *Knox College, by Whom Founded and Endowed.* Chicago: Press & Tribune Printing Office, 1860. 131 pp.

Knox College, Galesburg, Ill. *Record of the Centenary of Knox College and Galesburg.* Galesburg, Ill.: The College, 1938. 254 pp.

Muelder, Hermann R. *Missionaries and Muckrakers: The First Hundred Years of Knox College.* Urbana: University of Illinois Pr., 1984. 382 pp.

Plath, Paul J. "The Secularization of Knox College." Master's thesis, University of Illinois at Urbana-Champaign, 1977. 129 pp.

Webster, Martha F. *Seventy-Five Significant Years: The Story of Knox College, 1837-1919.* Galesburg, Ill.: Wagoner Printing Co., 1912. 210 pp.

Lake Forest College

Arpee, Edward. *The History of Lake Forest Academy.* Chicago: R. F. Seymour, 1944. 183 pp.

Lincoln College

Lindstrom, Andrew, and Carruthers, Olive. *Lincoln: The Namesake College; A Centennial History of Lincoln College, 1865-1965.* Lincoln, Ill.: n.p., 1965. 223 pp.

Loyola University of Chicago

Loyola University of Chicago. *One Hundred Years of Knowledge in the Service of Man.* Chicago: n.p., 1970. 48 pp.

Lutheran School of Theology at Chicago

Skillrud, Harold C. *LSTC: Decade of Decision; A History of the Merger of the Lutheran School of Theology at Chicago with Special Emphasis on the Decade 1958-1968.* Chicago: Lutheran School of Theology at Chicago, 1969. 327 pp.

McCormick Theological Seminary

Halsey, Leroy J. *A History of the McCormick Theological Seminary of the Presbyterian Church.* Chicago: The Seminary, 1893. 537 pp.

McKendree College

Walton, William C. *Centennial, McKendree College, with St. Clair County History.* Lebanon, Ill.: McKendree College, 1928. 643 pp.

Weil, Oscar A., Jr. "Origin and Establishment of McKendree College, 1828-1841." Master's thesis, Washington University, 1961. 301 pp.

MacMurray College

Hendrickson, Walter B. *Forward in the Second Century of MacMurray College: A History of 125 Years.* Jacksonville: MacMurray College, 1972. 93 pp.

Watters, Mary. *The First Hundred Years of MacMurray College.* Springfield, Ill.: Williamson Printing & Publishing Co., 1947. 652 pp.

Meadville/Lombard Theological Seminary

Swanson, James A. *A History of Lombard College, 1851-1930.* Macomb, Ill.: Western Illinois State College, 1955. 114 pp.

Monmouth College

Davenport, Francis G. *Monmouth College; The First Hundred Years, 1853-1953.* Cedar Rapids, Ia.: Torch Pr., 1953. 146 pp.

Urban, William L., et. al. *A History of Monmouth College through Its Fifth Quarter-Century.* Monmouth, Ill.: Monmouth College, 1979. 236 pp.

ILLINOIS / 189

Monticello College (Closed 1971)

Hamlin, Griffith A. *Monticello: The Biography of a College.* Fulton, Mo.: Published by William Woods College for the Monticello College Foundation, 1976. 223 pp.

Moody Bible Institute

De Remer, Bernard R. *Moody Bible Institute: A Pictorial History.* Chicago: Moody Pr., 1960. 128 pp.

Flood, Robert G., and Jenkins, Jerry B. *The Men Behind Moody.* Chicago: Moody Pr., 1984. 87 pp.

Getz, Gene A. "A History of Moody Bible Institute and Its Contributions to Evangelical Education." Ph.D. diss., New York University, 1968. 606 pp. *Dissertation Abstracts,* vol. 29A, p. 466.

--------. *MBI; The Story of Moody Bible Institute.* Chicago: Moody Pr., 1969. 393 pp.

--------. *MBI, the Story of Moody Bible Institute.* Rev. and Updated by James M. Vincent. Chicago: Moody Pr., 1986. 250 pp.

Martin, Dorothy M. *Moody Bible Institute: God's Power in Action.* Chicago: Moody Pr., 1977. 187 pp.

North Central College

Roberts, Clarence N. *North Central College; A Century of Liberal Education, 1861-1961.* Naperville: North Central College, 1960. 318 pp.

North Park College

Carlson, Leland H. *A History of North Park College, Commemorating the Fiftieth Anniversary, 1891-1941.* Chicago: North Park College, 1941. 432 pp.

Northeastern Illinois University

George, Melvin R. "Northeastern Illinois University: The History of a Comprehensive University." Ph.D. diss., University of Chicago, 1979. *Dissertation Abstracts International,* vol. 40A, p. 3141.

Northern Baptist Theological Seminary

Young, Warren C. *Commit What You Have Heard: A History of Northern Baptist Theological Seminary, 1913-1988.* Wheaton, Ill.: H. Shaw, 1988. 227 pp.

Northern Illinois University

Hayter, Earl W. *Education in Transition: The History of Northern Illinois University.* DeKalb: Northern Illinois University Pr., 1974. 541 pp.

Northwestern University

Hoadley, Grace. "Significant Chapters in the History of Northwestern University, 1905-1923." Master's thesis, Northwestern University, 1923. 150 pp.

A Pictorial History of Northwestern University, 1851-1951. Evanston: Northwestern University Pr., 1951. 198 pp.

Ward, Estelle F. *The Story of Northwestern University.* New York: Dodd, Mead, 1924. 376 pp.

Wilde, Arthur H., ed. *Northwestern University; A History, 1855-1905.* 4 vols. New York: University Publishing Co., 1905.

Williamson, Harold F., and Wild, Payson S. *Northwestern University: A History, 1850-1975.* Evanston: Northwestern University Pr., 1976. 403 pp.

Principia College

Leonard, Edwin S. *As the Sowing; The First Fifty Years of Principia.* St. Louis: n.p., 1948. 543 pp.

--------. *As the Sowing: The First Fifty Years of the Principia.* 2nd ed. St. Louis: Principia, 1951. 290 pp.

Rockford College

Cederborg, Hazel P. "History of Rockford College." 2 vols. Master's thesis, Wellesley College, 1926.

Nelson, C. Hal, ed. *Rockford College: A Retrospective Look.* Rockford, Ill.: Rockford College, 1980. 280 pp.

Rockford College, Rockford, Ill. *A Book of Views, Illustrating the Surroundings, Equipment, and Recreations of Rockford College for Women (1849-1920).* Rockford, Ill.: n.p., 1920. 32 pp.

--------. *The Celebration of the Ninetieth Year, the College Quadrangle, October 11, 1936.* Chicago: R. R. Donnelley & Sons Co., 1936. 16 pp.

Roosevelt University

Lelon, Thomas C. "The Emergence of Roosevelt College of Chicago: A Search for an Ideal." Ph.D. diss., University of Chicago, 1973. 525 pp.

Rosary College

Altenhofen, Aurelia. *Rosary College: Tradition and Progress, 1949-1974.* n.p., 1977. 122 pp.

Shurtleff College (Closed 1957)

DeBlois, Austen, K. *The Pioneer School; A History of Shurtleff College, the Oldest Educational Institution in the West.* Chicago: F. H. Revell, 1900. 356 pp.

Shurtleff College, Upper Alton, Ill. *Jubilee Memorial of Shurtleff College, Upper Alton, Ill., Consisting of Three Volumes in One.* Alton, Ill.: Daily Telegraph Steam Printing, 1877. 142 pp.

Southeastern Illinois College

Szymczak, Donald R. "Origin and Development of the Southeastern Illinois College, 1960-1976." Ph.D. diss., Southern Illinois University, 1977. 252 pp. *Dissertation Abstracts International,* vol. 38A, p. 2604.

Southern Illinois University at Carbondale

Lentz, Eli G. *Seventy-Five Years in Retrospect; From Normal School to Teachers College to University, Southern Illinois University, 1874-1949.*

Carbondale: University Editorial Board, Southern Illinois University, 1955. 169 pp.

Parkinson, Daniel B. *A Historical Bulletin of the Southern Illinois State Normal University.* Carbondale: Bureau of Publicity, 1914. 103 pp.

Plochmann, George K. *The Ordeal of Southern Illinois University.* Carbondale: Southern Illinois University, 1959. 662 pp.

Southern Illinois University at Edwardsville

Butler, David L. *Retrospective at a Tenth Anniversary, Southern Illinois University at Edwardsville.* Carbondale: Southern Illinois University Pr., 1976. 102 pp.

Wadell, Keith A. "The Establishment of Southern Illinois University at Edwardsville." Ph.D. diss., Southern Illinois University at Carbondale, 1983. 645 pp. *Dissertation Abstracts International,* vol. 44A, p. 2996.

Springfield College in Illinois

Trares, Thomas F. "Ecumenical Action: A History of Springfield College in Illinois, 1929-1969." Ph.D. diss., Saint Louis University, 1972. 87 pp. *Dissertation Abstracts International,* vol. 34A, p. 4585.

Trinity Evangelical Divinity School

Hanson, Calvin B. *The Trinity Story.* Minneapolis: Free Chruch Pr., 1983. 232 pp.

University of Chicago

Beadle, Muriel. *Where Has All the Ivy Gone? A Memoir of University Life.* Garden City, N. Y.: Doubleday, 1972. 395 pp.

Block, Jean F. *The Uses of Gothic: Planning and Building the Campus of the University of Chicago, 1892-1932.* Chicago: University of Chicago Library, 1983. 262 pp.

Flint, Nott W. *The University of Chicago, a Sketch.* Chicago: University of Chicago Pr., 1905. 40 pp.

Goodspeed, Thomas W. *A History of the University of Chicago, Founded by*

John D. Rockefeller; The First Quarter-Century. Chicago: University of Chicago Pr., 1916. 522 pp.

Goodspeed, Thomas W., ed.. *The University of Chicago Biographical Sketches.* 2 vols. Chicago: University of Chicago Pr., 1922-1925.

Levi, Edward H. *An Adventure in Discovery.* 1 vol. Chicago: University of Chicago, 1972.

Murphy, William M., and Bruckner, D. J. R. *The Idea of the University of Chicago: Selections from the Papers of the First Eight Chief Executives of the University of Chicago from 1891 to 1975.* Chicago: University of Chicago Pr., 1976. 533 pp.

Storr, Richard J. *Harper's University: The Beginnings; A History of the University of Chicago.* Chicago: University of Chicago Pr., 1966. 411 pp.

University of Illinois

Ebert, Roger, comp. *An Illini Century; One Hundred Years of Campus Life.* Urbana: University of Illinois Pr., 1967. 214 pp.

Hatch, Richard A., comp. *Some Founding Papers of the University of Illinois.* Urbana: University of Illinois Pr., 1967. 139 pp.

Illinois University. *Semi-Centennial History of the University of Illinois.* 1 vol. Urbana: University of Illinois Pr., 1918.

James, Edmund J. *Sixteen Years at the University of Illinois; A Statistical Study of the Administration of President Edmund J. James.* Urbana: University of Illinois Pr., 1920. 263 pp.

Johnson, Henry C. *Teachers for the Prairie: The University of Illinois and the Schools, 1868-1945.* Urbana: University of Illinois Pr., 1972. 508 pp.

Solberg, Winton U. *The University of Illinois, 1867-1894: An Intellectual and Cultural History.* Urbana: University of Illinois Pr., 1978. 494 pp.

Tilton, Leon D. *History of the Growth and Development of the Campus of the University of Illinois.* Urbana: University of Illinois, 1919. 52 pp.

Turner, Fred H. "The Illinois Industrial University." Ph.D. diss., University of Illinois at Urbana-Champaign, 1931. 14 pp.

Wabash Valley College

Gillespie, James R. "The Development of Wabash Valley College: 1960-1969." Ph.D. diss., Southern Illinois University at Carbondale, 1985. 296 pp. *Dissertation Abstracts International,* vol. 46A, p. 2899.

Western Illinois University

Hicken, Victor. *The Purple and the Gold; The Story of Western Illinois University.* Macomb: Western Illinois University Foundation, 1970. 224 pp.

Wheaton College

Bechtel, Paul M. *Wheaton College: A Heritage Remembered, 1860-1984.* Wheaton: H. Shaw Publishers, 1984. 415 pp.

Williard, Warren W. *Fire on the Prairie; The Story of Wheaton College.* Wheaton: Van Kamper Pr., 1950. 208 pp.

Winston Churchill College (Closed 1971)

Schindlbeck, David J. "The Formation and Development of Winston Churchill College." Master's thesis, Illinois State University, 1969. 202 pp.

INDIANA

Anderson University

Myers, Linfield. *As I Recall.* Anderson, Ind.: Anderson College Pr., 1973. 100 pp.

Ascension Seminary*

Lloyd, Garnet C. "The History of Ascension Seminary." Master's thesis, Indiana State Teachers College, 1937. 56 pp.

Ball State University

White, Glen. *The Ball State Story: From Normal Institute to University.* Muncie: Ball State University, 1967. 275 pp.

Bethel College

Beutler, Albert J. "The Founding and History of Bethel College of Indiana." Ph.D. diss., Michigan State University, 1970. 207 pp. *Dissertation Abstracts International,* vol. 31A, p. 2137.

Butler University

Fields, Thomas B. "A History of Butler University." Master's thesis, Indiana University, 1928. 156 pp.

Hollingsworth, Virginia N. "The History of the Teachers College of Indianapolis." Master's thesis, Butler University, 1946. 96 pp.

Jones, Alexander E. *Butler University: A Hoosier Tradition in Excellence.* New York: Newcomen Society in North America, 1968. 24 pp.

Canterbury College (Closed 1951)

Beeler, Kent D. "Canterbury College, 1946-1951: Its Decline and Demise." Ed.D. diss., Indiana University, 1969. 234 pp. *Dissertation Abstracts International,* vol. 31A, p. 2696.

Brown, Robert A. *The Story of Central Normal College, Danville (Hendricks County), Indiana, 1878-1946.* R. A. Brown, 1984. 122 pp.

Parr, James H. "A History of Central Normal College." Master's thesis, Indiana University, 1927. 76 pp.

Unruh, Alice E. "The Story of the Central Normal College." Master's thesis, Fort Hays Kansas State College, 1953. 75 pp.

Concordia Theological Seminary

Concordia College, Fort Wayne, Ind. *Das Concordia-College zu Fort Wayne Indiana in Wort und Bild.* St. Louis: L. Lange, 1909. 45 pp.

Heintzen, Erich H. *Prairie School of the Prophets: The Anatomy of a Seminary,1947-1976: History of Concordia Theological Seminary, Fort Wayne, Indiana.* St. Louis: Concordia, 1989. 245 pp.

Walle, Oscar T. *Lest We Forget-Lest We Forget!: A History of Concordia Senior College, 1957-1977.* Springfield, Ill.: Oscar T. Walle, 1978. 164 pp.

DePauw University

Manhart, George B. *DePauw Through the Years.* 2 vols. Greencastle, Ind.: DePauw University, 1962.

Sweet, William W. *Indiana Asbury-DePauw University, 1837-1937; A Hundred Years of Higher Education in the Middle West.* New York: Abingdon, 1937. 298 pp.

Earlham College

Earlham College. *Where the Roads of Quakerdom Cross: A Bit of History Important in the Annals of the Society of Friends: How a Pioneer Adventure in Faith Has Developed into a Powerhouse of Service.* Earlham: Earlham College, 1944. 16 pp.

Thornburg, Opal. *Earlham, the Story of the College, 1847-1962.* Richmond, Ind.: Earlham College Pr., 1963. 484 pp.

Franklin College

Cady, John F. *The Centennial History of Franklin College* Franklin, Ind.: n.p., 1934. 211 pp.

Franklin College, Franklin, Ind. Board of Trustees. *First Half Century of Franklin College, 1834-1884.* Cincinnati: Journal and Messenger, 1884. 178 pp.

Goshen College

Umble, John S. *Goshen College, 1894-1954: A Venture in Christian Higher Education.* Goshen, Ind.: Goshen College, 1955. 284 pp.

Hanover College

Baker, Frank S. *Glimpses of Hanover's Past, 1827-1977.* n.p.: Graessle-Mercer Co., 1978. 319 pp.

Dunn, William M. *Early History of Hanover College.* Madison, Ind.: The Courier Co., 1883. 20 pp.

Millis, William A. *The History of Hanover College from 1827 to 1927.* Hanover: Hanover College, 1927. 294 pp.

Moore, Archibald Y. *History of Hanover College.* Indianapolis: Hollenbeck Pr., 1900. 98 pp.

Huntington College

Chambers, Doris M. *Up from Stubble; A Sage of College Park, Ubee, Indiana.* Huntington, Ind.: Hill Crest Lithographing, 1973. 286 pp.

Pentzer, Orrin W. *Hartsville College, Hartsville, 1850-1897.* Columbus, Ind.: O. W. Pentzer & Sons, 1928. 48 pp.

Pfister, J. Ralph. *75 Years: Where Character and Culture Blend.* Huntington, Ind.: Huntington College, 1972. 99 pp.

Indiana State University

Allen, Max P. "History of the Indiana State Teachers College." Master's thesis, Indiana State Teachers College, 1931. 125 pp.

Indiana State College. *Exciting, Exacting, and Expansion Years at Indiana State Teachers College, 1934-1953.* Terre Haute: Indiana State Teachers College, 1953. 92 pp.

Indiana. State Teachers College, Terre Haute. *The Semi-Centennial Celebration of the Indiana State Normal School, January 6-9, 1920, in Commemoration of the Completion of Fifty Years of Work.* Terre Haute: Indiana State Normal School, 1920. 83 pp.

Lynch, William O. *A History of Indiana State Teachers College; Indiana State Normal School, 1870-1929.* Terre Haute: Indiana State Teachers College, 1946. 438 pp.

Indiana University

Baxter, Cynthia L. "Indiana University, 1917-1929." Master's thesis, Indiana University, 1953. 180 pp.

Clark, Thomas D. *Indiana University: Midwestern Pioneer.* 4 vols. Bloomington: Indiana University Pr., 1970-1977.

Harding, Samuel B., ed. *Indiana University, 1820-1904; Historical Sketch, Development of the Course of Instruction, Bibliography.* Bloomington: The University, 1904. 348 pp.

Indiana. University. *Indiana University, 1820-1920; Centennial Memorial Volume.* Bloomington: Indiana University, 1921. 345 pp.

Rawles, William A. *Historical Sketch of the University.* Indianapolis: Wm. B. Burford, 1904. 33 pp.

Wells, Herman B. *A Man, an Institution, and an Era.* New York: Newcomen Society in North America, 1952. 24 pp.

Woodburn, James A. *History of Indiana University.* 2 vols. Bloomington: Indiana University, 1940-.

Wylie, Theophilus A. *Indiana University, Its History from 1820, When Founded, to 1890.* Indianapolis: W. B. Burford Printer, 1890. 472 pp.

Indiana University-Purdue University at Fort Wayne

Ankenbruck, John. *The Creation Years: Indiana University-Purdue University at Fort Wayne.* Fort Wayne: Indiana-Purdue Foundation, 1983. 90 pp.

Indiana University-Purdue University at Indianapolis

Carr, Jack D. "History of Indiana Dental College, 1879-1925." Master's thesis, Butler University, 1957. 112 pp.

John Fletcher College (Closed)

Dewey, Clifford S. "A History of John Fletcher College with Special Reference to Its Religious Tradition." Master's thesis, University of Iowa, 1940.

Manchester College

Bollinger, Russell V., et. al. *The First Seventy-Five Years.* Elgin, Ill.: Brethren Pr., 1964. 235 pp.

Marian College

Whalen, Mary G. "Marian College, Indianapolis, Indiana: The First Quarter-Century, 1937-1962." Ed.D. diss., University of Cincinnati. 1966. 246 pp. *Dissertation Abstracts,* vol. 27A, p. 1637.

Mennonite Biblical Seminary

Pannabecker, Samuel F. *Ventures of Faith: The Story of Mennonite Biblical Seminary.* Elkhart: Mennonite Biblical Seminary, 1975. 117 pp.

Oakland City College

Robinson, Ivor J. "A History of Oakland City College." Master's thesis, Indiana University, 1930. 130 pp.

Shirley, Betty L. "A History of Oakland City College." Master's thesis, Indiana State Teachers College, 1957. 377 pp.

Purdue University

Freehafer, Ruth W. *R. B. Stewart and Purdue University.* West Lafayette: Purdue University, 1983. 221 pp.

Hepburn, William M., and Sears, L. M. *Purdue University; Fifty Years of Progress.* Indianapolis: Hollenbeck Pr., 1925. 203 pp.

Knoll, H. B., ed. *A Record of the University in the War Years, 1941-1945.* Lafayette: n.p., 1947. 213 pp.

Purdue University, Lafayette, Ind. *Purdue University, 1922-1932.* Lafayette: n.p., 1933. 176 pp.

Topping, Robert W. *A Century and Beyond: The History of Purdue University.* West Lafayette, Ind.: Purdue University Pr., 1988. 418 pp.

Rose-Hulman Institute of Technology

Bloxsome, John L. *Rose: The First One Hundred Years.* Terre Haute: Rose-Hulman Institute of Technology, 1973. 197 pp.

Rose Polytechnic Institute, Terre Haute, Ind. *Rose Polytechnic Institute; Memorial Volume: Embracing a History of the Institute, a Sketch of the Founder, Together with a Biographical Dictionary and Other Matters of Interest.* Terre Haute: Monfort & Co., 1909. 270 pp.

Saint Francis College

Scheetz, Mary J. "Service through Scholarship: A History of St. Francis College." Ph.D. diss., University of Michigan, 1970. 278 pp. *Dissertation Abstracts International,* vol. 31A, p. 6369.

Saint Mary-of-the Woods College

O'Neill, Margaret A. "A History of Saint Mary-of-the-Woods College." Master's thesis, Indiana State Teachers College, 1941. 196 pp.

St. Mary-of-the Woods College, St. Mary-of-the Woods, Ind. *The Story of St. Mary-of-the Woods.* n.p., n.d. 6 pp.

Schier, H. Tracy. "History of Higher Education for Women at Saint Mary-of-the Woods: 1840-1980." Ph.D. diss., Boston College, 1987. 294 pp. *Dissertation Abstracts International,* vol. 49A, p. 211.

Saint Mary's College

Creek, Mary E. *A Panorama: 1844-1977.* Notre Dame, Ind.: Saint Mary's College. 1977. 301 pp.

A Story of Fifty Years: Sisters of the Holy Cross, 1855-1905, from the Annals of the Congregation of the Sisters of the Holy Cross. Notre Dame, Ind.: The Ave Maria, 1905. 214 pp.

Taylor University

Ringenberg, William C. *Taylor University, the First 125 Years.* Grand Rapids, Mich.: Eerdmans, 1973. 184 pp.

Tri-State University

Orlosky, Elizabeth B. *From Carriage to Computer: The First One Hundred Years of Tri-State University.* Angola, Ind.: The University, 1984. 268 pp.

Parrott, Alice A. *History of Tri-State College, 1884-1956.* Angola, Ind.: Tri-State College Printshop, 1959. 229 pp.

Union Christian College (Closed)

Conlin, James W. "A History of Union Christian College, 1859-1924." Master's thesis, Indiana University, 1931. 178 pp.

Paddick, Kenneth L. "Union Christian College: 1858-1924." Ph.D. diss., Southern Illinois University at Carbondale, 1986. 182 pp. *Dissertation Abstracts International,* vol. 47A, p. 2479.

University of Evansville

Olmstead, Ralph E. *From Institute to University.* Evansville: University of Evansville, 1973. 340 pp.

University of Indianapolis

Henricks, Marvin L. *From Parochialism to Community: A Social-Historical Interpretation of Indiana Central University, 1902-1975.* n.p., 1977. 124 pp.

Vance, Russell E. *Fifty Years of Christian Education: A Short History of Indiana Central College, 1905-1955.* Indianapolis: Indiana Central College, 1955. 80 pp.

University of Notre Dame

Arthur, David J. "The University of Notre Dame, 1919-1933: An Administrative History." Ph.D. diss., University of Michigan, 1973. 452 pp. *Dissertation Abstracts International,* vol. 35A, p. 205.

A Brief History of the University of Notre Dame du Lac, Indiana from 1842 to 1892. Chicago: Werner, 1895. 256 pp.

Connelly, Joel, and Dooley, Howard J. *Hesburg's Notre Dame; Triumph in Transition.* New York: Hawthorne Books, 1972. 305 pp.

Fischer, Edward. *Notre Dame Remembered: An Autobiography.* Notre Dame: University of Notre Dame Pr., 1987. 191 pp.

Hope, Arthur J. *Notre Dame, One Hundred Years.* Notre Dame: University Pr., 1943. 482 pp.

Lyons, Joseph A., comp. *Silver Jubilee of the University of Notre Dame, June 23rd, 1869.* Chicago: E. B. Myers, 1869. 266 pp.

Schlereth, Thomas J. *The University of Notre Dame: A Portrait of Its History and Campus.* Notre Dame: University of Notre Dame Pr., 1976. 252 pp.

Schmuhl, Robert. *University of Notre Dame: A Contemporary Portrait.* Notre Dame: University of Notre Dame Pr., 1986. 149 pp.

Sullivan, Richard. *Notre Dame.* New York: Holt, 1951. 243 pp.

--------. *Notre Dame: Reminiscences of an Era.* Notre Dame: University of Notre Dame Pr., 1961. 259 pp.

Wack, John T. "The University of Notre Dame de Lac: Foundation, 1842-1857." Ph.D. diss., University of Notre Dame, 1966. 378 pp. *Dissertation Abstracts,* vol. 28A, p. 1777.

Wallace, Francis. *Notre Dame: Its People and Its Legends.* New York: McKay, 1969. 273 pp.

Valparaiso University

Albers, James W. *From Centennial to Golden Anniversary: The History of Valparaiso University from 1959-1975.* Valparaiso: The University, 1976. 87 pp.

Bigelow, Cecil L. "A History of Valparaiso University from 1873-1925." Master's thesis, University of Chicago, 1937. 64 pp.

Strietelmeier, John H. *Valparaiso's First Century; A Centennial History of Valparaiso University.* Valparaiso: The University, 1959. 189 pp.

Villanova University

Breslin, Richard D. "The Development of Villanova since Its Inception as a University in 1953." Ph.D. diss., Catholic University of America, 1969. 177 pp. *Dissertation Abstracts International,* vol. 30A, p. 1767.

Vincennes University

Burnett, Howard R. "A History of Vincennes University." Master's thesis, Indiana University, 1936. 294 pp.

Lawlis, Chelsea L. *Vincennes University in Transition: The Making of a Comprehensive Community College.* Vincennes, Ind.: The University, 1982. 309 pp.

Wabash College

Harvey, Robert S. *These Fleeting Years: Wabash College, 1832-1982; A Documentary History.* Crawfordsville, Ind.: Wabash College, 1982. 223 pp.

Osborne, James I., and Gronert, J. I. *Wabash College; The First Hundred Years, 1832-1932.* Crawfordsville, Ind.: Banta, 1932. 395 pp.

Tuttle, Joseph F. *The Origin and Growth of Wabash College.* Logansport, Ind.: Printed at the Daily Journal Office, 1876. 21 pp.

--------. *Wabash College, December 3. "Forty-Four Years Ago This Morning".* n.p., 1877. 12 pp.

IOWA

Buena Vista College

Cumberland, William H. *History of Buena Vista College.* Ames: Iowa State University Pr., 1966. 233 pp.

Central University

Thostenson, Josephine E. *One Hundred Years of Service, 1853-1933; A History of Central.* Pella: Central College, 1953. 50 pp.

Clarke College

Mulholland, Mary A.. *History of Clark College: The First 125 Years, 1843 to 1968.* Lake Mills, Iowa: Graphic Publishing Co., 1981. 54 pp.

--------. *History of Clarke College.* n.p., 1967. 145 pp.

Coe College

Eriksson, Erik M. *Cedar Rapids Collegiate Institute and Its Founders, 1853-1866: An Account of the Beginnings of Coe College.* Cedar Rapids: Coe College, 1928. 82 pp.

-------. *Coe Collegiate Institute and Its Founders, 1875-1881.* Cedar Rapids: Coe College, 1930. 106 pp.

Des Moines University (Closed 1929)

Wiggins, David. *An Iowa Tragedy: The Fall of Old Des Moines University.* Mount Horeb, Wisc.: Hist-Midwest Books, 1988. 131 pp.

Drake University

Blanchard, Charles. *Building for the Centuries: A Memorial of the Founders and Builders. Semicentennial: 1881-1931.* Des Moines, Ia.: Drake University, 1931. 273 pp.

Dahl, Orin L. *In Celebration of a Century: Drake University, 1881-1981.* Des Moines: Office of University Relations, Drake University, 1980. 132 pp.

Ritchey, Charles J. *Drake University through Seventy-Five Years, 1881-1956.* Des Moines: Drake University, 1956. 228 pp.

Faith Baptist Bible College

Patten, John L. *For the Truth's Sake: A History of Faith Baptist Bible College.* Ankeny, Iowa: The College, 1979. 62 pp.

Graceland College

Cheville, Roy A. *Through the West Door: The Story of the First Half Century of Graceland College.* Independence, Mo.: Herald Publishing House, 1946. 327 pp.

Edwards, Paul M. *The Hilltop Where: An Informal History of Graceland College.* Lamoni, Iowa: Venture Foundation, 1972. 189 pp.

Grand View College

Hansen, Thorvald. *We Laid Foundation Here: The Early History of Grand View College.* Des Moines: Grand View College, 1972. 144 pp.

Grinnell College

Nollen, John S. *Grinnell College.* Iowa City: State Historical Society of Iowa, 1953. 283 pp.

Iowa State University

Day, H. Summerfield. *The Iowa State University Campus and Its Buildings, 1859-1979.* Ames: Iowa State University, 1980. 517 pp.

Iowa State College of Agriculture and Mechanic Arts, Ames. *An Historical Sketch of the Iowa State College of Agriculture and Mechanic Arts.* Ames: n.p., 1920. 32 pp.

Ross, Earle D. *A History of the Iowa State College of Agriculture and Mechanic Arts.* Ames: Iowa State College Pr., 1942. 451 pp.

--------. *The Land Grant Idea at Iowa State College: A Centennial Trial Balance, 1858-1958.* Ames: Iowa State College Pr., 1958. 310 pp.

Iowa Wesleyan College

Haselmayer, Louis A. *History and Alumni Directory; Iowa Wesleyan College, 1842-1967.* n.p.: Iowa Wesleyan College, 1967. 146 pp.

Kirkwood Community College

The History of Kirkwood Community College: 20--1966-1986. Cedar Rapids: The College, 1986. 105 pp.

Loras College

Hoffmann, Mathias M. *The Story of Loras College, 1839-1939; The Oldest College in Iowa.* Dubuque: Loras College Pr., 1939. 255 pp.

Luther College

Bothne, Gisle C. J. *Det Norske Luther College, 1861-1897.* Decorah, Ia.: Forfalteren, 1897. 471 pp.

Luther College, Decorah, Ia. *Luther College through Sixty Years, 1861-1921.* Minneapolis: Augsburg Publishing House, 1922. 512 pp.

Nelson, David T. *Luther College, 1861-1961.* Decorah, Ia.: Luther College Pr., 1961. 419 pp.

Mount Mercy College

Roth, Mary A. *Courage and Change: Mount Mercy College, the First Fifty Years.* Cedar Rapids: Stamats Communications, 1980. 150 pp.

Northwestern College

De Jong, Gerald F. *From Strength to Strength: A History of Northwestern, 1882-1982.* Grand Rapids, Mich.: W. B. Eerdmans, 1982. 213 pp.

Hubers, Dale. "A History of the Northwestern Classical Academy, 1882-1957." Master's thesis, University of South Dakota, 1957. 102 pp.

Parsons College (Closed 1973)

Parsons, Willis E. *Fifty Years of Parsons College, 1875-1925.* Fairfield: Parsons College, 1925. 186 pp.

University of Iowa

Carstensen, Vernon. "The State University of Iowa: The Collegiate Department from the Beginning to 1878." Ph.D. diss., University of Iowa, 1936. 592 pp.

Crary, Ryland W. "History of the State University of Iowa: The Liberal Arts College in the Gilmore and Hancher Administrations." Ph.D. diss., University of Iowa, 1946. 229 pp.

Doty, Franklin A. "History of the State University of Iowa: The College of Liberal Arts, 1900-1916." Ph.D. diss., University of Iowa, 1947. 231 pp.

Fogdall, Vergil S. "History of the State University of Iowa: The

Governing Boards, 1847-1947." Ph.D. diss., University of Iowa, 1948.

Gerber, John C. *A Pictorial History of the University of Iowa.* Iowa City: University of Iowa Pr., 1988. 273 pp.

Haddock, William J. *A Retrospect, State University of Iowa.* Iowa City: n.p., 1904. 59 pp.

Perl, Larry. *Calm and Secure on Thy Hill: A Retrospective of the University of Iowa.* Iowa City: University of Iowa Alumni Association, 1978. 343 pp.

Pickard, Josiah L. *Historical Sketch of the State University of Iowa.* Iowa City: n.p., 1899. 66 pp.

Rich, Ellen M. *The State University of Iowa and the Civil War.* Iowa City: The State Historical Society of Iowa, 1918. 24 pp.

University of Northern Iowa

Hart, Irving H. *The First 75 Years.* Cedar Falls: Iowa State Teachers College, 1951. 160 pp.

Iowa. State Teachers College, Cedar Falls. *A Look at the 21-Year Period, 1929-30 to 1949-50.* Cedar Falls: Bureau of Research, Iowa State Teachers College, 1950. 27 pp.

--------. *Quarterly Centennial Register, of the State Normal School, Including a Brief History of the Founding, Organization, Growth and Development of the Institution.* Cedar Falls: The Normal School, 1901. 192 pp.

Molen, Clarence T., Jr. "The Evolution of a State University into a Teachers College: The University of Northern Iowa, 1876-1916." Ph.D. diss., University of Iowa, 1974. 426 pp. *Dissertation Abstracts International,* vol. 35A, p. 13797.

Wright, David S. *Fifty Years at the Teachers College; Historical and Personal Reminiscences, 1876-1926.* Cedar Falls: Iowa State Teachers College, 1926. 263 pp.

Wartburg College

Ottersberg, Gerhard S. *Wartburg College, 1852-1952: A Centennial History.* Waverly: Waverly Publishing Co., 1952. 111 pp.

--------. *Wartburg College, 1952-1977.* Waverly: The College, 1977. 46 pp.

Wartburg College, Clinton, Iowa. *Sixtieth Anniversary, 1868-1928.*
Clinton: n.p., 1928. 38 pp.

Westmar College

Kempers, Garrett. *A History of Westmar College.* Lakeland, Fla.: n.p.,
1965. 231 pp.

William Penn College

Watson, Sheppard A. *Penn College: A Product and a Producer.* Oskaloosa:
William Penn College, 1971. 417 pp.

KANSAS

Baker University

Ebright, Homer K. *The History of Baker University.* Baldwin, Kan.: n.p.,
1951. 356 pp.

Benedictine College

Moeder, Monica. "History of St. Benedict's College." Master's thesis,
University of Wichita, 1931. 154 pp.

Schuster, Mary F. *The Meaning of the Mountain; A History of the First
Century at Mount St. Scholastica.* Baltimore: Helion, 1963. 329 pp.

Bethany College

Lindquist, Emory K. *Bethany in Kansas: The History of a College.*
Lindsborg, Kan.: Bethany College, 1975. 309 pp.

Bethel College

Wedel, Peter J. *The Story of Bethel College.* North Newton, Kan.: Bethel
College, 1954. 632 pp.

Emporia State University

Fish, Everett D., and Kayser, Kathryn E. "An Outline of the History of the Kansas State Teachers College of Emporia, 1865-1934." 2 vols. Master's thesis, Kansas State Teachers College of Emporia, 1936.

Kansas State Teachers College of Emporia. *A History of the State Normal School of Kansas for the First Twenty-Five Years.* 2 vols. Topeka: Kansas Publishing House, 1889.

Fort Hays State University

Dickey, Otis. "A History of the Fort Hays Kansas State College." Master's thesis, Fort Hays Kansas State College, 1942. 314 pp.

Forsythe, James L. *The First 75 Years; A History of Fort Hays State University, 1902-1977.* Hays, Kan.: Fort Hays State University, 1977. 296 pp.

Wooster, Lyman D. *Fort Hays Kansas State College: An Historical Story.* Hays: n.p., 1961. 199 pp.

Friends University

Reeve, Juliet. *Friends, University: The Growth of an Idea.* Wichita: n.p., 1948. 325 pp.

Souders, Floyd, and Souders, Norma. *Friends University, 1898-1973.* Wichita: Friends University, 1974. 279 pp.

Hesston College

Miller, Mary. *A Pillar of Cloud; The Story of Hesston College, 1909-1959.* North Newton, Kan.: Mennonite Pr., 1959. 260 pp.

Kansas Newman College

Suellentrop, Joyce. *Kansas Newman College, Wichita, Kansas.* Wichita: Kansas Newman College, 1984. 76 pp.

Kansas State University

Carey, James C. *Kansas State University: The Quest for Identity.* Lawrence:

Regents Press of Kansas, 1977. 333 pp.

Quiring, Virginia M., ed. *The Milton S. Eisenhower Years at Kansas State University.* Manhattan: Friends of the Libraries of Kansas State University, 1986. 119 pp.

Walters, John D. *Columbian History of the Kansas Agricultural College, Located at Manhattan, Kansas.* Topeka: Press of the Hamilton Printing Co., 1893. 76 pp.

Williard, Julius T. *History of the Kansas State College of Agriculture and Applied Science.* Manhattan: Kansas State College Pr., 1940. 568 pp.

Kansas Wesleyan University

Mann, Gordon C. "An Outline History and Source Book of the Kansas Wesleyan University." Master's thesis, Kansas State Teachers College of Emporia, 1940. 66 pp.

Van Derhoff, Jack W. *"The Time ... Now Past," Matthew 14:15; Kansas Wesleyan University, 1886-1961.* Salina: Kansas Wesleyan University, 1962. 75 pp.

McPherson College

Craik, Elmer L. *History of the Church of the Brethren in Kansas.* McPherson, Kan.: Privately Printed, 1922. 397 pp.

Kolzow, Virden J. "An Outline History and Source Book of McPherson College." Master's thesis, Kansas State Teachers College of Emporia, 1940. 210 pp.

Ottawa University

Haworth, B. Smith. *Ottawa University: Its History and Its Spirit.* Ottawa: Ottawa University, 1957. 174 pp.

Le Page, Samuel M. *Short History of Ottawa University.* Ottawa: n.p., 1929. 39 pp.

Pittsburg State University

Bawden, William T. *History of Kansas State Teachers College of Pittsburg, 1903-1941.* Pittsburg: Kansas State Teachers College, 1952. 315 pp.

Kansas. State Teachers College, Pittsburg. *Historical Souvenir of the Kansas State Teachers College Giving a Brief History and Pictorial Review of the Growth and Development of the Institution during Its First Twenty-One Years from 1903 to 1924.* Pittsburg: Printing Department, Kansas State Teachers College, 1924. 32 pp.

Stryker, Mabel K. "A History of Kansas State Teachers College, Pittsburg, Kansas, 1903-1939." Master's thesis, Stanford University, 1939. 196 pp.

Sterling College

Buchanan, Tom, and Buchanan, Christine. *Sterling College: Co-Worker with God: The First 100 Years.* Sterling, Kan.: Sterling College, 1987. 119 pp.

Tabor College

Farquhar, Catherine B. "History of Tabor College." Master's thesis, University of Iowa, 1941.

Janzen, Abraham E. *A History of Tabor College; Part One.* Hillsboro, Kan.: Mennonite Brethren Publishing House, 1958. 39 pp.

Prieb, Wesley J., and Ratzlaff, Donald. *To a Higher Plane of Vision.* Hillsboro, Kan.: Tabor College, 1983. 48 pp.

Schmidt, William J. "History of Tabor College." Master's thesis, Wichita State University, 1961. 130 pp.

University of Kansas

Adams, Virginia, et. al., comps. *On the Hill: A Photographic History of the University of Kansas.* Lawrence: University Press of Kansas, 1983. 223 pp.

Fisher, Michael P. "The Turbulent Years: The University of Kansas, 1960-1975: A History." Ph.D. diss., University of Kansas, 1979. 270 pp. *Dissertation Abstracts International,* vol. 40A, p. 2500.

Griffin, Clifford S. *The University of Kansas; A History.* Lawrence: University Press of Kansas, 1974. 808 pp.

Sterling, Wilson, ed. *Quarter-Centennial History of the University of Kansas, 1866-1891.* Topeka: Crane, 1891. 198 pp.

Taft, Robert. *Across the Years on Mount Oread, 1866-1941: An Informal and Pictorial History of the University of Kansas.* Lawrence: University of Kansas, 1941. 202 pp.

--------. *The Years on Mount Oread.* Lawrence: University of Kansas Pr., 1955. 228 pp.

Western University (Closed)

Smith, Thaddeus T. "Western University: A Ghost College in Kansas." Master's thesis, Kansas State College of Pittsburg, 1966. 97 pp.

Wichita State University

Rydjord, John. *A History of Fairmont College.* Lawrence: Regents Press of Kansas, 1977. 251 pp.

KENTUCKY

Alice Lloyd College

Davis, Jerry C. *Miracle on Caney Creek.* Lexington: Thoroughbred Pr., 1982. 145 pp.

Asbury College

McKee, Earl S. "The Early History of Asbury College (1890-1910)." Master's thesis, University of Kentucky, 1926. 101 pp.

Berea College

Berea College, Ky. An Interesting History. Cincinnati: Elm Street Printing Co., 1875. 108 pp.

Brown, Dale W. *Berea College: Spiritual and Intellectual Roots.* Berea, Ky.: Berea College Pr., 1982. 39 pp.

Durham, James G. "A History of Berea College." Master's thesis, University of Kentucky, 1942. 253 pp.

Fairchild, Edward H. *Berea College Kentucky: An Interesting History.*

Cincinnati: Elm Street Printing Co., 1883. 87 pp.

Hutchins, Francis S. *Berea College: The Telescope and the Spade.* New York: Newcomen Society in North America, 1963. 24 pp.

Morgan, Charles T. *The Fruit of This Tree: The Story of a Great American College and Its Contribution to the Education of a Changing World.* Berea, Ky.: Berea College, 1946. 269 pp.

Peck, Elisabeth S. *Berea's First Century, 1855-1955.* Lexington: University of Kentucky Pr., 1955. 217 pp.

--------. *Berea's First One Hundred Twenty-Five Years: 1855-1980.* Lexington: University Press of Kentucky, 1982. 282 pp.

Rogers, John A. R. *Birth of Berea College; A Story of Providence.* Philadelphia: Coates, 1903. 174 pp.

Bethel College (Closed)

Haynes, William H. "History of Bethel College, Russellville, Kentucky." Master's thesis, University of Kentucky, 1941. 104 pp.

Centre College of Kentucky

Craig, Hardin. *Centre College of Kentucky; A Tradition and an Opportunity.* Danville, Ky.: Centre College of Kentucky, 1967. 170 pp.

Cumberland College

Hall, Ida J. "A History of Cumberland College." Master's thesis, University of Tennessee, 1962. 171 pp.

Eastern Kentucky University

Dorris, Jonathan T., ed. *Five Decades of Progress: Eastern Kentucky State College, 1906-1957.* Richmond, Ky.: Eastern Kentucky State College, 1957. 358 pp.

--------. *Three Decades of Progress; Eastern Kentucky State Teachers College, 1906-1936.* Richmond, Ky.: Eastern Kentucky State Teachers College, 1936. 363 pp.

Georgetown College

Daley, John M. "Georgetown College: The First Fifty Years." Ph.D. diss., Georgetown University, 1953.

Huddle, Orlando E. "A History of Georgetown College." Master's thesis, University of Kentucky, 1930. 160 pp.

Meyer, Leland W. *Georgetown College, Its Background and a Chapter in Its Early History.* Louisville: Printed by Western Recorder, 1929. 77 pp.

Snyder, Robert. *A History of Georgetown College.* Georgetown, Ky.: Georgetown College, 1979. 212 pp.

Yager, Arthur. *Historical Sketch of Georgetown College.* Georgetown, Ky.: Press of Times Job Rooms, 1904. 32 pp.

Kentucky State University

Coleman, Lena M. "A History of Kentucky State College for Negroes." Master's thesis, Indiana University, 1938. 59 pp.

Edward, Austin, Jr. "History of the Kentucky State Industrial College for Negroes." Master's thesis, Indiana State Teachers College, 1936. 121 pp.

Hardin, John A. *Onward and Upward: A Centennial History of Kentucky State University, 1886-1986.* Frankfort: Kentucky State University, 1987. 105 pp.

Lexington Theological Seminary

Pope, Richard M. *The College of the Bible - A Brief Narrative.* Lexington: College of the Bible, 1961. 28 pp.

Stevenson, Dwight. *Lexington Theological Seminary; 1865-1965: College of the Bible Century.* Saint Louis: Bethany Pr., 1964. 495 pp.

Louisville Presbyterian Theological Seminary

Sanders, Robert S. *History of Louisville Presbyterian Theological Seminary, 1853-1953.* Louisville: Louisville Presbyterian Theological Seminary, 1953. 100 pp.

Morehead State University

Rose, Harry E. "The Historical Development of a State College: Morehead Kentucky State College, 1887-1964." Ed.D. diss., University of Cincinnati, 1965. 560 pp. *Dissertation Abstracts,* vol. 26, p. 5207.

Murray State University

Jeffrey, Buron. "Origin and Development of the Murray State Teachers College." Master's thesis, University of Kentucky, 1936. 85 pp.

Woods, Ralph H. *Murray State University; Fifty Years of Progress, 1922-1972.* Murray, Ky.: Murray State University, 1973. 551 pp.

Simmons University (Closed 1930)

Prescott, Thomas B. *The History of Simmons University.* Kansas City, Kan.: Kansas City Baptist Theological Seminary, 1933. 126 pp.

Williams, Lawrence H. *Black Higher Education in Kentucky, 1879-1930: The History of Simmons University.* Lewiston, N.Y.: E. Mellen Pr., 1986.

--------. "A Peculiar People: Simmons University, Louisville, Kentucky, 1879-1930." Ph.D. diss., University of Iowa, 1985. 299 pp. *Dissertation Abstracts International,* vol. 47A, p. 952.

Southern Baptist Theological Seminary

Mueller, William A. *A History of Southern Baptist Theological Seminary.* Nashville: Broadman Pr., 1959. 256 pp.

Sue Bennett College

Jones, Clyde C. "A History of Sue Bennett College." Master's thesis, University of Kentucky, 1940. 232 pp.

Thomas More College

Hanna, Thomas H. "The History and Status of Villa Madonna College, 1921-1961." Ed.D. diss., University of Cincinnati, 1962. 497 pp. *Dissertation Abstracts,* vol. 25, p. 1712.

Saelinger, M. Irmina. *Retrospect and Vista: The First Fifty Years of*

Thomas More College, Formerly Villa Madonna College. Covington: Wendling Printing Co., 1971. 86 pp.

Transylvania University

Baker, Henry G. "Transylvania: A History of the Pioneer University of the West, 1780-1865." Ph.D. diss., University of Cincinnati, 1949. 368 pp.

Edwards, Dorothy L. "A History of Transylvania College from 1865 to 1940." Master's thesis, University of Kentucky, 1939. 148 pp.

Jennings, Walter W. *Transylvania: Pioneer University of the West.* New York: Pageant Pr., 1955. 321 pp.

Peter, Robert, and Peter, Johanna. *Transylvania University; Its Origin, Rise, Decline and Fall.* Louisville, Ky.: J. P. Morton & Co., 1896. 202 pp

Wright, John D. *Transylvania: Tutor to the West.* Lexington, Ky.: Transylvania University, 1975. 444 pp.

--------. *Transylvania: Tutor to the West.* 2nd rev. ed. Lexington, Ky.: University Press of Kentucky, 1980. 445 pp.

Wright, John D.; Kelly, William W.; and Young, William T. *Transylvania University, Pioneering a Third Century.* New York: Newcomen Society in North America, 1981. 24 pp.

Union College

Hembree, Sillous G. "A History of Union College." Master's thesis, University of Kentucky, 1938. 240 pp.

Marigold, W. G. *Union College, 1879-1979.* Barbourville, Ky.: Union College, 1979. 272 pp.

University of Kentucky

Donovan, Herman L. *At the Threshold of Greatness!* New York: Newcomen Society in North America, 1955. 28 pp.

Gillis, Ezra L. *The University of Kentucky: Its History and Development; A Series of Charts Depicting the Important Data, 1862-1955.* Lexington:

The University, 1956. 32 pp.

Hopkins, James F. *The University of Kentucky: Origins and Early Years.* Lexington: University of Kentucky Pr., 1951. 305 pp.

Irvin, Helen D. *Hail Kentucky! A Pictorial History of the University of Kentucky.* Lexington: University of Kentucky Pr., 1965. 102 pp.

State University of Kentucky. *Fiftieth Anniversary of the University of Kentucky, 1866-1916.* Lexington: Published by Order of Executive Committee of Board of Trustees of University of Kentucky, 1926. 45 pp.

Stevenson, Dwight E. *The Bacon College Story: 1836-1865.* Lexington: College of the Bible, 1962. 56 pp.

Talbert, Charles G. *The University of Kentucky: The Maturing Years.* Lexington: University of Kentucky Pr., 1965. 208 pp.

University of Kentucky. *The University of Kentucky: Its History and Development, Series of Charts Depicting Some of the More Important Data, 1866-1947.* Lexington: The University, 1948. 32 pp.

University of Louisville

Collins, Wellyn F. "Louisville Municipal College: A Study of the College Founded for Negroes in Louisville, Kentucky." Master's thesis. University of Louisville, 1976. 44 pp.

Cox, Dwayne D. "A History of the University of Louisville." Ph.D. diss., University of Kentucky, 1984. 226 pp. *Dissertation Abstracts International,* vol. 45A, p. 2973.

Federal Writers' Project. Kentucky. *A Centennial History of the University of Louisville.* Louisville: University of Louisville, 1939. 301 pp.

Hudson, James B. "The History of Louisville Municipal College: Events Leading to the Desegregation of the University of Louisville." Ed.D. diss., University of Kentucky, 1981. 142 pp. *Dissertation Abstracts International,* vol. 42A, p. 3029.

Western Kentucky University

Cornette, James P. "A History of the Western Kentucky State Teachers College." Ph.D. diss., George Peabody College for Teachers, 1939. 258 pp.

Harrison, Lowell H. *Western Kentucky University.* Lexington: University of Kentucky Pr., 1987. 348 pp.

Johnson, Jesse B. "The History of Ogden College." Master's thesis George Peabody College for Teachers, 1929. 148 pp.

Patterson, Charles E. "A History of the Bowling Green Business University." Master's thesis, University of Kentucky, 1937. 48 pp.

LOUISIANA

Centenary College of Louisiana

Bryson, Helen R. "A History of Centenary College." Master's thesis, Louisiana State University, 1941. 125 pp.

Lowrey, Walter M. *Centenary College of Louisiana: Sesquicentennial, 1825-1975.* Shreveport, La.: Centenary College Alumni Association, 1975. 32 pp.

Nelson, William H. *A Burning Torch and a Flaming Fire; The Story of Centenary College of Louisiana.* Nashville, Tenn.: Methodist Publishing House, 1931. 399 pp.

Dillard University

New Orleans University. *Seventy Years of Service, New Orleans University.* New Orleans: Faculty of New Orleans University, 1935. 106 pp.

Grambling State University

Gallot, Mildred B. "Grambling State University: A History, 1901-1977." Ed.D. diss., Louisiana State University and Agricultural and Mechanical College, 1982. 199 pp. *Dissertation Abstracts International,* vol. 43A, p. 698.

--------. *A History of Grambling State University.* Lanham, Md.: University Press of America, 1985. 262 pp.

Maxie, Earl. "The Development of Grambling College." Master's thesis, Tuskegee Institute, 1950.

Louisiana College

Hoffmeyer, Oscar. *Louisiana College 75 Years: A Pictorial History.* Pineville, La.: Louisiana College, 1981. 160 pp.

Louisiana State University and Agricultural and Mechanical College

Bedsole, Vergil L., ed. *Louisiana State University; A Pictorial Record of the First Hundred Years.* Baton Rouge: Louisiana State University Pr., 1959. 112 pp.

Dalrymple, W. H. *A Brief Sketch-Illustrated-of the Louisiana State University and Agricultural and Mechanical College, 1845-1922.* Baton Rouge: The University, 1922. 30 pp.

Fleming, Walter L. *Louisiana State University, 1860-1896.* Baton Rouge: Louisiana State University Pr., 1936. 499 pp.

Huff, Mary B. "Legal History of the Louisiana State University and Agricultural and Mechanical College." Master's thesis, Louisiana State University, 1935. 143 pp.

Reed, Germaine M. *David French Boyd: Founder of Louisiana State University.* Baton Rouge: Louisiana State University Pr., 1977. 315 pp.

Mount Lebanon University (Closed)

Pollard, Gerald W. "The History of Mount Lebanon University, 1851-1912." Master's thesis, Louisiana State University, 1971. 268 pp.

New Orleans Baptist Theological Seminary

Mueller, William A. *The School of Providence and Prayer; A History of the New Orleans Baptist Theological Seminary.* New Orleans: Printed by the Printing Department of the New Orleans Baptist Theological Seminary, 1969. 143 pp.

Northwestern State University of Louisiana

LeBreton, Marietta M. *Northwestern State University of Louisiana, 1884-1984: A History.* Natchitoches: Northwestern State University Pr., 1985. 304 pp.

Pettiss, John O. "Development of the Louisiana State Normal College, 1884-1927." Master's thesis, Louisiana State University, 1927. 97 pp.

Our Lady of Holy Cross College

Morrison, Betty L.. *A History of Our Lady of Holy Cross College, New Orleans.* Gretna, La.: HER Publishing Co., 1977. 203 pp.

--------. "A History of Our Lady of Holy Cross College, New Orleans, Louisiana." Ph.D. diss., Louisiana State University and Agricultural and Mechanical College, 1976. 183 pp. *Dissertation Abstracts International,* vol. 37A, p. 2685.

Silliman Junior College (Closed)

Harris, John F. "A History of Silliman College." Master's thesis, Louisiana State University, 1942. 63 pp.

Southeastern Louisiana University

Ancelet, Leroy. "A History of Southeastern Louisiana College." Ph.D. diss., Louisiana State University and Agricultural and Mechanical College, 1971. 150 pp. *Dissertation Abstracts International,* vol. 32A, p. 3736.

Southern University and Agricultural and Mechanical College

Lane, Ulysses S. "The History of Southern University, 1879-1960." Ed.D. diss., Utah State University, 1970. 189 pp. *Dissertation Abstracts International,* vol. 32A, p. 1229.

Vincent, Charles. *A Centennial History of Southern University and A & M College, 1880-1980.* Baton Rouge: Southern University, 1981. 351 pp.

Tulane University

Dixon, Brandt V. B. *A Brief History of H. Sophie Newcomb Memorial College, 1887-1919: A Personal Reminiscence.* New Orleans: Hauser Printing Co., 1928. 200 pp.

Dyer, John P. *Tulane: The Biography of a University, 1834-1965.* New York: Harper, 1966. 370 pp.

Longenecker, Herbert E. *Great Vision, Amply Justified: The Story of Tulane University.* New York: Newcomen Society in North America, 1968. 20 pp.

Tulane University Alumni Association. *The First Hundred Years.* New Orleans: The Alumni Association of the Tulane University of Louisiana, 1935. 27 pp.

University of Southwestern Louisiana

Hardy, Florent. *Brief History of the University of Southwestern Louisiana, 1900 to 1960.* Baton Rouge: Claitor's Publishing Division, 1973. 173 pp.

Seale, Lea L. *Brief History of the University of Southwestern Louisiana, 1901-1958.* Lafayette: n.p., 1960. 97 pp.

Stephens, Margaret. "A History of Southwestern Louisiana Institute, 1900-1935." Master's thesis, George Peabody College for Teachers, 1937. 177 pp.

MAINE

Bangor Theological Seminary

Clark, Calvin M. *History of Bangor Theological Seminary.* Boston: Pilgrim Pr., 1916. 408 pp.

Cook, Walter L. *Bangor Theological Seminary: A Sesquicentennial History.* Orono, Me.: University of Maine Pr., 1971. 217 pp.

Bates College

Anthony, Alfred W. *Bates College and Its Background; A Review of Origins and Causes.* Philadelphia: Judson Pr., 1936. 284 pp.

Phillips, Charles F. *Bates College in Maine; Enduring Strength and Scholarship.* New York: Newcomen Society in North America, 1952. 24 pp.

Bowdoin College

Anderson, Patricia M. *The Architecture of Bowdoin College.* Brunswick, Me.: Bowdoin College Museum of Art, 1988. 225 pp.

Bowdoin College. *Bowdoin College, 1802-1952; The Commemoration of the Opening of the College.* Brunswick, Me.: n.p., 1952. 79 pp.

Cleaveland, Nehemiah. *History of Bowdoin College: With Biographical Sketches of Its Graduates, 1806-1879.* Boston: J. R. Osgood & Co., 1882. 905 pp.

Greason, A. LeRoy. *Bowdoin and "The Common Good".* New York: Newcomen Society of the United States, 1985. 24 pp.

Hatch, Louis C. *The History of Bowdoin College.* Portland: Loring, Short & Harmon, 1927. 500 pp.

Sills, Kenneth C. M. *Joseph McKeen (1757-1807) and the Beginnings of Bowdoin College, 1802.* New York: Newcomen Society of England, American Branch, 1945. 28 pp.

Smyth, Egbert C. *Three Discourses upon the Religious History of Bowdoin College, during the Administrations of Presidents M'Keen, Appleton & Allen.* Brunswick: J. Griffin, 1858. 80 pp.

Wellington, Leah L. N. *History of the Bowdoin School, 1831-1907.* Manchester, N. H.: The Ruemely Pr., 1912. 178 pp.

Colby College

Bixler, Julius S. *Colby College (1813-1953); A Venture of Faith.* New York: Newcomen Society in North America, 1953. 32 pp.

Champlin, James T. *A Historical Discourse Delivered at the Fiftieth Anniversary of Colby University, August 2, 1870.* Lewiston: Journal Steam Pr., 1870. 30 pp.

Chipman, Charles P. *The Formative Period in Colby's History.* Waterville: n.p., 1912. 29 pp.

Marriner, Ernest C. *The History of Colby College.* Waterville: Colby College Pr., 1963. 659 pp.

Whittemore, Edwin C. *Colby College, 1820-1925: An Account of Its Beginnings, Progress and Service.* Waterville: Trustees of Colby College, 1927. 276 pp.

Maine Maritime Academy

Jordan, Howard. *Maine Maritime Academy: The Formative Years, 1941-1966.* Castine: Maine Maritime Academy, 1975. 75 pp.

Nasson College

Gay, Roger C. *Nasson College, 1912-1957; A Modern Parable of the Mustard Seed.* New York: Newcomen Society in North America, 1958. 24 pp.

University of Maine

Fernald, Merritt C. *History of the Maine State College and the University of Maine.* Orono: University of Maine, 1916. 450 pp.

Hauck, Arthur A. *Maine's University and the Land-Grant Tradition.* New York: Newcomen Society in North America, 1954. 28 pp.

Maine University. *Pride in the Past, Faith in the Future, 1865-1965, University of Maine.* Orono: n.p., 1965. 32 pp.

Smith, David C. *The First Century: A History of the University of Maine, 1865-1965.* Orono: University of Maine at Orono Pr., 1979. 295 pp.

University of Maine at Farmington

Mallett, Richard P. *University of Maine at Farmington: A Study in Educational Change, 1864-1974.* Freeport, Me.: Bond Wheelwright Co., 1984. 288 pp.

Purington, George C. *History of the State Normal School, Farmington, Maine: With Sketches of the Teachers and Graduates.* Farmington: Press of Knowlton, McLeary, 1889. 204 pp.

University of Southern Maine

Morton, Albert R. "A History of Gorham State Teachers College." Master's thesis, University of Maine, 1947. 320 pp.

MARYLAND

Anne Arundel Community College

Likins, Jeanne M.. "A Stepping Stone: The History of Anne Arundel Community College." Ph.D. diss., American University, 1981. 568 pp. *Dissertation Abstracts International,* vol. 42A, p. 4744.

--------. *A Stepping Stone: The History of Anne Arundel Community College, Augmented with Appendices Drawn from College Files.* Arnold, Md.: Anne Arundel Community College, 1981. 321 pp.

Bowie State College

Chapman, Oscar J. "A Brief History of the Bowie Normal School for Colored Students." Master's thesis, University of Michigan, 1936. 57 pp.

Jones Anglin, I. Patricia. "Bowie State College: From a Private Normal School to a Multi-Purpose State College." Ph.D. diss., University of Pittsburgh, 1983. 214 pp. *Dissertation Abstracts International,* vol. 44A, p. 2386.

Tipton, Elizabeth H. "A Descriptive Analysis of Selected Forces and Events which Influenced the Founding, Growth, and Development of Bowie State College from 1865 to 1975." Ed.D. diss., George Washington University, 1976. 266 pp. *Dissertation Abstracts International,* vol. 37A, p. 2022.

Charles County Community College

Larkin, Charles W. "Charles County Community College: The History of the First Twenty Years: 1958-1978." Ed.D. diss., George Washington University, 1982. 181 pp. *Dissertation Abstracts International,* vol. 43A, p. 642.

College of Notre Dame of Maryland

Cameron, Mary D. *The College of Notre Dame of Maryland: 1895-1945.* New York: D. X. McMullen, 1947. 219 pp.

MARYLAND / 225

Community College of Baltimore

Whitney, Herbert C. "The Origin and Development of the Baltimore Junior College." Master's thesis, University of Maryland, 1949. 108 pp.

Forest Park Junior College Center (Closed 1936)

Pedersen, Robert. *The Forest Park Junior College Center: Maryland's First Public Junior College.* 1987. 23 pp. ERIC Microfiche ED 282 606.

Goucher College

Knipp, Anna H., and Thomas, Thaddeus P. *The History of Goucher College.* Baltimore: Goucher College, 1938. 659 pp.

Hagerstown Junior College

Alford, Stanley C. "The Historical Development of Hagerstown Junior College, 1946 to 1975." Ed.D. diss., George Washington University, 1976. 238 pp. *Dissertation Abstracts International,* vol. 37A, p. 2006.

Crowl, Vaughn D. "Educating Rural Maryland: An Historical and Anecdotal Record of Hagerstown Junior College, 1946-1987." Ph.D. diss., American University, 1987. 341 pp. *Dissertation Abstracts International,* vol. 49A, p. 210.

Johns Hopkins University

French, John C. *A History of the University Founded by Johns Hopkins.* Baltimore: Johns Hopkins University Pr., 1946. 492 pp.

Gilman, Daniel C. *The Johns Hopkins University from 1873 to 1893.* Baltimore: n.p., 1893. 15 pp.

--------. *The Launching of the University.* New York: Dodd, Mead, 1906. 386 pp.

Hawkins, Hugh. "The Birth of a University: A History of Johns Hopkins University from the Death of the Founder to the End of the First Year of Academic Work, 1873-1877." Ph.D. diss., Johns Hopkins University, 1954.

--------. *Pioneer: A History of the Johns Hopkins University, 1874-1889.*

Ithaca, N. Y.: Cornell University Pr., 1960. 368 pp.

Schmidt, John C. *Johns Hopkins: Portrait of a University.* Baltimore: Johns Hopkins University, 1986. 251 pp.

Sharkey, Robert P. *Johns Hopkins: Centennial Portrait of a University.* Baltimore: Johns Hopkins University, 1975. 97 pp.

--------. *Johns Hopkins: Portrait of a University.* Baltimore: Johns Hopkins University, 1961. 64 pp.

Loyola College

Ryan, John J. *Historical Sketch of Loyola College, Baltimore, 1852-1902.* n.p., 1903. 247 pp.

Thompson, Mary M. "The Brief History of Mt. St. Agnes College, 1890-1958." Master's thesis, Loyola College, 1959.

Montgomery College

Fox, William L. *Montgomery College; Maryland's First Community College, 1946-1970.* Rockville, Md.: Montgomery College, 1970. 115 pp.

Morgan State University

Wilson, Edward N. *History of Morgan State College: A Century of Purpose in Action, 1867-1967.* New York: Vantage, 1975. 200 pp.

Mount Saint Mary's College

Meline, Mary M. *The Story of the Mountain: Mount St. Mary's College and Seminary, Emmitsburg, Maryland.* 2 vols. Emmitsburg: The Weekly Chronicle, 1911.

Peabody Conservatory of Music

Robinson, Ray E. "A History of the Peabody Conservatory of Music." Ed.D. diss., Indiana University, 1969. 704 pp. *Dissertation Abstracts,* vol. 30A, p. 5020.

Prince Georges Community College

Rennie, Thomas P. "A Historical Study of the Establishment and Development of Prince Georges Community College, 1958-1973." Ed.D. diss., George Washington University, 1975. 234 pp. *Dissertation Abstracts International,* vol. 36A, p. 2672.

St. Charles' College (Closed)

St. Charles' College, Md. *Golden Jubilee of St. Charles' College, Near Ellicott City, Maryland, 1848-1898.* Baltimore: J. Murphy & Co., 1898. 148 pp.

St. John's College

Tilghman, Tench F. *The Early History of St. John's College in Annapolis.* Annapolis: St. John's College Pr., 1984. 199 pp.

Weigle, Richard D. *Saint John's College, Annapolis; Pilot College in Liberal Arts Education.* New York: Newcomen Society in North America, 1953. 28 pp.

St. Joseph's College (Closed)

Crumlish, John M. "The History of St. Joseph's College, Emmitsburg, Maryland, 1809-1902." Master's thesis, Catholic University of America, 1948.

Saint Mary's College (Closed 1852)

Kartendick, James J. "The History of St. Mary's College, Baltimore, 1799-1852." Master's thesis, Catholic University of America, 1942.

Ruane, Joseph W. "The Founding of Saint Mary's College, Baltimore, 1799-1812." Master's thesis, Catholic University of America, 1933. 110 pp.

Salisbury State College

Purnell, Henrietta S., and Blackwell, Jefferson D. *The State Teachers College at Salisbury, Maryland: "Yesterday, Today and Tomorrow-a Chronology of Events from 1924-1954".* Salisbury: State Teachers College, 1954. 36 pp.

United States Naval Academy

Burr, Henry L. "Education in the Early Navy." Ed.D. diss., Temple University, 1939. 228 pp.

Crane, John de M. C., and Kieley, James F. *United States Naval Academy, the First Hundred Years.* New York: McGraw-Hill, 1945. 53 pp.

Hart, Casper P. "The Founding of the United States Naval Academy." Master's thesis, Columbia University, 1938.

Lovette, Leland P. *School of the Sea; The Annapolis Tradition in American Life.* New York: Frederick A. Stokes, 1941. 382 pp.

Norris, Walter B. *Annapolis, Its Colonial and Naval Story.* New York: Crowell, 1925. 323 pp.

Soley, James R. *Historical Sketch of the U. S. Naval Academy.* Washington: Government Printing Office, 1876. 348 pp.

Sweetman, Jack. *The United States Naval Academy: An Illustrated History.* Annapolis: Naval Institute Pr., 1979. 289 pp.

Todorich, Charles. *The Spirited Years: A History of the Antebellum Naval Academy.* Annapolis: Naval Institute Pr., 1984. 215 pp.

Warren, Mame, and Warren, Marion E. *Everybody Works but John Paul Jones: A Portrait of the U. S. Naval Academy, 1845-1915.* Annapolis: Naval Institute Pr. 1981. 110 pp.

University of Maryland

Callcott, George H. *A History of the University of Maryland.* Baltimore: Maryland Historical Pr., 1966. 422 pp.

Cordell, Eugene F. *The University of Maryland, 1807-1907.* 2 vols. New York: Lewis, 1907.

Hemmeter, John C. *The Centennial Celebration of the Foundation of the University of Maryland, May 30 and 31, June 1 and 2, 1907.* Baltimore: Williams & Wilkins Co., 1908. 267 pp.

University of Maryland Eastern Shore

Wilson, Wilbert R. "An Historical Analysis of Events and Issues Which Have Led to the Growth and Development of the University of Maryland

Eastern Shore from 1886-1975." Ed.D. diss., George Washington University, 1976. 195 pp. *Dissertation Abstracts International,* vol. 37A, p. 4914.

Washington College

Dumschott, Fred W. *Washington College.* Chestertown, Md.: The College, 1980. 286 pp.

Mead, Gilbert W. *A Chapter of Washington College History.* Chestertown, Md. Washington College, 1934. 7 pp.

Western Maryland College

Newcomer, Joe C. "The Origin and Early History of Western Maryland College." Master's thesis, University of Maryland, 1941. 65 pp.

Wills, George S. *History of Western Maryland College, 1866-1886.* Westminster, Md.: Historical Society of Carroll County, Maryland, 1949. 52 pp.

Woodstock College (Closed 1970)

Ryan, Edmund G. "An Academic History of Woodstock College in Maryland, 1869-1944: The First Jesuit Seminary in North America." Ph.D. diss., Catholic University of America, 1964. 269 pp. *Dissertation Abstracts,* vol. 25, p. 2838.

MASSACHUSETTS

American International College

Blake, C. E. *The Story of the French Protestant College.* Springfield, Mass., n.p., 1889. 16 pp.

Stryker, Garrett V. *A Brief History of the American International College.* Springfield, Mass., American International College, 1945. 36 pp.

Amherst College

Annals of Amherst College. The Soil, the Seed, the Sowers, the Presidents and Professors, Together with a Popular Guide to the College Buildings and Various Cabinets. Northampton: Trumbull & Gere, 1860. 70 pp.

Fuess, Claude M. *Amherst, the Story of a New England College.* Boston: Little, Brown, 1935. 372 pp.

Hitchcock, Edward. *Reminiscences of Amherst College, Historical, Scientific, Biographical and Autobiographical: Also of Other and Wider Life Experiences.* Northampton, Mass.: Bridgman & Childs, 1863. 412 pp.

Humphrey, Heman. *Sketches of the Early History of Amherst College.* Northampton, Mass.: Kingsbury Box & Printing Co., 1905. 32 pp.

King, Stanley. *"The Consecrated Eminence"; The Story of the Campus and Buildings of Amherst College.* Amherst, Mass.: Amherst College, 1951. 368 pp.

LeDuc, Thomas H. A. *Piety and Intellect at Amherst College, 1865-1912.* New York: Columbia University Pr., 1946. 165 pp.

Tyler, William S. *History of Amherst College during Its First Half Century, 1821-1871.* Springfield: Clark W. Bryan, 1873. 671 pp.

--------. *A History of Amherst College during the Administrations of Its First Five Presidents, from 1821 to 1891.* New York: F. H. Hitchcock, 1895. 312 pp.

Andover Newton Theological School

Rowe, Henry K. *History of Andover Theological Seminary.* Newton: n.p., 1933. 208 pp.

Woods, Leonard. *History of the Andover Theological Seminary.* Boston: J. R. Osgood & Co., 1885. 638 pp.

Atlantic Union College

Purdon, Rowena E. *That New England School.* South Lancaster, Mass.: The College Pr., 1956. 148 pp.

Wehtje, Myron F. *And There Was Light: A History of South Lancaster*

Academy, Lancaster Junior College, and Atlantic Union College. South Lancaster, Mass.: The Atlantic Pr., 1982.

Boston College

Dunigan, David R. "A History of Boston College." Ph.D. diss., Fordham University, 1945. 411 pp.

--------. *A History of Boston College.* Milwaukee: Bruce Publishing Co., 1947. 362 pp.

Frost, Jack. *The Crowned Hilltop: Boston College in Its Hundredth Year.* New York: Hawthorne Pr., 1962. 72 pp.

Boston University

Boston University. *First Quarter Centennial of Boston University.* Brookline, Mass.: The Riverdale Pr., 1898. 84 pp.

Case, Harold C. *Harvest from the Seed; Boston University in Mid-Century.* New York: Newcomen Society in North America, 1957. 24 pp.

Speare, Edward R. *Interesting Happenings in Boston University's History, 1839 to 1951.* Boston: Boston University Pr., 1957. 204 pp.

Waite, Frederick C. *History of the New England Female Medical College, 1848-1874.* Boston: Boston University School of Medicine, 1950. 132 pp.

Warren, William F. *The Historical Heritage of Boston University; Quarter-Centennial Address, June 1, 1898 by President William F. Warren.* Boston: The Riverdale Pr., 1898. 23 pp.

Bradford College

Pond, Jean S. *Bradford, a New England Academy.* Bradford, Mass.: Bradford Academy Alumnae Association, 1930. 368 pp.

--------. *Bradford, a New England School.* Rev. ed. Bradford, Mass.: n.p., 1955. 380 pp.

Brandeis University

Goldstein, Israel. *Brandeis University, Chapter of Its Founding.* New York: Bloch Publishing Co., 1951. 133 pp.

Sachar, Abram L. *A Host at Last.* Boston: Little, Brown, 1976. 308 pp.

Bridgewater State College

Boyden, Albert G. *History and Alumni Record of the State Normal School, Bridgewater, Mass. to July, 1876.* Boston: Noyes and Snow, 1876. 182 pp.

Boyden, Arthur C. *The History of Bridgewater Normal School.* Bridgewater: Bridgewater Normal Alumni Association, 1933. 156 pp.

Bridgewater State College: As We Were-As We Are, 1840-1976. Bridgewater: Alumni Association, Bridgewater State College, 1976. 160 pp.

Mass. State Teachers College, Bridgewater. *Seventy-Fifth Anniversary of the State Normal School, Bridgewater, Massachusetts, June 19, 1915.* Bridgewater: Arthur H. Willis, 1915. 87 pp.

Clark University

Atwood, Wallace W. *The First Fifty Years: An Administrative Report.* Worcester: Clark University, 1937. 120 pp.

Clark University, Worcester, Mass. *Twenty-Fifth Anniversary of Clark University, Worcester, Mass., 1889-1914.* Worcester: Clark University Pr., 1914. 77 pp.

Koelsch, William A. *Clark University, 1887-1987: A Narrative History.* Hanover, N. H.: University Press of New England, 1988. 320 pp.

Sanford, Edmund C. *A Sketch of the History of Clark University.* Worcester: Clark University Library, 1923. 16 pp.

Story, William E. *Clark University, 1889-1899, Decennial Celebration.* Worcester: Printed for the University, 1899. 566 pp.

College of the Holy Cross

Meagher, Walter J. "A History of Holy Cross, 1843-1901." Ph.D. diss., Fordham University, 1944. 149 pp.

Meagher, Walter J., and Grattan, William J. *The Spires of Fenwick; A History of the College of Holy Cross, 1843-1963.* New York: Vantage, 1966. 341 pp.

Eastern Nazarene College

Cameron, James R. *Eastern Nazarene College: The First Fifty Years, 1900-1950.* Kansas City, Mo.: Nazarene Publishing House, 1968. 420 pp.

Rice, George. "The History of Eastern Nazarene College." B. D. thesis, Nazarene Theological Seminary, 1952.

Emerson College

Coffee, John M., and Wentworth, Richard L. *A Century of Eloquence: The History of Emerson College, 1880-1980.* Boston: Alternative Publications, 1982. 661 pp.

O'Mara, Francis L., Jr. "A Partial History of Emerson College, 1903-1920." Master's thesis, Emerson College, 1964. 127 pp.

Woodnick, Michael L. "A History of Emerson College during the Administration of Charles Wesley Emerson, 1880-1903." Master's thesis, Emerson College, 1964. 113 pp.

Emmanuel College

Friel, Mary E. "History of Emmanuel College, 1919-1974." Ph.D. diss., Boston College, 1980. 308 pp. *Dissertation Abstracts International,* vol. 40A, p. 5745.

Fitchburg State College

Massachusetts. State Teachers College, Fitchburg. *A Normal School That is "Different", an Historical Sketch.* Fitchburg: Practical Arts Pr., 1912. 6 pp.

Framingham State College

Framingham State College. Alumnae Association. *First State Normal School in America: The State Teachers College at Framingham, Massachusetts.* Framingham: The Association, 1959. 109 pp.

Massachusetts. State College, Framingham. *Commemorating the Centennial Anniversary of the First State Normal School in America.* Framingham: Alumnae Association of the State Teachers College at Framingham, Mass., 1939. 28 pp.

Massachusetts. State Teachers College, Framingham. *Historical Sketches at the Framingham State Normal School.* Framingham: Alumni Association, 1914. 144 pp.

--------. *Semi-Centennial Celebration. State Normal School, Framingham, July 2, 1889.* Boston: Beacon Pr., 1889. 75 pp.

Gordon-Conwell Theological Seminary

Wood, Nathan, R. *A School of Christ.* Boston: Gordon College of Theology and Missions, 1953. 217 pp.

Hampshire College

Patterson, Franklin, and Longsworth, Charles. *The Making of a College.* Cambridge: MIT Pr., 1975. 364 pp.

Harvard University

Andrews, William L. *A Prospect of the Colledges in Cambridge in New England.* New York: Dodd, 1907. 38 pp.

Bail, Hamilton V. *Views of Harvard; A Pictorial Record to 1860.* Cambridge: Harvard University Pr., 1949. 264 pp.

Bailyn, Bernard, et. al., eds. *Glimpses of the Harvard Past.* Cambridge: Harvard University Pr., 1986. 149 pp.

Batchelder, Samuel F. *Bits of Harvard History.* Cambridge: Harvard University Pr., 1924. 338 pp.

Bentinek-Smith, William. *The Harvard Book: Selections from Three Centuries.* Cambridge: Harvard University Pr., 1953. 369 pp.

Bevis, Alma M. *Diets and Riots: An Interpretation of the History of Harvard University.* Boston: Marshall Jones Co., 1936. 127 pp.

Brown, Francis H. *Harvard University in the War of 1861-1865.* Boston: Cupples, Upham and Co., 1886. 407 pp.

Bush, George G. *Harvard, the First American University.* Boston: Cupples, Upham and Co., 1886. 160 pp.

Davis, Andrew M. *An Analysis of the Early Records of Harvard College, 1636-1750.* Cambridge: Library of Harvard University, 1895. 21 pp.

Eliot, Samuel A. *A Sketch of the History of Harvard College. And of Its Present State.* Boston: Little and Brown, 1848. 190 pp.

Gardiner, John H. *Harvard.* New York: Oxford University Pr., 1914. 333 pp.

Harvard University. *Building Harvard; Architecture of Three Centuries.* Cambridge: Information Center of Harvard University in Holyoke Center, 1964. 23 pp.

--------. *Historical Register of Harvard University, 1636-1936.* Cambridge: Harvard University, 1937. 484 pp.

Hill, George B. N. *Harvard College, by an Oxonian.* New York: Macmillan, 1894. 329 pp.

Jacquinot, Adrien. *An Historical Sketch of Harvard University.* n.p., 1880. 392 pp.

Kahn, Ely J. *Harvard; Through Change and Through Storm.* New York: Norton, 1969. 388 pp.

McCurdy, Michael. *The Illustrated Harvard; Harvard University in Wood Engravings and Words.* Chester, Conn.: The Globe Pequot Pr., 1986. 60 pp.

Moe, Alfred K. *A History of Harvard.* Cambridge: Harvard University, 1896. 121 pp.

Morison, Samuel E. *The Founding of Harvard College.* Cambridge: Harvard University Pr., 1968. 472 pp.

--------. *Harvard College in the Seventeenth Century.* 2 vols. Cambridge: Harvard University Pr., 1936-

--------. *Three Centuries of Harvard, 1636-1936.* Cambridge: Harvard University Pr., 1936. 512 pp.

Morison, Samuel E., ed. *The Development of Harvard University since the Inauguration of President Eliot.* Cambridge: Harvard University Pr., 1930. 660 pp.

Peirce, Benjamin. *A History of Harvard University, from Its Foundation, in the Year 1636 to the Period of the American Revolution.* Cambridge: Brown, Shattuck and Co., 1833. 316 pp.

Pier, Arthur S. *The Story of Harvard.* Boston: Little, Brown, 1913. 255 pp.

Quincey, Josiah. *The History of Harvard University.* 2 vols. Cambridge: J. Owen, 1840.

--------. *The History of Harvard Univesity.* 2 vols. Boston: Crosby, Nichols, Lee & Co., 1860.

Smith, Richard N. *The Harvard Century: The Making of the University to the Nation.* New York: Simon and Schuster, 1986. 397 pp.

The Story of Harvard, a Short History. Cambridge: University Information Center, 1964. 33 pp.

Vaille, Frederick O., and Clark, H. A., eds. *The Harvard Book; A Series of Historical, Biographical, and Descriptive Sketches.* 2 vols. Cambridge: Welch, Bigelow, 1875.

Wagner, Charles A. *Harvard: Four Centuries and Freedom.* New York: Dutton, 1950. 326 pp.

Lasell Junior College

Spooner, Ruth H. *Lasell's First Century, 1851-1951.* Boston: Abby Pr., 1951. 200 pp.

Winslow, Donald J. *Lasell: A History of the First Junior College for Women.* Newton, Mass.: Office of External Affairs, Lasell Junior College, 1988. 291 pp.

Massachusetts College of Pharmacy

Massachusetts College of Pharmacy, Boston. *The Massachusetts College of Pharmacy, 1823-1973; An Informal History.* Boston: Massachusetts College of Pharmacy, 1973. 82 pp.

Massachusetts Institute of Technology

Burchard, John E. *Q.E.D.; M.I.T. in World War II.* New York: Wiley, 1948. 354 pp.

Compton, Karl T. *Massachusetts Institute of Technology; "Tomb of the Dead Languages".* New York: Newcomen Society of England, American Branch, 1948. 32 pp.

Prescott, Samuel C. *When M.I.T. was "Boston Tech", 1861-1916.* Cambridge: Technology Pr., 1954. 350 pp.

Wylie, Francis E. *M.I.T. in Perspective.* Boston: Little, Brown, 1975. 220 pp.

Merrimack College

Roddy, Edward G. *Merrimack College: Genesis and Growth, 1947-1972.* North Andover, Mass.: n.p., 1972. 113 pp.

Mount Holyoke College

Cole, Arthur C. *A Hundred Years of Mount Holyoke College.* New Haven: Yale University Pr., 1940. 426 pp.

Gabriel, Ralph H. *The Founding of Holyoke; 1848.* Princeton: Princeton University Pr., 1936. 23 pp.

Green, Elizabeth A. *Mary Lyon & Mount Holyoke: Opening the Gates.* Hanover, N. H.: University Press of New England, 1979. 406 pp.

Mount Holyoke College. *The Centenary of Mount Holyoke College.* South Hadley, Mass.: The College, 1937. 195 pp.

Nutting, Mary O. *Historical Sketch of Mount Holyoke Seminary. Founded at South Hadley, Mass. in 1837.* Springfield, Mass.: C. W. Bryan and Co., 1878. 21 pp.

Shea, Charlotte K. "Mount Holyoke College, 1875-1910: The Passing of the Old Order." Ph.D. diss., Cornell University, 1983. 248 pp. *Dissertation Abstracts International,* vol. 44A, p. 1711.

Stow, Sarah D. *History of Mount Holyoke Seminary, South Hadley, Mass., during Its First Half Century, 1837-1887.* Springfield: Springfield Printing Co., 1887. 372 pp.

Stow, Sarah D., ed. *Semi-Centennial Celebration of Mount Holyoke Seminary,South Hadley, Mass., 1837-1887.* Springfield, Mass.: The Seminary, 1888. 155 pp.

Nichols College

Coyle, Darcy C. *Nichols College: A Brief History.* New York: Newcomen Society in North America, 1975. 20 pp.

Northeastern University

Ell, Carl S. *"Northeastern" at Boston; Adventures in Education to Develop Latent Details.* New York: Newcomen Society in North America, 1956. 24 pp.

Frederick, Antoinette. *Northeastern University, an Emerging Giant, 1959-1975.* Boston: Northeastern University Custom Book Program, 1982. 731 pp.

Marston, Everett C. *Origin and Development of Northeastern University, 1898-1960.* Boston: Cuneo, 1961. 234 pp.

Morris, Rudolph M. *Where? On Huntington Avenue: A Narrative of Northeastern.* North Quincy, Mass.: Christopher Publishing House, 1977. 191 pp.

Pine Manor College

Russell, Ruth W. *Pine Manor Junior College; The First Fifty Years, 1911-1961.* Chestnut Hill: Pine Manor Pr., 1969. 221 pp.

Radcliffe College

Howells, Dorothy E. *A Century to Celebrate: Radcliffe College, 1879-1979.* Cambridge: Radcliffe College, 1978. 152 pp.

McCord, David T. W. *An Acre for Education: Being Notes on the History of Radcliffe College.* Cambridge: Printed at the Crimson Printing Co., 1954. 90 pp.

--------. *An Acre for Education: Being Notes on the History of Radcliffe College.* Rev. Cambridge: Radcliffe College, 1958. 97 pp.

Schwager, Sally. "Harvard Women": A History of the Founding of Radcliffe College (Boston, Massachusetts)." Ph.D. diss., Harvard University, 1982. 505 pp. *Dissertation Abstracts International,* vol. 43A, p. 1857.

Thierry, Adelaide H. *When Radcliffe was Teen-Age.* Boston: Bruce Humphries, 1959. 113 pp.

St. John's Seminary

Sexton, John E., and Riley, Arthur J. *History of Saint John's Seminary, Brighton.* Boston: Roman Catholic Archbishop of Boston, 1945. 320 pp.

Salem State College

Massachusetts. State College, Salem. *Proceedings at the Quarter-Centennial Celebration of the State Normal School, at Salem, Mass.* Salem, Mass.: Observer Steam Printing Establishment, 1880. 60 pp.

Simmons College

Mark, Kenneth L. *Delayed by Fire, Being the Early History of Simmons College.* Concord, N. H.: Rumford Pr., 1945. 163 pp.

Smith College

Hanscom, Elizabeth D., and Greene, Helen F. *Sophie Smith and the Beginnings of Smith College.* Northampton, Mass.: Smith College, 1926. 120 pp.

Mendenhall, Thomas C. *Chance and Change in Smith College's First Century.* Northampton, Mass.: The College, 1976. 28 pp.

Seelye, Laurenus C. *The Early History of Smith College, 1871-1910.* Boston: Houghton Mifflin, 1923. 242 pp.

Smith College. *Celebration of the Quarter-Centenary of Smith College, October Second and Third, 1900.* Cambridge: Riverside Pr., 1900. 192 pp.

--------. *Historical Handbook of Smith College.* Northampton, Mass.: Smith College, 1932. 32 pp.

Southeastern Massachusetts University

Cass, Walter J. "A History of Southeastern Massachusetts Technological Institute in Cultural Perspective." Ed.D. diss., Boston University, 1967. 273 pp. *Dissertation Abstracts International*, vol. 29A, p. 4299.

Tufts University

Carmichael, Leonard. *Tufts College, Its Science and Technology, a Centennial View, 1852-1952.* New York: Newcomen Society in North America, 1952. 24 pp.

Miller, Russell E. *Light on the Hill; A History of Tufts College, 1852-1952.* Boston: Beacon Pr., 1966. 734 pp.

Start, Alaric B., ed. *Tufts College - Class of 1897. History of Tufts College.* Tufts, Mass.: Tufts College, 1896. 382 pp.

University of Massachusetts

Cary, Harold W. *The University of Massachusetts: A History of One Hundred Years.* Amherst: University of Massachusetts, 1962. 247 pp.

Caswell, Lilley B. *Brief History of the Massachusetts Agricultural College, Semicentennial, 1917.* Springfield, Mass.: F. A. Bassette Co. Printers, 1917. 72 pp.

Rand, Frank P. *Yesterdays at Massachusetts State College, 1863-1933.* Amherst: The Associate Alumni of Massachusetts State College, 1933. 245 pp.

Wellesley College

Converse, Florence. *The Story of Wellesley.* Boston: Little, Brown, 1915. 284 pp.

--------. *Wellesley College; A Chronicle of the Years, 1875-1938.* Wellesley: Hathaway House Bookshop, 1939. 311 pp.

Glassock, Jean, ed. *Wellesley College, 1875-1975: A Century of Women.* Wellesley: Wellesley College, 1975. 496 pp.

Hackett, Alice P. *Wellesley, Part of the American Story.* New York: Dutton, 1949. 320 pp.

Western New England College

Herman, Beaumont A. *Western New England College: A Calling to Fulfill.* Springfield, Mass.: B. A. Herman, 1980. 112 pp.

Westfield State College

Brown, Robert T. *The Rise and Fall of the People's Colleges: The Westfield Normal School, 1839 to 1914.* Westfield: Institute for Massachusetts Studies, Department of History, Westfield State College, 1988. 170 pp.

Massachusetts. State Teachers College, Westfield. *Alma Mater. Twenty-First Triennial. June 1, 1907.* Boston: Wright & Potter Printing Co., 1907. 52 pp.

Writers' Program (Mass.). *The State Teachers College at Westfield.* Boston: Jerome Pr., 1941. 114 pp.

Wheaton College

Clewes, Carolyn M. *Wheaton through the Years: 1835-1960.* Norton, Mass.: Wheaton College, 1960. 15 pp.

Helmreich, Paul C. *Wheaton College, 1834-1912: The Seminary Years.* Norton, Mass.: Class of 1949, Wheaton College, 1985. 143 pp.

Wheelock College

Bain, Winifred E. *Leadership in Childhood Education: A History of Wheelock College, 1888-89 to 1963-64.* Boston: Wheelock College, 1964. 74 pp.

Williams College

Botsford, Eli H. *Fifty Years at Williams under the Administrations of Presidents Chadbourne, Carter, Hewitt, Hopkins and Garfield.* 5 vols. Pittsfield: McClelland Pr., 1928-1940.

Durfee, Calvin. *A History of Williams College.* Boston: A. Williams and Co., 1860. 432 pp.

Perry, Arthur L. *Williamstown and Williams College.* New York: Scribner's, 1899. 847 pp.

Rudolph, Frederick. *Mark Hopkins and the Log; Williams College, 1836-1872.* New Haven: Yale University Pr., 1956. 267 pp.

Spring, Leverett W. *A History of Williams College.* Boston: Houghton Mifflin, 1917. 341 pp.

Wells, D. A. *Sketches of Williams College.* Williamstown: n.p., 1847. 99 pp.

Worcester Polytechnic Institute

Bronwell, Arthur B. *"W.P.I." 1865-1957; Cultivator of Yankee Ingenuity.* New York: Newcomen Society in North America, 1957. 24 pp.

Perry, Roger N. *Washburn: The Tradition Restored.* Worcester: Worcester

Polytechnic Institute, 1984. 31 pp.

Taylor, Herbert F. *Seventy Years of the Worcester Polytechnic Institute.* Worcester: Davis Pr., 1937. 415 pp.

Tymeson, Mildred M. *Two Towers; The Story of Worcester Tech, 1865-1965.* Barre, Mass.: Barre Publishing, 1965. 243 pp.

MICHIGAN

Adrian College

Adrian College. *The Story of a Noble Devotion, 1845-1945, One Hundred Years.* Adrian: Adrian College Pr., 1945. 160 pp.

Albion College

Fennimore, Keith J. *The Albion College Sesquicentennial History, 1835-1985.* Albion: Albion College, 1985. 738 pp.

Gildart, Robert. *Albion College, 1835-1960; A History.* Albion: Albion College, 1961. 280 pp.

Alma College

Bollinger, Donna S. *Pines, Prayers, and Perseverance: The Evolution of Alma College, Alma, Michigan.* Traverse City, Mich.: Village Pr., 1976. 92 pp.

Within Our Bounds: A Centennial History of Alma College. Alma: Alma College, 1986. 219 pp.

Andrews University

Vande Vere, Emmett K. *The Wisdom Seekers; The Intriguing Story of the Men and Women Who Made the First Institution for Higher Learning among Seventh-Day Adventist.* Nashville, Tenn.: Southern Publishing Association, 1972. 288 pp.

Calvin College

Calvin Seminary, Grand Rapids. *Semi-Centennial Volume: Theological*

School and Calvin College, 1876-1926. Grand Rapids, Mich.: Published for the Semi-Centennial Committee by Tradesman Co., 1926. 317 pp.

Timmerman, John J. *Promises to Keep: A Centennial History of Calvin College.* Grand Rapids, Mich.: Calvin College and Seminary, 1975. 197 pp.

Calvin Theological Seminary

Calvin Seminary, Grand Rapids. *Semi-Centennial Volume: Theological School and Calvin College, 1876-1926.* Grand Rapids, Mich.: Published for the Semi-Centennial Committee by Tradesman Co., 1926. 317 pp.

Cranbrook Academy of Art

Van Antwerp, Chiles. "A History of Cranbrook School." Master's thesis, University of Michigan, 1934.

Duns Scotus College (Closed)

Casey, Edgar. *Saint Anthony Shrine Duns Scotus College, Detroit, Michigan: A Brief History and Guide.* Detroit, Mich.: n.p., 1930. 32 pp.

Eastern Michigan University

Isbell, Egbert R. *A History of Eastern Michigan University, 1849-1965.* Ypsilanti: Eastern Michigan University, 1971. 413 pp.

Putnam, Daniel. *A History of the Michigan State Normal School (Now Normal College) at Ypsilanti, Michigan, 1849-1899.* Ypsilanti: Scharf Tag, Label & Box Co., 1899. 368 pp.

Ferris State College

Byrnes, Lawrence W. "Ferris Institute as a Private School, 1884-1952." Ph.D. diss., Michigan State University, 1970. 306 pp. *Dissertation Abstracts International,* vol. 32A, p. 210.

Deupree, Joseph E. *A Century of Opportunity: A Centennial History of Ferris State College.* Big Rapids, Mich.: The Author, 1982. 222 pp.

Flint Community College (Closed 1970)

Prahl, Marie R. "Case Study of the Development of a Junior College into a Community College." Ph.D. diss., University of Michigan, 1966. 406 pp. *Dissertation Abstracts,* vol. 27A, p. 2037.

GMI Engineering and Management Institute

Young, Clarence H., and Tuttle, Robert E. *The Years 1919-1969; A History of General Motors Institute.* Flint: General Motors Institute, 1969. 280 pp.

Grand Valley State College

Swets, Marinus M. "Study of the Establishment of Grand Valley State College." Ph.D. diss., Michigan State University, 1963. 380 pp. *Dissertation Abstracts,* vol. 24, p. 2350.

Zumberge, James H. *Grand Valley State College - Its Developing Years, 1964-1968.* Allendale, Mich.: Grand Valley State College, 1969. 172 pp.

Hillsdale College

Chamberlain, John. *Freedom and Independence: The Hillsdale Story.* Hillsdale, Mich.: Hillsdale College Pr., 1979. 56 pp.

Moore, Vivian E. *The First Hundred Years of Hillsdale College.* Ann Arbor: Ann Arbor Pr., 1944. 588 pp.

Hope College

Shackson, Marian. "History of Hope College." Master's thesis, Western Michigan University, 1942. 68 pp.

Stegenga, Preston J. *Anchor of Hope; The History of an American Denominational Institution, Hope College.* Grand Rapids: Eerdmans, 1954. 271 pp.

Wichers, Wynand. *A Century of Hope, 1866-1966.* Grand Rapids: Eerdmans, 1968. 304 pp.

Jordan College

Andersen, Niels T. *Sunrise Over Jordan: The Story of a 21st Century College.* Cedar Springs, Mich.: Jordan Pub., 1982. 283 pp.

Kalamazoo College

Goodsell, Charles T., and Dunbar, Willis F. *Centennial History of Kalamazoo College.* Kalamazoo: Kalamazoo College, 1933. 214 pp.

Haskell, Samuel. *Historical Sketch of Kalamazoo College.* Kalamazoo: Michigan Christian Herald Printing, 1864. 12 pp.

Hinkle, Marilyn. *On Such a Full Sea: Kalamazoo College Reaching 150 Years.* Kalamazoo: The College, 1982. 166 pp.

Mulder, Arnold. *The Kalamazoo College Story: The First Quarter of the Second Century of Progress, 1933-1958.* Kalamazoo: Kalamazoo College, 1958. 185 pp.

Madonna College

Kujawa, Rose M. "Madonna College: Its History of Higher Education, 1937-1977." Ph.D. diss., Wayne State University, 1979. 289 pp. *Dissertation Abstracts International,* vol. 40A, p. 1905.

Michigan State University

Beal, William J. *History of the Michigan Agricultural College: And Biographical Sketches of Trustees and Professors.* East Lansing: Agricultural College, 1915. 519 pp.

Blair, Lyle, and Kuhn, Madison. *A Short History of Michigan State.* East Lansing: Michigan State College Pr., 1955. 39 pp.

Blaisdell, Thomas C., ed. *Semi-Centennial Celebration of Michigan State Agricultural College, May 26-31, 1907.* Chicago: University of Chicago Pr., 1908. 377 pp.

Dressel, Paul L. *College to University: The Hannah Years at Michigan State, 1935-1969.* East Lansing: Michigan State University Pubns., 1987. 442 pp.

Kuhn, Madison. *Michigan State: The First Hundred Years, 1855-1955.* East Lansing: Michigan State University Pr., 1955. 501 pp.

246 / MICHIGAN

Michigan State College, 1855-1955. East Lansing: n.p., n.d. 688 pp.

Northern Michigan University

Hilton, Miriam E. *Northern Michigan University: The First Seventy-Five Years.* Marquette: Northern Michigan University Pr., 1975. 292 pp.

Oakland Community College

Manilla, Sunday J. "A History of Oakland Community College with Emphasis on Multi-Campus Administration, Systems Approach to Instruction, and the Educational Sciences." Ed.D. diss., Wayne State University, 1971. 497 pp. *Dissertation Abstracts International,* vol. 32A, p. 6157.

Oakland University

Riesman, David. *Academic Values and Mass Education; The Early Years of Oakland and Monteith.* Garden City, N. Y.: Doubleday, 1970. 332 pp.

Stoutenburg, Herbert N., Jr. "Oakland University: Its First Four Years: An Historical Analysis of Its Development and Its Administrative Policies." Ed.D. diss., Michigan State University, 1968. 245 pp. *Dissertation Abstracts,* vol. 29A, p. 3402.

Olivet College

Lignian, Mildred. *Folks & Oaks of Olivet.* Olivet: Olivet College Pr., 1975. 116 pp.

Williams, Wolcott B. *History of Olivet College, 1844-1900.* Olivet: n.p., 1901. 173 pp.

Sacred Heart Seminary

Silver Jubilee, 1919-1944. Detroit: Sacred Heart Seminary, 1944. 80 pp.

Saint Mary's College

Seventy-Five Years of the Orchard Lake Seminary. Orchard Lake, Mich.: Orchard Lake Schools, 1960. 104 pp.

Spring Arbor College

Killion, Mead W. "A History of Spring Arbor Seminary and Junior College." Master's thesis, University of Michigan, 1941. 106 pp.

Snyder, Howard A. *One Hundred Years at Spring Arbor: A History of Spring Arbor College, 1873-1973.* Spring Arbor, Mich.: Spring Arbor College, 1973. 160 pp.

University of Detroit

Muller, Herman J. *The University of Detroit, 1877-1977: A Centennial History.* Detroit: University of Detroit Pr., 1976. 397 pp.

University of Michigan

Adams, Charles K. *Historical Sketch of the University of Michigan.* Ann Arbor: The University, 1876. 56 pp.

Bordin, Ruth B. A. *University of Michigan: A Pictorial History.* Ann Arbor: University of Michigan Pr., 212 pp.

Davis, Phil. *The University; A Photographic Essay Composed of Pictures Selected from an Exhibition Displayed on the Campus of the University of Michigan on the Occasion of Its Sesquicentennial Celebration.* Ann Arbor: University of Michigan Pr., 1967.

Farrand, Elizabeth M. *History of the University of Michigan.* Ann Arbor: Register Publishing House, 1885. 300 pp.

Hatcher, Harlan H. *"The University of Michigan", 140 Years from Michigan Wilderness to a World Center of Learning, 1817-1957.* New York: Newcomen Society in North America, 1958. 32 pp.

Hinsdale, Burke A. *History of the University of Michigan.* Ann Arbor: University of Michigan, 1906. 376 pp.

Michigan University. *Records of the University of Michigan, 1817-1837.* Ann Arbor: University of Michigan, 1935. 211 pp.

Peckham, Howard H. *The Making of the University of Michigan, 1817-1967.* Ann Arbor: University of Michigan Pr., 1967. 276 pp.

Sagendorph, Kent. *Michigan: The Story of the University.* New York: Dutton, 1948. 384 pp.

Shaw, Wilfred B. *Short History of the University of Michigan.* Ann Arbor: Wahr, 1934. 157 pp.

-------. *The University of Michigan.* New York: Harcourt, 1920. 364 pp.

Shaw, Wilfred B., ed. *The University of Michigan, an Encyclopedic Survey.* 8 vols. Ann Arbor: University of Michigan Pr., 1941-1958.

University of Michigan-Dearborn

Campbell, Sharon A. C. " A History of the Development of the Flint and Dearborn Branches of the University of Michigan." Ph.D. diss., University of Michigan, 1973. 336 pp. *Dissertation Abstracts International,* vol. 34A, p. 4775.

Higgs, Elton D. *A Gift Renewed: The First Twenty-Five Years of the University of Michigan-Dearborn, 1959-1984.* Dearborn: The University, 1985. 105 pp.

University of Michigan-Flint

Campbell, Sharon A. C. "A History of the Development of the Flint and Dearborn Branches of the University of Michigan." Ph.D. diss., University of Michigan, 1973. 336 pp. *Dissertation Abstracts International,* vol. 34A, p. 4775.

Wayne State University

Halperin, Samuel. *A University in the Web of Politics.* New York: Holt, 1960. 16 pp.

Hanawalt, Leslie L. *A Place of Light; The History of Wayne State University.* Detroit: Wayne State University Pr., 1968. 512 pp.

Irwin, James R. "Wayne University - A History." Ed.D. diss., Wayne State University, 1952. 497 pp. *Dissertation Abstracts,* vol. 13, p. 338.

Riesman, David. *Academic Values and Mass Education; The Early Years of Oakland and Monteith.* Garden City, N. Y.: Doubleday, 1970. 332 pp.

Western Michigan University

Gagie, Martin R. J., ed. *Western Michigan University, a Pictorial History:*

75 Years of Growth. Kalamazoo: Western Michigan University, 1978. 46 pp.

Knauss, James O. *History of Western State Teachers College, 1904-1929.* Kalamazoo: Western Michigan Teachers College, 1929. 156 pp.

Stine, Leo C. *Western - A Twentieth Century University: A Case History of Western Michigan University.* Kalamazoo: New Issues Pr., 1980. 261 pp.

MINNESOTA

Augsburg College

Chrislock, Carl H. *From Fjord to Freeway: 100 Years, Augsburg College.* Minneapolis: Augsburg College, 1969. 262 pp.

Bemidji State University

Lee, Arthur O. *College in the Pines: A History of Bemidji State College.* Minneapolis: Dillon Pr., 1970. 215 pp.

--------. "A History of Bemidji State College: 1913-1937." Ph.D. diss., University of North Dakota, 1968. 312 pp. *Dissertation Abstracts,* vol. 29A, p. 4404.

Bethel Theological Seminary

Olson, Adolf, and Olson, Virgil A. *Seventy-Five Years: A History of Bethel Theological Seminary, St. Paul, Minnesota, 1871-1946.* Chicago: Conference Pr., 1946. 232 pp.

Carleton College

Dana, Malcolm M. *The History of the Origin and Growth of Carleton College, Northfield, Minnesota.* St. Paul: Office of the Pioneer Press Co., 1879. 36 pp.

Headley, Leal A., and Jarcow, Merrill E. *Carleton; The First Century.* Northfield, Minn.: Carleton College, 1966. 489 pp.

Leonard, Delavan L. *The History of Carleton College: Its Origin and*

250 / MINNESOTA

Growth, Environment and Builders. Chicago: Revell, 1904. 421 pp.

College of St. Scholastica

Duluth. College of St. Scholastica. *The First Fifteen Years of the College of St. Scholastica; A Report on the Effectiveness of Education for Women.* New York: D. X. McMullen, 1947. 184 pp.

College of Saint Teresa

Quinn, Bernetta. *Design in Gold: A History of the College of Saint Teresa, Winona, Minnesota, 1907-1957.* Winona: College of Saint Teresa, 1957. 80 pp.

College of St. Thomas

Keenan, Edward P. *The Story of St. Thomas College.* St. Paul: College of St. Thomas, 1933. 24 pp.

Tradition of Excellence: A Tribute and a Testimonial. St. Paul: The Mother's Club, College of St. Thomas, St. Thomas Military Academy, 1957. 115 pp.

Concordia College

Concordia College, St. Paul. *Concordia College.* St. Paul: n.p., 1943. 78 pp.

Overan, Oswald B. *A History of Concordia College, St. Paul, Minnesota.* St. Paul: Concordia College, 1968. 246 pp.

Rolfsrud, Erling N. *Cobber Chronicle: An Informal History of Concordia College.* Moorehead, Minn.: Concordia College, 1966. 240 pp.

--------. *Cobber Chronicle: An Informal History of Concordia College.* 2d ed. Moorehead, Minn.: Concordia College, 1976. 275 pp.

Dr. Martin Luther College

Schroeder, Morton A. *A Time to Remember: An Informal History of Dr. Martin Luther College, 1884-1984.* New Ulm, Minn.: Dr. Martin Luther College, 1984. 199 pp.

Gustavus Adolphus College

Lund, Doniver A.. *Gustavus Adolphus College: Celebrating 125 Years.* St. Peter, Minn.: Gustavus College, 1987. 117 pp.

--------. *Gustavus Adolphus College: A Centennial History, 1862-1962.* St. Peter, Minn.: Gustavus Adolphus College, 1963. 216 pp.

Peterson, Conrad. *Gustavus Adolphus College, a History of Eighty Years, 1862-1942.* Rock Island, Ill.: Augustana Book Concern, 1942. 128 pp.

--------. *Remember Thy Past: A History of Gustavus Adolphus College, 1862-1952.* St. Peter, Minn.: Gustavus Adolphus College Pr., 1953. 180 pp.

Hamline University

Johnson, David W. *Hamline University, a History.* St. Paul: North Central Publishing Co., 1980. 304 pp.

Pace, Charles N., ed. *Hamline University.* St. Paul: Hamline University Alumni Association, 1939. 142 pp.

Macalester College

Funk, Henry D. *A History of Macalester College: Its Origin, Struggle, and Growth.* St. Paul: Macalester College Board of Trustees, 1910. 304 pp.

Macalester College, a Century and Beyond. n.p., 1985. 96 pp.

Mankato State University

Giebel, Arlyn J. "Development of Mankato Normal School from 1877-1890." Master's thesis, Minnesota State College, Mankato, 1957.

Grev, Julian R. "Mankato State College, 1890 through 1900." Master's thesis, Mankato State University, 1964. 106 pp.

Larson, Sexton. "The Organization and Early Development of Mankato State Normal School." Master's thesis, Mankato State College, 1954. 49 pp.

Youel, Donald B. *Mankato State College; An Interpretive Essay.* Mankato:

Mankato State University, 1968. 140 pp.

Pillsbury Baptist Bible College*

Pettigrew, Larry D. *The History of Pillsbury Baptist Bible College.* Owatonna, Minn.: Pillsbury Baptist Bible College Pr., 1981. 180 pp.

St. Cloud State University

Brainard, Dudley S., and Cochrane, John C. *A History of the St. Cloud State Teachers College, 1869-1944.* St. Cloud: n.p., 1944. 47 pp.

Cates, Edwin H. *A Centennial History of St. Cloud State College.* Minneapolis: Dillan Pr., 1968. 256 pp.

Saint John's University

Barry, Colman J. *Worship and Work; St. John's Abbey and University, 1856-1956.* Collegeville: St. John's Abbey, 1956. 447 pp.

Hoffman, Alexius. *St. John's University, Collegeville, Minnesota: A Sketch of Its History.* Collegeville: Record Pr., 1907. 158 pp.

Saint Olaf College

Aasgaard, John A., ed. *Quarter Centennial, 1874-1899: Souvenir of St. Olaf College.* Northfield, Minn.: n.p., 1900. 134 pp.

Benson, William C. *High on Manitou; A History of St. Olaf College, 1874-1949.* Northfield, Minn.: St. Olaf College Pr., 1949. 266 pp.

Hegland, Georgina E. D. *As It Was in the Beginning.* Northfield, Minn.: St. Olaf College Pr., 1950. 163 pp.

Kelsey, Roger R. "Fram! Fram: Christmenn, Crossmenn: The St. Olaf College Program, 1912-1952." Ph.D. diss., George Peabody College for Teachers, 1954. 199 pp.

Shaw, Joseph M. *History of St. Olaf College, 1874-1974.* Northfield, Minn.: St. Olaf College Pr., 1974. 694 pp.

University of Minnesota

Ford, Guy S. *The Making of the University, an Unorthodox Report.*

Minneapolis: University of Minnesota Pr., 1940. 62 pp.

Gilfillan, John B. *History of the University of Minnesota.* St. Paul: University of Minnesota, 1906. 46 pp.

Gray, James. *Open Wide the Door; The Story of the University of Minnesota.* New York: Putnam, 1958. 256 pp.

--------. *The University of Minnesota, 1851-1951.* Minneapolis: University of Minnesota Pr., 1951. 609 pp.

Hall, Christopher W. *The University of Minnesota: An Historical Sketch.* Minneapolis: n.p., 1896. 75 pp.

Johnson, Elwin B., ed. *Forty Years of the University of Minnesota.* Minneapolis: General Alumni Association, 1910. 348 pp.

Roberts, Norene A. D. "An Early Political and Administrative History of the University of Minnesota, 1851-84." Ph.D., diss., University of Minnesota, 1978. 561 pp. *Dissertation Abstracts International,* vol. 39A, p. 7188.

University of Minnesota-Morris

McGrath, Gary L. "The Establishment and Early Development of the University of Minnesota, Morris." Ed.D. diss., Indiana University, 1974. 150 pp. *Dissertation Abstracts International,* vol. 35A, p. 5865.

Winona State University

DuFresne, Robert A. *Winona State University: A History of One Hundred Twenty-Five Years.* Winona: Winona State University, 1985. 366 pp.

Ruggles, Clyde O. *Historical Sketch and Notes; Winona State Normal School, 1860-1910.* Winona: Jones & Kroeger, 1910. 358 pp.

Selle, Erwin S., ed. *The Winona State Teachers College; Historical Notes, 1910-1935.* Winona: n.p., 1935. 158 pp.

Talbot, Jean. *First State Normal School, 1860 - Winona State College, 1960.* Winona: Winona State College, 1959-1961. 105 pp.

MISSISSIPPI

Alcorn State University

Bruss, Melvin. "The History of Oakland College, 1830-1871." Master's thesis, Louisiana State University, 1966. 268 pp.

Davis, Milan. *Pushing Forward: A History of Alcorn A. & M. College and Portraits of Some of Its Successful Graduates.* Okolona, Miss.: Okolona Industrial School, 1938. 124 pp.

Dunham, Melerson G. *The Centennial History of Alcorn Agricultural and Mechanical College.* Hattisburg: University and College Press of Mississippi, 1971. 198 pp.

Belhaven College

Gordon, James F., Jr. "A History of Belhaven College, Jackson, Mississippi, 1894-1981." Ph.D. diss., University of Mississippi, 1982. 298 pp. *Dissertation Abstracts International,* vol. 43A, p. 687.

Blue Mountain College

Sumrall, Robbie N. *A Light on a Hill; A History of Blue Mountain College.* Nashville, Tenn.: Benson Printing Co., 1947. 172 pp.

Tyler, Frances L. "Blue Mountain College under the Administration of Lawrence Tyndale Lowery, 1925-1960." Ph.D. diss., University of Mississippi, 1974. 192 pp. *Dissertation Abstracts International,* vol. 35A, p. 7095.

Clarke College

Reynolds, Thomas U. "A History of Clarke Memorial College." Master's thesis, Texas Christian University, 1952. 111 pp.

Copiah-Lincoln Junior College

Donnan, Annette W. "A Study of the History of Copiah-Lincoln Agricultural High School and Junior College from 1914 to May 31, 1976." Ed.D. diss., University of Southern Mississippi, 1977. 241 pp. *Dissertation Abstracts International,* vol. 38A, p. 2691.

Delta State University

Gunn, Jack W., and Castle, Gladys C. *A Pictorial History of Delta State University.* Jackson: University Press of Mississippi, 1980. 216 pp.

Gulf Park College (Closed 1971)

Elias, Louis, Jr. "A History of Gulf Park College for Women, 1917-1971." Ed.D. diss., University of Mississippi, 1981. 151 pp. *Dissertation Abstracts International,* vol. 42A, p. 4735.

Jackson State University

Dansby, B. Baldwin. *A Brief History of Jackson College; A Typical Story of the Survival of Education among Negroes in the South.* Jackson: Jackson College, 1953. 286 pp.

Rhodes, Lelia G. *Jackson State University: The First Hundred Years, 1877-1977.* Jackson: University Press of Mississippi, 1979. 340 pp.

Jefferson College (Closed)

Blain, William T. *Education in the Old Southwest: A History of Jefferson College, Washington, Mississippi.* Washington, Miss.: Friends of Jefferson College, Inc., 1976. 155 pp.

Dobbs, Sharron L. "Jefferson College: A Study of the Origins of Higher Education in Mississippi, 1802-1848." Ph.D. diss., University of Mississippi, 1987. 112 pp. *Dissertation Abstracts International,* vol. 48A, p. 574.

Fowler, William B. "History of Jefferson College of Washington, Mississippi, Prior to the War for Southern Independence." Master's thesis, Louisiana State University, 1937.

Jones County Junior College

Tisdale, Thomas T. "From Agricultural High School to Comprehensive Junior College: Jones County Junior College, 1910 to 1970." Ed.D. diss., University of Southern Mississippi, 1972. 176 pp. *Dissertation Abstracts International,* vol. 33A, p. 4768.

Mary Holmes College

Pfeifer, Helen E. *Something of a Faith; A Brief History of Mary Holmes College.* West Point, Miss.: n.p., 1967. 37 pp.

Millsaps College

Harmon, George M. *Millsaps College: Determining the Agenda.* New York: Newcomen Society of the United States, 1985. 26 pp.

Mississippi College

McLemore, Richard A., and McLemore, Nannie. *The History of Mississippi College.* Jackson: Hederman Brothers, 1979. 285 pp.

Nobles, Lewis. *A College for Mississippians: The Story of Mississippi College.* New York: Newcomen Society in North America, 1976. 24 pp.

Mississippi State University

Betterworth, John K. *People's College; A History of Mississippi State.* University, Ala.: University of Alabama Pr., 1953. 471 pp.

--------. *People's University: The Centennial History of Mississippi State.* Jackson: University Press of Mississippi, 1980. 504 pp.

Colvard, Dean W. *The "Land Grant" Way in Mississippi; The Story of Mississippi State University.* New York: Newcomen Society in North America, 1962. 24 pp.

Lee, Stephen D. *The Agricultural and Mechanical College of Mississippi. Its Origin, Object, Management and Results, Discussed in a Series of Papers.* Jackson: Clarion-Ledger Publishing House, 1889. 18 pp.

McComas, James D. *Mississippi State University: A New Century, a New Dimension.* New York: Newcomen Society in North America, 1978. 20 pp.

Mississippi State University. *The First One Hundred Years, Mississippi State University.* Mississippi State: The University, 1978. 150 pp.

Mississippi University for Women

Pieschel, Bridget S., and Pieschel, Stephen R. *Loyal Daughters: One*

Hundred Years at Mississippi University for Women, 1884-1984. Jackson: University Press of Mississippi, 1984. 208 pp.

Mississippi Valley State University

Baker, Clemon. "A Historical Investigation of the Goal Evolution of Mississippi Valley State University, 1946-1976." Ph.D. diss., Southern Illinois University, 1977. 177 pp. *Dissertation Abstracts International,* vol. 38A, p. 648.

Tinsley, Sammy J. "A History of Mississippi Valley State College." Ph.D. diss., University of Mississippi, 1972. 293 pp. *Dissertation Abstracts International,* vol. 33A, p. 3339.

White, James H. *Up from a Cotton Patch: J. H. White and the Development of Mississippi Valley State College.* Itta Bena, Miss.: n.p., 1979. 176 pp.

Okolona College (Closed 1966)

Stewart, Richard A. "The History and Educational Programs of Okolona College, Okolona Mississippi." Master's thesis, Tennessee Agricultural & Industrial State University, 1962.

Rust College

Baker, Webster B. *A History of Rust College.* Greensboro, N. C.: The Author, 1924. 221 pp.

Tougaloo College

Campbell, Clarice T. "The Founding of Tougaloo College." Master's thesis, University of Mississippi, 1967. 115 pp.

--------. "History of Tougaloo College." Ph.D. diss., University of Mississippi, 1970. 410 pp. *Dissertation Abstracts International,* vol. 31A, p. 1181.

Campbell, Clarice T., and Rogers, Oscar A., Jr. *Mississippi: The View from Tougaloo.* Jackson: University Press of Mississippi, 1979. 276 pp.

Woodworth, Frank G. *Tougaloo University, Tougaloo, Mississippi.* New York: The Winthrop Pr., 18--. 11 pp.

University of Mississippi

Cabaniss, James A. *A History of the University of Mississippi.* University: University of Mississippi, 1949. 242 pp.

--------. *The University of Mississippi; Its First Hundred Years.* 2d ed. Hattiesburg: University College Press of Mississippi, 1971. 207 pp.

Lloyd, James B., et. al. *The University of Mississippi: The Formative Years, 1848-1906.* University: Library, Department of Archives and Special Collections, University of Mississippi, 1979. 93 pp.

Lucas, Aubrey D. *Developing the Human Capital of Mississippi: A Challenge for Higher Education.* New York: Newcomen Society of the United States, 1986. 16 pp.

Measells, Dewitt T., Jr. "History of the Expansion of the University of Mississippi, 1848-1947." Master's thesis, University of Mississippi, 1947. 130 pp.

Read, James C. "The Williams Chancellorship at the University of Mississippi, 1946-68." Ed.D. diss., University of Mississippi, 1978. 340 pp. *Dissertation Abstracts International,* vol. 39A, p. 3408.

University of Southern Mississippi

Hickman, Alma. *Southern as I Saw It; Personal Remembrances of an Era, 1912 to 1954.* Hattiesburg: University of Southern Mississippi Pr., 1966. 144 pp.

Morgan, Chester M. *Dearly Bought, Deeply Treasured: The University of Southern Mississippi, 1912-1987.* Jackson: University Press of Mississippi, 1987. 181 pp.

Utica Junior College

Washington, Walter. "Utica Junior College, 1903-1957: A Half Century of Education for Negroes." Ed.D. diss., University of Southern Mississippi, 1970. 202 pp. *Dissertation Abstracts International,* vol. 31A, p. 4506.

Whitworth College

Rice, Kathleen G. "A History of Whitworth College for Women." Ph.D. diss., University of Mississippi, 1985. 145 pp. *Dissertation Abstracts*

International, vol. 46A, p. 3622.

MISSOURI

Central Methodist College

Tucker, Frank C. *Central Methodist College: One Hundred and Ten Years.* Nashville: Parthenon Pr., 1967. 195 pp.

Central Missouri State University

Anders, Leslie. *Education for Service: Centennial History of Central Missouri State College.* Warrensburg: Central Missouri State College, 1971. 85 pp.

Christian Brothers College (Closed)

Witt, Michael J. "The Devolution of Christian Brothers College: 1900-1931." Ph.D. diss., Saint Louis University, 1980. 270 pp. *Dissertation Abstracts International,* vol. 41A, p. 3220.

Columbia College

Hale, Allean L. *Petticoat Pioneer: The Christian College Story, 1851-1951.* Columbia, Mo.: n.p., 1956. 263 pp.

--------. *Petticoat Pioneer; The Story of Christian College, Oldest College for Women West of the Mississippi.* Rev. ed. St. Paul, Minn.: North Central Publishing Co., 1968. 314 pp.

Hughes, Mary K. "A History of Christian College, 1851-1900." Master's thesis, University of Missouri, 1944. 165 pp.

Concordia Seminary

Graebner, Theodore C. *Concordia Seminary; Its History, Architecture, and Symbolism.* St. Louis: Concordia Publishing House, 1926. 128 pp.

Meyer, Carl S. *Log Cabin to Luther Tower.* St. Louis: Concordia Publishing House, 1965. 322 pp.

Suelflow, Roy A. "The History of Concordia Seminary, St. Louis, 1839-

1865." Master's thesis, Washington University, 1946. 113 pp.

Culver-Stockton College

Lee, George R. *Culver-Stockton College: The First 130 Years.* Canton, Mo.: Culver-Stockton College, 1984. 199 pp.

Peters, George L. *Dreams Come True, a History of Culver-Stockton College.* Canton, Mo.: Culver-Stockton College, 1941. 144 pp.

Shrout, Mildred R. "A History of Culver-Stockton College, 1937-1956." Master's thesis, Northeast Missouri State College, 1971. 148 pp.

Drury College

Clippinger, Frank W. *The Drury Story.* Springfield, Mo.: Drury College, 1982. 3519 pp.

Pope, Richard M. "Drury College: An Intrepretation." Ph.D. diss., University of Chicago, 1955. 224 pp.

Roulet, Paul. *History of Drury College at Springfield, Green County, Missouri: Preceeded by a Notice of the Early Educational Efforts to Found Schools in Southwest Missouri before the War.* Springfield, Mo.: The Author, 1899. 191 pp.

Eden Theological Seminary

Arndt, Elmer J. F., ed. *The Heritage of the Reformation; Essays Commemorating the Centennial of Eden Theological Seminary.* New York: R. R. Smith, 1950. 264 pp.

Brueggemann, Walter A. "Ethos and Ecumenism: The History of Eden Theological Seminary, 1925-1970." Ph.D. diss., Saint Louis University, 1974. 290 pp. *Dissertation Abstracts International,* vol. 35A, p. 2737.

Harris-Stowe State College

Harris, Ruth M. *Stowe Teachers College and Her Predecessors.* Boston: Christopher Publishing House, 1967. 162 pp.

St. Louis. Board of Education. *One Hundred Years of Teacher Education in the St. Louis Public School System.* St. Louis: Board of Education, 1958-

Kansas City College of Osteopathy and Surgery

Johnston, Mamie, and Knickerbocker, M. R. *A History of the Kansas City College of Osteopathy and Surgery, 1916-1966.* Kansas City, Mo.: Lowell Pr., 1967. 72 pp.

Lincoln University

Foster, R. B. *Historical Sketch of Lincoln Institute.* Jefferson City: n.p., 1871. 18 pp.

Marshall, Albert P. *Soldiers' Dream: A Centennial History of Lincoln University of Missouri.* Jefferson City: Lincoln University, 1966. 40 pp.

Savage, William S. *The History of Lincoln University.* Jefferson City: Lincoln University, 1939. 302 pp.

Lindenwood College

Templin, Lucinda D., comp. *Reminiscences of Lindenwood College: A Souvenir for the Homecoming.* St. Charles: n.p., 1920. 166 pp.

Marillac College (Closed 1975)

Monahan, Danno R. "Education Women Religious: The History of Marillac College, 1955-1969." Ph.D. diss., St. Louis University, 1972. 127 pp. *Dissertation Abstracts International,* vol. 33A, p. 2745.

Midwestern Baptist Theological Seminary

Hester, Hubert I. *The Founding of Midwestern Baptist Theological Seminary.* Kansas City: Midwestern Baptist Theological Seminary, 1964. 20 pp.

Missouri Valley College

Parsons, Nellie F. "The History of Missouri Valley College." Master's thesis, University of Missouri, 1940. 141 pp.

Missouri Western State College

Flanagan, Frances. *Missouri Western State College: A History, 1915-1983.* Saint Joseph: Board of Regents, 1983. 138 pp.

Moberly Junior College

Ricker, Paul A. "A History of the Growth and Development of Moberly Area Junior College, 1926-1984." Ed.D. diss., University of Missouri, 1984. 157 pp. *Dissertation Abstracts International,* vol. 45A, p. 3293.

Northeast Missouri State University

Ryle, Walter H. *Centennial History of the Northeast Missouri State Teachers College.* Kirksville: Northeast Missouri State Teachers College, 1972. 768 pp.

Simmons, Lucy. *History of Northeast Missouri State Teachers College.* Kirksville: n.p., 1927. 99 pp.

Violette, Eugene M. *History of the First District State Normal School, Kirksville, Missouri.* Kirksville: Journal Printing Co., 1905. 280 pp.

Northwest Missouri State University

Albertini, Virgil. *The Towers in the Northwest: A History of Northwest Missouri State University, 1956-1980.* Maryville: Northwest Missouri State University, 1980. 325 pp.

Dykes, Mattie M. *Behind the Birches; A History of Northwest Missouri State College.* Maryville: Northwest Missouri State College, 1956. 297 pp.

Park College

McAfee, Joseph E. *College Pioneering: Problems and Phases of the Life at Park College during Its Early Years.* Kansas City, Mo.: Alumni Parkana Committee, 1938. 264 pp.

--------. *A Mid-West Adventure in Education; Problems and Phases of Life at Park College during Its Early Days.* Kansas City, Mo.: Alumni Parkana Committee, 1937. 167 pp.

MISSOURI / 263

Rockhurst College

Owens, Hugh M. "History of Rockhurst College: The First Quarter-Century." Master's thesis, Saint Louis University, 1953. 185 pp.

Saint Louis College of Pharmacy

Winkelmann, John P. *History of the St. Louis College of Pharmacy.* St. Louis: Privately Printed, 1964. 175 pp.

Saint Louis University

Adams, Rita G., et. al. *Saint Louis University-One Hundred Fifty Years.* St. Louis: Saint Louis University, 1968. 176 pp.

Faherty, William B. *Better the Dream; Saint Louis: University and Community, 1818-1968.* St. Louis: Saint Louis University, 1968. 445 pp.

Fanning, William H. W. *Historical Sketch of the St. Louis University.* St. Louis: Saint Louis University, 1908. 64 pp.

Ganss, George E. *The Jesuit Educational Tradition and Saint Louis University; Some Bearings for the University's Sesquicentennial, 1818-1968.* St. Louis: Sesquicentennial Committee of Saint Louis University, 1969. 60 pp.

Heithaus, Claude H. *The Truth About Saint Louis University.* St. Louis: Saint Louis University, 1940, 40 pp.

Hill, Walter, H. *Historical Sketch of the Saint Louis University; The Celebration of Its Fiftieth Anniversary or Golden Jubilee on June 24, 1879.* St. Louis: P. Fox, 1879. 268 pp.

Saint Louis University. *Memorial Volume of the Diamond Jubilee of St. Louis University, 1829-1904.* St. Louis: Little and Becker Printing Co., 1904. 330 pp.

St. Paul's College*

MacKey, Katharine W. *The Story of St. Paul's College: Tales of the College Yard.* n. p., 1931. 60 pp.

School of the Ozarks

Godsey, Helen, and Godsey, Townsend. *Flight of the Phoenix: A Biography of the School of the Ozarks--A Unique American College: The First 75 Years.* Point Lookout, Mo.: School of the Ozarks, 1984. 643 pp.

Southeast Missouri State University

Farmer, Ernest K. "Southeast Missouri State Normal, 1873-1921." Ph.D. diss., Southern Illinois University at Carbondale, 1987. 261 pp. *Dissertation Abstracts International,* vol. 48A, p. 2551.

Mattingly, Arthur. *Normal to University: A Century of Service.* Cape Girardeau, Mo.: Southeast Missouri State University, 1979. 304 pp.

Southwest Baptist University

Hamlett, Mayme L. *To Noonday Bright: The Story of Southwest Baptist University 1878-1984.* Bolivar, Mo.: Southwest Baptist University, 1984. 428 pp.

Mahan, Lessie D. J. "A History of Southwest Baptist College, 1878-1946." Master's thesis, University of Missouri, 1948. 102 pp.

Southwest Missouri State University

Ellis, Roy. *Shrine of the Ozarks; A History of Southwest Missouri State College, 1905-1965.* Springfield: Southwest Missouri State College, 1968. 283 pp.

Stephens College

Crighton, John C. *Stephens; A Story of Educational Innovation.* Columbia: American Pr., 1970. 432 pp.

Three Rivers Community College

Burke, Thomas R. "Three Rivers Community College: The Formative Years, 1966-1979." Ph.D. diss., University of Mississippi, 1981. 225 pp. *Dissertation Abstracts International,* vol. 42A, p. 2991.

University of Missouri

Babb, Joseph G. *A Short History of the University.* Columbia: University of Missouri, 1915. 197 pp.

Lowry, Thomas J. *A Sketch of the University of Missouri.* Columbia: Herald Publishing House, 1890. 126 pp.

Missouri. University. *The University of Missouri, First State University in the Louisiana Purchase.* Columbia: n.p., 1953.

Olson, James, and Olson, Vera. *The University of Missouri: An Illustrated History.* Columbia: University of Missouri Pr., 1988. 296 pp.

Stephens, Frank F. *A History of the University of Missouri.* Columbia: University of Missouri Pr., 1962. 661 pp.

Viles, Jonas. *The University of Missouri, a Centennial History.* Columbia: University of Missouri, 1929. 508 pp.

University of Missouri-Kansas City

Scofield, Carlton F. *History of the University of Kansas City: Prologue to a Public Urban University.* Kansas City, Mo.: Lowell Pr., 1976. 52 pp.

University of Missouri-Rolla

Christensen, Lawrence O., and Ridley, Jack B. *UM-Rolla: A History of MSM/UMR.* Columbia: University of Missouri Printing Services, 1983. 324 pp.

Mann, Bonita H., and Mann, Clair V. *The History of the Missouri School of Mines and Metallurgy.* Rolla: Phelps County Historical Society, 1941. 1020 pp.

Washington University

Hayes, Donn W. "A History of Smith Academy of Washington University." Ph.D. diss., Washington University, 1950. 117 pp.

Shepley, Ethan A. H. *What Does Washington University Stand For?* New York: Newcomen Society in North America, 1958. 32 pp.

Westminster College

Fisher, Michael M., and Rice, John J. *History of Westminster College, 1851-1903*. Columbia: Press of E. W. Stephens, 1903. 380 pp.

Lamkin, Charles F. *A Great Small College; A Narrative History of Westminster College, Fulton, Missouri, 1946.* St. Louis: Horace Barks Pr., 568 pp.

Parrish, William E. *Westminster College, an Informal History, 1851-1969.* Fulton: Westminster College, 1971. 280 pp.

William Jewell College

Clark, James G., comp. *History of William Jewell College, Liberty, Clay County, Missouri.* St. Louis: Central Baptist Printing, 1893. 278 pp.

Hester, Hubert I. *Jewell: A 125th Anniversary History.* Liberty, Mo.: William Jewell College, 1975. 39 pp.

--------. *Jewell is Her Name: A History of William Jewell College.* Liberty, Mo.: William Jewell College, 1967. 257 pp.

William Woods College

Hamlin, Griffith A. *In Faith and History: The Story of William Woods College.* St. Louis: Bethany Pr., 1965. 239 pp.

MONTANA

College of Great Falls

Cronin, Kathleen J. "An Historical Perspective of the College of Great Falls." Ed.D. diss., Boston University, 1974. 393 pp. *Dissertation Abstracts International,* vol. 35A, p. 232.

Northern Montana College

Caskey, Gerald C. "A History of Northern Montana College to 1951." Master's thesis, University of North Dakota, 1953. 95 pp.

University of Montana

Merriam, Harold G. *The University of Montana: A History.* Missoula: University of Montana Pr., 1970. 194 pp.

Miller, Donald C., and Cohen, Stan. *University of Montana, Missoula: A Pictorial History.* Missoula: Pictorial Histories Publishing Co., 1980. 86 pp.

Western Montana College

Pyeatt, Margaret F. "A Historical Study of the Growth of Montana State Normal College, 1914 through 1941. Master's thesis, Western Montana College, 1965. 130 pp.

NEBRASKA

Bellevue College

Creigh, Dorothy W. *Bellevue College, 1880-1919: A Brief History.* Hastings, Neb.: Hastings College, 1962. 114 pp.

Concordia Teachers College

Brandhorst, Carl T. *A Short Story of Concordia Teachers College, Seward, Nebraska; Measurable Growth, Immeasurable Grace.* n.p., 1969. 31 pp.

Freitag, Alfred J. "A History of Concordia Teachers College, 1864-1964." Ed.D. diss., University of Southern California, 1965. 561 pp. *Dissertation Abstracts,* vol. 26, p. 849.

Simon, Martin P. "A History of Concordia Teachers College, Seward, Nebraska." Ph.D. diss., University of Oregon, 1953. 323 pp.

Creighton University

Dowling, Michael P. *Creighton University.* Omaha: Press of Burkley Printing Co., 1903. 272 pp.

Kirby, Maurice W. "History of Creighton University, 1878-1926." Master's thesis, University of Nebraska, 1954. 142 pp.

Vosper, James M. "A History of Selected Factors in the Development of Creighton University." Ph.D. diss., University of Nebraska, 1976. 268 pp. *Dissertation Abstracts International,* vol. 37A, p. 4176.

Dana College

Christensen, William E. *Saga of the Tower; A History of Dana College and Trinity Seminary.* Blair: Lutheran Publishing House, 1959. 271 pp.

Petersen, Peter L. *A Place Called Dana: The Centennial History of Trinity Seminary and Dana College, 1884-1984.* Blair: The College, 1984. 231 pp.

Doane College

History of Doane College, Crete, Nebraska, 1872 to 1912. Crete, Neb.: n.p., 1957. 312 pp.

Hastings College

Weyer, Frank E. *Hastings College, Seventy-Five Years in Retrospect, 1882-1957.* Hastings: Hastings College Anniversary Committee, 1957. 164 pp.

Kearney State College

Holmgren, Philip. *Kearney State College, 1905-1980: A History of the First Seventy-Five Years.* Kearney, Neb.: Kearney State College Pr., 1980. 224 pp.

Nebraska State College, Wayne. *Nebraska Normal College: A History of Nebraska Normal College, the Faculty, Students, the Progress and Development of the New School.* Lincoln: n.p., 1939. 176 pp.

Midland Lutheran College

Dowie, James I. "Luther Academy, 1883 to 1903; A Facet of Swedish Pioneer Life in Nebraska." Ph.D. diss., University of Minnesota, 1957. 367 pp. *Dissertation Abstracts,* vol. 20, p. 4382.

Nebraska Wesleyan University

Booth, Ethel. *Where Sunflowers Grew; The Story of Nebraska Wesleyan throught Its Early Years.* Lincoln: Nebraska Wesleyan Pr., 1962. 88 pp.

Rogers, Vance D. *Nebraska Wesleyan University: Pioneers Laying Foundations for Generations to Come.* New York: Newcomen Society in North America, 1977. 20 pp.

Winship, Frank L. "Early History of Nebraska Wesleyan University." Master's thesis, University of Nebraska, 1930. 190 pp.

Peru State College

Longfellow, Ernest. *The Normal on the Hill; One Hundred Years of Peru State College.* Grand Island: Augustine Co., 1967. 68 pp.

Union College

Dick, Everett N. *Union: College of the Golden Cords.* Lincoln: Union College Pr., 1967. 441 pp.

Rees, David D., and Dick, Everett. *Union College; Fifty Years of Service.* Lincoln: Union College Pr., 1941. 230 pp.

University of Nebraska

Aughey, Samuel. *The Ideas and the Men That Created the University of Nebraska.* Lincoln: Journal Company, State Printers, 1881. 23 pp.

Berquist, David H. "The Latin School and the Emergence of a State University in Nebraska: A History of Preparatory Education at the University of Nebraska, 1871-1897." Ed.D. diss., University of Nebraska, 1973. 223 pp. *Dissertation Abstracts International,* vol. 34A, p. 3930.

Biehn, Albert L. "The Development of the University of Nebraska, 1871-1900." Master's thesis, University of Nebraska, 1934. 183 pp.

Manley, Robert N. *Centennial History of the University of Nebraska.* 2 vols. Lincoln: University of Nebraska Pr., 1969.

Nebraska. University. *Semi-Centennial Anniversary Book. The University of Nebraska, 1867-1919.* Lincoln: The University, 1919. 144 pp.

University of Nebraska at Omaha

Campen, Lillian H. "The Early History of the University of Omaha." Master's thesis, University of Nebraska at Omaha, 1951. 148 pp.

Thompson, Tommy R. *A History of the University of Nebraska at Omaha, 1908-1983.* Omaha: University of Nebraska at Omaha, 1983. 160 pp.

York College

Larsen, Dale R. "A History of York College." Ed.D. diss., University of Nebraska, 1966. 221 pp. *Dissertation Abstracts,* vol. 27A, p. 3293.

NEVADA

University of Nevada

Church, J. E., Jr., ed. *Nevada State University Tri-decennial Celebration, May 28 to June 2, 1904.* Reno: Barndollar and Durley, 1904. 204 pp.

Doten, Samuel B. *An Illustrated History of the University of Nevada.* Carson City: University of Nevada, 1924. 235 pp.

Hulse, James W. *University of Nevada: A Centennial History.* Reno: University of Nevada Pr., 1974. 258 pp.

NEW HAMPSHIRE

Colby-Sawyer College

Rowe, Henry K. *A Centennial History, 1837-1937, Colby Academy.* New London: Colby Junior College, 1937. 435 pp.

Dartmouth College

Brown, Samuel G. *An Historical Discourse, Delivered before the Alumni of Dartmouth College, July 21, 1869, One Hundred Years after the Founding of That Institution.* Hanover: Printed at the Dartmouth Pr., 1870. 38 pp.

Chase, Frederick. *A History of Dartmouth College and the Town of Hanover, New Hampshire.* 2d ed. Brattleboro, Vt.: Vermont Printing Co., 1928.

--------. *A History of Dartmouth College, 1815-1909.* Concord: The Rumford Pr., 1913. 725 pp.

Crosby, Nathan. *The First Half Century of Dartmouth College: Being Historical Collections and Personal Reminiscences.* Hanover: J. B. Parker, 1876. 56 pp.

Dartmouth College. *Centennial Celebration at Dartmouth College, July 21, 1869.* Hanover: J. B. Parker, 1870. 101 pp.

--------. *150 Years of Dartmouth College, an Account of the Celebration of the Sesqui-Centennial Anniversary of the Founding of the College.* Boston: Pinkham Pr., 1921. 169 pp.

Dickey, John S. *Eleazar Wheelock, 1711-1779, Daniel Webster, 1782-1852, and Their Pioneer Dartmouth College.* New York: Newcomen Society in North America, 1954. 28 pp.

Hill, Ralph N. *The College on the Hill; A Dartmouth Chronology.* Hanover: Dartmouth Pubns., 1964. 357 pp.

Hill, William C., comp. *Dartmouth Traditions; Being a Compilation of Facts and Events Connected with the History of Dartmouth College and the Lives of Its Graduates, from the Early Founding of the College to the Present Day.* Hanover: Dartmouth Pr., 1901. 213 pp.

Quint, Wilder D. *The Story of Dartmouth.* Boston: Little, Brown, 1921. 285 pp.

Richardson, Leon B. *History of Dartmouth College.* 2 vols. Hanover: Dartmouth College, 1932.

Smith, Baxter P. *The History of Dartmouth College.* Boston: Houghton, Osgood and Co., 1878. 474 pp.

--------. *The Origin of Dartmouth College; Its Progress during a Century; And Its Various Relations to History.* Cambridge: Riverside Pr., 1877.

Wheelock, John. *Sketches of the History of Dartmouth College and Moors' Charity School.* n.p., 1815. 88 pp.

Franklin Pierce College

DiPietro, Frank S. "Franklin Pierce College: A Case Study." Ed.D. diss., Boston University, 1971. 260 pp. *Dissertation Abstracts International,* vol. 32A, p. 1827.

Keene State College

Smart, James G. *Striving: Keene State College, 1909-1984: The History of a Small Public Institution.* Canaan, N. H.: Phoenix Pub., 1984. 350 pp.

Rivier College

Cormier, Marie C. "A Brief History of Rivier College, 1933-1953." Master's thesis, Rivier College, 1955. 71 pp.

Saint Anselm College

McKeon, Valarie A. "History of Saint Anselm College: 1889-1985." Ph.D. diss., Boston College, 1985. 485 pp. *Dissertation Abstracts International,* vol. 46A, p. 3628.

University of New Hampshire

Bardwell, John D., and Bergeron, Ronald P. *Images of a University: A Photographic History of the University of New Hampshire.* Durham, N. H.: University of New Hampshire, 1984. 127 pp.

History of the University of New Hampshire, 1866-1941. Durham, N. H.: University of New Hampshire, 1941. 333 pp.

Johnson, Eldon L. *From Turnip Patch to University; The University of New Hampshire.* New York: Newcomen Society in North America, 1956. 28 pp.

Sackett, Everett B. *New Hampshire's University: The Story of a New England Land-Grant College.* Somersworth: New Hampshire Publishing Co., 1974. 210 pp.

Walker, Joseph B. *Genesis of the N. H. College of Agriculture and the Mechanic Arts: An Historical Address at the Dedication of the New Hampshire College of Agriculture and the Mechanic Arts at Durham, on*

Wednesday, August 30, 1893. Concord, N. H.: Printed by the Republican Pr., 1894. 15 pp.

NEW JERSEY

Alma White College (Closed 1979)

Lawrence, Evan J. "Alma White College: A History of Its Relationship to the Development of the Pillar of Fire." Ed.D. diss., Columbia University, 1966. 152 pp. *Dissertation Abstracts,* vol. 27A, p. 908.

Bloomfield College

Taylor, Harry T. *Bloomfield College; The First Century: 1868-1968.* Bloomfield, N. J.: Bloomfield College, 1970. 228 pp.

Centenary College

Custard, Leila R. *Through Golden Years, 1867-1943: A History of Centenary, Published for the Seventy-Fifth Anniversary.* New York: Lewis Historical Publishing Co., 1947. 269 pp.

College of Saint Elizabeth

McEniry, Blanche M. *Three Score and Ten; History of the College of Saint Elizabeth, 1899-1969.* Convent Station, N. J.: College of Saint Elizabeth, 1969. 136 pp.

Drew University

Cunningham, John T. *University in the Forest; The Story of Drew University.* Florham Park, N. J.: Afton Publishing Co., 1972. 288 pp.

Sitterly, Charles F. *The Building of Drew University.* New York: Methodist Book Concern, 1938. 302 pp.

Evelyn College (Closed)

Healy, Frances P. "A History of Evelyn College for Women, Princeton,

New Jersey, 1887 to 1897." Ph.D. diss., Ohio State University, 1967. 207 pp. *Dissertation Abstracts,* vol. 28A, p. 3478.

Fairleigh Dickinson University

Lengyel, Emil, and Mackensen, Heina F. *The First Quarter Century; A History of Fairleigh Dickinson University, 1942-1967.* South Brunswick: A. S. Barnes, 1974. 282 pp.

Sammartino, Peter. *I Dreamed a College.* South Brunswick: A. S. Barnes, 1977. 172 pp.

--------. *Of Castles and Colleges; Notes Toward an Autobiography.* New York: A. S. Barnes, 1972. 189 pp.

Georgian Court College

Geis, M. Christina. *Georgian Court: An Estate of the Gilded Age.* Philadelphia: Art Alliance Pr., 1982. 195 pp.

Jersey City State College

Sherman, John. "The Origin and Development of Jersey City State College, 1927-1962." Ed.D. diss., New York University, 1968. 338 pp. *Dissertation Abstracts,* vol. 29A, p. 420.

Kean College of New Jersey

Raichle, Donald R. *From a Normal Beginning: The Origins of Kean College of New Jersey.* Rutherford, N. J.: Fairleigh Dickinson University Pr., 1980. 432 pp.

Montclair State College

Davis, Earl C. "The Origin and Development of the New Jersey State Teachers College at Montclair, 1908-1951." Ph.D. diss., New York University, 1954. 235 pp. *Dissertation Abstracts,* vol. 15, p. 221.

New Brunswick Theological Seminary

Bruins, Elton J. "The New Brunswick Theological Seminary, 1884-1959." Ph.D. diss., New York University, 1962. 223 pp. *Dissertation*

Abstracts, vol. 24, p. 1719.

Hageman, Howard G. *Two Centuries Plus: The Story of New Brunswick Seminary.* Grand Rapids, Mich.: W. B. Eerdmans Publishing Co., 1984. 215 pp.

Raven, John H., comp. *Biographical Record, Theological Seminary New Brunswick, 1784-1911.* New Brunswick: Printed for the Seminary by the Rev. Archibald Laidlie Memorial Fund, 1912. 305 pp.

--------. *Biographical Record, Theological Seminary, New Brunswick, New Jersey, 1784-1934.* 2d ed. New Brunswick: Printed for the Seminary by the Rev. Laidlie Memorial Fund, 1934. 276 pp.

Princeton Theological Seminary

A Brief History of the Theological Seminary of the Presbyterian Church, at Princeton, New Jersey: Together with Its Constitution, Bye-Laws,etc. Princeton: Printed by John Bogart, 1838. 45 pp.

Clutter, Ronald T. "The Reorientation of Princeton Theological Seminary, 1900-1929." Th.D. diss., Dallas Theological Seminary, 1982. 249 pp.

Haines, George L. "The Princeton Theological Seminary, 1925-1960." Ph.D. diss., New York University, 1966. 263 pp. *Dissertation Abstracts,* vol. 27, p. 2599.

Scovel, Raleigh D. "Orthodoxy in Princeton: A Social and Intellectual History of Princeton Theological Seminary, 1812-1860." Ph.D. diss., University of California, Berkeley, 1970. 358 pp. *Dissertation Abstracts International,* vol. 31A, p. 5336.

Princeton University

Alexander, Samuel D. *Princeton College during the Eighteenth Century.* New York: A. D. F. Randolph & Co., 1872. 326 pp.

Breese, Gerald W. *Princeton University Land, 1752-1984.* Princeton: Princeton University, 1986. 261 pp.

Collins, Varnum L. *Princeton.* New York: Oxford University Pr., 1914. 416 pp.

--------. *Princeton, Past and Present.* Rev. ed. Princeton: Princeton University Pr., 1945. 172 pp.

Dod, William A. *History of the College of New Jersey, from Its Commencement, A. D., 1746-1783.* Princeton: J. T. Robinson, 1844. 50 pp.

Edgar, Robert. *An Historical Sketch of the College of New Jersey.* Philadelphia: J. M. Wilson, 1859. 66 pp.

Gambee, Robert. *Princeton.* New York: W. W. Norton, 1987. 272 pp.

Greiff, Constance M.; Gibbons, Mary W.; and Menzies, Elizabeth G. C. *Princeton Architecture; A Pictorial History of Town and Campus.* Princeton: Princeton University Pr., 1967. 200 pp.

Lane, Wheaton J., ed. *Pictorial History of Princeton.* Princeton: Princeton University Pr., 1947. 199 pp.

Leitch, Alexander. *A Princeton Companion.* Princeton: Princeton University Pr., 1978. 559 pp.

McCosh, James. *Twenty Years of Princeton College.* New York: Scribner, 1888. 68 pp.

MacLean, John. *History of the College of New Jersey from Its Origin in 1746 to the Commencement of 1854.* 2 vols. Philadelphia: J. B. Lippincott, 1877.

Norris, Edwin M. *The Story of Princeton.* Boston: Little, Brown, 1917. 270 pp.

Osgood, Charles G. *Lights in Nassau Hall; A Book of Bicentennial Princeton, 1746-1946.* Princeton: Princeton University Pr., 1951. 276 pp.

--------. *The Modern Princeton.* Princeton: Princeton University Pr., 1947. 158 pp.

Princeton College: Published by Authority of the Alumni Association of Philadelphia. Philadelphia: J. B. Chandler, 1869. 12 pp.

Princeton University. *The Princeton Book: A Series of Sketches Pertaining to the History, Organization and Present Condition of the College of New Jersey.* Boston: Houghton, 1879. 457 pp.

Schmidt, George P. *Princeton and Rutgers: The Two Colonial Colleges of New Jersey.* Princeton: Van Nostrand, 1964. 137 pp.

Selden, William K. *Princeton the Best Old Place of All: Vignettes of*

Princeton University, 1884, 1934, 1984. Princeton: Office of Printing Services, Princeton University, 1987. 118 pp.

Wallace, George R. *Princeton Sketches. The History of Nassau Hall.* New York: Putnam, 1893. 200 pp.

Wertenbaker, Thomas J. *Princeton, 1746-1896.* Princeton: Princeton University Pr., 1846. 424 pp.

Rider College

Brower, Walter A., Jr. "Rider College: The First One Hundred Years." Ed.D. diss., Temple University, 1965. 280 pp. *Dissertation Abstracts,* vol. 26, p. 4419.

Rutgers, The State University of New Jersey

Bennett, Hugh F. "A History of the University of Newark, 1908-1946." Ph.D. diss., New York University, 1956. 262 pp. *Dissertation Abstracts,* vol. 16, p. 2083.

Demarest, William H. S. *A History of Rutgers College, 1766-1924.* New Brunswick: Rutgers College, 1924. 570 pp.

History of Rutgers College, or, An Account of the Union of Rutgers College, and the Theological Seminary of the General Synod of the Reformed Dutch Church. New York: Anderson & Smith, Printers, 1833. 24 pp.

Holsten, George H. *Bicentennial Year: The Story of a Rutgers Celebration.* New Brunswick: Rutgers University Pr., 1968. 294 pp.

Lukac, George J., ed. *Aloud to Alma Mater.* New Brunswick: Rutgers University Pr., 1966. 241 pp.

McCormick, Richard P. *Rutgers: A Bicentennial History.* New Brunswick: Rutgers University Pr., 1966. 336 pp.

Moffatt, Michael. *The Rutgers Picture Book: An Illustrated History of Student Life in the Changing College and University.* New Brunswick: Rutgers University Pr., 1985. 265 pp.

Rutgers College, New Brunswick, N. J. *The Centennial Celebration of Rutgers College, June 21, 1870.* Albany, N. Y.: J. Munsell, 1870. 98 pp.

Schmidt, George P. *Douglass College; A History.* New Brunswick: Rutgers University Pr., 1968. 282 pp.

--------. *Princeton and Rutgers: The Two Colonial Colleges of New Jersey.* Princeton: Van Nostrand, 1964. 137 pp.

Saint Peter's College

Cronin, Richard J. *Jesuits and the Beginning of St. Peter's College.* Itasca, Ill.: Peacock Publications, 1983. 91 pp.

O'Donnell, Jim. *Jesuit College in Jersey City.* Jersey City, N. J.: Saint Peter's College, 1972.

Seton Hall University

Kennelly, Edward F. "A Historical Study of Seton Hall College." Ph.D. diss., New York University, 1944. 201 pp.

Marshall, William F. *A Sketch of Seton Hall College.* South Orange, N. J.: Photo Engraving Co., 1895. 97 pp.

The Summit of a Century: The Centennial Story of Seton Hall University, 1856-1956. South Orange, N. J.: Seton Hall University, 1956. 108 pp.

Stevens Institute of Technology

Furman, Franklin D. *Morton Memorial; A History of the Stevens Institute of Technology.* Hoboken, N. J.: Stevens Institute of Technology, 1905. 641 pp.

Rogers, Kenneth C. *Fundamentals First: The Story of Stevens Institute of Technology.* New York: Newcomen Society in North America, 1979. 28 pp.

Stevens Institute of Technology, Hoboken, N. J. Alumni Association. *Stevens 75th Anniversary, Commemorating Seventy-Five Years of Accomplishment in Engineering Education.* Hoboken, N. J.: The Alumni Association of the Stevens Institute of Technology, 1945. 83 pp.

Stockton State College

Alton, Elizabeth B. *The Stockton Story: A History of the Founding of*

Richard Stockton State College. Pomona, N. J.: Richard Stockton State College Alumni Association, 1983. 140 pp.

Trenton State College

Fromm, Glenn E. "A History of the New Jersey State Teachers College at Trenton, 1855-1950." Ed.D. diss., New York University, 1951. 526 pp. *Dissertation Abstracts,* vol. 11, p. 565.

Union County College

Raichle, Donald R. *New Jersey's Union College: A History, 1933-1983.* Rutherford, N. J.: Fairleigh Dickinson University Pr., 1983. 270 pp.

Upsala College

Calman, Alvin R. *Upsala College: The Early Years.* New York: Vantage Pr., 1983. 206 pp.

Westminister Choir College

Bristol, Lee H. *Westminister Choir College: A College of Music to Sing About.* New York: Newcomen Society in North America, 1965. 24 pp.

Page, Patricia A. "The Westminister Choir College." Master's thesis, Union Theological Seminary, 1953. 62 pp.

Schisler, Charles H. "A History of Westminister Choir College." Ph.D. diss., Indiana University, 1976. 566 pp. *Dissertation Abstracts International,* vol. 37A, p. 6834.

William Paterson College of New Jersey

White, Kenneth B. *Paterson State College; A History, 1855-1966.* Paterson: Student Cooperative Association of Paterson State College, 1967. 208 pp.

NEW MEXICO

College of Santa Fe

Saint Michael's College, Santa Fe, N. M. *75 Years of Service, 1859-1934: An Historical Sketch of Saint Michael's College.* Santa Fe, N. M.: Saint Michael's College, 1934. 139 pp.

Eastern New Mexico University

Golden, Floyd D. *Eastern New Mexico University: The Golden Years, 1928-1960.* Portales: Eastern New Mexico University, 1975. 142 pp.

Mann, Aubrey E. "The History and Development of Eastern New Mexico University." Ed.D. diss., University of Northern Colorado, 1959. 233 pp.

New Mexico Highlands University

Price, Hugh W. "A History of the New Mexico Normal University: 1893-1931." Master's thesis, New Mexico Normal University, 1932. 175 pp.

New Mexico Institute of Mining and Technology

Christiansen, Paige W. *Of Earth and Sky; A History of New Mexico Institute of Mining and Technology, 1889-1964.* Socorro: New Mexico Institute of Mining and Technology, 1964. 107 pp.

New Mexico Military Institute

Jackman, Eugene T. "The New Mexico Military Institute, 1891-1966: A Critical History." Ph.D. diss., University of Mississippi, 1967. 525 pp. *Dissertation Abstracts,* vol. 28A, p. 110.

Kelly, James R. *A History of New Mexico Military Institute, 1891-1941.* Albuquerque: University of New Mexico Pr., 1953. 404 pp.

New Mexico State University

Kropp, Simon F. *That All May Learn; New Mexico State University, 1888-1964.* Las Cruces: New Mexico State University, 1972. 401 pp.

University of New Mexico

Horn, Calvin. *The University in Turmoil and Transition: Crisis Decades at the University of New Mexico.* Albuquerque: Rocky Mountain Publishing Co., 1981. 361 pp.

Hughes, Dorothy. *Pueblo on the Mesa, the First Fifty Years at the University of New Mexico.* Albuquerque: University of New Mexico Pr., 1939. 151 pp.

Popejoy, Thomas L. "U. of N. M.," University of New Mexico, a Calculated Risk. New York: Newcomen Society in North America, 1952. 24 pp.

Reeve, Frank D. "History of the University of New Mexico." Master's thesis, University of New Mexico, 1928. 271 pp.

Western New Mexico University

Overturf, Donald S. "The History of New Mexico Western College Silver City." Ph.D. diss., University of Nebraska at Lincoln, 1966. 759 pp. *Dissertation Abstracts,* vol. 21, p. 2562.

NEW YORK

Adelphi University

Barrows, Chester L. *Fifty Years of Adelphi College.* Garden City: Adelphi College Pr., 1946. 255 pp.

Albany Medical College

Beebe, Richard T. *Albany Medical College and Albany Hospital: A History, 1839-1982.* Albany: New Art Printers, 1983. 458 pp.

Alfred University

Norwood, John N. *Fiat Lux; The Story of Alfred University with Its Constituent and Affiliated Schools.* Alfred: Alfred University, 1957. 287 pp.

Owler, Martha R. T., comp. *Semi-Centennial Souvenir; Alfred University, the Mountain College; Its Patriotic Aim and Noble Work, 1857-1907.* n.p., 1907. 82 pp.

Auburn Community College

Skinner, Albert T. "A History of Auburn Community College during Its Founding Period, 1953-1959." Ph.D. diss., Syracuse University, 1961. 540 pp. *Dissertation Abstracts,* vol. 23, p. 145.

Bard College

Hopson, George B. *Reminiscences of St. Stephen's College, Annandale, New York.* New York: S. Gorham, 1910. 54 pp.

Kline, Reamer. *Education for the Common Good: A History of Bard College -- The First 100 Years, 1860-1960.* Annandale-on-Hudson, N. Y.: The College, 1982. 244 pp.

Barnard College

Barnard College. *A History of Barnard College, Published in Honor of the Seventy-Fifth Anniversary of the College.* New York: Barnard College, 1964. 126 pp.

Meyer, Annie N. *Barnard Beginnings.* Boston: Houghton Mifflin, 1935. 196 pp.

Miller, Alice D. *Barnard College: The First Fifty Years.* New York: Columbia University Pr., 1939. 194 pp.

White, Marian C. *A History of Barnard College.* New York: Columbia University Pr., 1954. 222 pp.

Bernard M. Baruch College of the City University of New York

Berrol, Selma C. *Getting Down to Business: Baruch College in the City of New York, 1847-1987.* Westport, Conn.: Greenwood Pr., 1989. 267 pp.

Brooklyn College of the City University of New York

Coulton, Thomas E. *A City College in Action; Struggle and Achievement at Brooklyn College, 1930-1955.* New York: Harper, 1955. 233 pp.

Horowitz, Murray M. *Brooklyn College - The First Half Century.* New York: Brooklyn College Pr., 1981. 290 pp.

Canisius College

Brady, Charles A. *The First Hundred Years: Canisius College, 1870-1979.* Buffalo: Holling Pr., 1969. 388 pp.

Demske, James M. *A Promise of Quality: The First 100 Years of Canisius College.* New York: Newcomen Society in North America, 1970. 32 pp.

Harney, Thomas E. *AMDG, a History of Canisius College, 1883-1913: Under the New York State Regents' Charter, on Washington Street, Buffalo.* Smithtown, N. Y.: Exposition Pr., 1981. 171 pp.

--------. *Canisius College: The First Nine Years, 1870-1879.* New York: Vantage Pr., 1971. 259 pp.

City College of the City University of New York

Cozenza, Mario E. *The Establishment of the College of the City of New York as the Free Academy in 1847.* New York: The Associate Alumni of the College of the City of New York, 1925. 234 pp.

Rudy, Willis. "The College of the City of New York: A History, 1847-1947." Ph.D. diss., Columbia University, 1950. 492 pp.

--------. *The College of the City of New York: A History, 1847-1947.* New York: Arno Pr., 1977. 492 pp.

City University of New York

Gordon, Sheila C. "The Transformation of the City University of New York, 1945-1970." Ph.D. diss., Columbia University, 1975. 322 pp. *Dissertation Abstracts International,* vol. 38A, p. 4325.

Colgate University

Colgate University. *The Colgate University Centennial Celebration, 1818-1919.* Hamilton, N. Y.: The University, 1920. 183 pp.

Colgate University, Hamilton, N. Y. *The First Half Century of Madison University, (1819-1869).* New York: Sheldon & Co., 1872. 503 pp.

Rosenberger, Jesse L. *Rochester and Colgate; Historical Backgrounds of the Two Universities.* Chicago: University of Chicago Pr., 1925. 173 pp.

Williams, Howard D. *A History of Colgate University, 1819-1969.* New York: Van Nostrand, 1969. 358 pp.

--------. "The History of Colgate University to 1869." Ph.D. diss., Harvard University, 1949. 171 pp.

College of Saint Rose

Soulier, Catherine F. "A History of the College of Saint Rose, Albany, New York, 1920-1950." Master's thesis, College of Saint Rose, 1951. 140 pp.

Columbia University

Arrowsmith, Robert. *Columbia of Yesterday, 1754-1897.* n.p., 1926. 32 pp.

Burgess, John W. *Reminiscences of an American Scholar; The Beginnings of Columbia University.* New York: Columbia University Pr., 1934. 430 pp.

Columbia University. *Historical Sketch and Present Condition.* New York: n.p., 1893. 94 pp.

--------. *An Historical Sketch of Columbia College, in the City of New York, 1754-1876.* New York: Printed for the College, 1876. 243 pp.

--------. *The Rise of a University.* 2 vols. New York: Columbia University Pr., 1937.

Coon, Horace. *Columbia, Colossus on the Hudson.* New York: Dutton, 1947. 388 pp.

First, Wesley, ed. *Columbia Remembered.* 1 vol. New York: Columbia

University Pr., 1967.

--------. *University on the Heights.* New York: Doubleday, 1969. 199 pp.

A History of Columbia College on Morningside. New York: Columbia University Pr., 1954. 284 pp.

A History of Columbia University, 1754-1904. New York: Columbia University Pr., 1904. 493 pp.

Humphrey, David C. *From King's College to Columbia, 1746-1800.* New York: Columbia University Pr., 1976. 413 pp.

--------. "King's College in the City of New York, 1754-1776." Ph.D. diss., Northwestern University, 1968. 669 pp. *Dissertation Abstracts,* vol. 29A, p. 2643.

Jay, John. *Columbia College.* New York: Alumni Association of Columbia College, 1876. 48 pp.

Keppel, Frederick P. *Columbia.* New York: Oxford University Pr., 1914. 297 pp.

Moore, Clement C. *The Early History of Columbia College.* New York: Columbia University Pr., 1940. 41 pp.

Moore, George H. *Collegium Regale Novi Eboraci. The Origin and Early History of Columbia College.* New York: Printed for the Author, 1890. 46 pp.

Moore, Nathaniel F. *An Historical Sketch of Columbia College, in the City of New York.* New York: Printed for Columbia College, 1846. 126 pp.

Pine, John B. *King's College and the Early Days of Columbia College.* New York: University Printing Office, Columbia University, 1917. 20 pp.

--------. *King's College, Now Columbia University.* New York: J. J. Little, 1896.

Progress and Promise of Columbia University in the City of New York. New York: n.p., 1967. 144 pp.

Robson, John W., ed. *A Guide to Columbia University, with Some Account of Its History and Traditions.* New York: Columbia University Pr., 1937. 213 pp.

Concordia College

Steinberg, Allan G. *We Will Remember: Concordia College, the First Century.* Bronxville: Concordia College, 1981. 120 pp.

Cornell University

Becker, Carl L. *Cornell University: Founders and the Founding.* Ithaca: Cornell University Pr., 1943. 246 pp.

Berry, Romeyn. *Behind the Ivy; Fifty Years in One University with Visits to Sundry Others.* Ithaca: Cornell University Pr., 1950. 337 pp.

Bishop, Morris. *A History of Cornell.* Ithaca: Cornell University Pr., 1962. 663 pp.

Colman, Gould P. *Education and Agriculture; A History of the New York State College of Agriculture.* Ithaca: Cornell University, 1963. 603 pp.

Hewett, Waterman T. *Cornell University, a History.* 4 vols. New York: University Publishing Society, 1905.

Parsons, Kermit C. *The Cornell Campus: A History of Its Planning & Development.* Ithaca: Cornell University Pr., 1968. 352 pp.

Poole, Murray E. *A Story Historical of Cornell University with Biographies of Distinguished Cornellians.* Ithaca: The Cayuga Pr., 1916. 227 pp.

Wright, Albert H. *Pre-Cornell and Early Cornell.* Ithaca: n.p., n.d.

Young, Charles V. P., comp. *Cornell in Pictures: The First Century.* Ithaca: Quill and Dagger Alumni Association, 1965. 176 pp.

Daemen College

Dunn, Georgia. *Hillsides, a Memoir; 1948-1972; The First Twenty-Four Years of Rosary Hill College.* Buffalo: Rosary Hill College, 1973. 326 pp.

Elmira College

Barber, William C. *Elmira College, the First Hundred Years.* New York: McGraw-Hill, 1955. 290 pp.

Meltzer, Gilbert W. "Beginnings of Elmira College, 1851-1868." Master's thesis, University of Rochester, 1941. 251 pp.

--------. *The Beginnings of Elmira College, 1851-1868.* Elmira, N. Y.: Commercial Pr., 1941. 146 pp.

Fordham University

Gannon, Robert I. *Up to the Present; The Story of Fordham.* Garden City, N. Y.: Doubleday, 1967. 332 pp.

McGinley, Laurence J. *Fordham, Part of an Ancient Tradition.* New York: Newcomen Society in North America, 1954. 28 pp.

Taaffe, Thomas G. *A History of St. John's College, Fordham, N. Y.* New York: The Catholic Publication Society, 1891. 154 pp.

General Theological Seminary

Dawley, Powel M. *The Story of the General Theological Seminary; A Sesquicentennial History, 1817-1967.* New York: Oxford University Pr., 1969. 390 pp.

Genesee Community College

Peters, David E. *The Founding of Genesee Community College.* Batavia, N. Y.: Genesee Community College, 1970. 75 pp.

--------. "The Founding of Genesee Community College: A Case Study." Ph.D. diss., State University of New York at Buffalo, 1969. 266 pp. *Dissertation Abstracts,* vol. 30A, p. 2267.

Hamilton College

Allison, Charles E. *A Historical Sketch of Hamilton College, Clinton, New York.* Yonkers, N. Y.: n.p., 1889. 85 pp.

A Documentary History of Hamilton College. Clinton, N. Y.: The College, 1922. 292 pp.

Pilkington, Walter. *Hamilton College, 1812-1962.* Clinton, N. Y.: Hamilton College, 1962. 311 pp.

Hartwick College

Heins, Henry H. *Throughout All the Years, the Bicentennial Story of Hartwick in America, 1746-1946.* Oneonta, N. Y.: Board of Trustees of Hartwick College, 1946. 239 pp.

Schmitthenner, John W. "The Origin and Educational Contribution of Hartwick Seminary." Ph.D. diss., New York University, 1934. 185 pp.

Hebrew Union College-Jewish Institute of Religion

Hebrew Union College-Jewish Institute of Religion. *Jubilee Volume (1875-1925).* Cincinnati: n.p., 1925. 521 pp.

Hobart and William Smith Colleges

Brown, Alan W. *Hobart College; Oldest Episcopal College in U. S. A.* New York: Newcomen Society in North America, 1956. 32 pp.

Dunfee, Walter H., and Schoen-Rene, Otto E. *William Smith College, 1908-1958: A History.* Geneva, N. Y.: Hobart and William Smith Colleges, 1959. 64 pp.

Smith, Warren H. *Hobart and William Smith; The History of Two Colleges.* Geneva, N. Y.: Hobart and William Smith Colleges, 1972. 299 pp.

Turk, Milton H. *Hobart; The Story of a Hundred Years, 1822-1922.* Geneva. N. Y.: Hobart College, 1921. 154 pp.

Hofstra University

Lord, Clifford L. *The Hofstra Adventure; The Story of an Emerging University.* New York: Newcomen Society in North America, 1970. 28 pp.

--------. *The Hofstra Story, 1935-1971.* Hampstead, N. Y.: Hofstra University Pr., 1972. 24 pp.

Houghton College

Wilson, Kenneth L., ed. *Consider the Years: Houghton College, 1883-1958.* n.p., 1958. 40 pp.

Hunter College of the City University of New York

Patterson, Samuel W. *Hunter College; Eighty-Five Years of Service.* New York: Lantern Pr., 1955. 263 pp.

Ithaca College

Harcourt, John. *The Ithaca College Story.* Ithaca, N. Y.: Ithaca College, 1983. 153 pp.

Jamestown Community College

Schlifke, William H. "The Beginnings of the Jamestown Community College, Jamestown, New York." Master's thesis, State University of New York at Buffalo, 1953. 84 pp.

Jewish Theological Seminary of America

Soltis-Cohen, Solomon. *The Jewish Theological Seminary, Past and Future; Address Delivered at the Twenty-Fifth Annual Commencement, New York, June 2, 1918.* New York: The Jewish Theological Seminary of America, 1919. 46 pp.

The Juilliard School

Damrosch, Frank H. *Institute of Musical Art: 1905-1926.* New York: Privately Printed for Juilliard School of Music, 1936. 272 pp.

Hayes, Marie T. "The History of the Juilliard School from Its Inception to 1973." Master's thesis, Catholic University of America, 1974. 216 pp.

Keuka College

Africa, Philip A. *Keuka College: A History.* Valley Forge: Judson Pr., 1973. 320 pp.

Griffin, Zebina F. *The Builders of Keuka College.* Penn Yan, N. Y.: Penn Yan Printing Co., 1937. 75 pp.

Le Moyne College

Kenny, James E. *A History of Le Moyne College: The First Twenty-Five Years.* Syracuse: J. E. Kenney, 1972. 97 pp.

Long Island University

Gantner, Elliot S. M. "Long Island: The History of a Relevant and Responsive University, 1926-1968." Ed.D. diss., Columbia University, 1975. 732 pp. *Dissertation Abstracts International,* vol. 35A, p. 7679.

Manhattan College

Casimir Gabriel, Brother. *The Tree Bore Fruit: Manhattan College, 1853-1953.* Riverdale, N. Y.: Manhattan College, 1953. 159 pp.

Costello, Gabriel. *The Arches of the Years: Manhattan College, 1853-1979.* Bronx, N. Y.: Manhattan College, 1980. 382 pp.

Sullivan, Jeremiah S. *Manhattan College.* New York: Newcomen Society in North America, 1978. 20 pp.

Manhattan School of Music

Schenck, Janet W. *Adventure in Music, a Reminiscence; Manhattan School of Music, 1918-1960.* New York: Manhattan School of Music, 1961. 107 pp.

Marymount College

Doran, Micheileen J. "A History of Marymount College, Tarrytown." Ed.D. diss., Columbia University, Teachers College, 1979. 393 pp. *Dissertation Abstracts International,* vol. 40A, p. 5333.

New School for Social Research

Rutkoff, Peter M., and Scott, William B. *New School: A History of the New School for Social Research.* New York: Free Pr., 1986. 314 pp.

New York City Technical College of the City University of New York

Frommer, Harvey. *City Tech: The First 40 Years.* Brooklyn: Technical College Pr., 1986. 192 pp.

New York Law School

Thornton, John V. *New York Law School: A Heritage.* New York: New York Law School, 1978. 24 pp.

New York Theological Seminary

Pazmino, Robert W. *The Seminary in the City: A Study of New York Theological Seminary.* Lanham, Md.: University Press of America, 1988. 135 pp.

New York University

Chamberlain, Joshua L., ed. *New York University: Its History, Influence, Equipment and Characteristics, with Benefactors, Officers and Alumni.* 2 vols. Boston: R. Herndon Co., 1901-

Hester, James M. *New York University; The Urban University Coming of Age.* New York: Newcomen Society in North America, 1971. 24 pp.

Jones, Theodore F. *New York University, 1832-1932.* New York: New York University Pr., 1933. 459 pp.

Niagara County Community College

Millar, Graham. *Niagara County Community College: A Brief History.* Cambria, N. Y.: Niagara County Community College, 1982. 69 pp.

Niagara University

McKey, Joseph P. *History of Niagara University, Seminary of Our Lady of Angels, 1856-1931.* Niagara: Niagara University, 1931. 377 pp.

That All May Know Thee; Addresses Delivered on the Occasions Commemorating the One Hundredth Anniversary of the Establishment of Niagara University. Niagara: The University, 1956. 69 pp.

Pace University

Pace: *The First 75 Years.* New York: Pace University, n.d. 21 pp.

Packer Collegiate Institute (Closed 1972)

Nickerson, Marjorie L. *A Long Way Forward; The First Hundred Years of the Packer Collegiate Institute.* Brooklyn: Packer Collegiate Institute, 1945. 284 pp.

Parsons School of Design

Jones, Marjorie F. "A History of the Parsons School of Design, 1896-1966." Ph.D. diss., New York University, 1968. 465 pp. *Dissertation Abstracts International,* vol. 30A, p. 148.

Levy, David C. "An Historical Study of Parsons School of Design and Its Merger/Affiliation with the New School for Social Research." Ph.D. diss., New York University, 1979. 395 pp. *Dissertation Abstracts International,* vol. 40, p. 5674.

Paul Smiths College of Arts and Science

Woods, James R. *Paul Smith's College, 1937-1980: A Saga of Strife, Struggle, and Success.* Paul Smiths, N. Y.: The College, 1980. 275 pp.

Polytechnic University of New York

Brooklyn. Polytechnic Institute. *First Quarter Century of the Brooklyn Collegiate and Polytechnic Institute.* Brooklyn: n.p., 1880. 27 pp.

--------. *The Polytechnic Institute of Brooklyn: Retrospect and Outlook.* Brooklyn: Issued by the Corporation, 1890. 25 pp.

Bugliarello, George. *Towards the Technological University: The Story of Polytechnic Institute of New York.* New York: Newcomen Society in North America, 1975. 36 pp.

Kastendieck, Miles M. *The Story of Poly.* Wilmington: H. Matthews and Co., 1940. 255 pp.

O'Connor, John J. *Polytechnic Institute of Brooklyn: An Account of the Educational Purposes and Development of the Institute during Its*

First Century. Brooklyn: Polytechnic Institute of Brooklyn, 1956? 20 pp.

Queens College of the City University of New York

Queens College, Flushing, N. Y. *Queens College of the City University of New York, 1837-1962.* Flushing: Twenty-Fifth Anniversary Committee of Queens College, 1963. 76 pp.

Rensselaer Polytechnic Institute

Baker, Raymond P. *A Chapter in American Education; Rensselaer Polytechnic Institute, 1824-1924.* New York: Scribners, 1924. 170 pp.

Reznek, Samuel. *Education for a Technological Society; A Sesquicentennial History of Rensselaer Polytechnic Institute.* Troy: Rensselaer Polytechnic Institute, 1968. 520 pp.

Ricketts, Palmer C. *History of the Renssealaer Polytechnic Institute, 1824-1894.* New York: Wiley, 1895. 193 pp.

--------. *History of Rensselaer Polytechnic Institute, 1824-1914.* New York: Wiley, 1914. 269 pp.

--------. *History of Rensselaer Polytechnic Institute, 1824-1934.* 3d ed. New York: Wiley, 1934. 293 pp.

--------. *Rensselaer Polytechnic Institute; A Short History.* Troy: n.p., 1930. 28 pp.

Rochester Institute of Technology

Hoke, George W.. *Blazing New Trails, The Biography of a Pioneer in Education.* Rochester: Rochester Athenaeum and Mechanics Institute, 1937. 164 pp.

Rockefeller University

Corner, George W. *A History of the Rockefeller Institute, 1901-1953: Origins and Growth.* New York: Rochester Institute Pr., 1964. 635 pp.

Institute to University: A Seventy-Fifth Anniversary Colloquium, June 8, 1976. New York: Rockefeller University, 1977. 108 pp.

Roberts Wesleyan College

Pfouts, Neil E. *A History of Roberts Wesleyan College.* Master's thesis, University of Rochester, 1950. 218 pp.

Russell Sage College

Patton, Julia. *Russell Sage College, the First Twenty-Five Years, 1916-1941.* Troy: Press of W. Snyder, 1941. 237 pp.

Spears, George J. *Russell Sage College; The Second Quarter Century, 1941-1966.* Troy: Birkmayer, 1966. 263 pp.

St. Bonaventure University

Angelo, Mark V. "The History of St. Bonaventure University." Ph.D. diss., Fordham University, 1958.

--------. *The History of St. Bonaventure University.* St. Bonaventure: Franciscan Institute, 1961. 253 pp.

Hammon, Walter. *The First Bonaventure Men: The Early History of St. Bonaventure University and the Allegany Franciscans.* St. Bonaventure: St. Bonaventure University, 1958. 249 pp.

Herscher, Irenaeus J. *The History of St. Bonaventure University.* St. Bonaventure: The Franciscan Institute, 1951. 424 pp.

St. Francis College

Florentz, Christopher J., ed. *St. Francis College: The First One Hundred Years.* New York: St. Francis College, 1984. 165 pp.

St. John Fisher College

Haffey, Hugh J. *The Beginnings of St. John Fisher College.* Rochester, N. Y.: St. John Fisher College, 1977. 80 pp.

Saint Joseph's Seminary

Scanlan, Arthur J. *St. Joseph's Seminary, Dunwoodie, New York, 1896-1921, with an Account of the Other Seminaries of New York.* New York: The United States Catholic Historical Society, 1922. 237 pp.

St. Lawrence University

Black, Malcolm S. *Sixty Years of St. Lawrence.* Canton: St. Lawrence University, 1916. 375 pp.

Blankman, Edward J., and Cannon, Thurlow O. *The Scarlet and the Brown: A History of St. Lawrence University, 1856-1981.* Canton: St. Lawrence University, 1987. 285 pp.

Pink, Louis H., and Delmage, Rutherford E., eds. *Candle in the Wilderness; A Centennial History of the St. Lawrence University, 1856-1956.* New York: Appleton, 1957. 304 pp.

St. Lawrence University, Canton, N. Y. Class of 1916. *Sixty Years of Saint Lawrence.* Canton: St. Lawrence University, 1916. 375 pp.

St. Vladimir's Orthodox Theological Seminary

St. Vladimir's Orthodox Theological Seminary, New York. *Thirtieth Anniversary, St. Vladimir's Orthodox Theological Seminary, 1938-1968.* Tuckahoe, N. Y.: n.p., 1968. 49 pp.

Sarah Lawrence College

McDonough, Colleen. "The Founding of Sarah Lawrence College." Master's thesis, Sarah Lawrence College, 1978.

Seminary of the Immaculate Conception

Cantley, Michael J. *A City with Foundations: A History of the Seminary of the Immaculate Conception, 1930-1980.* Huntington, N. Y.: Seminary of the Immaculate Conception, 1980. 135 pp.

Siena College

Mooney, Donald J. "A History of Siena College from the Beginning to July, 1943." Master's thesis, Siena College, 1945. 57 pp.

Skidmore College

Hoffman, Allan M.. *History of an Idea.* Washington: University Press of America, 1981. 305 pp.

--------. "History of an Idea: Skidmore College, 1903-1925." Ed.D. diss., Columbia University, 1976. 267 pp. *Dissertation Abstracts International,* vol. 37A, p. 6312.

Palamountain, Joseph C. *"Such Growth Bespeaks the Work of Many Hands," the Story of Skidmore College.* New York: Newcomen Society in North America, 1976. 27 pp.

State University of New York at Albany

French, William M. *College of the Empire State; A Centennial History of the New York College for Teachers at Albany.* Albany: n.p., 1944. 271 pp.

Graves, Frank P. *The University of the State of New York; Its History and Functions.* Albany: The University of the State of New York Pr., 1931. 8 pp.

Hough, Franklin B. *Historical and Statistical Record of the University of the State of New York during the Century from 1784 to 1884.* Albany: Weed, Parsons and Co., 1885. 867 pp.

New York. State University, Albany. *An Historical Sketch of the State Normal College at Albany, N. Y. and a History of Its Graduates for Fifty Years, 1844-1894.* Albany: Brandow Printing Co., 1894. 350 pp.

--------. *A Historical Sketch of the State Normal School at Albany, New York and a History of Its Graduates for Forty Years.* Albany: Press for Barton Brandow, 1884. 234 pp.

Sherwood, Sidney. *The University of the State of New York: History of Higher Education in the State of New York.* Washington: U. S. Bureau of Education, 1900. 538 pp.

State Universtiy of New York at Binghamton

Hambalek, Stephen. *Alma Mater: A Popular History of Harpur College, 1946-1964.* Binghamton: State University of New York at Binghamton, 1975. 128 pp.

McIntire, Stephen W. *Harpur College in the Bartle Era.* Binghamton: Foundation of the State University of New York at Binghamton, 1975. 308 pp.

State University of New York College at Brockport

Butler, M. Alene. "A History of the Brockport Collegiate Institute, 1832 to 1867." Master's thesis, University of Rochester, 1939. 194 pp.

Dedman, W. Wayne. *Cherishing This Heritage; The Centennial History of the State University College at Brockport, New York.* New York: Appleton, 1969. 317 pp.

State University of New York at Buffalo

Park, Julian. *The Evolution of a College; A Century of Higher Education in Buffalo.* Buffalo: University of Buffalo, 1938. 101 pp.

--------. *A History of the University of Buffalo.* Buffalo: n.p., 1917. 87 pp.

State University College at Buffalo. *New York State Teachers College at Buffalo; A History, 1871-1946.* Buffalo: n.p., 1946. 183 pp.

State University of New York College at Cortland

Brush, Carey W. "The Cortland Normal School Response to Changing Needs and Professional Standards, 1866-1942." Ph.D. diss., Columbia University, 1961. 382 pp. *Dissertation Abstracts,* vol. 22, p. 3915.

Park, Bessie L. *Cortland - Our Alma Mater; A History of Cortland Normal School and State University of New York Teachers College at Cortland, 1869-1959.* Ithaca: Cayuga Pr., 1960. 337 pp.

State University of New York College at Fredonia

Ohles, John F. "The Historical Development of State University of New York College at Fredonia as Representative of the Evolution of Teacher Education in the State University of New York." Ed.D. diss., State University of New York at Buffalo, 1964. 448 pp. *Dissertation Abstracts,* vol. 25, p. 3376.

State University of New York
College at Geneseo

Fisher, Rosalind R. *The Stone Strength of the Past. Centennial History of the State University College of Arts and Sciences at Geneseo, New York.* n.p., 1971. 283 pp.

Mau, Clayton C. *Brief History of the State University Teachers College, Geneseo, New York.* Geneseo: State University of New York, 1956. 23 pp.

State University of New York
College at New Paltz

Klotzberger, Edward L. "The Growth and Development of State Teachers College, New Paltz, State University of New York with Implications of Education in the State of New York." Ph.D. diss., University of Connecticut, 1958. 310 pp. *Dissertation Abstracts,* vol. 19, p. 1009.

State University of New York
College at Oneonta

Brush, Carey W. *In Honor of Good Faith; A History of the State University College at Oneonta, New York.* Oneonta: n.p., 1965. 330 pp.

State University of New York
College at Oswego

Hollis, Andrew P. *The Contribution of the Oswego Normal School to Educational Progress in the United States.* Boston: D. C. Heath, 1898. 160 pp.

New York. State University College, Oswego. *Historical Sketches Relating to the First Quarter Century of the State Normal and Training School at Oswego, N. Y.* Oswego: n.p., 1888. 303 pp.

Rogers, Dorothy. *Oswego: Fountainhead of Teacher Education; A Century in the Seldon Tradition.* New York: Appleton, 1961. 305 pp.

State University of New York
College at Plattsburgh

Cooper, Frank A. *The Plattsburgh Idea in Education, 1889-1964.* Plattsburgh: n.p., 1964. 175 pp.

State University of New York College at Potsdam

Lahey, William C. *The Potsdam Tradition; A History and a Challenge.* New York: Appleton, 1966. 255 pp.

New York. State University College, Potsdam. *First Quarto-Centennial History of the State Normal and Training School, Potsdam, N. Y., 1869-1894.* Potsdam: n.p., 1895. 227 pp.

State University of New York College of Environmental Science and Forestry

Armstrong, George R., ed. *Forestry College: Essays on the Growth and Development of New York State's College of Forestry, 1911-1961.* Syracuse: Alumni Association, State University College of Forestry at Syracuse University, 1961. 300 pp.

Syracuse University

Allen, James E. *An Uncommon Man; The Story of Dr. William Pearson Tolley and Syracuse University.* New York: Newcomen Society in North America, 1963. 24 pp.

Galpin, William F. *Syracuse University.* 2 vols. Syracuse: Syracuse University Pr., 1952-

Teachers College, Columbia University

Cremin, Lawrence A. *A History of Teachers College, Columbia University.* New York: Columbia University Pr., 1954. 289 pp.

Mix, Mary D. "New College of Teachers College: A History, 1932-1939." Ph.D. diss., Columbia University, 1968. 464 pp. *Dissertation Abstracts,* vol. 29A, p. 3436.

Russell, James E. *Founding Teachers College; Reminiscences of the Dean Emeritus.* New York: Teachers College, Columbia University, 1937. 106 pp.

Union College

Fortenbaugh, Samuel B. *In Order to Form a More Perfect Union: An Inquiry into the Origins of a College.* Schenectady: Union College Pr., 1978. 130 pp.

Fox, Dixon R. *Union College: An Unfinished History.* Schenectady: Graduate Council, Union College, 1945. 84 pp.

Hough, Franklin B. *Historical Sketch of Union College.* Washington: Government Printing Office, 1876. 81 pp.

Huntley, C. William. *Thirty Years in the Life of a College.* Schenectady: Union College, 1985. 273 pp.

Raymond, Andrew V. *Union University, Its History, Influence, Characteristics and Equipment.* 3 vols. New York: Lewis Publishing Co., 1907.

Union College (Schenectady, N. Y.). *Union College, 1795-1895; A Record of the Commemoration, June Twenty-First to the Twenty-Seventh, 1895, of the One Hundredth Anniversary of the Founding of Union College, Including a Sketch of Its History.* New York: n.p., 1897. 524 pp.

Union University, Schenectady. *The First Semi-Celebration Anniversary of Union College. Celebrated July 22, 1845.* Albany: W. C. Little & Co., 1845. 186 pp.

Union Theological Seminary

Coffin, Henry S. *A Half Century of Union Theological Seminary, 1896-1945: An Informal History.* New York: Scribner, 1954. 261 pp.

Handy, Robert T. *A History of Union Theological Seminary in New York.* New York: Columbia University Pr., 1987. 388 pp.

Hatfield, Edwin F. *The Early Annals of Union Theological Seminary in the City of New York.* New York: n.p., 1876. 27 pp.

Prentiss, George L. *The Union Theological Seminary in the City of New York: Historical and Biographical Sketches of Its First Fifty Years.* New York: A. D. F. Randolph and Co., 1889. 294 pp.

--------. *The Union Theological Seminary in the City of New York: Its Design and Another Decade of Its History.* Asbury Park: Pennypacker, 1899. 576 pp.

United States Merchant Marine Academy

Mitchell, C. Bradford. *We'll Deliver: Early History of the United States Merchant Marine Academy, 1938-1956.* Kings Point, N. Y.: United States Merchant Marine Academy Alumni Association, 1977. 253 pp.

United States Military Academy

Ambrose, Stephen E. *Duty, Honor, Country: A History of West Point.* Baltimore: Johns Hopkins University Pr., 1966. 357 pp.

Baumer, William H. *West Point, Moulder of Men.* New York: Appleton-Century, 1942. 264 pp.

Berry, Sidney B. *The United States Military Academy, a Fundamental National Institution: West Point, a Special Place.* New York: Newcomen Society in North America, 1977. 28 pp.

Denton, Edgar, III. "The Formative Years of the United States Military Academy, 1775-1833." Ph.D. diss., Syracuse University, 1964. 307 pp. *Dissertation Abstracts,* vol. 25, p. 4669.

Dillard, Walter S. "The United States Military Academy, 1865-1900: The Uncertain Years." Ph.D. diss., University of Washington, 1972. 418 pp. *Dissertation Abstracts International,* vol. 33A, p. 2281.

Farley, Joseph P. *West Point in the Early Sixties, with Incidents of the War.* Troy: Pafraets, 1902. 201 pp.

Fleming, Thomas J. *West Point; The Men and Times of the United States Military Academy.* New York: Morrow, 1969. 402 pp.

Forman, Sidney. *West Point: A History of the United States Military Academy.* New York: Columbia University Pr., 1950. 255 pp.

Godson, William F. H. "History of West Point, 1852-1902." Ed.D. diss., Temple University, 1934. 108 pp.

Holden, Edward S., comp. *The Centennial of the United States Military Academy at West Point, New York, 1802-1902.* 2 vols. Washington: Government Printing Office, 1904.

Morrison, James L. *"The Best School in the World": West Point, the Pre-Civil War Years, 1833-1866.* Kent, Ohio: Kent State University Pr., 1986. 255 pp.

--------. "The United States Military Academy, 1833-1866: Years of

Progress and Turmoil." Ph.D. diss., Columbia University, 1970. 377 pp. *Dissertation Abstracts International,* vol. 31A, p. 4684.

Nye, Roger H. "The United States Military Academy in an Era of Educational Reform, 1900-1925." Ph.D. diss., Columbia University, 1968. *Dissertation Abstracts,* vol. 29A, p. 856.

Pappas, George S. *West Point Sesquicentennial, 1801-1952: A Pictorial History of the One Hundred and Fifty Years of the United States Military Academy.* West Point, N. Y.: United States Military Academy, 1952. 45 pp.

University of Rochester

May, Arthur J. *A History of the University of Rochester, 1850-1962.* Edited and Abridged by Lawrence E. Kline. Rochester: University of Rochester, 1977. 359 pp.

An Outline History of the University of Rochester. Rochester: E. R. Andrews, Printer, 1886. 70 pp.

Rochester, N. Y. University. *The University of Rochester, the First Hundred Years.* Rochester: University of Rochester Centennial Committee, 1950. 96 pp.

Rosenberger, Jesse L. *Rochester and Colgate; Historical Backgrounds of the Two Universities.* Chicago: University of Chicago Pr., 1925. 173 pp.

--------. *Rochester: The Making of a University.* Rochester: The University of Rochester, 1927. 333 pp.

Slater, John R. *Rochester at Seventy-Five.* Bulletin of the University of Rochester, 1925. 31 pp.

Valentine, Alan C. *Rochester's University (1850-1950) a 100th Anniversary Address.* New York: Newcomen Society in North America, 1950. 24 pp.

Vassar College

Borton, Mark C. *Vassar: A Photographic Celebration.* Haddam, Conn.: Embarry Imp., 1984. 111 pp.

Herman, Debra. "College and After: The Vassar Experiment in Women's Education, 1861-1924." Ph.D. diss., Stanford University, 1979. 365 pp. *Dissertation Abstracts International,* vol. 40A, p. 1027.

Life at Vassar; Seventy-Five Years in Pictures. Poughkeepsie: Vassar Cooperative Bookshop, 1940. 124 pp.

Linner, Edward R. *Vassar: The Remarkable Growth of a Man and His College, 1855-1865.* Poughkeepsie: Vassar College, 1984. 210 pp.

Lossing, Benson J. *Vassar College and Its Founder.* New York: Alvord, 1867. 175 pp.

Norris, Mary H. *The Golden Age of Vassar.* Poughkeepsie: Vassar College, 1915. 164 pp.

Plum, Dorothy A., and Dowell, George B. *The Great Experiment; A Chronicle of Vassar.* Poughkeepsie: n.p., 1961. 124 pp.

Plum, Dorothy A., and Dowell, George B., comps. *The Magnificent Enterprise; A Chronicle of Vassar College.* Poughkeepsie: Vassar College, 1961. 138 pp.

Raymond, John H. *Vassar College. A College for Women, in Poughkeepsie, N. Y. A Sketch of Its Foundation, Aims, and Resources, and of the Development of Its Scheme of Instruction to the Present Time.* New York: S. W. Green Printer, 1873. 78 pp.

Taylor, James M. *Before Vassar Opened: A Contribution to the History of the Higher Education of Women in America.* Farmingdale, N. Y.: Dabor Social Sciences Publications, 1978. 287 pp.

Taylor, James M., and Haight, Elizabeth H. *Vassar.* New York: Oxford University Pr., 1915. 232 pp.

Vassar College. *Historical Sketch of Vassar College. Founded at Poughkeepsie, N. Y., January 18, 1861.* New York: S. W. Green Printer, 1876. 54 pp.

Wells College

Lowe, Walter I. *Wells College and Its Founders, an Historical Sketch.* Aurora: The College, 1901. 24 pp.

Russ, Anne J. *Divergent Realities: The Wells College Experience, 1876-1905.* Boston: Paper Presented at the Annual Meeting of the American Educational Research Association, April, 1980. 15 pp. ERIC Microfiche ED 185 929.

---------. "Higher Education for Women: Intent, Reality, and Outcomes, Wells College, 1868-1913." Ph.D. diss., Cornell University, 1980. 138 pp. *Dissertation Abstracts International,* vol. 41A, p. 135.

Wells College Aurora, N. Y. *Seventy-Fifth Anniversary of Wells College: October the Fifteenth, Nineteen Hundred and Forty-Three, Aurora, New York.* Aurora: n.p., 1943. 31 pp.

Yeshiva University

Klaperman, Gilbert. "The Beginnings of Yeshiva University: The First Jewish University in America." D.H.L. diss., Yeshiva University, 1955. 397 pp. *Dissertation Abstracts,* vol. 18, p. 1774.

---------. *The Story of Yeshiva University, the First Jewish University in America.* New York: Macmillan, 1969. 301 pp.

NORTH CAROLINA

Atlantic Christian College

Ware, Charles C. *A History of Atlantic Christian College, Culture in Coastal Carolina.* Wilson, N. C.: Atlantic Christian College, 1956. 248 pp.

Belmont Abbey College

Doris, Sebastian. "Belmont Abbey-Its History and Educational Influence." Master's thesis, Catholic University of America, 1933. 68 pp.

Black Mountain College (Closed 1959)

Duberman, Martin B. *Black Mountain; An Exploration in Community.* New York: Dutton, 1972. 527 pp.

Campbell University

Pearce, J. Winston. *Campbell College: The Miracle at Little Buies Creek, 1887-1974.* Nashville, Tenn.: Broadman Pr., 1976. 284 pp.

---------. *Campbell University: Big Miracle at Little Buies Creek.* vol. 2.

Nashville, Tenn.: Broadman Pr., 1985. 304 pp.

Catawba College

Keppel, Alvin R. *"A College of Our Own": A Brief History of Catawaba College, 1851-1951.* Salisbury: Catawba College, 1951. 54 pp.

Leonard, Jacob C. *History of Catawba College, Formerly Located at Newton, Now at Salisbury, North Carolina.* Salisbury: Catawba College, 1927. 352 pp.

Chowan College

Gatewood, Herman W., and Taylor, R. Hargus. *Through the Years: A Pictorial History, Issued in Observance of the 125th Academic Year in the Life of Chowan College, Murfreesboro, North Carolina.* Murfreesboro, N. C.: n.p., 1972. 52 pp.

McKnight, Edgar V. *A History of Chowan College.* Murfreesboro, N. C.: Chowan College, 1964. 330 pp.

Davidson College

Shaw, Cornelia R. *Davidson College; Intimate Facts.* New York: Revell Pr., 1923. 317 pp.

Duke University

Chaffin, Nora C. *Trinity College, 1839-1892; The Beginnings of Duke University.* Durham: Duke University Pr., 1950. 584 pp.

Duke University, Durham, N. C. *History and Government of Duke University.* Durham, N. C.: n.p., 1943. 22 pp.

Porter, Earl W. *Trinity & Duke, 1892-1924: Foundations of Duke University.* Durham: Duke University Pr., 1964. 274 pp.

East Carolina University

Bratton, Mary Jo J. *East Carolina University: The Formative Years, 1907-1982.* Greenville, N. C.: East Carolina University Alumni Association, 1986. 535 pp.

Elizabeth City State University

Johnson, Evelyn A. *History of Elizabeth City State University: A Story of Survival.* New York: Vantage Pr., 1980. 277 pp.

Elon College

Stokes, Durwood T. *Elon College, Its History and Traditions.* Chapel Hill: Elon College Alumni Association, 1982. 564 pp.

Fayetteville State University

Jones, Mildred P. *History of Fayetteville State College.* Fayetteville: Fayetteville State College Pr., 1969. 113 pp.

Murphy, Ella L. "Origin and Development of Fayetteville State Teachers College, 1867-1959. -- A Chapter in the History of the Education of Negroes in North Carolina." Ph.D. diss., New York University, 1960. 371 pp. *Dissertation Abstracts,* vol. 21, p. 3431.

Gardner-Webb College

Dedmond, Francis B. *Lengthened Shadows; A History of Gardner-Webb College, 1907-1956.* Boiling Springs, N. C.: Gardner-Webb College, 1957. 219 pp.

Greensboro College

Gobbel, Luther L. *Greensboro College, 1935-1952: My Seventeen Years as Its President: With a Resume of the Years before 1935.* Greensboro: Greensboro College Alumni Association, 1977. 225 pp.

Guilford College

Gilbert, Dorothy L. *Guilford, a Quaker College.* Greensboro, N. C.: Printed for Guilford College, 1937. 359 pp.

High Point College

Locke, William R. *No Easy Task: The First Fifty Years of High Point College.* High Point, N. C.: High Point College, 1975. 140 pp.

Johnson C. Smith University

George, Arthur A. "The History of Johnson C. Smith University, 1867 to the Present." Ed.D. diss., New York University, 1954. 352 pp. *Dissertation Abstracts,* vol. 15, p. 222.

--------. *100 Years, 1867-1967: Salient Factors in the Growth and Development of Johnson C. Smith University, Charlotte, N. C.: A History.* Charlotte: Johnson C. Smith University, 1968. 60 pp.

Parker, Inez M. *The Biddle-Johnson C. Smith University Story.* Charlotte, N. C.: Charlotte Publishing, 1975. 133 pp.

Livingstone College

Davis, Lenwood G. "A History of Livingstone College: 1879-1957." D. A. diss., Carnegie-Mellon University, 1979. 323 pp. *Dissertation Abstracts International,* vol. 40A, p. 2819.

Livingstone College, Salisbury, N. C. *Quarter Centennial of Livingstone College and Industrial School, Salisbury, N. C., May 19-24, 1907.* Salisbury, N. C.: J. E. Mason, Secretary, 1907. 16 pp.

Louisburg College

Russell, Miriam L. "A History of Louisburg College, 1787-1958." Master's thesis, Appalachian State Teachers College, 1959. 181 pp.

Willard, George-Anne. *Louisburg College Echoes: Voices from the Formative Years, 1787-1917: With a Summary of the Expansion Years, 1917-1987.* Louisburg, N. C.: Louisburg College, 1988. 200 pp.

Mars Hill College

Carter, Edward J. "A History of Mars Hill College." Master's thesis, University of North Carolina, 1940. 110 pp.

McLeod, John A. *From These Stones; Mars Hill College, the First Hundred Years.* Mars Hill, N. C.: Mars Hill College, 1955. 291 pp.

Roueche, John E. "An Analysis of the Transition of a Junior College into a Four-Year Liberal Arts College: A Case Study." Ph.D. diss., Florida State University, 1964. *Dissertation Abstracts,* vol. 26, p. 231.

Meredith College

Johnson, Mary L. *A History of Meredith College.* Raleigh: Meredith College, 1956. 301 pp.

--------. *History of Meredith College.* 2d ed. Raleigh: Edward and Broughton, 1972. 497 pp.

North Carolina Agricultural and Technical State University

Gibbs, Warmoth T. *History of the North Carolina Agricultural and Technical College, Greensboro, North Carolina.* Dubuque: William C. Brown, 1966. 209 pp.

North Carolina Central University

Seay, Elizabeth I. "A History of North Carolina College for Negroes." Master's thesis, Duke University, 1941. 117 pp.

North Carolina State University

Allen, Christopher E. "The Land Grant Act of 1862 and Practical Education in North Carolina: The Founding of North Carolina College of Agriculture and Mechanic Arts." Master's thesis, North Carolina State University, 1984. 108 pp.

Lockmiller, David A. *History of the North Carolina State College of Agriculture and Engineering of the University of North Carolina, 1889-1939.* Raleigh: Printed by Edwards & Broughton, 1939. 310 pp.

Reagan, Alice E. *North Carolina State University: A Narrative History.* Ann Arbor, Mich.: Edwards Brothers, 1987. 285 pp.

Queens College

Hoyle, Hughes B., Jr. "The Early History of Queens College to 1872." Ph.D. diss., University of North Carolina, 1963. 319 pp. *Dissertation Abstracts,* vol. 25, p. 4520.

McEwen, Mildred M. *Queens College: Yesterday and Today.* Charoltte, N. C.: Queens College Alumnae Association, 1980. 297 pp.

St. Andrews Presbyterian College

Bracey, William R. "A History of Flora MacDonald College." Master's thesis, Appalachian State Teachers College, 1962. 119 pp.

Saint Augustine's College

Halliburton, Cecil D. *A History of Saint Augustine's College, 1867-1937.* Raleigh: St. Augustine's College, 1937. 97 pp.

St. Augustine's School, Raleigh, N. C. *A Record of Fifty Years: 1867-1917.* Raleigh: The School, 1917. 39 pp.

Salem College

Fries, Adelaide L. *Historical Sketch of Salem Female Academy.* Salem, N. C.: Crist and Kehln, 1902. 32 pp.

Griffin, Frances. *Less Time for Meddling: A History of Salem Academy and College, 1772-1866.* Winston-Salem: J. F. Blair, 1979. 311 pp.

Shaw University

Carter, Wilmoth A. *Shaw's Universe: A Monument to Educational Innovation.* Raleigh, N. C.: Shaw University, 1973. 229 pp.

Jenkins, Clara B. "A Historical Study of Shaw University, 1865-1963." Ed.D. diss., University of Pittsburgh, 1964. 153 pp. *Dissertation Abstracts,* vol. 26, p. 3738.

University of North Carolina at Chapel Hill

Allcott, John V. *The Campus at Chapel Hill: Two Hundred Years of Architecture.* Chapel Hill: Chapel Hill Historical Society, 1986. 108 pp.

Battle, Kemp P. *History of the University of North Carolina.* 2 vols. Raleigh: Edwards and Broughton, 1907-1912.

Connor, Robert D. W. *A Documentary History of the University of North Carolina, 1776-1799.* 2 vols. Chapel Hill: University of North Carolina Pr., 1953.

Fordham, Christopher C. *University of North Carolina at Chapel Hill: The*

First State University. New York: Newcomen Society of the United States, 1985. 24 pp.

Henderson, Archibald. *The Campus of the First State University.* Chapel Hill: University of North Carolina Pr., 1949. 412 pp.

House, Robert B. *The Light That Shines; Chapel Hill, 1912-1916.* Chapel Hill: University of North Carolina Pr., 1964. 216 pp.

Love, James L. *'Tis Sixty Years Since.* Chapel Hill: University of North Carolina Pr., 1945. 55 pp.

North Carolina University. *Sketches of the History of the University with a Catalogue of Officers and Students, 1789-1889.* Chapel Hill: n.p., 1889. 242 pp.

Powell, William S. *The First State University; A Pictorial History of the University of North Carolina.* Chapel Hill: University of North Carolina Pr., 1972. 309 pp.

--------. *The First State University: A Pictorial History of the University of North Carolina.* Rev. ed. Chapel Hill: University of North Carolina Pr., 1979. 348 pp.

Russell, Phillips. *These Old Stone Walls.* Chapel Hill: Chapel Hill Historical Society, 1972. 147 pp.

Vickers, James. *Chapel Hill, an Illustrated History.* Chapel Hill: Barclay Publishers, 1985. 208 pp.

Waddell, Alfred M. *The Ante-Bellum University. Oration Delivered at the Celebration of the Centennial of the University of North Carolina, June 5, 1895.* Wilmington, N. C.: Jackson & Bell, 1895. 17 pp.

Wagstaff, Henry M. *Impressions of Men and Movements at the University of North Carolina.* Chapel Hill: University of North Carolina Pr., 1950. 110 pp.

Weeks, Stephen B. *"The University of North Carolina in the Civil War." An Address Delivered at the Centennial Celebration of the Opening of the Institution, June 5th, 1895.* Richmond: W. E. Jones, Printer, 1896. 38 pp.

Wilson, Louis R. *Louis Round Wilson's Historical Sketches.* Durham, N. C.: Moore Publishing Co., 1976. 435 pp.

--------. *The University of North Carolina, 1900-1930; The Making of a*

Modern University. Chapel Hill: University of North Carolina Pr., 1957. 633 pp.

--------. *The University of North Carolina under Consolidation, 1931-1963; History and Appraisal.* Chapel Hill: University of North Carolina Consolidated Office, 1964. 483 pp.

University of North Carolina at Charlotte

Rieke, Robert. *A Retrospective Vision: The University of North Carolina at Charlotte, 1965-1975.* Charlotte: The University, 1977. 121 pp.

Sanford, J. Kenneth. *The First Decade, UNCC.* Charlotte: UNCC Development Office, 1975. 28 pp.

University of North Carolina at Greensboro

Bowles, Elisabeth A. *A Good Beginning; The First Four Decades of the University of North Carolina at Greensboro.* Chapel Hill: University of North Carolina Pr., 1967. 193 pp.

University of North Carolina at Wilmington

Crewes, J. Marshall. *From These Beginnings: Wilmington College, 1946-1969.* Wilmington: University of North Carolina at Wilmington, 1984. 113 pp.

Wake Forest University

Hearn, Thomas K. *Wake Forest and the Spirit of Opportunity.* New York: Newcomen Society of the United States, 1984. 27 pp.

Paschal, George W. *History of Wake Forest College.* Wake Forest: Wake Forest College, 1935-

Warren Wilson College

Jensen, Henry W. *History of Warren Wilson College: On the Occasion of the College's Eightieth Anniversary.* n.p., 1974. 122 pp.

Western Carolina University

Bird, William E. *The History of Western Carolina College: The Progress of an Idea.* Chapel Hill: University of North Carolina Pr., 1963. 294 pp.

Smith, Jo Ann. *By Chance or By Plan.* Raleigh, N. C.: Business Services, 1982. 48 pp.

Wingate College

Hester, Hubert I. *The Wingate College Story; An Epic of Vision, Faith, Work, and Achievement.* Wingate, N. C.: Wingate College, 1972. 201 pp.

Yadkin College (Closed 1924)

Fick, Virginia G. *Country College on the Yadkin: A Historical Narrative.* Winston-Salem, N. C.: Historical Division, Hunter Publishing Co., 1984. 89 pp.

Freeman, Randall B. "The History of Yadkin College, 1865-1924." Master's thesis, Wake Forest University, 1987. 131 pp.

Michael, Olin B. *Yadkin College, 1856-1924; A Historic Sketch.* Salisbury, N. C.: Rowan Printing Co., 1939. 182 pp.

NORTH DAKOTA

Dickinson State College

Belsheim, Osbourne T. *The Story of Dickinson State; A History of Dickinson State College, 1918-1968.* Dickinson: Dickinson State College, 1968. 226 pp.

Jamestown College

Kroeze, Barend H. *A Prairie Saga.* St. Paul: North Central Publishing Co., 1952. 175 pp.

Mayville State College

Neilson, James W. *The School of Personal Service: History of Mayville State College.* Mayville, N. D.: n.p., 1979. 158 pp.

Minot State University

Stee, Agnes M. "History of the Minot State Teachers College." Master's thesis, University of North Dakota, 1948. 121 pp.

North Dakota State University

Hunter, William C. *Beacon Across the Prairie; North Dakota's Land Grant College.* Fargo: North Dakota Institute for Regional Studies, 1961. 309 pp.

Northwest Bible College (Closed)

Doktor, Guy, and Doktor, Hazel. *Let Us Go Forward: History of Northwest Bible College, Minot, North Dakota.* Cleveland, Tenn.: Pathway Pr., 1976. 239 pp.

Spence, G. H. "History of the Northwest Bible College." B. S. thesis, Minot State College, 1974.

University of North Dakota

Geiger, Louis G. *University of the Northern Plains; A History of the University of North Dakota, 1833-1958.* Grand Forks: University of North Dakota Pr., 1958. 491 pp.

Starcher, George W. *"Beacon O'er Our Western Land": The University of North Dakota.* New York: Newcomen Society in North America, 1964. 24 pp.

Wilkins, Robert P., ed. *A Century on the Northern Plains: The University of North Dakota at 100.* Grand Forks: University of North Dakota Pr., 1983. 206 pp.

Valley City State College

Hanna, Glenn A. "History of the Valley City State Teachers College." Master's thesis, University of North Dakota, 1951. 116 pp.

314 / OHIO

Hennessey, Daniel L. "History of the Valley City State College, 1890-1970." Master's thesis, University of North Dakota, 1971. 236 pp.

Yankton College

Alstad, Adrien D. "Fargo College: A Study in Liberal Arts Education on the Dakota Prairie." Master's thesis, Moorehead State College, 1974. 82 pp.

OHIO

Alfred Holbrook College (Closed 1941)

Roush, Chester A. *The History of Alfred Holbrook College.* Kettering, Ohio: C. A. Roush, 1980. 97 pp.

Antioch College

Allen, Ira W. *A Collection of Facts. History of the Rise, Difficulties and Suspension of Antioch College.* Columbus: J. Geary & Son, 1858. 240 pp.

Clark, Burton R. *The Distinctive College Antioch, Reed and Swarthmore.* Chicago: Aldine, 1970. 280 pp.

Henderson, Algo D., and Hall, Dorothy. *Antioch College: Its Design for Liberal Education.* New York: Harper, 1946. 280 pp.

Morgan, Lucy G. *Pioneering Days at Antioch.* Yellow Springs, Ohio: Antioch Pr., 1947. 24 pp.

Vallance, Harvard F. "A History of Antioch College." Ph.D. diss., Ohio State University, 1936. 501 pp.

Ashland College

Ashland College, Ashland, Ohio. *A Brief History of Ashland College.* Ashland: n.p., 1932. 20 pp.

Miller, Clara W., and Mason, Edward G. *A Short History of Ashland College, 1878-1953.* Ashland: Ashland College Diamond Jubilee Committee, 1953. 99 pp.

Athenaeum of Ohio

Miller, Francis J. "A History of the Athenaeum of Ohio, 1829-1960." Ed.D. diss., University of Cincinnati, 1964. 468 pp. *Dissertation Abstracts,* vol. 25, p. 3959.

Bluffton College

Bluffton College, an Adventure in Faith, 1900-1959. Bluffton: Berne Witness Pr., 1950. 268 pp.

Hardesty, Von D. *A Narrative of Bluffton College.* Bluffton: The College, 1974. 48 pp.

Smith, C. Henry, and Hirschler, E. J., eds. *The Story of Bluffton College.* Bluffton: Bluffton College, 1925. 296 pp.

Bowling Green State University

Givens, Stuart R. *The Falcon Soars; Bowling Green State University: The Years of Growing Distinction, 1963-1985.* Bowling Green: Bowling Green State University Popular Pr., 1986. 183 pp.

McFall, Kenneth. "From Normal School to State University - The Development of Bowling Green State University." Ph.D. diss., Western Reserve University, 1947. 258 pp.

Overman, James R. *The History of Bowling Green State University.* Bowling Green: Bowling Green University Pr., 1967. 234 pp.

Capital University

Owens, David B. *These Hundred Years; The Centennial History of Capital University.* Columbus: Capital University, 1950. 255 pp.

Case Western Reserve University

Cramer, Clarence H. *Case Western Reserve University: A History of the University, 1826-1976.* Boston: Little, Brown, 1976. 401 pp.

Cutler, Carroll. *A History of Western Reserve College, during Its First Half Century, 1826-1876.* Cleveland: Crocker Publishing House, 1876. 88 pp.

Dorrance, David B. "Cleveland College: Genesis-Ethos-Exodus." Ph.D. diss., Case Western Reserve University, 1977. 195 pp. *Dissertation Abstracts International*, vol. 38A, p. 4601.

Glennan, Thomas K. *Case Institute of Technology, 75 Years of Service to American Industry.* New York: Newcomen Society in North America, 1954. 24 pp.

Haydn, Hiram C. *Western Reserve University from Hudson to Cleveland, 1878-1890; An Historical Sketch.* Cleveland: Western Reserve University, 1905. 211 pp.

Herrick, Clay. *But It's So! A Collection of Historical Sketches of Western Reserve.* Cleveland: The Independent Pr., 1934. 64 pp.

Kitzmiller, H. H. *One Hundred Years of Western Reserve.* Hudson, Ohio: James W. Ellsworth Foundation, 1926. 52 pp.

Martin, Claude T. *From School to Institute; An Informal Story of Case.* Cleveland: World Publishing Co., 1967. 125 pp.

Millis, John S. *Western Reserve at Cleveland: One Hundred and Thirty-Two Years of a Venture in Faith.* New York: Newcomen Society in North America, 1957. 28 pp.

Thwing, Charles F. *Notes on the History of the College for Women of Western Reserve University for Its First Twenty-Five Years, 1888-1913.* Cleveland: Western Reserve University Pr., 1913. 60 pp.

Waite, Frederick C. *Western Reserve University, the Hudson Era; A History of Western Reserve College and Academy at Hudson, Ohio, from 1826 to 1882.* Cleveland: Western Reserve University Pr., 1943. 540 pp.

Cedarville College

McDonald, Cleveland. "The History of Cedarville College." Ph.D. diss., Ohio State University, 1966. 235 pp. *Dissertation Abstracts,* vol. 27A, p. 2056.

---------. *The History of Cedarville College.* Cedarville, Ohio: Cedarville College, 1966. 170 pp.

Central State University

Goggins, Lathardus. *Central State University: The First One Hundred*

Years, 1887-1987. Kent, Ohio: Kent State University Pr., 1988. 194 pp.

--------. "The Evolution of Central State College under Dr. Charles H. Wesley from 1942-1965: An Historical Analysis." Ed.D. diss., University of Akron, 1983. 217 pp. *Dissertation Abstracts International,* vol. 44A. p. 339.

Cleveland Institute of Art

Wixom, Nancy C. *Cleveland Institute of Art: The First Hundred Years, 1882-1982.* Cleveland: Cleveland Institute of Art, 1983. 80 pp.

Cleveland State University

Earnest, G. Brooks. *History of Fenn College.* Cleveland: Fenn Educational Fund of the Cleveland Foundation, 1974. 718 pp.

Fenn College, Cleveland. *A Decade of Achievement, Fenn College, Cleveland.* Cleveland: n.p., 1961. 51 pp.

College of Wooster

McKee, John D. *After Fifty Years: Reminiscences, 1920-1979, of the College of Wooster.* Wooster, Ohio: McKee, 1975. 92 pp.

Notestein, Lucy L. *Wooster of the Middle West.* New Haven: Yale University Pr., 1937. 333 pp.

--------. *Wooster of the Middle West.* 2 vols. Kent, Ohio: Kent State University Pr., 1971.

Columbus College of Art and Design

Stockwell, Rachel N. *The Columbus College of Art and Design: First Hundred Years, 1879-1979.* Columbus: Columbus College of Art and Design, 1979. 122 pp.

Denison University

Chessman, G. Wallace. *Denison: The Story of an Ohio College.* Granville: Denison University, 1957. 451 pp.

Chessman, G. Wallace, and Southgate, Wyndham M. *Heritage and Promise, Denison, 1831-1981.* Granville: Sesquicentennial, 1981. 192 pp.

Denison University. *Memorial Volume of Denison University, 1831-1906.* Granville: Published by the University, 1907. 286 pp.

Shepardson, Francis W. *Denison University, 1831-1931: A Centennial History.* Granville: n.p., 1931. 438 pp.

Dyke College

Dyke College. *125 Years of Education for Business; The History of Dyke College, 1848-1973.* Cleveland: Dyke College, 1973. 44 pp.

Findlay College

Kern, Richard. *Findlay College: The First Hundred Years.* Nappanee, Ind.: Evangel Pr., 1984. 480 pp.

Hebrew Union College-Jewish Institute of Religion

Chyet, Stanley F. *The Hebrew Union College, Jewish Institute of Religion, 1947-1961.* Cincinnati: Hebrew Union College Pr., 1961. 28 pp.

Cohn, Bernard N. *A Brief History of Hebrew Union College-Jewish Institute of Religion.* Cincinnati: Hebrew Union College-Jewish Institute of Religion, 1975. 8 pp.

Karff, Samuel E., ed. *Hebrew Union College-Jewish Institute of Religion at One Hundred Years: 1875-1975.* Cincinnati: Hebrew Union College Pr., 1976. 501 pp.

Heidelberg College

Williams, Edward I. F. *Heidelberg, Democratic Christian College, 1850-1950.* Menasha, Wisc.: Banta Publishing Co., 1952. 321 pp.

Williard, George W. *The History of Heidelberg College.* Cincinnati: Elm Street Printing, 1879. 347 pp.

Hiram College

Green, Francis M. *Hiram College & Western Reserve Eclectic Institute:*

Fifty Years of History, 1850-1900. Cleveland: O. S. Hubbell Printing Co., 1901. 425 pp.

Historical Sketch of Hiram College, 1887. Garrettsville, Ohio: The Item Printing and Publishing Co., 1887. 23 pp.

Treudley, Mary B. *Prelude to the Future; The First Hundred Years of Hiram College.* New York: Association Pr., 1950. 288 pp.

John Carroll University

Gavin, Donald P. *John Carroll University: A Century of Service.* Kent, Ohio: Kent State University Pr., 1985. 553 pp.

Kent State University

Lowry, Mary A. *Past Dream, Present Reality: KSU Trumbull Campus.* Warren, Ohio: Kent State University Trumbull Campus, 1984. 125 pp.

Shriver, Philip R. *The Years of Youth; Kent State University, 1910-1960.* Kent, Ohio: Kent State University Pr., 1960. 266 pp.

Kenyon College

Bodine, William B. *Historical Sketch of the Theological Seminary of the Diocese of Ohio and Kenyon College.* n.p., 1875. 32 pp.

Chalmers, Gordon K. *The College in the Forest, 1824.* New York: Newcomen Society of England, American Branch, 1948. 24 pp.

Greenslade, Thomas B. *Kenyon College, Its Third Half Century.* Gambier, Ohio: Kenyon College, 1975. 301 pp.

Piatt, John J. *How the Bishop Built His College in the Woods.* Cincinnati: Western Literary Pr., 1906. 74 pp.

Smythe, George F. *Kenyon College: Its First Century.* New Haven: Yale University Pr., 1924. 349 pp.

Malone College

Osborne, Byron L. *The Malone Story; The Dream of Two Quaker Young People.* Newton, Kan.: Printed by United Printing, 1970. 359 pp.

Marietta College

Andrews, Israel W. *Historical Sketch of Marietta College, Founded at Marietta, Ohio.* Cincinnati: n.p., 1876. 33 pp.

Beach, Arthur G. *A Pioneer College; The Story of Marietta.* Chicago: John F. Cuneo Co., 1935. 325 pp.

Marietta College. *Marietta College in the War of Secession, 1861-1865.* Cincinnati: P. G. Thomson, 1878. 96 pp.

--------. *The Seventy-Fifth Anniversary of the Present Charter of Marietta College and the 113th of the Founding of Muskingun Academy.* Marietta, Ohio: The College, 1910. 235 pp.

Miami University

Flower, Olive. *The History of Oxford College for Women, 1830-1928.* Oxford, Ohio: Miami University Alumni Association, 1949. 329 pp.

Havighurst, Walter. *Miami Album.* Oxford, Ohio: King Library, Miami University, 1981. 100 pp.

--------. *The Miami Years: 1809-1959.* New York: Putnam, 1958. 254 pp.

--------. *The Miami Years: 1809-1969.* Rev. ed. New York: Putnam, 1969. 332 pp.

Miami University, Oxford, Ohio. *Centennial Year 1809 & 1909, Miami University.* Oxford, Ohio: n.p., 1909. 40 pp.

Nelson, Narka. *The Western College for Women, 1853-1953.* Oxford, Ohio: Western College, 1954. 248 pp.

Rodabaugh, James H. "A History of Miami University from Its Origin to 1845." Master's thesis, Miami University, 1933. 266 pp.

--------. "A History of Miami University from Its Origin to 1885." Ph.D. diss., Ohio State University, 1937.

Thompson, Bertha B. "The History of Miami University from 1873 to 1900." Master's thesis, Miami University, 1954. 381 pp.

Upham, Alfred H. *Old Miami, the Yale of the Early West.* Hamilton, Ohio: Republican Publishing Co., 1909. 274 pp.

Mount Union College

Osborne, Newell Y. *A Select School: The History of Mount Union College and an Account of a Unique Educational Experiment, Scio College.* Alliance, Ohio: n.p., 1967. 645 pp.

Muskingum College

Bright, John H. "Historical Development of Present-Day Problems of Muskingum College." Ph.D. diss., University of Cincinnati, 1951.

Fisk, William L. *A History of Muskingum College.* New Concord, Ohio: The College, 1978. 276 pp.

North Central Technical College

Sliney, Bruce. "The History of North Central Technical College: 1961-1981." Ed.D. diss., University of Akron, 1983. 411 pp. *Dissertation Abstracts International,* vol. 44A. p. 406.

Oberlin College

Ballantine, W. G., ed. *The Oberlin Jubilee: 1833-1883.* Oberlin: E. J. Goodrich, 1883. 356 pp.

Barnard, John. *From Evangelism to Progressivism at Oberlin College, 1866-1917.* Columbus: Ohio State University Pr., 1969. 171 pp.

Blodgett, Geoffrey. *Oberlin Architecture, College and Town: A Guide to Its Social History.* Oberlin: Oberlin College, 1985. 239 pp.

Fairchild, Edward H. *Historical Sketch of Oberlin College.* Springfield: Republic Printing Co., 1868. 34 pp.

Fairchild, James H. *Oberlin: Its Origin, Progress and Results.* Oberlin: Shankland and Harmon, 1860. 70 pp.

--------. *Oberlin: Its Origin, Progress and Results.* Oberlin: R. Butler, Printer, 1871. 88 pp.

--------. *Oberlin: The Colony and the College, 1833-1883.* Oberlin: E. J. Goodrich, 1883. 377 pp.

Fletcher, Robert S. *A History of Oberlin College from Its Foundation through the Civil War.* 2 vols. Oberlin: Oberlin College, 1943.

――――. "Oberlin College, 1833-1866." Ph.D. diss., Harvard University, 1939.

Hosford, Frances J. *Father Shipherd's Magna Charta; A Century of Coeducation in Oberlin College.* Boston: Marshall Jones Co., 1937. 180 pp.

Leonard, Delavan L. *Story of Oberlin: The Institution, the Community, the Idea, the Movement.* Boston: n.p., 1898. 447 pp.

Shumway, Arthur L., and Brower, C. D. *Oberlinians. A Jubilee Volume of Semi-Historical Anecdotes Connected with the Past and Present of Oberlin College, 1833-1883.* Cleveland: Home Publishing Co., 1883. 175 pp.

Smith, Delazon. *A History of Oberlin; or, New Lights of the West.* Cleveland: S. Underhill, 1837. 82 pp.

Ohio Northern University

Belch, George E. *Tempered by Crises; The Centennial Year History of Ohio Northern University.* Ada, Ohio: Ohio Northern University, 1971. 42 pp.

Rogers, James T. "A History of Ohio Northern University." Master's thesis, Ohio State University, 1933. 145 pp.

The Ohio State University

Department of Photography & Crime Staff. *First Hundred Years: A Family Album of the Ohio State University, 1870-1970.* Columbus: Ohio State University Pr., 1970. 160 pp.

Fawcett, Novice G. *The Ohio State University: A Centennial of Increasing Commitment.* New York: Newcomen Society in North America, 1971. 24 pp.

Kinnison, William A. *Building Sullivant's Pyramid: An Administrative History of the Ohio State University.* Columbus: Ohio State University Pr., 1970. 225 pp.

Mendenhall, Thomas C., ed. *History of Ohio State University, 1870-1910.* 5 vols. Columbus: Ohio State University Pr., 1920-1941.

Pollard, James E. *History of the Ohio State University; The Story of Its*

First Seventy-Five Years, 1873-1948. Columbus: Ohio State University Pr., 1952. 434 pp.

Underwood, Paul. *The Enarson Years.* Columbus: Ohio State University, 1985. 213 pp.

Ohio University

Fontaine, Paul. *Ohio University, the Baker Years.* Athens: Ohio University Pr., 1961. 174 pp.

Hoover, Thomas N. *The History of Ohio University.* Athens: Ohio University Pr., 1954. 274 pp.

Lovenstein, Meno. *The Decade of the University: Ohio University and the Alden Years.* Athens: Ohio University, 1971. 246 pp.

Martzloff, Clement L. *Ohio University, the Historic College of the Old Northwest.* Athens: Ohio University, 1910. 37 pp.

Peters, William E. *The Legal History of the Ohio University, Athens, Ohio.* Cincinnati: Press of the Western Methodist Book Concern, 1910. 336 pp.

Ping, Charles J. *Ohio University in Perspective: The Annual Convocation Addresses of President Charles J. Ping, 1975-1984.* Athens: Ohio University Pr., 1985. 292 pp.

Super, Charles W. *A Pioneer College and Its Background: The Ohio University.* Salem, Mass.: Newcomb & Gauss, Printers, 1924. 133 pp.

Ohio Wesleyan University

Hubbart, Henry C. *Ohio Wesleyan's First Hundred Years.* Delaware, Ohio: Ohio Wesleyan University, 1943. 358 pp.

Nelson, Edward T., ed. *Fifty Years of History of the Ohio Wesleyan University, Delaware, Ohio, 1844-1894.* Cleveland: The Cleveland Printing and Publishing Co., 1895. 547 pp.

Otterbein College

Bartlett, Willard W. *Education for Humanity; The Story of Otterbein College.* Westerville: Otterbein College, 1934. 285 pp.

--------. "An Historical Study of Otterbein College at Westerville in the State of Ohio." Ph.D. diss., The Ohio State University, 1933.

Garst, Henry. *Otterbein University, 1847-1907.* Dayton, Ohio: United Brethren Publishing House, 1907. 316 pp.

Hancock, Harold B. *The History of Otterbein College, 1930-1972.* Westerville: Otterbein College, 1971. 197 pp.

Rio Grande College

Evans, Benjamin R. "A History of Rio Grande College." Master's thesis, Ohio State University, 1939. 125 pp.

Sinclair Community College

Bussey, Charles C. *Origin and Development of Sinclair Community College, Dayton, Ohio, 1887-1970.* Dayton, Ohio: n.p., 112 pp.

Trinity Lutheran Seminary

Huber, Donald L. *Educating Lutheran Pastors in Ohio, 1830-1980: A History of Trinity Lutheran Seminary and Its Predecessors.* Lewiston, N. Y.: E. Mellen Pr., 1989. 303 pp.

University of Akron

Auburn, Norman P. *Akron's Municipal University; An Example of Town and Gown Rapport.* New York: Newcomen Society in North America, 1953. 32 pp.

--------. *The First Hundred Years are the Hardest: The Story of the University of Akron.* New York: Newcomen Society in North America, 1970. 24 pp.

Knepper, George W. *New Lamps for Old; One Hundred Years of Urban Higher Education at the University of Akron.* Akron: University of Akron, 1970. 407 pp.

Kolbe, Parker R. *A History of the Establishment of the Municipal University of Akron.* Akron: The Municipal University of Akron, 1914. 36 pp.

Spanton, Albert I., ed. *Fifty Years of Buchtel, 1870-1920.* Akron:

Buchtel College Alumni Association, 1922. 446 pp.

University of Cincinnati

Hamel, Dana B. "A History of the Ohio Mechanics Institute, Cincinnati, Ohio." Ed.D. diss., University of Cincinnati, 1962. 173 pp.

McGrane, Reginald C. *The University of Cincinnati: A Success Story in Urban Higher Education.* New York: Harper, 1963. 364 pp.

Walters, Raymond. *Historical Sketch of the University of Cincinnati.* Cincinnati: The Mountel Pr., 1940. 48 pp.

--------. *University of Cincinnati: Highlights, Past and Present.* New York: Newcomen Society in North America, 1952. 28 pp.

University of Dayton

Knust, Edward H., comp. *Hallowed Memories: A Chronological History of the University of Dayton.* 1 vol. Dayton: University of Dayton, 1953.

--------. *Miscellanea: Some Interesting Facts in the History of the University of Dayton, 1850-1950.* 1 vol. Dayton: University of Dayton, 1951.

Roesch, Raymond A. *The University of Dayton Proudly Growing with a Proud and Growing Community.* New York: Newcomen Society in North America, 1962. 24 pp.

Wehrle, William O. *A History of the University of Dayton.* Dayton: University of Dayton, 1937. 44 pp.

Whetro, R. Kathleen. *Highlights of Twenty-Five Years of Coeducation at the University of Dayton.* Dayton: University of Dayton, 1959. 19 pp.

University of Toledo

Hickerson, Frank R. "A History of the University of Toledo." Ph.D. diss., University of Cincinnati, 1941. 588 pp.

--------. *The Tower Builders; The Centennial Story of the University of Toledo.* Toledo: University of Toledo Pr., 1972. 464 pp.

Urbana University

Higgins, Francis J. *"The Will to Survive": Urbana College, 1850-1975.*
Urbana, Ohio: Urbana College, 1977. 168 pp.

Wilberforce University

Arnett, Benjamin W., and Mitchell, Samuel T., comp. *The Wilberforce Alumnal. A Comprehensive Review of the Origin, Development and Present Status of Wilberforce University.* Xenia, Ohio: Printed at the Gazette Office, 1885. 64 pp.

McGinnis, Frederick A. *A History and an Interpretation of Wilberforce University.* Blanchester: Brown Publishing Co., 1941. 215 pp.

--------. "A History of Wilberforce University." Ed.D. diss., University of Cincinnati, 1940. 132 pp.

Mitchell, Samuel T. *Wilberforce University: Its Inception, Growth and Present Status.* Indianapolis: Freeman Publishing Co., 1895.

Talbert, Horace. *The Sons of Allen. Together with a Sketch of the Rise and Progress of Wilberforce University, Wilberforce, Ohio.* Xenia, Ohio: Aldine Pr., 1906. 286 pp.

Wilmington College

Beauregard, Erving E. *Old Franklin, the Eternal Touch: A History of Franklin College, New Athens, Harrison County, Ohio.* Lanham, Md.: University Press of America, 1983. 253 pp.

Read, James M. *The Making of Sensible Men.* New York: Newcomen Society in North America, 1967. 24 pp.

Wittenberg University

Clark, G. Gerlaw. *History of Wittenberg College, Springfield, Ohio.* Springfield, Ohio: J. A. Work, 1887. 201 pp.

Kinnison, William A. *Wittenberg: A Concise History.* Springfield, Ohio: Wittenberg University, 1976. 97 pp.

--------. *Wittenberg in Clark County, 1845-1970.* Springfield, Ohio: Clark County Historical Society, 1970. 80 pp.

Lentz, Harold H. *A History of Wittenberg College, (1845-1945)*.
Springfield, Ohio: Wittenberg Pr., 1946. 330 pp.

Xavier University

Bennish, Lee J. *Continuity and Change: Xavier University, 1831-1981*.
Chicago: Loyola University Pr., 1981. 252 pp.

McNulty, Helen P. "One Hundred and Ten Years of Education at Xavier."
Ph.D. diss., Fordham University, 1958.

O'Connor, Paul L. *Xavier University*. New York: Newcomen Society in
North America, 1956. 28 pp.

Youngstown State University

Skardon, Alvin W. *Steel Valley University: The Origin of Youngstown State*.
Youngstown: Youngstown State University, 1983. 288 pp.

OKLAHOMA

Bacone College

Bode, Coeryne. "The Origin and Development of Bacone College." Master's
thesis, University of Tulsa, 1957. 127 pp.

Williams, John, and Meredith, Howard L. *Bacone Indian University: A
History*. Oklahoma City, Ok.: Western Heritage Books, 1980.
163 pp.

East Central University

Gillespie, John, and Story, Dale. *A History of East Central State College,
1909-1949*. Ada, Ok.: East Central University, 1980. 126 pp.

Langston University

Patterson, Zella J. B., and Wert, Lynette L. *Langston University: A
History*. Norman: University of Oklahoma Pr., 1979. 319 pp.

Northeastern State University

Caywood, Elzie R. "The History of Northeastern State College." Master's thesis, University of Oklahoma, 1950. 172 pp.

Northern Oklahoma College

Bradley, Mac H. *From UPS to NOC: 1901-1976.* Tonkawa, Ok.: Northern Oklahoma College, 1976. 179 pp.

Oklahoma Baptist University

Bruster, Bill G. "A History of Oklahoma Baptist University with Special Reference to the Contribution of John Wesley Raley." Ph.D. diss., Southwest Baptist Theological Seminary, 1972.

Owens, James N. *Annals of O. B. U.* Shawnee: Historical Commission, Baptist General Convention of Oklahoma, 1956. 246 pp.

Oklahoma Christian College

Beeman, William O. *Oklahoma Christian College: Dream to Reality: The Story of the First Twenty Years, 1950-1970.* Delight, Ark.: Gospel Light Publishing Co., 1970. 180 pp.

Oklahoma City University

Brill, Harry E. *Story of Oklahoma University and Its Predecessors: Texas Wesleyan College, Fort Worth University, Epworth University, Methodist University, Oklahoma City College.* Oklahoma City University Pr., 1938. 263 pp.

Smith, Cluster Q. *Building for Tomorrow; The Story of Oklahoma City University.* Nashville, Tenn.: Parthenon Pr., 1961. 391 pp.

Oklahoma Panhandle State University

Sexton, Kathryn A. *The Heritage of the Panhandle - The History of Panhandle State University: 1909-1979.* Norman: Oklahoma University Pr., 1979. 548 pp.

Oklahoma Presbyterian College

Semple, Anne R. "The Origin and Development of the Oklahoma Presbyterian College." Ph.D. diss., Oklahoma State University, 1955.

Oklahoma State University

Davis, Larry D. "The History of the Oklahoma State University Technical Branch, Okmulgee, Oklahoma." Ed.D. diss., Oklahoma State University, 1988. 508 pp. *Dissertation Abstracts International,* vol. 49A, p. 2948.

Fischer, LeRoy H. *Oklahoma State University: Historic Old Central.* Stillwater: Oklahoma State University, 1988. 321 pp.

Rulon, Philip R. "The Founding of the Oklahoma Agricultural and Mechanical College, 1890-1908." Ed.D. diss., Oklahoma State University, 1968. 317 pp. *Dissertation Abstracts,* vol. 30A, p. 1056.

--------. *Oklahoma State University since 1890.* Stillwater: Oklahoma State University Pr., 1975. 368 pp.

Oral Roberts University

Roberts Oral. *Oral Roberts University, 1965-1983: "True to a Heavenly Vision".* New York: Newcomen Society of the United States, 1983. 26 pp.

Phillips University

Marshall, Frank H. *Phillips University's First Fifty Years, 1906-1956.* 3 vols. Enid: Phillips University, 1957.

Southern Nazarene University

Cantrell, Roy H. "The History of Bethany Nazarene College." Ph.D. diss., Southwestern Baptist Theological Seminary, 1955. 313 pp.

Southwestern Oklahoma State University

Fiegel, Melvin F. "A History of Southwestern State College, 1903-1953." Ed.D. diss., Oklahoma State University, 1968. 272 pp. *Dissertation Abstracts International.* vol. 30A, p. 1836.

University of Oklahoma

Cross, George L. *The University of Oklahoma and World War II: A Personal Account, 1941-1956.* Norman: University of Oklahoma Pr., 1980. 298 pp.

Gittenger, Roy. *The University of Oklahoma, 1892-1942.* Norman: University of Oklahoma Pr., 1942. 282 pp.

Long, Charles F., and Hart, Carolyn G. *The Sooner Story, 1890-1980.* Norman: University of Oklahoma Foundation, 1980. 120 pp.

Sorrels, Carolyn S. *Eight Early Buildings on the Norman Campus of the University of Oklahoma.* Norman: n.p., 1985. 136 pp.

Weidman, John M. "A History of the University of Oklahoma." Master's thesis, University of Oklahoma, 1928. 202 pp.

Wood, Edwin K. "The University of Oklahoma in the World War." Master's thesis, University of Oklahoma, 1923. 46 pp.

University of Tulsa

Delfraisse, Betty D. "The History of the University of Tulsa." Master's thesis, University of Texas, 1929. 88 pp.

Logsdon, Guy W.. *University of Tulsa: A History, 1882-1972.* Norman: University of Oklahoma Pr., 1977. 358 pp.

--------. "The University of Tulsa: A History from 1882 to 1972." Ed.D. diss., University of Oklahoma, 1975. 381 pp. *Dissertation Abstracts International,* vol. 37A, p. 157.

OREGON

Colegio Cesar Chavez (Closed 1983)

Maldonado, Carlos S. ""The Longest Running Death in History": A History of Colegio Cesar Chavez, 1973-1983." Ph.D. diss., University of Oregon, 1986. 179 pp. *Dissertation Abstracts International,* vol. 47A, p. 3335.

Dallas College (Closed)

Coad, Nola E. "A History of Dallas College." Master's thesis, University of Oregon, 1930. 45 pp.

George Fox College

Stanbrough, Amos C. "History of Pacific College." Master's thesis, Oregon State College, 1929. 49 pp.

Lewis and Clark College

Montague, Martha F. *Lewis and Clark College, 1867-1967.* Portland: Binford & Mort, 1968. 244 pp.

Linfield College

Holmes, Kenneth L., ed. *Linfield's Hundred Years; A Centennial History of Linfield College, McMinnville, Oregon.* Portland: Binford & Mort, 1956. 198 pp.

Jonasson, Jonas A. *Bricks Without Straws: The Story of Linfield College.* Caldwell, Id.: Caxton Printers, 1938. 215 pp.

Mount Angel Seminary

Hodes, Ursula. "Mt. Angel, Oregon, 1848-1912." Master's thesis, University of Oregon, 1932. 136 pp.

Northwest Christian College

Goodrich, Martha H. "A History of Northwest Christian College." Master's thesis, University of Oregon, 1949. 226 pp.

Oregon Institute of Technology

Purvine, W. D. *OVS, OTI, OIT: Oregon Tech's First 30 Years, 1946-1976.* Eugene, Ore.: University of Oregon, 1979. 636 pp.

Oregon State University

Groshong, James W. *The Making of a University, 1868-1968.* Corvallis: Oregon State University, 1968. 32 pp.

Smith, John E. *Corvallis College.* Corvallis: n.p., 1953. 60 pp.

Van Loan, Lillian S. "Historical Perspective of Oregon State College." Ed.D. diss., Oregon State University, 1959. 389 pp. *Dissertation Abstracts,* vol. 20, p. 947.

Pacific University

Long, Watt A. "A History of Pacific University." Master's thesis, University of Oregon, 1932. 37 pp.

Pacific University, Forest Grove, Oregon. *Exercises of the Semi-Centennial Anniversary of Tualatin Academy and Pacific University, Held at Forest Grove, Oregon, July 9, 1898.* Forest Grove: n.p., 1898. 86 pp.

Philomath College (Closed)

Springer, Clair G. "A History of Philomath College." Master's thesis, Oregon State College, 1929. 49 pp.

Portland State University

Allen, John E., ed. *Portland State University: The First 25 Years, 1955-1980.* Portland: The University, 1980. 144 pp.

Reed College

Clark, Burton R. *The Distinctive College: Antioch, Reed and Swarthmore.* Chicago: Aldine, 1970. 280 pp.

University of Oregon

Belknap, George N. *An Episode in the Documentaray History of the University of Oregon: The Blue Ribbon University.* Eugene, Ore.: University of Oregon, 1976. 29 pp.

Fortt, Inez L. *Early Days at the University of Oregon.* Fort, 1976. 60 pp.

Sheldon, Henry D. *History of the University of Oregon.* Portland: Binfords & Mort, 1940. 288 pp.

University of Portland

Covert, James T. *A Point of Pride: The University of Portland Story.* Portland: University of Portland Pr., 1976. 328 pp.

Western Conservative Baptist Seminary

Englizian, H. Crosby. *A Brief History of Western Conservative Baptist Seminary, 1927-1977.* Portland: n.p., 1977? 13 pp.

Western Evangelical Seminary

Williamson, Glen. *Born for Such a Day: The Amazing Story of Western Evangelical Seminary.* Portland: Le Sabre Pr., 1974. 94 pp.

Willamette University

Doney, Carl G. *Cheerful Yesterdays and Confident Tomorrows.* Portland: Binfords & Mort, 1942. 190 pp.

Gatke, Robert M. *Chronicles of Willamette, the Pioneer University of the West.* 2 vols. Portland: Binfords & Mort, 1943. 702 pp.

Gregg, Robert D. *Chronicles of Willamette, Volume II: Those Eventful Years of the President Smith Era.* Portland: n.p., 1970. 238 pp.

Hines, Gustavus. *Oregon and Its Institutions: Comprising a Full History of the Williamette University, the First Established on the Pacific Coast.* New York: Carlton & Porter, 1868. 326 pp.

Matthews, James T. *Turn Right to Paradise.* Portland: Binfords & Mort, 1942. 196 pp.

PENNSYLVANIA

Academy of the New Church

Gladish, Richard R. *A History of the Academy of New Church (From Its*

Beginnings to 1966). Bryn Athyn, Pa.: General Church Religion Lessons, 1967. 223 pp.

Albright College

Gingrich, Felix W., and Barth, Eugene H. *A History of Albright College, 1856-1956.* Reading, Pa.: Albright College, 1956. 562 pp.

Allegheny College

Pelletier, Lawrence L. *From a Reliance on the Smiles of Heaven; The Story of Allegheny College.* New York: Newcomen Society in North America, 1966. 28 pp.

Smith, Ernest A. *Allegheny-A Century of Education, 1815-1915.* Meadville, Pa.: Allegheny College History Co., 1916. 599 pp.

Bloomsburg University of Pennsylvania

Edwards, Eda B. *Profile of the Past, a Living Legacy: Bloomsburg State College, 1839-1979.* Bloomsburg: Bloomsburg State College, 1982. 240 pp.

Bryn Mawr College

Meigs, Cornelia. *What Makes a College? A History of Bryn Mawr.* New York: Macmillan, 1956. 277 pp.

Rittenhouse, Caroline S., and Dolenski, Leo M. *Bryn Mawr College.* Bryn Mawr, Pa.: Bryn Mawr College Library, 1985. 48 pp.

Bucknell University

Gretzinger, William C., and Walker, Charles A., eds. *An Historical Sketch of Bucknell University.* Lewisburg, Pa.: The Editors, 1890. 50 pp.

Oliphant, James O. *The Beginnings of Bucknell University; A Sampling of the Documents.* Lewisburg, Pa.: Bucknell University Pr., 1954. 79 pp.

--------. *The Rise of Bucknell University.* New York: Appleton-Century-Crofts, 1965. 448 pp.

Theiss, Lewis E. *Centennial History of Bucknell University, 1846-1946.*

Williamsport, Pa.: Grit Publishing Company Pr., 1946. 484 pp.

California University of Pennsylvania

Serinko, Regis J. "California State College of Pennsylvania: From Private Normal College to Multi-Purpose Public Institution." Ph.D. diss., University of Pittsburgh, 1974. 557 pp. *Dissertation Abstracts International,* vol. 35A, p. 2026.

--------. *California State College: The People's College in the Monongahela Valley.* Dubuque, Iowa: Kendall/Hunt, 1975. 352 pp.

Carnegie-Mellon University

Cleeton, Glen U. *The Story of Carnegie Tech, II. The Doherty Administration, 1936-1950.* Pittsburgh: Carnegie Pr., 1965. 371 pp.

Tarbell, Arthur W. *The Story of Carnegie Tech: Being a History of Carnegie Institute of Technology from 1900 to 1935.* Pittsburgh: Carnegie Institute of Technology, 1937. 270 pp.

Cedar Crest College

Klein, Harry M. J. *Cedar Crest College, 1867-1947.* Allentown: Trustees of Cedar Crest College, 1948. 142 pp.

Chatham College

Dysart, Laberta. *Chatham College: The First Ninety Years.* Pittsburgh: Chatham College, 1960. 283 pp.

McBane, Edith L. *Pennsylvania College for Women, Historical Sketch, 1869-1944.* Pittsburgh: Alumnae Association of Pennsylvania College for Women, 1944. 32 pp.

Chestnut Hill College

Luckacs, John. *A Sketch of the History of Chestnut Hill College, 1924-1974.* Chestnut Hill: Chestnut Hill College, 1975. 64 pp.

Cheyney University of Pennsylvania

Conyers, Charline F. "A History of the Cheyney State Teachers College, 1837-1951." Ed.D. diss., New York University, 1960. 389 pp. *Dissertation Abstracts,* vol. 21, p. 3002.

Clarion University of Pennsylvania

Farmerie, Samuel A. *Clarion State College: A Centennial History.* Clarion: Alumni Association, 1968. 64 pp.

College Misericordia

Ference, Regina C. "A History of College Misericordia." Master's thesis, University of Scranton, 1964. 89 pp.

College of Philadelphia (Closed 1779)

Gordon, Ann D. "The College of Philadelphia, 1749-1779: Impact of an Institution." Ph.D. diss., University of Wisconsin, 1975. 342 pp. *Dissertation Abstracts International,* vol. 37A, p. 544.

Crozer Theological Seminary*

Crozer Theological Seminary, Chester, Pa. *Historical Sketch of Crozer Theological Seminary: Souvenir of the Thirtieth Anniversary of the Foundation of the Seminary and of the Presidency of Henry G. Weston.* Chester, Pa.: Printed for the Seminary, 1897. 32 pp.

Delaware Valley College of Science and Agriculture

Allman, Herbert D. *A Unique Institution: The Story of the National Farm School.* Philadelphia: Jewish Publication Society of America, 1935. 322 pp.

Dickinson College

Crooks, George R. *Dickinson College. The History of a Hundred Years.* Carlisle, Pa.: n.p., 1883. 36 pp.

Dickinson College. *Bulwark of Liberty: Early Years at Dickinson.* New York: Revell, 1950. 174 pp.

Edel, William W. *John and Mary's College Over Susquehanna.* New York: Newcomen Society in North America, 1956. 24 pp.

Himes, Charles F. *A Sketch of Dickinson College, Carlisle, Penn'a, Including the List of Trustees and Faculty from the Foundation, and a More Particular Account of the Scientific Department.* Harrisburg: L. S. Hart, 1879. 155 pp.

King, Horatio C. *History of Dickinson College.* New York: American University Publishing Co., 1897. 45 pp.

Morgan, James H. *Dickinson College; The History of One Hundred and Fifty Years, 1783-1933.* Carlisle, Pa.: Dickinson College, 1933. 460 pp.

Sellers, Charles. *Dickinson College; A History.* Middletown, Conn.: Wesleyan University Pr., 1973. 626 pp.

Super, Charles W. *A Pioneer College and Its Background (Dickinson).* Salem, Mass., Newcomb & Gauss, 1923. 103 pp.

Drexel University

Kotzin, Miriam N. *A History of Drexel University, 1941-1963.* Philadelphia: Drexel University, 1983. 251 pp.

McDonald, Edward D., and Hinton, Edward M. *Drexel Institute of Technology, 1891-1941; A Memorial History.* Camden: Haddon Craftsmen, 1942. 336 pp.

Dropsie University (Closed 1988)

Ratsh, Abraham I., and Nemoy, Leon, eds. *Essays on the Occasion of the Seventieth Anniversary of the Dropsie University, 1909-1979.* Philadelphia: Dropsie University, 1979. 462 pp.

Rubenstein, Frank J. *The Early Years, 1908-1919; The Dropsie College for Hebrew and Cognate Learning.* Philadelphia: Dropsie University, 1977. 48 pp.

Duquesne University

Clees, William J. "Duquesne University: Its Years of Struggle, Sacrifice, and Service." Ed.D. diss., University of Pittsburgh, 1970. 204 pp. *Dissertation Abstracts International,* vol. 31A, p. 2138.

Hanley, Francis X. "Duquesne University: Evolution from College to University, Administration of Martin A. Hehir, C. S. SP., 1899-1931." Ph.D. diss., University of Pittsburgh, 1979. 351 pp. *Dissertation Abstracts International,* vol. 40A, p. 4325.

Eastern College

Baird, John A. *A Leap of Faith: The First Twenty Years of Eastern College.* St. Davids, Pa.: Eastern College, 1972. 121 pp.

Claghorn, George S. *Mount Up with Wings; A History of Eastern Baptist College.* St. Davids, Pa.: Eastern Baptist College, 1962. 78 pp.

Edinboro University of Pennsylvania

Neel, George W. "A History of the State Teachers College at Edinboro, Pennsylvania." Ph.D. diss., Rutgers University, 1950. 117 pp.

Vance, Russell E. *A Portrait of Edinboro: From Private Academy to State College, 1856-1976.* Rochester, N. Y.: PSI Publishers, 1977. 272 pp.

Elizabethtown College

Schlosser, Ralph W. *History of Elizabethtown College, 1899-1970.* Elizabethtown: Elizabethtown College, 1971. 358 pp.

Franklin and Marshall College

Dubbs, Joseph H. *History of Franklin and Marshall College; Franklin College, 1787-1853; Marshall College, 1836-1853; Franklin and Marshall College, 1853-1903.* Lancaster, Pa.: Franklin and Marshall College Alumni Association, 1903. 402 pp.

Klein, Frederick S. *Since 1787: The Franklin and Marshall College Story.* Lancaster, Pa.: Franklin and Marshall College, 1968. 45 pp.

Geneva College

Galbreath, Clarence R. "A Christian College in Contemporary America: Geneva College, 1956-1976." Ph.D. diss., University of Pittsburgh, 1981. 121 pp. *Dissertation Abstracts International,* vol. 43A, p. 86.

Glasgow, William M. *The Geneva Book, Comprising a History of Geneva*

College and a Biographical Catalogue of the Alumni and Many Students.
Philadelphia: Westbrook Publishing Co., 1908. 445 pp.

Gettysburg College

Breidenbaugh, Edward S., ed. *The Pennsylvania College Book, 1832-1882.*
Philadelphia: Lutheran Publication Society, 1882.

Dunkelberger, Harold A. *Gettysburg College and the Lutheran Connection: An Open-Ended Story of a Proud Relationship.* Gettysburg: Gettysburg College, 1975. 32 pp.

Glatfelter, Charles H. *A Salutary Influence: Gettysburg College, 1832-1985.* 2 vols. Gettysburg: Gettysburg College, 1987.

Hefelbower, Samuel G. *The History of Gettysburg College, 1832-1932.* Gettysburg: Gettysburg College, 1932. 485 pp.

Wentz, Abdel R. *Gettysburg Lutheran Theological Seminary.* 2 vols. Harrisburg: The Evangelical Pr., 1965.

--------. *History of the Gettysburg Theological Seminary of the General Synod of the Evangelical Lutheran Church in the United States and of the United Lutheran Church in America, Gettysburg, Pennsylvania, 1826-1926.* Philadelphia: United Lutheran Publication House, 1927. 624 pp.

Gratz College

King, Diane A. "A History of Gratz College, 1893-1928." Ph.D. diss., Dropsie University, 1979.

Grove City College

Bartok, Leslie A. "Grove City College and the United States Government since 1977: A Case Study of Autonomy vs. Authority." Ph.D. diss., University of Pittsburgh, 1983. 78 pp. *Dissertation Abstracts International,* vol. 44A, p. 2370.

Dayton, David M. "Building 'Mid the Pines: An Historical Study of Grove City College." Ph.D. diss., University of Pittsburgh, 1971. 440 pp. *Dissertation Abstracts International,* vol. 32A, p. 4999.

--------. *'Mid the Pines: An Historical Study of Grove City College.* Grove City: Grove City College Alumni Association, 1973. 281 pp.

Dietrich, Marietta. "The History of Grove City College." Master's thesis, University of Pittsburgh, 1933. 96 pp.

Ketler, Weir C. *An Adventure in Education: 75 Years of Grove City College, 1876-1951.* New York: Newcomen Society in North America, 1953. 32 pp.

Ramsey, W. M. *Making of a University; What We Have to Learn from Educational Ideals in America.* London: Hodder and Stoughton, 1915. 46 pp.

Hahnemann University

Bradford, Thomas L. *History of the Homeopathic Medical College of Pennsylvania; The Hahnemann Medical College and Hospital of Philadelphia.* Philadelphia: Boericke and Tafel, 1898. 904 pp.

Haverford College

Garrett, Philip C. *A History of Haverford College for the First Sixty Years of Its Existence.* Philadelphia: Potter & Coates, 1892. 732 pp.

Jones, Rufus M. *Haverford College; A History and an Interpretation.* New York: Macmillan, 1933. 244 pp.

Sharpless, Isaac. *The Story of a Small College, by Isaac Sharpless, President of Haverford College, 1887-1917.* Philadelphia: John C. Winston Co., 1918. 237 pp.

Stevens, Robert. *Philadelphia Friends and Higher Education: The Case of Haverford College.* New York: Newcomen Society in North America, 1983. 24 pp.

Hershey Junior College (Closed 1965)

Klotz, Richard R. "The Hershey Junior College, Hershey, Pennsylvania, 1938-1965." Ed.D. diss., Pennsylvania State University, 1970. 406 pp. *Dissertation Abstracts International,* vol. 32A, p. 762.

Holy Family College

Frey, Peter W. *Holy Family College: A History of Its Growth and Development.* Philadelphia: Holy Family College, 1979. 44 pp.

PENNSYLVANIA / 341

Indiana University of Pennsylvania

Merryman, John E. *The Indiana Story, 1875-1975: Pennsylvania's First State University.* Indiana, Pa.: Merryman, 1976. 458 pp.

--------. "Indiana University of Pennsylvania: From Private Normal School to Public University, 1871-1968." Ph.D. diss., University of Pittsburgh, 1972. 506 pp. *Dissertation Abstracts International,* vol. 33A, p. 4142.

Juanita College

Ellis, Charles C. *Juanita College; The History of Seventy Years, 1876-1946.* Elgin, Ill.: Brethren Publishing House, 1947. 298 pp.

Emmert, David. *Reminiscences of Juanita College, Quarter Century, 1876-1901.* Huntington, Pa.: The Author, 1901. 183 pp.

Kaylor, Earl C. *Truth Sets Free: Juanita Independent College in Pennsylvania, Founded by the Brethren, 1876: A Centennial History.* South Brunswick: A. S. Barnes, 1977. 431 pp.

Kutztown University

Graver, Lee. *Beacon on the Hill: A Centennial History of Kutztown State College.* Kutztown: The State College, 1966. 173 pp.

Myers, Clara A. "History of the State Teacher's College, Kutztown, Pennsylvania." Master's thesis, Temple University, 1934. 154 pp.

Lackawanna Junior College

Zaydon, Jemille A. "The Growth of Lackawanna Junior College." Master's thesis, Wilkes College, 1978. 108 pp.

Lafayette College

Coffin, Seldon J. *The Men of Lafayette, 1828-1893; Lafayette College, Its History, Its Men, Their Record.* Easton, Pa.: G. W. West, 1891. 342 pp.

Gendebien, Albert W. *The Biography of a College: Being the History of the Third Half-Century of Lafayette College.* Easton, Pa.: Lafayette College, 1986. 698 pp.

Kosanovich, William T. *Lafayette College, 1826-1976.* n.p., 1976. 80 pp.

Lafayette College, Easton, Pa. *Illustrated History of Lafayette College, Easton, Pa.* Easton, Pa.: n.p., 1888. 44 pp.

Owen, William B. *Historical Sketches of Lafayette College: With an Account of Its Present Organization and Courses of Study.* Easton, Pa.: G. W. West, 1876. 74 pp.

Skillman, David B. *The Biography of a College; Being the History of the First Century of the Life of Lafayette College.* 2 vols. Easton, Pa.: Lafayette College, 1932.

La Salle University

Donaghy, Thomas J. *Conceived in Crisis: A History of La Salle College, 1863-1965.* Philadelphia: La Salle College, 1966. 219 pp.

Lebanon Valley College

Wallace, Paul A. W. *Lebanon Valley College; A Centennial History.* Annville, Pa.: Lebanon Valley College, 1966. 280 pp.

Lehigh University

Bowen, Catherine D. *A History of Lehigh University.* South Bethlehem: Lehigh Alumni Bulletin, 1924. 105 pp.

Hyde, Edmund M. *The Lehigh University, a Historical Sketch.* South Bethlehem: n.p., 1986. 45 pp.

Lehigh University, Bethlehem, Pa. Anniversary Committee. *Seventy-Five Years of Lehigh University; A Chronology.* Bethlehem: Lehigh University, 1942. 55 pp.

Stevens, William B. *The Lehigh University, Its Origins and Aims: An Historical Discourse.* Philadelphia: A. C. Bryson & Co., 1869. 25 pp.

Lincoln University

Bond, Horace M. *Education for Freedom: A History of Lincoln University, Pennsylvania.* Lincoln University, Pa.: Lincoln University, 1976. 616 pp.

Rendall, John B. *A Historical Sketch of Lincoln University.* Philadelphia: Wood Printing Co., 1904. 19 pp.

Webb, Edward. *Lincoln University, Pennsylvania: Its History and Work.* Philadelphia: Allen, Lane and Scott, 1890.

Lock Haven University

Wisor, Harold C. "A History of Teacher Education at Lock Haven State College, Lock Haven, Pennsylvania, 1870-1969." Ed.D. diss., Pennsylvania State University, 1966. 334 pp. *Dissertation Abstracts,* vol. 27A, p. 3687.

Lutheran Theological Seminary at Philadelphia

Tappert, Theodore G. *History of the Lutheran Theological Seminary at Philadelphia: 1864-1964.* Philadelphia: Lutheran Theological Seminary, 1964. 168 pp.

Lycoming College

Williams, Charles S. *History of Lycoming College and Its Predecessor Institutions: Williamsport Academy, Dickinson Seminary, Williamsport Dickinson Junior College.* Baltimore: King Brothers, 1959. 154 pp.

Marywood College

Turnbach, Catherine R. "The Origin, Growth, and Development of Mary Wood College, 1919-1953." Master's thesis, Marywood College, 1954. 37 pp.

Medical College of Pennsylvania

Alsop, Gulielma F. *History of the Woman's Medical College, Philadelphia, Pennsylvania, 1850-1959.* Philadelphia: Lippincott, 1950. 256 pp.

Messiah College

Sider, E. Morris. *Messiah College: A History.* Nappanee, Ind.: Evangel Pr., 1984. 314 pp.

Millersville University of Pennsylvania

Graver, Lee A. *A History of the First Pennsylvania State Normal School, Now the State Teachers College at Millersville.* Millersville: State Teachers College, 1955. 258 pp.

Lingenfelten, Linwood S., and Kent, Charles I., eds. *One Hundred Years at the State Teachers College, Millersville, Pennsylvania; With a History in Words and Pictures, 1855-1955.* Lancaster, Pa.: Commercial Printing House, 1955. 30 pp.

Moore College of Art

Design for Women: A History of the Moore College of Art. Wynnewood, Pa.: Livingston Publishing Co., 1968. 111 pp.

Moravian College

Reichel, William C. *A History of the Rise, Progress, and Present Condition of the Bethlehem Female Seminary.* Philadelphia: J. B. Lippincott, 1858. 468 pp.

--------. *A History of the Rise, Progress, and Present Condition of the Moravian Seminary for Young Ladies at Bethlehem, Pa.,* 2d ed. Philadelphia: J. B. Lippincott, 1870. 570 pp.

--------. *A History of the Rise, and Present Condition of the Moravian Seminary for Young Ladies at Bethlehem, Pennsylvania.* Rev. Philadelphia: Lippincott, 1881. 608 pp.

Reichel, William C., and Bigler, William H. *A History of the Moravian Seminary for Young Ladies, at Bethlehem, Pa., with a Catalogue of Its Pupils, 1785-1870.* 4th ed. Bethlehem: Published for the Seminary, 1901. 636 pp.

Schwarze, William N. *History of the Moravian College and Theological Seminary, Founded at Nazareth, Pennsylvania, October 2, 1807.* Bethlehem, Pa.: Times Publishing Co. Printers, 1910. 304 pp.

Weinlick, John R. *Twentieth Century Moravian College: Challenge and Response.* Bethlehem, Pa.: Alumni Association of Moravian College, 1977. 192 pp.

Muhlenberg College

Ochsenford, Solomon E., ed. *Muhlenberg College. A Quarter-Centennial Memorial Volume, Being a History of the College and a Record of Its Men.* Allentown, Pa.: Muhlenberg College, 1892. 584 pp.

Swain, James E. *A History of Muhlenberg College: 1848-1967.* New York: Appleton-Century-Crofts, 1967. 212 pp.

Pennsylvania State University

Bezilla, Michael. *Penn State: An Illustrated History.* University Park: Pennsylvania State University Pr., 1985. 415 pp.

Dunaway, Wayland F. *History of the Pennsylvania State College.* State College: Pennsylvania State College, 1946. 540 pp.

Warnock, Arthur R. *"Your Penn State"; A Brief History of the Pennsylvania State College for Freshmen.* State College: n.p., 1941. 35 pp.

Philadelphia College of Osteopathic Medicine

Peterman, Cy. *The Seventy-Fifth Anniversary History of Philadelphia College of Osteopathic Medicine: A Condensed Record of the Courage, Convictions, and the Transcending Determination of the Early Osteopathic Pioneers, and Those Who Have since Carried on Their Concept of Better Healing and Health Care.* Kutztown: Kutztown Publishing Co., 1974. 143 pp.

Philadelphia College of Pharmacy

England, Joseph W., ed. *The First Century of the Philadelphia College of Pharmacy, 1821-1921.* Philadelphia: Franklin Printing Co., 1922. 728 pp.

Philadelphia College of the Bible

Showers, Renald. "A History of Philadelphia College of the Bible." Th. M. thesis, Dallas Theological Seminary, 1962. 207 pp.

Point Park College

Bern, Paula R.. "Point Park College: A History." Ph.D. diss., University of Pittsburgh, 1980. 463 pp. *Dissertation Abstracts International,* vol. 41A, p. 565.

--------. "Point Park College, 1960-1973." Master's thesis, University of Pittsburgh, 1978. 75 pp.

McLean, Albert F., ed. *Point Park College, the First 25 Years: An Oral History.* Pittsburgh: Point Park College, 1985. 222 pp.

Saint Charles Borromeo Seminary

Connelly, James F. *Saint Charles Seminary, Philadelphia: A History of the Theological Seminary of Saint Charles Borromeo, Overbrook, Philadelphia, Pennsylvania, 1832-1979.* Philadelphia: The Seminary, 1979. 674 pp.

Saint Joseph's University

Burton, David H., and Gerrity, Frank. *Saint Joseph's College: A Family Portrait, 1851-1976.* Philadelphia: Saint Joseph's College Pr., 1977. 76 pp.

Talbot, Francis X. *Jesuit Education in Philadelphia; St. Joseph's College, 1851-1926.* Philadelphia: St. Joseph's College, 1927. 146 pp.

Seton Hill College

Troutman, R. Dwight. "Hazard Yet Forward: A History of Seton Hill College." Ph.D. diss., University of Pittsburgh, 1978. 323 pp. *Dissertation Abstracts International,* vol. 39A, p. 1385.

Shippensburg University

Hubley, John E. *Fountainhead of Good Teachers; A History of the First Ninety Years of Shippensburg State College.* Shippensburg: News-Chronicle Publishing Co., 1964. 176 pp.

--------. *Hilltop Heritage: Shippensburg State's First Hundred Years.* Shippensburg: Shippensburg State College, 1971. 85 pp.

--------. "A History of the Cumberland Valley State Normal School and the State Teachers College, Shippensburg, Pennsylvania." Ed.D. diss., Pennsylvania State University, 1963. 275 pp. *Dissertation Abstracts,* vol. 24, p. 1064.

Slippery Rock University

Watson, Robert J.. *Slippery Rock State College: The Legend Behind the Name.* Slippery Rock: Slippery Rock State College Alumni Association, 1982. 183 pp.

--------. "Slippery Rock's Journey from Normal School to Multi-Purpose State College." Ph.D. diss., University of Pittsburgh, 1979. 210 pp. *Dissertation Abstracts International,* vol. 40A, p. 2517.

Susquehanna University

Clark, William S. *The Story of Susquehanna University.* Selinsgrove: Susquehanna University Pr., 1958. 382 pp.

Swarthmore College

An Adventure in Education; Swarthmore College under Frank Aydolette. New York: Macmillan, 1941. 236 pp.

Babbidge, Homer D. "Swarthmore College in the Nineteenth Century: A Quaker Experience in Education." Ph.D. diss., Yale University, 1953. 323 pp.

Clark, Burton R. *The Distinctive College: Antioch, Reed and Swarthmore.* Chicago: Aldine, 1970. 280 pp.

Walton, Richard J. *Swarthmore College, an Informal History.* Swarthmore, Pa.: Swarthmore College, 1986. 152 pp.

Temple University

Johnson, Robert L. *The Case for Temple University, One of America's Most Unusual Institutions.* New York: Newcomen Society in North America, 1954. 24 pp.

Temple University, Philadelphia. *Five Years of Progress at Temple University,1926-1931.* Philadelphia: n.p., 1931? 14 pp.

Thiel College

Johnson, Roy H. *The History of Thiel College, 1866-1974.* Philadelphia: Dorrance Publishing Co., 1974. 264 pp.

Thomas Jefferson University

Gould, George M. *The Jefferson Medical College of Philadelphia: Benefactors, Alumni, Hospital, etc., Its Founders, Officers, Instructors, 1826-1904: A History.* 2 vols. New York: Lewis Publishing Co., 1904.

Wagner, Frederick B., Jr., ed. *Thomas Jefferson University: Tradition and Heritage.* Philadelphia: Lea & Febiger, 1989. In Press.

University of Pennsylvania

Chamberlain, Joshua L. *University of Pennsylvania; Its History, Influence, Equipment and Characteristics.* 2 vols. Boston: R. Herndon Co., 1901-1902.

Cheyney, Edward P. *History of the University of Pennsylvania, 1740-1940.* Philadelphia: University of Pennsylvania Pr., 1940. 461 pp.

Gilbert, William K. *A History of the College and Academy of Philadelphia, Now Called the University.* Philadelphia: Trent, 1963.

Gordon, Ann D. "The College of Philadelphia, 1749-1779: Impact of an Institution." Ph.D. diss., University of Wisconsin-Madison, 1975. 342 pp. *Dissertation Abstracts International,* vol. 37A, p. 544.

Lippincott, Horace M. *The University of Pennsylvania, Franklin's College; Being Some Account of Its Beginnings and Development, Its Customs and Traditions and Its Gifts to the Nation.* Philadelphia: Lippincott, 1919. 248 pp.

Meyerson, Martin, and Winegrad, Dilys P. *Gladly Learn and Gladly Teach: Franklin and His Heirs at the University of Pennsylvania, 1740-1976.* Philadelphia: University of Pennsylvania Pr., 1978. 263 pp.

Montgomery, Thomas H. *A History of the University of Pennsylvania, from Its Foundation to A. D. 1770.* Philadelphia: G. W. Jacobs & Co., 1900. 566 pp.

Nitzsche, George E. *University of Pennsylvania; Its History, Traditions, Buildings and Memorials.* 5th ed. Philadelphia: John C. Winston Co., 1914. 256 pp.

--------. *University of Pennsylvania: Its History, Traditions, Buildings and Memorials: Also a Brief Guide to Philadelphia.* 6th ed. Philadelphia: International Printing Co., 1916. 312 pp.

--------. *University of Pennsylvania: Its History, Traditions, Buildings,*

PENNSYLVANIA / 349

and Memorials: Also a Brief Guide to Philadelphia. 7th ed. Philadelphia: International Printing Co., 1918. 328 pp.

Smith, William. *Account of the College, Academy, and Charitable School of Philadelphia in Pennsylvania.* Philadelphia: University of Pennsylvania Library, 1951. 43 pp.

Turner, William L. "The College, Academy, and Charitable School of Philadelphia: The Development of a Colonial Institution of Learning, 1740-1779." Ph.D. diss., University of Pennsylvania, 1952.

Wood, George B. *Early History of the University of Pennsylvania from Its Origin to 1827.* 3d ed. Philadelphia: n.p., 1896. 275 pp.

--------. *The History of the University of Pennsylvania, from Its Origin to the Year 1827.* Philadelphia: McCarty & Davis, 1834. 112 pp.

University of Pittsburgh

Alberts, Robert C. *Pitt: The Story of the University of Pittsburgh, 1787-1987.* Pittsburgh: University of Pittsburgh Pr., 1986. 537 pp.

Baynham, Edward G. "The Founding of the University of Pittsburgh." Master's thesis, University of Pittsburgh, 1935. 63 pp.

Starrett, Agnes L. *Through One Hundred and Fifty Years: The University of Pittsburgh.* Pittsburgh: University of Pittsburgh Pr., 1937. 581 pp.

University of Pittsburgh at Johnstown

Shaffer, Lowell D. "A Comparison and Interpretation of the Historical Development of the University of Pittsburgh at Johnstown and the Altona Campus of Pennsylvania State University." Ph.D. diss., University of Pittsburgh, 1982. 311 pp. *Dissertation Abstracts International,* vol. 44A, p. 86.

Ursinus College

Brown, Revelle W. *The Builders of Ursinus, a College in the American Tradition in Old Pennsylvania.* New York: Newcomen Society in North America, 1951. 28 pp.

Yost, Calvin D. *Ursinus College: A History of Its First Hundred Years.* Collegeville, Pa.: The College, 1985. 206 pp.

Valley Forge Military Junior College

Pearson, Willard. *Valley Forge Military Academy and Junior College: Dedicated to Excellence.* New York: Newcomen Society of the United States, 1985.

Villanova University

Middleton, Thomas C. *Historical Sketch of the Augustinian Montastery, College, and Mission of the St. Thomas of Villanova, Delaware County, Pa., during the First Half Century of Their Existence, 1842-1892.* Villanova: Villanova College, 1893. 146 pp.

Washington and Jefferson College

Coleman, Hellen T. W. *Banners in the Wilderness; The Early Years of Washington and Jefferson College.* Pittsburgh: University of Pittsburgh Pr., 1956. 285 pp.

Hobbs, Jane E. "Old Jefferson College." Master's thesis, University of Pittsburgh, 1929. 133 pp.

Moffat, James D. *Historical Sketch of Washington and Jefferson College.* Washington, Pa.: n.p., 1890. 29 pp.

Smith, Joseph. *History of Jefferson College: Including an Account of the Early "Log-Cabin" Schools, and the Cannonsburg Academy.* Pittsburgh: J. T. Shryock, 1857. 433 pp.

Waynesburg College

Dusenberry, William H. *The Waynesburg College Story, 1849-1974.* Kent, Ohio: Kent State University Pr., 1975. 476 pp.

West Chester University

Lee, Kathryn J. "West Chester Academy, 1811-1871: Formative Years of West Chester State College." Master's thesis, West Chester State College, 1966. 174 pp.

Lewis, Joseph J. *History of the West Chester Academy, or, Cornerstone Writings.* Devon, Pa.: Arno Pr., 1972. 23 pp.

Smith, Andrew T. *Quarto - Centennial History of the West Chester State*

Normal School, of the First District, at West Chester, Chester County, Penn'a. West Chester, Pa.: Village Record Printing, 1896. 63 pp.

Sturzebecker, Russell L. *Centennial History of West Chester State College.* West Chester, Pa.: Tinicum Pr., 1971. 272 pp.

Westminster College

Gamble, Paul. *History of Westminister College, 1852-1977.* New Wilmington: Westminister College, 1977. 97 pp.

--------. *Westminister's First Century.* New Wilmington: Westminister College, 1952. 76 pp.

Widener University

Moll, Clarence R. "A History of Pennsylvania Military College, 1821-1954." Ph.D. diss., New York University, 1955. 481 pp. *Dissertation Abstracts,* vol. 16, p. 906.

Wilson College

The History of an Idea: A Brief Sketch of Wilson College. Chambersburg, Pa.: n.p., 1945. 23 pp.

RHODE ISLAND

Brown University

Barry, Jay. *A Tale of Two Centuries: A Warm and Richly Pictorial History of Brown University, 1764-1985.* Providence: Brown Alumni Monthly, 1985. 319 pp.

Bronson, Walter C. *The History of Brown University, 1764-1914.* Providence: The University, 1914. 547 pp.

Brown University. *Celebration of the One Hundredth Anniversary of the Founding of Brown University, September 6th, 1864.* Providence: S. S. Rider & Bro., 1865. 178 pp.

--------. *The Growth of Brown University in Recent Years, 1899-1909.* Providence: The University, 1909. 14 pp.

––––––––. *The Sesquicentennial of Brown University, 1764-1914; A Commemoration.* Providence: The University, 1915. 306 pp.

Fleming, Donald H. *Science and Technology in Providence, 1700-1914; An Essay in the History of Brown University in the Metropolitan Community.* Providence: Brown University, 1952. 54 pp.

Gerold, William. *College Hill; A Photographic Study of Brown University in Its Two Hundredth Year.* 1 vol. Providence: Brown University Pr., 1965.

Guild, Reuben A. *Early History of Brown University.* Providence: Printed by Snow and Farnham, 1897. 631 pp.

––––––––. *Historical Sketch of Brown University.* Providence: Snow & Greene, 1858. 8 pp.

––––––––. *History of Brown University, with Illustrative Documents.* Providence: Providence Press Company, Printers, 1867. 443 pp.

––––––––. *Life, Times and Correspondence of James Manning, and the Early History of Brown University.* Boston: Gould and Lincoln, 1864. 523 pp.

Keen, William W. *The Early Years of Brown University, 1764-1770.* Boston: Merrymount Pr., 1914. 36 pp.

Locke, Edwin A., ed. *Brown University. An Illustrated Historical Souvenir.* Providence: Preston & Rounds Co., 1897. 123 pp.

Providence College

McCaffrey, Donna T. "The Origins and Early History of Providence College through 1947." Ph.D. diss., Providence College, 1985. 537 pp. *Dissertation Abstracts International,* vol. 45A, p. 3728.

Rhode Island College

Bicknell, Thomas W. *A History of the Rhode Island Normal School.* Providence: T. W. Bicknell, 1911. 231 pp.

Carbone, Hector R. "The History of the Rhode Island Institute of Instruction and the Rhode Island Normal School as Agencies and Institutions of Teacher Education, 1845-1920." Ph.D. diss., University of Connecticut, 1971. 440 pp.

University of Rhode Island

Eschenbacher, Herman F. "Rhode Island and Its Land Grant College, 1863-1914: A Case Study of the Establishment of a Morrill Act College in New England." Ph.D. diss., Harvard University, 1963.

--------. *The University of Rhode Island: A History of Land Grant Education in Rhode Island.* New York: Appleton, 1967. 548 pp.

Woodward, Carl R. *Education's "Lively Experiment" in Rhode Island.* New York: Newcomen Society in North America, 1957. 28 pp.

--------. *From College to University, 1941-1958; A Summary Report.* Kingston, R. I.: n.p., 1960. 60 pp.

SOUTH CAROLINA

Anderson College

Campbell, Marie K. "A Historical Study of Anderson College, 1911 through 1930." Master's thesis, Clemson College, 1961. 110 pp.

Hester, Hubert I. *They That Wait; A History of Anderson College.* Anderson: Anderson College, 1969. 204 pp.

Benedict College

Richardson, Frederick. "A Power for Good in Society: The History of Benedict College." Ph.D. diss., Florida State University, 1973. 275 pp. *Dissertation Abstracts International,* vol. 35A, p. 1028.

Bob Jones University

Tice, Margaret B. *Bob Jones University: 50 Years under God.* Greenville, S. C.: The University, 1976. 114 pp.

Wright, Melton. *Fortress of Faith: The Story of Bob Jones University.* New enl. ed. Greenville, S. C.: Bob Jones University Pr., 1960. 336 pp.

--------. *Fortress of Faith: The Story of Bob Jones University.* 3d ed. Grand Rapids: Eerdmans, 1984. 439 pp.

The Citadel, The Military College of South Carolina

Bond, Oliver J. *The Story of the Citadel.* Richmond: Garrett and Massie, 1936. 242 pp.

Citadel, the Military College of South Carolina. Association of Graduates. *Semi-Centennial of the South Carolina Military Academy.* Charleston: Walker, Evans & Cogswell, 1893. 63 pp.

Grimsley, James A. *The Citadel: Educating the Whole Man.* New York: Newcomen Society in North America, 1983. 20 pp.

Thomas, John P. *The History of the South Carolina Military Academy.* Charleston: Walker, Evans & Cogswell, 1893. 579 pp.

Clemson University

Bryan, Wright. *Clemson: An Informal History of the University, 1889-1979.* Columbia: R. L. Bryan, 1979. 288 pp.

Mellette, Frank. *Old Clemson College -- It Was a Hell of a Place.* Deep Run, N. C.: F. Mellette, 1981. 301 pp.

Coker College

Parrish, William S. "A History of Coker College." Master's thesis, University of South Carolina, 1938. 122 pp.

College of Charleston

Easterby, James H. *A History of the College of Charleston, Founded 1770.* Charleston: Trustees of the College of Charleston, 1935. 379 pp.

Columbia Bible College and Seminary

Matthews, R. Arthur. *Towers Pointing Upward.* Columbia: Columbia Bible College, 1973. 175 pp.

Columbia College

Ariail, James M. *Columbia College, 1912-1968.* Columbia: n.p., 1969. 50 pp.

SOUTH CAROLINA / 355

Griffin, Anne F. *Columbia College Centennial: An Historical Pageant.* Columbia: Farrell Pr., 1956. 89 pp.

Savory, Jerold J. *Columbia College: The Ariail Era.* Columbia: R. L. Bryan, 1979. 246 pp.

Winn, Evelyn B. "A History of Columbia College." Master's thesis, University of South Carolina, 1927. 127 pp.

Converse College

Kibler, Lillian A. *History of Converse College, 1889-1971.* Spartanburg: Converse College, 1973. 547 pp.

Erskine College

Boyce, Annabel. S. *Bryson College, 1919-1929: A History.* Fayetteville, Tenn.: Bryson College Alumni Association, 1976. 148 pp.

Kennedy, Walter A., Jr. "Erskine College before the Civil War." Master's thesis, University of South Carolina, 1945. 174 pp.

Lesesne, Joab M., Jr. "A Hundred Years of Erskine College, 1839-1939." Ph.D. diss., University of South Carolina, 1967. 318 pp. *Dissertation Abstracts,* vol. 28A, p. 3608.

Wingard, Kathleen M. "History of the Women's College of Due West." Master's thesis, University of South Carolina, 1928. 197 pp.

Francis Marion College

West, Thomas W. *Marion College, 1873-1967.* Strasburg, Va.: Shenandoah Publishing House, 1970. 298 pp.

Furman University

Daniel, Robert N. *Furman University, a History.* Greenville: Furman University, 1951. 289 pp.

McGlothlin, William J. *Baptist Beginnings in Education: A History of Furman University.* Nashville: Sunday School Board of the Southern Baptist Convention, 1926. 249 pp.

Reid, Alfred S. *Furman University: Toward a New Identity, 1925-1975.*

Durham, N. C.: Duke University Pr., 1976. 288 pp.

Limestone College

McMillan, Montague. *Limestone College, a History: 1845-1970.* Gaffney: Limestone College, 1970. 516 pp.

Taylor, Walter C. "History of Limestone College." Master's thesis, University of South Carolina, 1934. 106 pp.

--------. *History of Limestone College, Gaffney, S. C.* Gaffney: Limestone College, 1937. 128 pp.

Lutheran Theological Southern Seminary

Hahn, Stephen S. "A History of the Lutheran Theological Southern Seminary and Its Library, 1830-1934." Thesis, University of Chicago, 1977. 142 pp.

Medical University of South Carolina

Edwards, James B. *The Southeast's Oldest Medical School: Now a Leading Research and Treatment Center.* New York: Newcomen Society of the United States, 1986. 23 pp.

Lynch, Kenneth M. *Medical Schooling in South Carolina, 1823-1969.* Columbia: R. L. Bryan, 1970. 153 pp.

Morris College

Sims, Frank K. "A Socio-Historical Study of Morris College, Sumter, South Carolina." Master's thesis, Tennessee Agricultural & Industrial State University, 1960.

Newberry College

Bedenbaugh, J. Holland. "A History of Newberry College." Master's thesis, University of South Carolina, 1930. 207 pp.

Henry, Gordon C., ed. *A History of Newberry College, Newberry, South Carolina, 1856-1976: 120 Years of Service to the Lutheran Church and to South Carolina.* Rev. Newberry, S. C.: Newberry College, 1976. 34 pp.

North Greenville College

Flynn, Jean M. *A History of North Greenville Junior College.* Tigerville, S. C.: North Greenville Junior College, 1953. 173 pp.

Presbyterian College

Hammet, Ben H. *The Spirit of PC: A Centennial History of Presbyterian College.* Clinton, S. C.: Jacobs Pr., 1982. 204 pp.

South Carolina State College

Potts, John F. *The History of South Carolina State College, 1896-1978.* Orangeburg: South Carolina State College, 1978. 215 pp.

Summerland College (Closed 1930)

McKenzie, Pearle. "A History of Summerland College." Master's thesis, University of South Carolina, 1929. 72 pp.

University of South Carolina

Bryan, John M. *An Architectural History of the South Carolina College, 1801-1855.* Columbia: University of South Carolina Pr., 1976. 133 pp.

Green, Edwin L. *A History of the University of South Carolina.* Columbia: State Co., 1916. 475 pp.

Hollis, Daniel W. "South Carolina College." Ph.D. diss., Columbia University, 1953.

--------. *University of South Carolina.* 2 vols. Columbia: University of South Carolina Pr., 1951-1956.

Jones, Thomas F. *The University of South Carolina; Faithful Index to the Ambitions and Fortunes of the State.* New York: Newcomen Society in North America, 1964. 24 pp.

LaBorde, Maximillian. *History of the South Carolina College, from Its Incorporation, Dec. 19, 1801 to Dec. 19, 1865, Including Sketches of Its Presidents and Professors.* 2d ed. Charleston: Walker Evans & Cogswell Printers, 1874. 596 pp.

--------. *History of the South Carolina College, from Its Incorporation in 1801 to 1857.* Columbia: n.p., 1859. 463 pp.

Voorhees College

Blanton, Robert J. *The Story of Voorhees College: From 1897 to 1982.* Denmark, S. C.: Voorhees College, 1983. 266 pp.

Jabs, Albert E. "The Mission of Voorhees College: Its Roots and Its Future." Ed.D. diss., University of South Carolina, 1983. 205 pp. *Disseration Abstracts International,* vol. 45A, p. 94.

Winthrop College

Crowson, Elmer T. *The Winthrop Story, 1886-1960.* Baltimore: Gateway Pr., 1987. 599 pp.

Odom, Jane H. "The Struggle for Coeducation at Winthrop College: Two Decades of Progress, 1954-1974." Master's thesis, Winthrop College, 1982. 125 pp.

Wofford College

Treanor, John M. *Founding Fathers of Wofford College, 1776-1976: A Series of Biographical Sketches.* Spartanburg, S. C.: Wofford Library Pr., 1976-

Wallace, David D. *History of Wofford College, 1854-1949.* Nashville, Tenn.: Vanderbilt University Pr., 1951. 287 pp.

SOUTH DAKOTA

Augustana College

Erpestad, Emil. *A History of Augustana College.* Sioux Falls: Augustana College, 1971. 320 pp.

Hanson, Richard S. "Augustana College, Canton, South Dakota, 1884-1919." Master's thesis, University of South Dakota, 1939. 56 pp.

Jordahl, Sivert A. *Memorial History: Lutheran Normal School, Sioux Falls,*

South Dakota, 1889-1918. *Sioux Falls: Brown & Saenger, 1954. 125 pp.*

Sneen, Donald J. *Through Trials and Triumphs: A History of Augustana College.* Sioux Falls: Center for Western Studies, 1985. 192 pp.

Black Hills State College

Haivala, Paul A. *The Friendly College: The First 100 Years of Black Hill State College, 1883-1983.* Spearfish: Black Hills State College, 1983. 192 pp.

Dakota State College

Lowry, Vayne A. *Forty Years at General Beadle, 1922-1962.* Madison, S. D.: Dakota State College, 1984. 74 pp.

Stewart, Charles J. "A History of Eastern South Dakota State Normal School." Master's thesis, University of South Dakota, 1938. 66 pp.

Dakota Wesleyan University

Coursey, Oscar W. *A History of Dakota Wesleyan University for Fifty Years, 1885-1935.* Mitchell: Dakota Wesleyan University, 1935. 170 pp.

Goerig, Violet M. "Dakota Wesleyan University, 1885-1960." Master's thesis, University of South Dakota, 1970. 197 pp.

Huron College

Huron College, Huron, South Dakota. *Huron College, Beginning and Growth.* Huron: n.p., 1923. 24 pp.

Sioux Falls College

Jeschke, Reuben P. *Dream of the Pioneers; A Brief and Informal History of Sioux Falls College in Commemoration of Its Seventy-Fifth Anniversary.* Sioux Falls: Sioux Falls College, 1958. 175 pp.

South Dakota State University

Powers, William H. *A History of South Dakota State College.* Brookings: South Dakota State College, 1931. 144 pp.

Sewrey, Charles L. *A History of South Dakota State College, 1884-1959.*
Brookings: South Dakota State College, 1959. 98 pp.

University of South Dakota

Akeley, Lewis E. *This Is What We Had in Mind; Early Memories of the University of South Dakota.* Vermillion: University of South Dakota, 1959. 69 pp.

Christol, Carl. *The Early History of the University of South Dakota.* 1 vol. Vermillion: n.p., 1964.

Clow, Richmond L. *The University of South Dakota, 1967-1982.* Vermillion: Dakota Pr., 1983. 113 pp.

Cummins, Cedric C. *The University of South Dakota, 1862-1966.* Vermillion: Dakota Pr., 1975. 334 pp.

Dow, John G. *Early History of the University, 1862-1889.* Vermillion: South Dakota Alumni Association, 1907. 110 pp.

Stockton, Frank T. *This Is What We Tried to Do in Cayote Land, 1917-1924.* Vermillion: University of South Dakota, 1968. 59 pp.

Wessington Springs Junior College (Closed 1964)

Waller, Fred L. "A History of Wessington Springs College." Master's thesis, University of South Dakota, 1935. 124 pp.

Yankton College (Closed 1984)

McMurtry, William J. *Yankton College; A Historical Sketch.* Yankton: n.p., 1907. 160 pp.

Stewart, Edgar I. *Yankton College; The Second Twenty-Five Years.* Yankton: n.p., 1932. 220 pp.

TENNESSEE

Austin Peay State University

Condell, Robert. "A History of Austin Peay State University." Master's thesis, University of Tennessee, 1971. 173 pp.

Waters, Charles M., ed. *The First Fifty Years of Austin Peay State University.* Clarksville: Austin Peay State University, 1977. 213 pp.

Belmont College

Duncan, Ivar L. M. *A History of Belmont College.* Nashville: Belmont College, 1967. 15 pp.

Bethel College

Oliver, Mary C. "A History of Bethel Woman's College." Master's thesis, Murray State Teachers College, 1944. 75 pp.

Bryan College

Lasley, Jess W. "The History of Bryan College." Ph.D. diss., Baylor University, 1960.

Burritt College (Closed 1949)

West, Francis M. "Pioneer of the Cumberlands: A History of Burritt College, 1848-1938." Master's thesis, Tennessee Technological University, 1969. 174 pp.

Carson-Newman College

Carr, Isaac N. *History of Carson-Newman College.* Jefferson City: Carson-Newman College, 1959. 367 pp.

Hall, William F. "The History of Carson-Newman College." Master's thesis, University of Tennessee, 1936. 87 pp.

Christian Brothers College

Battersby, William J. *The Christian Brothers in Memphis; A Chronicle of One Hundred Years, 1871-1971.* Memphis: Christian Brothers College, 1971. 101 pp.

Cumberland University

Bone, Winstead P. *A History of Cumberland University, 1842-1935.* Lebanon: The Author, 1935. 303 pp.

Nunley, Joe E. "A History of Cumberland Female College, McMinnville, Tennessee." Ed.D. diss., University of Tennessee, 1965. 153 pp. *Dissertation Abstracts,* vol. 26, p. 4423.

Stephens, John V. *The Cumberland University Theological School - Lebanon Theological Seminary.* Cincinnati: n.p., 1939. 38 pp.

David Lipscomb College

Neil, Robert G. "The History of David Lipscomb College." Master's thesis, George Peabody College for Teachers, 1938. 106 pp.

Pittman, Samuel P. *Lipscomb's Golden Heritage, 1891-1941.* Nashville: Associated Ladies for Lipscomb, David Lipscomb College, 1983. 64 pp.

East Tennessee State University

Burleson, David S. *History of East Tennessee State College.* Johnson City: East Tennessee State College, 1947. 102 pp.

Fisk University

Jones, Thomas E. *Progress at Fisk University: A Summary of Recent Years.* Nashville: Fisk University, 1930. 55 pp.

Merrill, James G. *Fisk University after Forty Years.* New York: C. Holt, (19?). 12 pp.

Richardson, Joe M. *History of Fisk University, 1865-1946.* University, Ala.: University of Alabama Pr., 1980. 227 pp.

Johnson Bible College

Black, Robert E. *The Story of Johnson Bible College.* Kimberlin Heights, Tenn.: Johnson Bible College, 1951. 118 pp.

Lambuth College

Clement, Sarah V. *A College Grows: MCFI-Lambuth.* Jackson: Lambuth College Alumni Association, 1972. 242 pp.

Hinton, David E. "Origin, Development and Aims of Lambuth College." Master's thesis, George Peabody College for Teachers, 1936. 66 pp.

Lane College

Cooke, Anna L. *Lane College: Its Heritage and Outreach, 1882-1982.* Jackson: The College, 1987. 150 pp.

Lee College

Horton, E. Gene. "A History of Lee Junior College, Cleveland, Tennessee." Master's thesis, University of South Dakota, 1953. 89 pp.

Johnson, Robert G. "Establishment and Development of Lee College, 1918-1954." Master's thesis, Memphis State University, 1955.

Ray, Mauldon A. "A Study of the History of Lee College, Cleveland, Tennessee." Ed.D. diss., University of Houston, 1964. 242 pp. *Dissertation Abstracts,* vol. 25, p. 2336.

Underwood, James L. "Historical Development of Lee Junior College." Master's thesis, University of Tennessee, 1954.

LeMoyne-Owen College

Qualls, J. Winfield. "The Beginning and Early History of the LeMoyne School at Memphis--1871-1874." Master's thesis, Memphis State University, 1952. 58 pp.

Lincoln Memorial University

Shumate, Mildred. *A Brief History of Lincoln Memorial University.* Harrogate, Tenn.: Lincoln Memorial University Pr., 1972. 20 pp.

Suppiger, Joseph E. *Phoenix of the Mountains: The Story of Lincoln Memorial University.* Harrogate, Tenn.: Lincoln Memorial University Pr., 1977. 159 pp.

Madison College

Sandborn, William C. "The History of Madison College." Ed.D. diss., George Peabody College for Teachers, 1953. 201 pp.

Martha Washington College (Closed 1931)

Curtis, Claude D. *Three Quarters of a Century at Martha Washington College.* Bristol: King Printing Co., 1928. 223 pp.

Martin Methodist College

Allen, Paul F. *A History of Martin College: The First One Hundred Years.* Pulaski, Tenn.: Martin College, 1971. 48 pp.

Maryville College

Lloyd, Ralph W. *Maryville College: A History of 150 Years, 1819-1969.* Maryville, Tenn.: Maryville College Pr., 1969. 287 pp.

Wilson, Samuel T. *A Century of Maryville College, 1819-1919, a Story of Altruism.* Maryville, Tenn.: The Directors at Maryville College, 1916. 265 pp.

--------. *Chronicles of Maryville College; A Story of Altruism.* Maryville, Tenn.: The Directory of Maryville College, 1935. 334 pp.

Meharry Medical College

Roman, Charles V. *Meharry Medical College: A History.* Nashville: Sunday School Publishing Board of the National Baptist Convention, 1934. 224 pp.

--------. *Meharry Medical College: A History.* Freeport, N. Y.: Books for Libraries Pr., 1972. 224 pp.

Summerville, James. *Educating Black Doctors: A History of Meharry Medical College.* University, Ala.: University of Alabama Pr., 1983. 279 pp.

Memphis State University

Sorrels, William. *The Exciting Years: The Cecil C. Humphreys Presidency of Memphis State University, 1960-1977.* Memphis: Memphis State University Pr., 1987. 283 pp.

Stathis, John C. "The Establishment and Early Development of the West Tennessee State Normal School, 1909-1914." Master's thesis, Memphis State University, 1951. 112 pp.

Wooten, Rebecca G. "A History of Memphis State College." Master's thesis, University of Texas, 1942. 128 pp.

Middle Tennessee State University

Pittard, Homer. *First Fifty Years.* Murfreesboro: Middle Tennessee State College, 1961. 273 pp.

--------. "Middle Tennessee State College: Its Historical Aspects and Its Relation to Significant Teacher Education Movements." Ed.D. diss., George Peabody College for Teachers, 1957. 482 pp. *Dissertation Abstracts,* vol. 18, p. 513.

Morristown College

Hammond, Brenda H. "A Historical Analysis of Selected Forces and Events Which Influenced the Founding, Growth, and Development of Morristown College, a Historically Black Two-Year College from 1881 to 1981." Ed.D. diss., George Washington University, 1983. 374 pp. *Dissertation Abstracts International,* vol. 44A, p. 696.

Rhodes College

Cooper, Waller R. *Southwestern at Memphis, 1848-1948.* Richmond, Va.: John Knox Pr., 1949. 172 pp.

Roper, James E. *Southwestern at Memphis, 1948-1975.* Memphis: Southwestern, 1975. 118 pp.

Scarritt Graduate School (Closed 1988)

Cobb, Alice. *"Yes, Lord, I'll Do It": Scarritt's Century of Service.* Nashville: Scarritt College, 1987. 206 pp.

Sequatchie College*

Baskin, Patricia N. "Sequatchie College, 1860-1892: A Link in the History of Education in Tennessee." Master's thesis, Baylor University, 1979. 116 pp.

Southern College of Seventh-Day Adventists

Gardner, Elva B. *Southern Missionary College, a School of His Planning: A Narrative of Seventy Years of Growth and Development of SMC, 1892-1962.* Chattanooga, Tenn.: Published by the Board of Trustees, 1962. 240 pp.

Tennessee State University

Fancher, Evelyn P. "Tennessee State University: A History of an Institution with Implications for the Future." Ph.D. diss., George Peabody College for Teachers of Vanderbilt University, 1975. 302 pp. *Dissertation Abstracts International,* vol. 36A, p. 5098.

Lloyd Raymond G. *Tennessee Agricultural and Industrial State University, 1912-1962; Fifty Years of Leadership Through Excellence, 1912-1962.* Nashville: n.p., 1962. 73 pp.

Tennessee Technological University

Smith, Austin W. *The Story of Tennessee Tech.* Nashville: McQuiddy Printing Co., 1957. 326 pp.

Tennessee Wesleyan College

Martin, LeRoy A. *A History of Tennessee Wesleyan College, 1857-1957.* Athens, Tenn.: n.p., 1957. 296 pp.

Trevecca Nazarene College

Downey, J. Paul. "History of Trevecca Nazarene College." Master's thesis, University of Alabama, 1938. 101 pp.

Wynkoop, Mildred B. *The Trevecca Story: 75 Years of Christian Service.* Nashville: Trevecca Pr., 1976. 304 pp.

Tusculum College

Bailey, Gilbert L. "A History of Tusculum College, 1944-1964." Master's thesis, Tennessee State University, 1965.

Ragan, Allen E. *A History of Tusculum College, 1794-1944.* Greenville: The Tusculum Sesquicentennial Committee, 1945. 274 pp.

Union University

Ward, Richard H. *A History of Union University.* Jackson, Tenn.: Union University Pr., 1975. 211 pp.

University of Tennessee

Folmsbee, Stanley J. *Blount College and East Tennessee College, 1794-1840: The First Predecessors of the University of Tennessee.* Knoxville: University of Tennessee Pr., 1946. 50 pp.

--------. *East Tennessee University, 1840-1879: Predecessor of the University of Tennessee.* Knoxville: University of Tennessee, 1959. 143 pp.

--------. *Tennessee Establishes a State University; First Years of the University of Tennessee, 1879-1887.* Knoxville: University of Tennessee Pr., 1961. 214 pp.

Holt, Andrew D. *The University of Tennessee; Dynamic Spirit of the Volunteer State.* New York: Newcomen Society in North America, 1966. 28 pp.

Montgomery, James R. *Threshold of a New Day; The University of Tennessee, 1919-1946.* Knoxville: University of Tennessee, 1971. 432 pp.

--------. *The University of Tennessee Builds for the Twentieth Century; A History of the University of Tennessee during the Administration of President Brown Ayers, 1904-1919.* Knoxville: University of Tennessee, 1957. 97 pp.

--------. "The University of Tennessee during the Administration of President Brown Ayers, 1904-1919." Master's thesis, University of Tennessee, 1956. 203 pp.

--------. "The University of Tennessee, 1887-1919." Ph.D. diss.,

Columbia University, 1961. 375 pp. *Dissertation Abstracts*, vol. 22, p. 3261.

--------. *The Volunteer State Forges Its University; The University of Tennessee, 1887-1919.* Knoxville: University of Tennessee, 1966. 231 pp.

Montgomery, James R.; Folmsbee, Stanley J.; and Greene, Lee S. *To Foster Knowledge: A History of the University of Tennessee, 1794-1970.* Knoxville: University of Tennessee Pr., 1984. 482 pp.

Orr, Bill M. "A History of Tennessee Medical College, 1889-1914." Master's thesis, University of Tennessee, 1960. 93 pp.

Sanford, Edward T. *Blount College and the University of Tennessee. An Historical Address Delivered before the Alumni Association and Members of the University of Tennessee.* Knoxville: The University, 1894. 119 pp.

University of Tennessee (Knoxville Campus). *The University of Tennessee Sesqui-centennial, 1794-1944.* Knoxville: University of Tennessee Pr., 1945. 217 pp.

University of Tennessee at Chattanooga

Govan, Gilbert E., and Livingood, James W. *The University of Chattanooga: Sixty Years.* Chattanooga: University of Chattanooga, 1947. 271 pp.

University of Tennessee at Martin

Inman, Elmer B. "A History of the Development of the University of Tennessee, Martin Branch." Ed.D. diss., University of Tennessee, 1960. 250 pp. *Dissertation Abstracts,* vol. 21, p. 311.

University of the South

Baker, Lily, et.al., eds. *Sewanee.* Sewanee: Published for the Benefit of the University Library College of Sewanee, 1937. 156 pp.

Chitty, Arthur B. *Reconstruction at Sewanee; The Founding of the University of the South and Its First Administration, 1857-1872.* Sewanee: The University Pr., 1954. 206 pp.

Fairbanks, George R. *History of the University of the South at Sewanee,*

Tennessee, from Its Founding by the Southern Bishops, Clergy and Laity of the Episcopal Church in 1857 to the Year 1905. Jacksonville, Fla.: H. and W. B. Drew Co., 1905. 403 pp.

Haskins, David G. *A Brief Account of the University of the South.* New York: Dutton, 1877. 47 pp.

McCrady, Edward. *Sewanee; Domain of the University of the South, 1858-1958.* New York: Newcomen Society in North America, 1958. 28 pp.

Strode, William. *Sewanee, the University of the South.* Louisville: Harmony House Pub., 1984. 96 pp.

Thomas, Charles E. *The University of the South: Sewanee, "The Oxford of America".* Sewanee: The University Pr., 1934. 31 pp.

Vanderbilt University

Austin, Ben. *The 40 Year Cycle.* South Pasadena, Calif.: Kilmarnock Pr., 1980-

Branscomb, Bennett H. *Vanderbilt University; The Commodore's Best Investment.* New York: Newcomen Society in North America, 1950. 24 pp.

Conkin, Paul K. *Gone With the Ivy: A Biography of Vanderbilt University.* Knoxville: University of Tennessee Pr., 1985. 810 pp.

Crabb, Alfred L. *The Genealogy of George Peabody College for Teachers Covering a Period of One Hundred and Fifty Years.* Nashville: n.p., 1935. 56 pp.

Cullum, Edward N. "George Peabody College for Teachers, 1914-1937." Ed.D. diss., George Peabody College for Teachers, 1963. 620 pp. *Dissertation Abstracts,* vol. 24, p. 5168.

Dillingham, George A. "Peabody Normal College in Southern Education, 1875-1909." Ph.D. diss., George Peabody College for Teachers, 1970. 227 pp. *Dissertation Abstracts International,* vol. 31A, p. 2839.

George Peabody College for Teachers, Nashville. *The Semicentennial of George Peabody College for Teachers, 1875-1925.* Nashville: George Peabody College for Teachers, 1925. 188 pp.

Kelton, Allen. "The University of Nashville, 1850-1875." Ph.D. diss., George Peabody College for Teachers, 1969. 968 pp. *Dissertation Abstracts, International* vol. 30A, p. 4794.

McGaw, Robert A. *A Brief History of Vanderbilt University, 1873-1973.* Nashville: Vanderbilt University Pr., 1973. 48 pp.

--------. *The Vanderbilt Campus: A Pictorial History.* Nashville: Vanderbilt University, 1978. 160 pp.

Mims, Edwin. *A History of Vanderbilt University.* Nashville: Vanderbilt University Pr., 1946. 197 pp.

--------. *A History of Vanderbilt University.* Reprint. New York: Arno Pr., 1977. 497 pp.

Morgan, Kenimer H. "The University of Nashville, 1825-1850." Ph.D. diss., George Peabody College for Teachers, 1960. 883 pp. *Dissertation Abstracts,* vol. 21, p. 539.

Washington College (College Program Discontinued 1923)

Alexander, John E. *A Historical Sketch of Washington College, Tennessee.* Bristol, Tenn.: Printed on Washington College Press by Students, 1902. 55 pp.

Carr, Howard E. *Washington College; A Study of an Attempt to Provide Higher Education in Eastern Tennessee.* Knoxville: S. B. Newman and Co., 1935. 282 pp.

TEXAS

Abilene Christian University

Craig, Earl L. "The Development of Abilene Christian College." Master's thesis, West Texas State College, 1940. 161 pp.

Morris, Don H., and Leach, Max. *Like Stars Shining Brightly; The Story of Abilene Christian College.* Abilene: Abilene Christian College Pr., 1953. 236 pp.

Amarillo College

Curl, Carroll A. "The History of Amarillo College, 1929-1946." Master's thesis, West Texas State College, 1947. 139 pp.

Angelo State University

Rawls, Ruth E. "Angelo State College, 1926-1965." Master's thesis, Southwest Texas State College, 1969. 82 pp.

Austin College

Landolt, George L. *Search for the Summit; Austin College through XII Decades, 1849-1970.* Sherman: Austin College Alumni Association, 1970. 360 pp.

Wallace, Percy E. "The History of Austin College." Master's thesis, University of Texas, 1924. 196 pp.

Austin Presbyterian Theological Seminary

Currie, Thomas W. *Austin Presbyterian Theological Seminary: A Seventy-Fifth Anniversary History.* San Antonio: Trinity University Pr., 1978. 285 pp.

Baylor College of Medicine

Moursund, Walter H. *A History of Baylor University College of Medicine, 1900-1953.* Houston: Gulf Publishing Co., 1956. 242 pp.

Baylor University

Dickinson, William C. "Baylor University - A Century of Discipline, 1845-1947." Master's thesis, Baylor University, 1962. 174 pp.

Edwards, Margaret R. "A Sketch of Baylor University." Master's thesis, Baylor University, 1920. 292 pp.

Gambrell, Herbert P. "The Early Baylor University, 1841-1961." Master's thesis, Southern Methodist University, 1924. 141 pp.

Guemple, John R. "A History of Waco University." Master's thesis, Baylor University, 1964. 149 pp.

McCain, Clara E. "Schools of Baylor University in Dallas." Master's thesis, Southern Methodist University, 1946. 84 pp.

Murray, Lois S. *Baylor at Independence.* Waco: Baylor University Pr., 1972. 421 pp.

Simmons, Laura. *"Out of Our Past"; Texas History Stories.* Waco: Texian Pr., 1967. 99 pp.

Watson, Bert A. "Baylor University: A Military History." Master's thesis, Baylor University, 1968.

White, Michael A. "History of Baylor University, 1845-1861." Master's thesis, Baylor University, 1962. 135 pp.

--------. *History of Baylor University, 1845-1861.* Waco: Texian Pr., 1968. 135 pp.

Williams, Earl F. "History of Baylor University." Master's thesis, Baylor University, 1941. 159 pp.

Bishop College

Toles, Caesar F. "The History of Bishop College." Master's thesis, University of Michigan, 1947. 135 pp.

Blinn College

Schmidt, Charles F.. *History of Blinn College (1883-1958).* Rev. ed. Fort Worth: University Supply and Equipment Co., 1958. 100 pp.

--------. *History of Blinn Memorial College, 1883-1934.* San Antonio: Lodovic Printing Co., 1935. 103 pp.

Burleson College*

Smith, Jesse G. "History of Burleson College, Greenville, Texas." Master's thesis, Southern Methodist University, 1931.

Carr-Burdette College*

Shumacher, Billy G. "A History of Carr-Burdette College." Master's thesis, Texas Christian University, 1951. 107 pp.

Clarendon College

Talley, Kate. "A History of Clarendon College." Master's thesis, West Texas State Teachers College, 1933. 99 pp.

Concrete College*

Wildman, Edward L. "Concrete College and Its Founders." Master's thesis, Southwest Texas State Teachers College, 1944. 36 pp.

Dallas College*

Haley, May B. "Origin and History of Dallas College through the Clough Administration, 1915-1948." Master's thesis, Southern Methodist University, 1950. 98 pp.

Dallas Community College

Gibbons, Harold E. "The Historical Development of the Dallas Community College District: A Study of a Multi-College District." Ph.D. diss., University of Oklahoma, 1975. 151 pp. *Dissertation Abstracts International,* vol. 36A, p. 5099.

Dallas Theological Seminary

Renfer, Rudolf A. "A History of Dallas Theological Seminary." Ph.D. diss., University of Texas, 1959. 326 pp. *Dissertation Abstracts,* vol. 20, p. 2258

East Texas Baptist University

Boyd, James H. "History of the College of Marshall." Master's thesis, Baylor University, 1944. 71 pp.

Westmoreland, Olene. *History of East Texas Baptist College.* Nacogdoches, Tex.: n.p., 1950. 36 pp.

East Texas State University

Bledsoe, James M. *A History of Mayo and His College.* Commerce: n.p., 1946. 159 pp.

Hankins, Martha L. "History of the East Texas State Teachers College." Master's thesis, University of Texas, 1937. 114 pp.

Smith, Lewis I. "A Survey of the History and Growth of the East Texas State Teachers College." Master's thesis, Southern Methodist University, 1928. 86 pp.

El Paso Junior College

Agee, Forrest J. "A History of the El Paso Junior College, 1920-1927." Master's thesis, University of Texas, 1937. 121 pp.

Franklin College*

Glazener, Stephen M. "The History of Franklin College, Pilot Point, Denton County, Texas." Master's thesis, Southern Methodist University, 1932. 238 pp.

Gonzales College*

Lacy, George R. "A History of Gonzales College." Master's thesis, University of Texas, 1936. 133 pp.

Goodnight College*

Fanning, James B. "The History of Goodnight College." Master's thesis, West Texas State University, 1967. 100 pp.

Grayson College*

McMahon, Aileen. "History of Grayson College." Master's thesis, Southern Methodist University, 1940. 137 pp.

Hardin-Simmons University

Jay, Ike W. "History of Hardin-Simmons University, 1890-1940." Master's thesis, Texas Tech College, 1941. 49 pp.

Prescott, Thomas B. "The History of Simmons University." Master's thesis, University of Texas, 1930. 104 pp.

--------. "The History of Simmons University." Th.D. diss., Kansas City Baptist Theological Seminary, 1933. 126 pp.

Richardson, Rupert N. *Famous Are Thy Halls: Hardin-Simmons University As I Have Known It.* Abilene: n.p., 1964. 296 pp.

Hillsboro College

Little, Faye M. "History of Hillsboro (Texas) Junior College." Master's thesis, Baylor University, 1965. 141 pp.

Houston Baptist University

Sibley, Marilyn M. *To Benefit a University: The Union Baptist Association College Property Committee, 1958-1975.* Houston: Treaty Oak Pr., 1978. 86 pp.

Houston Community College

Liddell, Marilyn N. B. "Historical Documentary of Socio-Political and Socio-Economic Factors in Creating Houston Community College (1967-1971)." Ed.D. diss., University of Houston, 1982. 156 pp. *Dissertation Abstracts International,* vol. 43A, p. 3522.

Howard Payne University

Hinton, William H. "A History of Howard Payne College with Emphasis on the Life and Administration of Thomas H. Taylor." Ph.D. diss., University of Texas, 1957.

Hitt, Bowling M. "History of Howard Payne College." Master's thesis, Sul Ross State College, 1951. 209 pp.

Williams, Mima A. "History of Daniel Baker College." Master's thesis, University of Texas, 1940. 168 pp.

Huston-Tillotson College

Jones, William H. *Tillotson College from 1930-1940; A Study of the Total Institution.* Austin: n.p., 1940. 303 pp.

Shackles, Chrystine I. *Reminiscences of Hutson Tillotson College.* Austin: n.p., 1973. 116 pp.

Williams, Mabel C. "The History of Tillotson College, 1881-1952." Master's thesis, Texas Southern University, 1967. 182 pp.

Incarnate Word College

Power, Alacoque, ed. *In Words Commemorated: Essays Celebrating the Centennial of Incarnate Word College, San Antonio, Texas.* San Antonio: The College, 1982. 314 pp.

Reitemeyer, Mary. "The History of Incarnate Word Academy, San Antonio, Texas." Master's thesis, George Peabody College for Teachers, 1938. 84 pp.

Jarvis Christian College

Noe, Minnie A. "History of Jarvis Christian College." Master's thesis, Texas Christian University, 1966. 107 pp.

Kidd-Key College (Closed 1935)

Connelly, Annie L. "The History of Kidd-Key College, Sherman, Grayson County, Texas." Master's thesis, Southern Methodist University, 1942. 137 pp.

Kilgore College

Bolt, Doris, and Durning, Bonnie. *A History of Kilgore College, 1935-1981.* Kilgore, Tex.: Kilgore College, 1981. 223 pp.

Lamar University

Asbury, Ray. *The South Park Story, 1891-1971, and the Founding of Lamar University, 1923-1941; A Documented 80 Year History.* Beaumont: South Park Historical Committee, 1972. 245 pp.

Hutchison, Earl E. "The History of Lamar Junior College." Master's thesis, Texas College of Arts and Industries, 1938. 54 pp.

McLaughlin, Marvin L. "Reflections on the Philosophy and Practices of Lamar State College of Technology as Shown through Its History." Ed.D. diss., University of Houston, 1955. 295 pp. *Dissertation Abstracts,* vol. 15, p. 1021.

Welch, Joe B. "A History of the Growth and Development of Lamar University from 1949-1973." Ed.D. diss., McNeese State University, 1974. 217 pp. *Dissertation Abstracts International,* vol. 35A, p. 4108.

Lon Morris College

Jones, Glendell A. "A History of Lon Morris College." Ph.D. diss., North Texas State University, 1973. 359 pp. *Dissertation Abstracts International,* vol. 34A, p. 1668.

--------. *Mid the Pine Hills of East Texas: The Methodist Centennial History of Lon Morris College.* Jacksonville, Tex.: Progress Publishing Co., 1973. 136 pp.

Strother, Martha D. "A History of Lon Morris College." Master's thesis, Southern Methodist University, 1941. 109 pp.

McMurry College

Newman, Vernie. "A History of McMurry College, 1920-1936." Master's thesis, Texas Tech College, 1937. 76 pp.

Marvin College*

Cobb, Berry B. *History of Marvin College.* Dallas: n.p., 1933. 15 pp.

Midland College

Hickman, Lillian W. "The History of Midland College." Master's thesis, University of Oregon, 1949. 360 pp.

Our Lady of the Lake University

Duncan, Virginia C. "An Analysis of the Evolution of the Purposes of Our Lady of the Lake College." Ph.D. diss., University of Texas, 1967. 335 pp. *Dissertation Abstracts,* vol. 28A, p. 3920.

Paris Junior College

Newton, James H. "History of the Paris Junior College." Master's thesis, Southern Methodist University, 1935. 93 pp.

Paul Quinn College

Harvey, McClennon P. *A Brief History of Paul Quinn College, Waco, Texas:*

1872-1965: With Pictorial Illustrations. Waco: Smith Printing Co., 1965. 72 pp.

Prairie View Agricultural and Mechanical University

Gee, Ruth E. "The History and Development of the Prairie View Training School, 1916-1946." Master's thesis, Prairie View College, 1946. 37 pp.

Sims, Van E. "The Willette Rutherford Banks Administration: A Study in the Historical Development of Prairie View Agricultural and Mechanical College." Master's thesis, Prairie View College, 1950. 105 pp.

Woolfolk, George R. *Prairie View; A Study in Public Conscience, 1878-1946.* New York: Pagent Pr., 1962. 404 pp.

Ranger Junior College

Baskin, Henry L. "History of Ranger Junior College." Master's thesis, University of Texas, 1937. 151 pp.

Rice University

Fitts, Dora A. "A History of Rice Institute." Master's thesis, Butler University, 1934. 128 pp.

Meiners, Fredericka. *A History of Rice University: The Institute Years, 1907-1963.* Houston: Published in Cooperation with the Rice University Historical Commission by Rice University Studies, 1982. 249 pp.

Winningham, Geoff. *Rice University: A 75th Anniversary Portrait.* Houston: Rice University Pr., 1987. 160 pp.

Rusk Baptist College*

Quillen, Herbert N. "A History of the Rusk Baptist College from 1895 to 1928." Master's thesis, Stephen F. Austin State College, 1968. 140 pp.

St. Edward's University

Dunn, William. *Saint Edward's University: A Centennial History.* St.

Edward's University, 1986. 444 pp.

St. Philip's College

Buxton, Alfred G. "A Study of St. Philip's College, San Antonio, Texas." Master's thesis, Trinity University, 1955. 75 pp.

Norris, Clarence W. "St. Philip's College: A Case Study of a Historically Black Two-Year College." Ed.D. diss., University of Southern California, 1975. 327 pp. *Dissertation Abstracts International,* vol. 36A, p. 148.

Sam Houston State University

Bunting, David E. "A Documentary History of Sam Houston Normal Institute." Master's thesis, University of Texas, 1933. 316 pp.

Estill, Mary S. *Vision Realized; A History of Sam Houston State University.* Huntsville, Tex.: Sam Houston Pr., 1970. 246 pp.

Smith, Willis L. "The Development of Sam Houston State Teachers College." Master's thesis, Southern Methodist University, 1928. 154 pp.

San Antonio College

Pope, Wilbur A. "A Study of the Growth and Development of the San Antonio College." Master's thesis, Trinity University, 1952. 73 pp.

Ralson, Hugh E. "History of the San Antonio Junior College." Master's thesis, University of Texas, 1933. 127 pp.

Southern Methodist University

Blair, John E. "The Founding of Southern Methodist University from 1915 to 1926." Master's thesis, Southern Methodist University, 1926. 249 pp.

Hillerbrand, Bonnie B., and Salacuse, Donna B., eds. *SMU Reflections.* Dallas: Southern Methodist University Pr., 1986. 148 pp.

Petit, Judith L. "The Founding of Southern Methodist University, 1910-1916." Master's thesis, Southern Methodist University, 1965. 154 pp.

Thomas, Mary M. H. *Southern Methodist University: Founding and Early Years.* Dallas: SMU Pr., 1974. 224 pp.

--------."Southern Methodist University, the First Twenty-Five Years, 1915-1940." Ph.D. diss., Emory University, 1971. 373 pp. *Dissertation Abstracts International,* vol. 32A, p. 2045.

White, James F. *Architecture at SMU: 50 Years and 50 Buildings.* Dallas: Southern Methodist University Pr., 1966. 32 pp.

Southwest Texas Junior College

Gray, Leona S. "The History of Southwest Texas Junior College." Master's thesis, East Texas State College, 1961. 120 pp.

Nielsen, Ida L., and Gray, Leona S. *From Barracks to Bricks; The Southwest Texas Junior College Story, First Twenty-Five Years.* Uvalde: Southwest Texas Junior College, 1972. 127 pp.

Southwest Texas State University

Brown, Ronald C. *Beacon on the Hill: Southwest Texas State University.* Dallas: Taylor, 1979. 103 pp.

French, Roger, F. "A History of the Southwest Texas State Teachers College." Master's thesis, Southwest Texas State Teachers College, 1939. 106 pp.

Nichols, Tom W. *Rugged Summit.* San Marcos: University Press, Southwest Texas State University, 1970. 483 pp.

Southwestern Assemblies of God College

Farmer, Blake L. "Southwestern Assemblies of God College's Founding, Growth, and Development, 1927-1965." Ed.D. diss., Baylor University, 1965. 169 pp. *Dissertation Abstracts,* vol. 26, p. 4421.

Southwestern Baptist Theological Seminary

Baker, Robert A. *Tell the Generations Following: A History of Southwestern Baptist Theological Seminary, 1908-1983.* Nashville: Broadman Pr., 1983. 526 pp.

Scarborough, Lee R. *A Modern School of the Prophets; A History of the*

Southwestern Baptist Theological Seminary, a Product of Prayer and Faith, Its First Thirty Years, 1907-1937. Nashville: Broadman Pr., 1939. 213 pp.

Southwestern Christian College

Evans, Jack. "The History of Southwestern Christian College, Terrell, Texas." Master's thesis, University of Texas at El Paso, 1963. 67 pp.

Southwestern University

Jones, Ralph W. "A History of Southwestern University, 1873-1949." Ph.D. diss., University of Texas, 1960. 676 pp. *Dissertation Abstracts,* vol. 20, p. 4576.

--------. *Southwestern University, 1840-1961.* Austin: Jenkins Publishing Co., 1973. 373 pp.

Willbern, Glen D. "A History of Southwestern University, Georgetown, Texas." Master's thesis, University of Texas, 1928. 193 pp.

Stephen F. Austin State University

Craddock, Bettye. "The Golden Years: The First Half Century of Stephen F. Austin State University." Master's thesis, Stephen F. Austin State University, 1972. 188 pp.

Sul Ross State University

Pollitt, Frank C. "A History of Sul State Teachers College from 1917 to 1939." Master's thesis, Sul Ross State College, 1939. 83 pp.

Tarleton State University

Cockrell, Frank S. "History of John Tarleton Agricultural College." Master's thesis, Southwest Texas State Teachers College, 1941. 65 pp.

Grissom, Preston B. "The Development of John Tarleton College." Master's thesis, West Texas State Teachers College, 1933. 160 pp.

Temple Junior College

Farrell, Harry C., Jr. "Temple Junior College, Its Founding, Growth, and Development, 1926-1964." Ed.D. diss., Colorado State College, 1964. 567 pp. *Dissertation Abstracts,* vol. 26, p. 6496.

Havekost, Irene. "History of Temple Junior College." Master's thesis, Southwest Texas State Teachers College, 1943. 100 pp.

Texas Agricultural and Mechanical University

Cofer, David B. *The First Five Administrators of Texas A & M College, 1876-1890.* College Station: n.p., 1952. 48 pp.

--------. *Fragments of Early History of Texas A. and M. College.* College Station: n.p., 1953. 96 pp.

--------. *The Second Five Administrators of Texas A & M College, 1890-1905.* College Station: n.p., 1954. 132 pp.

Cofer, David B., ed. *Early History of Texas A & M College through Letters and Papers.* College Station: n.p., 1952. 143 pp.

Dethloff, Henry C. *A Pictorial History of Texas A & M University, 1876-1976.* College Station: Texas A & M University Pr., 1975. 232 pp.

Kellam, Nettie L. "The History of the Texas College of Arts and Industries." Master's thesis, University of Texas, 1938. 169 pp.

Perry, George S. *The Story of Texas A & M.* New York: McGraw-Hill, 1951. 264 pp.

Tomlinson, Marie G. "The State Agricultural and Mechanical College of Texas, 1871-1879: The Personalities, Politics, and Uncertainties." 2 vols. Master's thesis, Texas Agricultural and Mechanical University, 1976.

Texas Christian University

Corder, Jimmie W. *More than a Century.* Fort Worth: Texas Christian University Pr., 1973. 66 pp.

Hall, Colby D. *History of Texas Christian University, a College of the Cattle Frontier.* Fort Worth: Texas Christian University Pr., 1947. 380 pp.

Mason, Frank M. "The Beginnings of Texas Christian University." Master's thesis, Texas Christian University, 1930. 147 pp.

Moore, Jerome A. *Texas Christian University: A Hundred Years of History.* Fort Worth: Texas Christian University Pr., 1973. 306 pp.

Powell, Mae M. "The History of Texas Christian University from 1895 to 1939." Master's thesis, Southern Methodist University, 1939. 185 pp.

Sadler, McGruder E. *Texas Christian University; The Recent Developments.* New York: Newcomen Society in North America, 1965. 24 pp.

Texas Lutheran College

Brown, Dorothy A. *We Sing to Thee: A Story About Clifton College.* Waco: Texian Pr., 1974. 142 pp.

Klages, Alfred D. "A History of Texas Lutheran College, 1851-1951." Master's thesis, University of Texas, 1952. 74 pp.

Moore, Elif A. "The History of Clifton College." Master's thesis, University of Texas, 1927. 220 pp.

Wiederaenders, Arthur G. *Coming of Age: A History of Texas Lutheran College.* San Antonio: Paul Anderson Co., 1978. 238 pp.

Texas Presbyterian College (Closed)

Woodward, Mary T. "History of Texas Presbyterian College, Milford, Texas." Master's thesis, Southern Methodist University, 1945. 133 pp.

Texas Southern University

Bryant, Ira B. *Texas Southern University: Its Antecedents, Political Origin, and Future.* Houston: Bryant, 1975. 127 pp.

Lanier, Raphael O. "The History of Higher Education for Negroes in Texas 1930-1955, with Particular Reference to Texas Southern University." Ed.D. diss., New York University, 1957. 331 pp. *Dissertation Abstracts,* vol. 18, p. 2045.

Terry, William E. "Origin and Development of Texas Southern University, Houston, Texas." Ed.D. diss., University of Houston, 1968. 323 pp. *Dissertation Abstracts International,* vol. 31A, p. 988.

Texas Tech University

Andrews, Ruth H. *The First Thirty Years; A History of Texas Technological College, 1925-1955.* Lubbock: Texas Tech Pr., 1956. 393 pp.

Barrick, Nolan E. *Texas Tech, the Unobserved Heritage.* Lubbock: Texas Tech Pr., 1985. 63 pp.

Gibbs, Clifford L. "The Establishment of Texas Technological College." Master's thesis, Texas Tech College, 1939. 59 pp.

Rushing, Jane G., and Nall, Kline A. *Evolution of a University: Texas Tech at Fifty Years.* Austin: Madrona Pr., 1975. 207 pp.

Wade, Homer D. *The Establishment of Texas Technological College, 1916-1923.* Lubbock: Texas Tech Pr., 1956. 167 pp.

Texas Wesleyan College

Corely, Carol W. *A Brief Survey of the Development of Texas Wesleyan College and Judge George W. Armstrong.* Denton: Texas Woman's University, 1970. 68 pp.

Cox, John E. "A Brief History of Texas Wesleyan College." Ed.D. diss., University of Northern Colorado, 1953. 140 pp.

Matthews, Ben A. "The History of Polytechnic College." Master's thesis, Southern Methodist University, 1930. 124 pp.

Texas Woman's University

Bellamy, Caroline B. "A Study of the Significant Changes in the Growth and Development of the Texas State College for Women." Master's thesis, Texas State College for Women, 1939. 79 pp.

James, Eleanor. *A Summary History of the University, 1901-1961.* Denton: Texas Woman's University, 1961. 48 pp.

Thompson, Joyce. *Marking a Trail: A History of the Texas Woman's University.* Denton: Texas Woman's University Pr., 1982. 238 pp.

Trinity University

Everett, Donald E. *Trinity University; A Record of One Hundred Years.*

San Antonio: Trinity University Pr., 1968. 276 pp.

Hetherington, Martha A. "Trinity University, 1939-1952: The Story of Relocation in San Antonio, Texas." Master's thesis, University of Texas, 1965. 120 pp.

Hornbeak, Samuel L. *Trinity University; Project of Pioneers.* San Antonio: Trinity University Development Council, 1951. 42 pp.

Mason, Blanche M. "Trinity University: The Waxachachie Period." Master's thesis, Trinity University, 1966.

Mitchell, Yetta G. "The History of the Trinity University from 1869 to 1934." Master's thesis, Southern Methodist University, 1936. 213 pp.

Reiwald, Eugenia D. "Trinity University: Aspects of the Tehuacana Period." Master's thesis, Trinity University, 1964.

Tyler Junior College

Ballard, Robert M., Jr. "Tyler Junior College: Its Founding, Growth and Development." Ph.D. diss., East Texas State University, 1971. 192 pp. *Dissertation Abstracts International,* vol. 33A, p. 582.

University of Houston

Houston, Texas. University. *The Growth and Development of the University of Houston, a Summation, March, 1927-May, 1950.* Houston: n.p., 1950. 134 pp.

Mohr, Eleanor S. "The History of the Houston Junior College." Master's thesis, University of Texas, 1936. 181 pp.

Nicholson, Patrick J. *In Time: An Anecdotal History of the First Fifty Years of the University of Houston.* Houston: Pacesetter Pr., 1977. 486 pp.

University of Mary Hardin-Baylor

Edwards, Frederick W. "An Administrative History of Mary Hardin-Baylor College with Special Attention to the Administration of Gordon G. Singleton, 1937-1952." Master's thesis, Baylor University, 1977. 364 pp.

James, Eleanor. *Forth from Her Portals: The First 100 Years in Belton:*

University of Mary Hardin-Baylor. Belton, Tex.: University of Mary Hardin-Baylor Pr., 1986. 180 pp.

Walker, Thomas T. "Mary Hardin-Baylor College, 1845-1937." Ed.D. diss., George Peabody College for Teachers, 1962. 241 pp. *Dissertation Abstracts,* vol. 23. p. 3758.

University of North Texas

Hall, Morris E. "The Development of North Texas State College, 1890-1949." Ed.D. diss., New York University, 1954. 277 pp. *Dissertation Abstracts,* vol. 14, p. 1609.

Higginbotham, Robert L. "A History of North Texas State Teachers College." Master's thesis, North Texas State Teachers College, 1936. 82 pp.

Rogers, James L. *The Story of North Texas, from Texas Normal College, 1890 to North Texas State University, 1965.* Denton: North Texas State University, 1965. 377 pp.

University of Texas at Arlington

Hudspeth, Junia E. "A History of North Texas Agricultural College." Master's thesis, Southern Methodist University, 1935. 172 pp.

University of Texas at Austin

Benedict, Harry Y. *A Source Book Relating to the History of the University of Texas: Legislative, Legal, Bibliographical, and Statistical.* Austin: The University, 1917. 854 pp.

Berry, Margaret C. *The University of Texas: A Pictorial Account of Its First Century.* Austin: University of Texas Pr., 1980. 425 pp.

Eckhardt, Carl J. *In the Beginning of the University of Texas.* n.p., 1979. 120 pp.

Frantz, Joe B. *The Forty-Acre Follies.* Austin: Texas Monthly Pr., 1983. 349 pp.

Lane, John J. *A History of the University of Texas.* Austin: H. Hutchings, 1891. 322 pp.

Long, Walter E. *For All Time to Come.* Austin: n.p., 1964. 111 pp.

University of Texas at El Paso

Fugate, Francis L. *Frontier College: Texas Western at El Paso, the First Fifty Years.* El Paso: Texas Western Pr., 1964. 162 pp.

Hamilton, Nancy. *Lamaseries on the Hill: A Pictorial History of the University of Texas at El Paso, 1913-1988.* El Paso: Texas Western Pr., 1988. 200 pp.

Ray, Joseph M. *On Becoming a University; Report on an Octennium.* El Paso: Texas Western Press of the University of Texas at El Paso, 1968. 109 pp.

University of Texas Medical Branch at Galveston

The University of Texas Medical Branch at Galveston: A Seventy-Five Year History by the Faculty and Staff. Austin: University of Texas Pr., 1967. 435 pp.

Wesley College (Closed 1938)

Houser, John H. "The History of Wesley College, Greenville, Texas." Master's thesis, Southern Methodist University, 1939. 133 pp.

McMullin, William C. "A Descriptive History of Wesley College." Ed.D. diss., North Texas State University, 1987. 580 pp. *Dissertation Abstracts International,* vol. 48A, p. 581.

West Texas State University

Cleveland, Truman. "A Historical Study of the West Texas State College." Master's thesis, West Texas State College, 1953. 53 pp.

Craig, Richard H. "The Development of West Texas State Teachers College, 1932-1945." Master's thesis, West Texas State College, 1947. 137 pp.

Hill, Joseph A. *More than Brick and Mortar; West Texas State College, 1909-1959.* Canyon, Tex. n.p., 1959. 368 pp.

Rowan, Jonnie. "A History of the West Texas State Teachers College." Master's thesis, West Texas State Teachers College, 1932. 116 pp.

Wiley College

Allen, Jewel. "The History of Negro Education at Wiley College." Master's thesis, East Texas State Teachers College, 1940. 67 pp.

UTAH

Brigham Young University

Bergera, Gary J., and Priddis, Ronald. *Brigham Young University: A House of Faith.* Salt Lake City: Signature Books, 1985. 513 pp.

Butterworth, Edwin. *Brigham Young University: 1,000 Views of 100 Years.* Provo: Brigham Young University Pr., 1975. 354 pp.

Smith, Keith L. "Brigham Young University: The Early Years, 1875-1921." Ph.D. diss., Brigham Young University, 1972. 281 pp. *Dissertation Abstracts International,* vol. 33A, p. 1002.

Wilkinson, Ernest L. *Brigham Young University; A University of Destiny.* New York: Newcomen Society in North America, 1971. 36 pp.

--------. *Brigham Young University: The First One Hundred Years.* 4 vols. Provo: Brigham Young University Pr., 1975-

Wilkinson, Ernest L., and Skousen, W. Cleon. *Brigham Young University: A School of Destiny.* Provo: Brigham Young University Pr., 1976. 925 pp.

Dixie College

Colvin, Lloyd W. "The Rise, Progress, and Development of Dixie Junior College." Master's thesis, University of Utah, 1962. 194 pp.

Gregerson, Edna J. "The Evolution of Dixie College as a Public Institution of Higher Education in Utah from 1871 to 1935." Ed.D. diss., University of Nevada, Las Vegas, 1981. 431 pp. *Dissertation Abstracts International,* vol. 43A, p. 2258.

Snow College

Christensen, Edward L. *Snow College Historical Highlights: The First 100 Years.* Ephraim, Utah: Snow College, 1988. 210 pp.

Findlay, Ross P. "Snow College, Its Founding and Development, 1888-1932." Master's thesis, Utah State Agricultural College, 1952. 137 pp.

Southern Utah State College

Sherratt, Gerald R. "A History of the College of Southern Utah, 1897 to 1947." Master's thesis, Utah State Agricultural College, 1954. 114 pp.

University of Utah

Chamberlin, Ralph V. *The University of Utah, a History of Its First Hundred Years, 1850-1950.* Salt Lake City: University of Utah Pr., 1960. 616 pp.

Haglund, Elizabeth, ed. *Remembering the University of Utah.* Salt Lake City: University of Utah Pr., 1981. 235 pp.

Hodson, Paul W. *Crisis on Campus: The Exciting Years of Campus Development at the University of Utah.* Salt Lake City: Keeban Corp., 1987. 330 pp.

Olpin, Albert R. *Cosmopolitan Provincialism: Utah!* New York: Newcomen Society in North America, 1956. 28 pp.

Utah State University

Ricks, Joel E. *The Utah State Agricultural College; A History of Fifty Years, 1888-1938.* Salt Lake City: Deseret News Pr., 1938. 184 pp.

Simmonds, A. J. *Pictures Past: A Centennial Celebration of Utah State University.* Logan: Utah State University Pr., 1988. 126 pp.

Westminster College

Buzza, David E. "Contributions to a History of Utah's Westminister College." Master's thesis, University of Chicago, 1939.

Nyman, Emil. *A Short History of Westminster College, Salt Lake City: The First Century, 1875-1975.* n.p., 1976. 70 pp.

Webster, Lewis G. "A History of Westminister College of Salt Lake City, Utah, 875-1969." Master's thesis, Utah State University, 1970. 171 pp.

VERMONT

Bennington College

Brockway, Thomas P. *Bennington College in the Beginning.* Bennington: Bennington College Pr., 1981. 244 pp.

Jones, Barbara S. *Bennington College; The Development of an Educational Idea.* New York: Harper & Brothers, 1946. 239 pp.

Newcomb, Theodore M., et. al. *Persistence and Change: Bennington College and Its Students After Twenty-Five Years.* New York: Wiley, 1967. 292 pp.

Goddard College

Benson, Ann G., and Adams, Frank. *To Know for Real: Royce S. Pitkin and Goddard College.* Adamant, Vt.: Adamant Pr., 1987. 278 pp.

Green Mountain College

Knieriemen, Ruth-Ann D. *Green Mountain College, In Loco Parentis: A History of the Troy Conference Academy, Ripley Female College, Green Mountain Junior College, Green Mountain College.* Poultney, Vt.: Journal Pr., 1984. 371 pp.

Johnson State College

Raymond, Kenneth. *The History of Johnson State College: 1828-1984.* Johnson: Johnson State College, 1985. 142 pp.

Middlebury College

Lee, William S. *Father Went to College; The Story of Middlebury.* New York: Wilson-Erickson, Inc., 1936. 149 pp.

Stameshkin, David M. "The Town's College: Middlebury College, 1800-1915." Ph.D. diss., University of Michigan, 1978. 690 pp. *Dissertation Abstracts International,* vol. 39A, p. 1064.

--------. *The Town's College: Middlebury College, 1800-1915.* Middlebury: Middlebury College Pr., 1985. 368 pp.

Norwich University

Davenport, Walter R. *Montpelier Seminary and Its Students; With Brief Sketches of Newbury Seminary, Springfield Wesleyan Seminary, Bakersfield North Academy and the Celebration of the First Centennial.* Montpelier: Capital City Pr., 1934. 547 pp.

Ellis, William A., comp. *Norwich University. Her History, Her Graduates, Her Roll of Honor.* Concord, N. H.: Rumford Pr., 1898. 624 pp.

Ellis, William A., ed. *Norwich University, 1819-1911; Her History, Her Graduates, Her Roll of Honor.* 3 vols. Montpelier: Capital City Pr., 1911.

Harmon, Ernest N. *Norwich University, Its Founder and His Ideals.* New York: Newcomen Society in North America, 1951. 32 pp.

Martin, Eldon H. *Vermont College, a Famous Old School.* Nashville: Parthenon Pr., 1962. 247 pp.

Shepard, William A. *The Hospital that Became a College: Sloan U. S. Army General Hospital, Montpelier, Vermont.* Northfield, Vt.: Norwich University Pr., 1983. 28 pp. ERIC Microfiche ED 288 416.

Smith, Peter P. "The Transformation of Norwich University: 1971-1981." Ed.D. diss., Harvard University, 1983. 128 pp. *Dissertation Abstracts International,* vol. 44A, p. 3238.

White, Homer, *History of Norwich University.* Northfield, Vt.: C. N. Whitemarsh, Printer, 1891. 30 pp.

Trinity College

Roth, Stephen. *A History of Trinity College, 1925-1975.* Burlington: Privately Published, 1975. 65 pp.

University of Vermont

Borgmann, Carl W. *"UVM": The University of the State of Vermont, 1791.* New York: Newcomen Society in North America, 1956. 28 pp.

Huntington, Charles A. *The University of Vermont Fifty Years Ago.* Burlington: Whitney & Stanley, 1892. 336 pp.

Lindsay, Julian I. *Tradition Looks Forward; The University of Vermont: A History, 1791-1904.* Burlington: University of Vermont and State

Agricultural College, 1954. 285 pp.

University of Vermont Centennial, 1804-1904. Burlington: Centennial Committee of the Associate Alumni, 1903. 23 pp.

Vermont. University. *The University of Vermont and State Agricultural College, Burlington, Vermont.* Boston: Merrymount Pr., 1913. 29 pp.

VIRGINIA

Averett College

Gray, David W. "A History of Averett College." Master's thesis, University of Richmond, 1961. 175 pp.

Hayes, J. I. *A History of Averett College.* Danville: Averett College Pr., 1984. 216 pp.

Bridgewater College

Warden, James E. "Bridgewater College, 1880-1972." Ed.D. diss., University of Pittsburgh, 1973. 279 pp. *Dissertation Abstracts International,* vol. 34A, p. 4126.

Wayland, John W., ed. *Fifty Years of Education Endeavor; Bridgewater College, 1880-1930, Daleville College, 1890-1930.* Staunton: McClure Co., 1930. 414 pp.

Clinch Valley College

Zehmer, George B. *The Story of the Founding of Clinch Valley College.* Charlottesville: n.p., 1958. 69 pp.

College of William and Mary

Adams, Herbert B. *The College of William and Mary: A Contribution to the History of Higher Education with Suggestions for Its National Promotion.* Washington: U. S. Government Printing Office, 1887. 89 pp.

College of William and Mary. *The College of William and Mary, Highlights of Progress, 1960-1970: A Report on the Decade and a Look* to 1970-1980. *Williamsburg: The College, 75 pp.*

--------. *Historical Sketch of the College of William and Mary, in Virginia.* Richmond: Gary and Clemmitt, 1866. 20 pp.

--------. *History of the College of William and Mary from Its Foundation, 1660, to 1874.* Richmond: J. W. Randolph & English, 1874. 183 pp.

--------. *Vital Facts: A Chronology of the College of William and Mary.* Williamsburg: The College, 1976. 42 pp.

--------. *Vital Facts: A Chronology of the College of William and Mary.* Williamsburg: The College, 1978. 44 pp.

--------. *Vital Facts: A Chronology of the College of William and Mary.* Rev. Williamsburg: The College, 1982. 44 pp.

--------. *Vital Facts, a Chronology of the College of William and Mary.* Rev. Williamsburg: The College, 1983. 44 pp.

--------. *Vital Facts, a Chronology of the College of William and Mary.* Rev. Williamsburg: The College, 1985. 46 pp.

--------. *Vital Facts: A William and Mary Chronology, 1693-1963.* Williamsburg: n.p., 1963. 22 pp.

Graves, Thomas A. *The College of William and Mary in Virginia.* New York: Newcomen Society in North America, 1976. 24 pp.

Kale, Wilford. *Hark Upon the Gale: An Illustrated History of the College of William and Mary.* Norfolk: Donning Co., 1985. 228 pp.

Morpurgo, J. E. *Their Majesties' Royall College: William and Mary in the Seventeenth and Eighteenth Centuries.* Williamsburg: College of William and Mary, 1976. 247 pp.

Osborne, Ruby O. "The College of William and Mary in Virginia, 1800-1827." Ed.D. diss., College of William and Mary in Virginia, 1981. 627 pp. *Dissertation Abstracts International,* vol. 42A, p. 3889.

Smith, Russell T. "Distinctive Traditions at the College of William and Mary and Their Influence on the Modernization of the College, 1865 to 1919." Ed.D. diss., College of William and Mary in Virginia, 1981. 245 pp. *Dissertation Abstracts International,* vol. 46A, p. 84.

Tyler, Lyon G. *The College of William and Mary in Virginia; Its History and Work, 1693-1907.* Richmond: Whittet & Shepperson, 1907. 96 pp.

――――. *The College of William and Mary: Its Work, Discipline and History, from Its Founding to the Present Time.* Williamsburg: n.p., 1917. 38 pp.

Eastern Mennonite College

Pellman, Hubert R. *Eastern Mennonite College, 1917-1967: A History.* Harrisonburg, Va.: Eastern Mennonite College, 1967. 291 pp.

Emory and Henry College

Curtis, Claude D. *Three Quarters of a Century at Martha Washington College.* Bristol: King Printing Co., 1928. 223 pp.

Stevenson, George J. *Increase in Excellence, a History of Emory and Henry College.* New York: Appleton, 1963. 224 pp.

Ferrum College

Ayers, Ethel S. "A History of Ferrum College: The First Fifty Years, 1913-1963." Master's thesis, Appalachian State Teachers College, 1963. 143 pp.

Hurt, Franklin B. *A History of Ferrum College; An Uncommon Challenge.* Roanoke, Va.: Stone Printing Co., 1977. 303 pp.

Hampden-Sydney College

Bradshaw, Herbert C. *History of Hampden-Sydney College: From the Beginnings to the Year 1856.* Durham, N. C.: Fisher-Harrison Corp., 1976. 503 pp.

Dabney, Virginius. *America's Becentennial '76 College; The Story of Hampden-Sydney College in Virginia.* New York: Newcomen Society in North America, 1973. 19 pp.

Hampton University

Armstrong, Mary F. *Hampton Institute, 1868-1885: Its Work for Two Races.* Hampton: Normal School Pr., 1885. 34 pp.

Armstrong, Samuel C. *The Founding of Hampton Institute.* Boston: Directors of the Old South Work, 1904. 16 pp.

Hampton Institute, Hampton, Va. *A Decade (1893-1903) of the Hampton School.* Hampton: Hampton Institute Pr., 1903. 24 pp.

--------. *Hampton Institute.* Hampton: Hampton Institute Pr., 1930. 12 pp.

--------. *Hampton Institute, 1868-1943. Seventy-Five Years of Education for Life.* Hampton: Hampton Institute Pr., 1943. 16 pp.

--------. *Twenty-Two Years' Work of the Hampton Normal and Agricultural Institute at Hampton, Virginia.* Hampton: Normal School Pr., 1893. 520 pp.

Hunter, Wilma D. "Coming of Age: Hollis B. Frissell and the Emergence of Hampton Institute, 1893-1917." Ph.D. diss., Indiana University, 1982. 257 pp. *Dissertation Abstracts International,* vol. 43A, p. 3677.

John, Walton C. *Hampton Normal and Agricultural Institute: Its Evolution and Contribution to Education as a Land-Grant College.* Washington: Government Printing Office, 1923. 118 pp.

Peabody, Francis G. *Education for Life: The Story of Hampton Institute.* Garden City, N. Y.: Doubleday, 1918. 393 pp.

Puryear, B. N. *Hampton Institute, a Pictorial Review of Its First Century, 1868-1968.* Hampton, Va.: n.p., 1962(?). 131 pp.

Robinson, William H. "The History of Hampton Institute, 1868-1949." Ph.D. diss., New York University, 1954. 467 pp. *Dissertation Abstracts,* vol. 15, p. 223.

Schall, Keith L., ed. *Stony the Road: Chapters in the History of Hampton Institute.* Charlottesville: University Press of Virginia, 1977. 183 pp.

Hollins College

Logan, John A. *Hollins, an Act of Faith for 125 Years.* New York: Newcomen Society in North America, 1968. 28 pp.

Niederer, Frances J. *Hollins College; An Illustrated History.* Charlottesville: University Press of Virginia, 1973. 221 pp.

--------. *Hollins College: An Illustrated History.* 2d ed. Charlottesville: University Press of Virginia, 1985. 232 pp.

Vickery, Dorothy S. *Hollins College, 1842-1942; An Historical Sketch, Being an Account of the Principal Developments in the One-Hundred-Year History of Hollins College.* Hollins College: Hollins College, 1942. 83 pp.

James Madison University

Dingeldine, Raymond C. *Madison College: The First Fifty Years, 1908-1958.* Harrisonburg: Madison College, 1959. 315 pp.

Sonner, Ray V. "Madison College: The Miller Years, 1949-1970." Ed.D. diss., University of Virginia, 1974. 153 pp. *Dissertation Abstracts International,* vol. 35A, p. 4103.

Longwood College

Dalton, Thomas C. "Institutional Changes in a State Teachers College: An Analysis of the Decision Making at Longwood College, 1946-1967." Ed.D. diss., University of Virginia, 1976. 238 pp. *Dissertation Abstracts International,* vol. 37A, p. 1901.

Lynchburg College

Wake, Orville W. "A History of Lynchburg College, 1903-1953." Ph.D. diss., University of Virginia, 1957. 375 pp. *Dissertation Abstracts,* vol. 17, p. 2493.

Marion College (Closed 1967)

Hunter, Katrina V. "A History of Marion College, Marion, Virginia." Master's thesis, East Tennessee State University, 1969. 97 pp.

Wilson, Goodridge. *A Brief History of Marion College.* Marion, Va.: n.p., 1948. 55 pp.

Mary Baldwin College

Waddell, Joseph A. *History of Mary Baldwin Seminary (Originally Augusta Female Seminary) from 1842 to 1905 Inclusive.* Staunton, Va.: Augusta Printing Corp., 1908. 84 pp.

Watters, Mary. *The History of Mary Baldwin College, 1842-1942; Augusta Female Seminary, Mary Baldwin Seminary, Mary Baldwin College.*

Staunton, Va.: Mary Baldwin College, 1942. 629 pp.

Mary Washington College

Alvey, Edward. *History of Mary Washington College, 1908-1972.* Charlottesville: University Press of Virginia, 1974. 682 pp.

Carlson, Alden L. "A History of Mary Washington College." Master's thesis, University of Virginia, 1948. 105 pp.

Marymount University

Walsh, Walter. "The Growth and Development of Marymount College, Arlington, Virginia, 1948-1965." Master's thesis, Catholic University of America, 1966.

Norfolk State University

Brooks, Lyman B. *Upward: A History of Norfolk State University, 1935 to 1975.* Washington, D. C.: Howard University Pr., 1983. 395 pp.

Old Dominion University

Rutyna, Richard A., and Kuehl, John W. *Old Dominion University: Heritage and Horizons.* Norfolk: Donning Co., 1987. 200 pp.

Sweeney, James R. *Old Dominion University-A Half Century of Service.* Norfolk: Old Dominion University Office of Printing and Publications, 1980. 136 pp.

Protestant Episcopal Theological Seminary in Virginia

Goodwin, William A. R., ed. *History of the Theological Seminary in Virginia and Its Historical Background.* 2 vols. New York: E. S. Gorham, 1923-1924.

Radford University

Moffett, M'Ledge. *A History of the State Teachers College at Radford, Virginia, 1910-1930.* Radford: n.p., 1933. 413 pp.

Randolph-Macon College

Irby, Richard. *History of Randolph-Macon College, Virginia, the Oldest Incorporated Methodist College in America.* Richmond: Whittet & Shepperson, 1898. 330 pp.

Scanlon, James E. *Randolph-Macon College: A Southern History, 1825-1967.* Charlottesville: University Press of Virginia, 1983. 480 pp.

Randolph-Macon Woman's College

Cornelius, Roberta D. *The History of Randolph-Macon Woman's College from the Founding in 1891 through the Year of 1949-1950.* Chapel Hill: University of North Carolina Pr., 1951. 428 pp.

Jones, Wilfred. "The History of Randolph-Macon Academy, Front Royal, Virginia." Master's thesis, University of Virginia, 1952. 96 pp.

Roanoke College

Eisenberg, William E. *The First Hundred Years: Roanoke College, 1842-1942.* Salem: The Trustees of Roanoke College, 1942. 511 pp.

Saint Paul's College

Russell, James S. *Adventure in Faith; An Autobiographic Story of St.Paul Normal and Industrial School, Lawrenceville, Virginia.* New York: Morehouse Pub., 1936. 117 pp.

Thurman, Frances A. "The History of Saint Paul's College, Lawrenceville, Virginia, 1888-1959." Ph.D. diss., Howard University, 1978. 320 pp. *Dissertation Abstracts International,* vol. 40A, p. 1655.

Shenandoah College and Conservatory of Music

Connor, Clarence H. "A Study of the Functions of Shenandoah College and Shenandoah Conservatory of Music." Ed.D. diss., University of Virginia, 1955. 265 pp. *Dissertation Abstracts,* vol. 16, p. 1956.

Wilkins, James R. *The Impossible Task: A History of Shenandoah College and Conservatory, 1875 to 1985, and the Moving and Rebuilding of the Colleges in Winchester, Virginia, 1955 to 1985: Also a Brief History of the Old John Kerr School and Early Education in the Winchester,*

Virginia Area. Winchester: J. R. Wilkings, 1985. 371 pp.

Southern Seminary Junior College

Kling, Frederick W. "The History of Southern Seminary." Master's thesis, University of Virginia, 1937. 103 pp.

Robey, Margaret D. "A History of the Southern Seminary and Junior College since 1937." Master's thesis, University of Virginia, 1952. 214 pp.

Stonewall Jackson College*

Britt, Samuel S. "A History of Stonewall Jackson College, 1868-1930." Master's thesis, University of Virginia, 1949. 114 pp.

Sweet Briar College

Stohlman, Martha L. *The Story of Sweet Briar College.* Sweet Briar: Alumnae Association of Sweet Briar College, 1956. 255 pp.

Von Briesen, Martha, and Vickery, Dorothy S. *Sweet Briar College: Seven Decades, 1901-1971.* Sweet Briar: n.p., 1972. 64 pp.

University of Richmond

Alley, Reuben E. *History of the University of Richmond, 1830-1971.* Charlottesville: University Press of Virginia, 1977. 286 pp.

Heilman, E. Bruce. *The Story of the University of Richmond: A Sequicentennial Address.* New York: Newcomen Society in North America, 1979. 28 pp.

University of Virginia

Abernathy, Thomas P. *Historical Sketch of the University of Virginia.* Richmond: Dietz Pr., 1948. 51 pp.

Barringer, Paul B. *The University of Virginia; Its History, Influence, Equipment and Characteristics with Biographical Sketches and Portraits of Founders, Benefactors, Officers, and Alumni.* 2 vols. New York: Lewis Publishing Co., 1904.

Bruce, Philip A. *History of the University of Virginia, 1819-1919.* 5 vols. New York: Macmillan, 1920.

Cabell, Nicholas F., ed. *Early History of the University of Virginia as Contained in the Letters of Thomas Jefferson and Joseph C. Cabell.* Richmond: J. W. Randolph, 1856. 528 pp.

Dabney, Virginius. *Mr. Jefferson's University: A History.* Charlottesville: University Press of Virginia, 1981. 642 pp.

Light, R. Chambliss, Jr., ed. *An Historical Sketch of the University of Virginia.* Logos Three Enterprises, 1977. 174 pp.

O'Neal, William B. *Pictorial History of the University of Virginia.* Charlottesville: University Press of Virginia, 1968. 177 pp.

--------. *Pictorial History of the University of Virginia.* 2d ed. Charlottesville: University Press of Virginia, 1976.

Patton, John S. *Jefferson, Cabell, and the University of Virginia.* New York: Neale Publishing Co., 1906. 380 pp.

Patton, John S., ed. *Jefferson's University: Glimpses of the Past and Present of the University of Virginia.* Charlottesville: Michie Co., 1915. 97 pp.

Patton, John S., and Doswell, Sallie J. *The University of Virginia: Glimpses of Its Past and Present.* Lynchburg: J. P. Bell Co., 1900. 96 pp.

Shannon, Edgar F. *The University of Virginia: A Century and a Half of Innovation.* New York: Newcomen Society in North America, 1969. 20 pp.

A Sketch of the History of the University of Virginia. Washington, D. C.: H. Polkinhorn, 1859. 36 pp.

A Sketch of the University of Virginia. Richmond: Whittet & Shepperson, 1885. 42 pp.

Virginia. University. *The Centennial of the University of Virginia, 1819-1921.* New York: Putnam, 1922. 235 pp.

--------. *Historical Sketch.* Charlottesville: n.p., 1948. 13 pp.

--------. *A Sketch of the History of the University of Virginia.* Charlottesville: Chronicle Steam Book and Job Printing House, 1880. 66 pp.

Virginia Commonwealth University

Dabney, Virginius. *Virginia Commonwealth University: A Sesquicentennial History.* Charlottesville: University Press of Virginia, 1987. 429 pp.

Williams, Ann L. "In Search of a Home: An Historical Analysis of the Major Factors Concerning the Location of Virginia Commonwealth University." Ed.D. diss., College of William and Mary in Virginia, 1985. 104 pp. *Dissertation Abstracts International,* vol. 47A, p. 444.

Virginia Military Institute

Byrd, Harry F. *The Virginia Military Institute, "In Peace a Glorious Asset, In War a Tower of Strength".* New York: Newcomen Society of the United States, 1984. 23 pp.

Couper, William. *One Hundred Years at V.M.I.* 4 vols. Richmond: Garrett and Massie, 1939.

Smith, Francis H. *The Virginia Military Institute, Its Building and Rebuilding.* Lynchburg: J. P. Bell Co., 1912. 277 pp.

Wise, Henry A. *Drawing Out the Men: The VMI Story.* Charlottesville: University Press of Virginia, 1978. 581 pp.

Wise, Jennings C. *The Military History of the Virginia Military Institute from 1839 to 1865.* Lynchburg: J. P. Bell Co., 1915. 576 pp.

--------. *V.M.I. Papers.* n.p., 19?. 53 pp.

Virginia Polytechnic Institute and State University

Cochran, John P. "The Virginia Agricultural and Mechanical College: The Formative Half Century, 1872-1919, of Virginia Polytechnic Institute." Ph.D. diss., University of Alabama, 1961. 328 pp. *Dissertation Abstracts,* vol. 22, p. 1596.

Kinnear, Duncan L. *The First 100 Years; A History of Virginia Polytechnic Institute and State University.* Blacksburg: V P I Education Foundation, 1972. 498 pp.

Robertson, Jenkins M., comp. *Virginia Polytechnic Institute and State University Historical Data Book.* Centennial edition. Blacksburg: Virginia Polytechnic Institute and State University, 1972. 124 pp.

Virginia State University

Claiborne, Judith H. "Virginia State College as Portrayed by the Petersburg *Progress-Index*." Master's thesis, Virginia State College, 1979. 55 pp.

Jeffreys, Richard L. "A History of Virginia State College for Negroes, Ettrick, Virginia." Master's thesis, University of Michigan, 1937. 281 pp.

Virginia Union University

Corey, Charles H. *A History of Richmond Theological Seminary, with Reminiscences of Thirty Years' Work among the Colored People of the South.* Richmond: J. W. Randolph Co., 1895. 240 pp.

Fisher, Miles M., ed. *Virginia Union University and Some of Her Achievements: Twenty-Fifth Anniversary, 1897-1924.* Richmond: Brown Printing Shop, Inc., 1924. 110 pp.

Taliaferro, Cecil R. "Virginia Union University, the First One Hundred Years, 1865-1965." Ph.D. diss., University of Pittsburgh, 1975. 144 pp. *Dissertation Abstracts International,* vol. 36A, p. 2065.

Washington and Lee University

Crenshaw, Ollinger. *General Lee's College; The Rise and Growth of Washington and Lee University.* New York: Random House, 1969. 366 pp.

Washington and Lee University, Lexington, Va. *Historical Papers.* 2 vols. Lexington: Washington and Lee University, 1890-1904.

WASHINGTON

Central Washington University

Mohler, Samuel R. *The First Seventy-Five Years; A History of Central Washington State College, 1891-1966.* Ellensburg: Central Washington State College, 1967. 374 pp.

Eastern Washington University

Dryden, Cecil P. *Light for an Empire; The Story of Eastern Washington State College.* Cheney, Wash.: Eastern Washington State College, 1965. 269 pp.

Haag, Edmund V. *The Centennial Album: An Illustrated History of Eastern Washington University.* Cheney, Wash.: Eastern Washington University, 1982. 88 pp.

Oliphant, James O. *History of the State Normal School at Cheney.* Spokane: Inland-American Printing Co., 1924. 175 pp.

Evergreen State College

Jones, Richard M. *Experiment at Evergreen.* Cambridge, Mass.: Schenkman Publishing Co., 1981. 163 pp.

Stevens, William H. "The Philosophical and Political Origins of the Evergreen State College." Ph.D. diss., University of Washington, 1983. 392 pp. *Dissertation Abstracts International,* vol. 44A, p. 2382.

Gonzaga University

Gonzaga's Silver Jubilee: A Memoir. Spokane: n.p., 1912. 280 pp.

Schoenberg, Wilfred P. *Gonzaga University; Seventy-Five Years, 1887-1962.* Spokane: Gonzaga University, 1963. 612 pp.

Northwest College of the Assemblies of God

Williams, Mary M. "A History of Northwest College of the Assemblies of God, 1934-1966." Master's thesis, University of Washington, 1966. 153 pp.

Pacific Lutheran University

Schnackenberg, Walter C. *The Lamp and the Cross, Sagas of Pacific Lutheran University from 1890 to 1965.* Tacoma: Pacific Lutheran University Pr., 1965. 182 pp.

Seattle Pacific University

Hedges, Richard G. "A Historical Study of Seattle Seminary and Seattle Pacific College, 1891-1926." Master's thesis, University of Washington, 1962. 62 pp.

Seattle University

Cronin, Timothy F. "Seattle University: 1891-1966." Ed.D. diss., Seattle University, 1982. 401 pp. *Dissertation Abstracts International,* vol. 43A, p. 1856.

Richardson, Archie J. *Reminiscing: A Seventy Year Collection of Memoirs and Stories about the Jesuits Who Built Seattle University.* Seattle: Seattle University Alumni Association in Cooperation with the Seattle University Office of Publications, 1980. 97 pp.

University of Puget Sound

Matthews, Alfred W. "History of the College of Puget Sound." Master's thesis, University of Washington, 1926. 83 pp.

Tacoma. University of Puget Sound. *75 Years in Retrospect and Prospect, 1888-1963-2038.* Tacoma: n.p., 1963. 62 pp.

University of Washington

Gates, Charles M. *The First Century at the University of Washington, 1861-1961.* Seattle: University of Washington Pr., 1961. 252 pp.

Odegaard, Charles E. *The University of Washington; Pioneering in Its First and Second Century.* New York: Newcomen Society in North America, 1964. 24 pp.

Peterson, Daniel E. "University of Washington History, 1887-1902." Master's thesis, University of Washington, 1985. 205 pp.

Sanders, Jane. *Into the Second Century: The University of Washington, 1961-1986.* Seattle: University of Washington Pr., 1987. 56 pp.

Walla Walla College

60 Years of Progress: Walla Walla College. College Place: The College Pr., 1952. 400 pp.

Washington State University

Bryan, Enoch A. *Historical Sketch of the State College of Washington, 1890-1925.* Spokane: The Alumni Association and the Associated Students, 1928. 556 pp.

Landeen, William M. *E. O. Holland and the State College of Washington, 1916-1944.* Pullman: Washington State University Pr., 1958. 454 pp.

Lindsay, Ernest L. *The State College of Washington, a Land Grant College.* New York: American Historical Co., 1940. 43 pp.

Murdock, Patrick M. "A Critical History of the College of Agriculture, State College of Washington, 1892-1916." Ph.D. diss., Washington State University, 1955. 262 pp. *Dissertation Abstracts,* vol. 15, p. 810.

Neill, Thomas. *Incidents in the Early History of Pullman and the State College of Washington.* Fairfield, Wa.: Ye Galleon Pr., 1977. 28 pp.

Thornton, Richard S. *The Hill; A Collection of Pen-and-Ink Illustrations and an Essay.* Pullman: Alumni Association of Washington State University, 1963. 125 pp.

--------. *WSU, the Hill; A Collection of Pen-and-Ink Illustrations and an Essay Highlighting the History of Washington State University.* 2d ed. Pullman: Alumni Association of Washington State University, 1966. 131 pp.

Western Washington University

Hicks, Arthur C. *Western at 75.* Bellingham: Western Washington State College Foundation, 1974. 132 pp.

Whitman College

Maxey, Chester C. *Marcus Whitman, 1802-1847: His Courage, His Deeds & His College.* New York: Newcomen Society in North America, 1950. 40 pp.

Penrose, Stephen B. *Whitman, an Unfinished Story.* Walla Walla: Whitman Publishing Co., 1935. 256 pp.

Whitworth College

Gray, Alfred O. *Not by Might: The Story of Whitman College, 1890-1965.* Spokane: Whitworth College, 1965. 279 pp.

WEST VIRGINIA

Alderson-Broaddus College

Simpson, Ervin P. Y. *A History of Adlerson-Broaddus College, 1812-1951.* 2 vols. Philippi, WV.: The College, 1983.

Appalachian Bible College

Winters, Richard W. "Metamorphosis of a Dream: The History of Appalachian Bible College (1950-1983)." Ed.D. diss., Virginia Polytechnic Institute and State University, 1985. 447 pp. *Dissertation Abstracts International,* vol. 46A, p. 2186.

Bethany College

Funk, Dorothy R. *Unique Profile of Bethany College.* Martins Ferry, Ohio: Times-Leader, 1972. 32 pp.

Gresham, Perry E., comp. *The Saga of Bethany; A Pioneer in Broadcloth.* St. Louis: Bethany Pr., 1960. 189 pp.

Woolery, William K. *Bethany Years; The Story of Old Bethany from Her Founding Years through a Century of Trial and Triumph.* Huntington: Standard Printing & Publishing Co., 1941. 290 pp.

Bluefield State College

Garrett, R. Thomas. "A Study of the Transition of Bluefield State College from a Black Teacher Preparation College to a Predominantly White Liberal Arts College." Ed.D. diss., Rutgers, the State University of New Jersey, 1979. 111 pp. *Dissertation Abstracts International,* vol. 40A, p. 3827.

Concord College

Sizemore, Virginia L. "A History of Concord College." Master's thesis, Marshall University, 1950. 127 pp.

Davis and Elkins College

Ross, Thomas R. *Davis and Elkins College: The Diamond Jubilee History.* Elkins: The College, 1980. 325 pp.

Fairmont State College

Boughter, Isaac F., ed. *Fairmont State Normal School: A History.* Fairmont: Fairmont State Normal School, 1929. 142 pp.

Marshall University

Marshall University, Huntington, W.Va. *One Hundred Years of Marshall College.* Huntington: Centennial Committee of Marshall College, 1937. 167 pp.

Moffat, Charles H. *Marshall University, an Institution Comes of Age; 1837-1980.* Huntington: Marshall University Alumni Association, 1981. 326 pp.

Toole, Robert C. "History of Marshall College, 1837 to 1915." Master's thesis, Marshall College, 1951.

Shepherd College

Slonaker, Arthur G. "A History of Shepherd College, Shepherdstown, West Virginia." Ed.D. diss., University of Virginia, 1958. 293 pp. *Dissertation Abstracts,* vol. 19, p. 1639.

--------. *A History of Shepherd College, Shepherdstown, West Virginia.* Parsons: McClain Printing Co., 1967. 197 pp.

University of Charleston

Coburn, Frances G. "An Historical Study of the Growth of Morris Harvey College from 1888-1952." Master's thesis, Marshall College, 1952. 101 pp.

Krebs, Frank J. *Where There Is Faith: The Morris Harvey College Story, 1888-1970.* Charleston, W.Va.: Morris Harvey College, 1974. 371 pp.

West Liberty State College

Regier, Cornelius C. *West Liberty Yesterday and Today.* Wheeling: Wheeling News Lithograph Co., 1939. 221 pp.

Reuter, Frank T. *West Liberty State College; The First 125 Years.* West Liberty: n.p., 1963. 208 pp.

West Virginia State College

Drain, John R. "The History of West Virginia State College from 1892-1950." Master's thesis, West Virginia State College, 1958.

Harlan, John C. *A History of West Virginia State College, 1891-1965.* Dubuque, Iowa: W. C. Brown, 1968. 185 pp.

West Virginia University

Chapman, Berlin B. *West Virginia University: A Memoir.* Parsons: McClain Printing Co., 1975. 22 pp.

Doherty, William T., and Summers, Festus P. *West Virginia University, Symbol of Unity in a Sectionalized State.* Morgantown: West Virginia University Pr., 1982. 385 pp.

Ernst, Harry W. *West Virginia University: A Pictorial History, 1867-1979.* Morgantown: West Virginia University Office of Publications, 1980. 106 pp.

West Virginia Wesleyan College

Haught, Thomas W. *West Virginia Wesleyan College, First Fifty Years, 1890-1940.* Buckhannon: West Virginia Wesleyan College, 1940. 192 pp.

Plummer, Kenneth M. *A History of West Virginia Wesleyan College, 1890-1965.* Buckhannon: West Virginia Wesleyan College Pr., 1965. 160 pp.

WISCONSIN

Beloit College

Ballard, Lloyd. *Beloit College, 1917-1923: The Brannon Years.* Beloit: Beloit College, 1971. 144 pp.

Beliot College, Beloit, Wis. *Historical Sketch of Beloit College, Founded at Beloit, Wis., June 24, 1847.* Madison: Atwood & Culver Printers, 1876. 31 pp.

Eaton, Edward D. *Historical Sketches of Beloit College.* New York: A. S. Barnes, 1928. 319 pp.

Whitney, Henry M. *A History of Beloit College and a Sketch of Aaron L. Chapin, One of Its Founders and President from 1850 to 1886.* Milwaukee: n.p., 1893. 23 pp.

Cardinal Stritch College

Flahive, Robert F. "Cardinal Stritch College: Yesterday, Today and Tomorrow." Ed.D. diss., Marquette University, 1973. 383 pp. *Dissertation Abstracts International,* vol. 34A, p. 2328.

Carroll College

Langill, Ellen. *Carroll College: The First Century, 1846-1946.* Waukesha, Wisc.: Carroll College Pr., 1980. 223 pp.

Pelton, Carol. "A Chronicle of Carroll College." Master's thesis, Marquette University, 1940. 99 pp.

Carthage College

Lentz, Harold H. *The Miracle of Carthage: History of Carthage College, 1847-1974.* Lima, Ohio: C. S. S. Publishing Co., 1975. 414 pp.

Spielman, William C. *The Diamond Jubilee History of Carthage College, 1870-1945.* Carthage, Ill.: Carthage College Historical Society, 1945. 220 pp.

Edgewood College

Beyenka, Barbara. *A Jubilee History.* Madison: Edgewood College, 1977. 76 pp.

Institute of Paper Chemistry

Strange, John G. *Fifty Years of Aspiration: An Abridged History of the Institute of Paper Chemistry.* Appleton, Wisc.: Institute of Paper Chemistry, 1980. 134 pp.

Lakeland College

Jaberg, Eugene C. *A History of Mission House-Lakeland.* Philadelphia: Christian Education Pr., 1962. 277 pp.

Lawrence University

Busch, Stephen E. "A History of the Lawrence Conservatory of Music." Ed.D. diss., University of Michigan, 1961. 211 pp. *Dissertation Abstracts,* vol. 21. p. 3806.

Kieckhefer, Grace N. *The History of Milwaukee-Downer College, 1851-1951.* Milwaukee: n.p., 1950. 124 pp.

Plantz, Samuel. *Lawrence College.* Menasha, Wisc.: Wisconsin State Historical Society, 1922. 21 pp.

Schumann, Marguerite E. *Creation of a Campus; A Chronicle of Lawrence College Buildings and the Men Who Made Them.* Appleton: Lawrence College Pr., 1957. 99 pp.

Marquette University

Hamilton, Rapheal N. *The Story of Marquette University: An Object Lesson in the Development of Catholic Higher Education.* Milwaukee: Marquette University Pr., 1953. 434 pp.

Milton College

Whitford, Albert. *An Historical Sketch of Milton College.* Milton, Wisc.: Milton College Alumni Association, 1916. 24 pp.

Mount Mary College

Fitzpatrick, Edward A., ed. *The Autobiography of a College, by the President, Faculty, and Students of Mount Mary College, Milwaukee, Wisc.* Milwaukee: Bruce Publishing Co., 1939. 271 pp.

Northland College

Dexter, Nathaniel B. *Northland College: A History.* Ashland, Wisc.: Northland College, 1968. 296 pp.

Northwestern College

Hormann, Arthur. *Our Northwestern College, the Story of Its Origin and Growth.* Milwaukee: Northwestern Publishing House, 1915. 96 pp.

Kowalke, Erwin E. *Centennial Story: Northwestern College, 1865-1965.* Watertown, Wisc.: Northwestern College, 1965. 320 pp.

Ripon College

Merrell, Edward H. *Ripon College, an Historical Sketch.* Ripon: Ripon Free Pr., 1893. 40 pp.

Saint Francis Seminary, School of Pastoral Ministry

Johnson, Peter L. *Halcyon Days; The Story of St. Francis Seminary, Milwaukee, 1856-1956.* Milwaukee: Bruce Publishing Co., 1956. 416 pp.

University of Wisconsin-Eau Claire

Carter, Hilda R., and Jenswold, John R. *The University of Wisconsin-Eau Claire: A History, 1916-1976.* Eau Claire: University of Wisconsin-Eau Claire Foundation, 1976. 162 pp.

University of Wisconsin-La Crosse

Gilkey, George R. *The First Seventy Five Years: A History of the University of Wisconsin-La Crosse, 1909-1979.* La Crosse: University of Wisconsin-La Crosse Foundation, 1981. 258 pp.

University of Wisconsin-Madison

Bogue, Allan G., and Taylor, Robert. *The University of Wisconsin: One Hundred and Twenty-Five Years.* Madison: University of Wisconsin Pr., 1975. 289 pp.

Butterfield, Consul W. *History of the University of Wisconsin, from Its First Organization to 1879.* Madison: University Press Co., 1879. 233 pp.

Carpenter, Stephen H. *An Historical Sketch of the University of Wisconsin from 1849 to 1876.* Madison: Atwood & Culver, Printers, 1876. 66 pp.

Curti, Merle. *The University of Wisconsin: A History, 1848-1925.* 2 vols. Madison: University of Wisconsin Pr., 1949.

Fred, Edwin B., ed. *A University Remembers.* Madison: University of Wisconsin, 1969. 118 pp.

Gard, Robert E. *University, Madison, U. S. A.* Madison: Wisconsin House, 1970. 308 pp.

Pyre, James F. A. *Wisconsin.* New York: Oxford University Pr., 1920. 419 pp.

Selley, George C. *Some Ferments at Wisconsin, 1901-1947, Memories and Reflections.* Madison: University of Wisconsin Pr., 1960. 124 pp.

Thwaites, Reuben G. *The University of Wisconsin; Its History and Its Alumni, with Historical and Descriptive Sketches of Madison.* Madison: J. N. Purcell, 1900. 889 pp.

University of Wisconsin-Madison. *A Resourceful University: The University of Wisconsin-Madison in Its 125th Year.* Madison: University of Wisconsin Pr., 1975. 279 pp.

University of Wisconsin-Milwaukee

Klotsche, J. Martin. *The University of Wisconsin--Milwaukee, an Urban University.* Milwaukee: University of Wisconsin-Milwaukee, 1972. 151 pp.

University of Wisconsin-Platteville

Gamble, Richard D. *From Academy to University, 1866-1966; A History of*

Wisconsin State University, Platteville, Wisconsin. Platteville: Wisconsin State University, 1966. 270 pp.

Wisconsin. State Teachers College, Platteville. *During Seventy-Five Years, a History of the State Teachers College, Platteville, Wisconsin, 1866-1941.* Platteville: n.p., 1941. 147 pp.

University of Wisconsin-River Falls

King, James T., and Wyman, Walker D. *Centennial History: The University of Wisconsin-River Falls, 1874-1974.* River Falls: University of Wisconsin-River Falls Pr., 1975. 330 pp.

University of Wisconsin-Stevens Point

Specht, Ellen L. *History of the Wisconsin State University at Stevens Point.* Stevens Point: The University, 1969. 26 pp.

University of Wisconsin-Whitewater

Bohi, Mary J. *A History of Wisconsin State University, Whitewater, 1868-1968.* Whitewater: Wisconsin State University Foundation, 1967. 274 pp.

Salisbury, Albert. *Historical Sketches of the First Quarter-Century of the State Normal School at Whitewater, Wisconsin, with a Catalogue of Its Graduates and a Record of Their Work, 1868-1893.* Madison: Tracy, Gibbs & Company Printers, 1893. 198 pp.

WYOMING

Casper College

McCollom, Stewart F. "A History of Casper College with Reference to Selected Historical Aspects of the Junior College Movement in the United States and Wyoming." Ph.D. diss., University of Wyoming, 1965.

Sheridan College

Cavanna, Robert C. "A History of Sheridan College, 1948-1973." Ed.D.

diss., University of Wyoming, 1977. 232 pp. *Dissertation Abstracts International,* vol. 38A, p. 5148.

University of Wyoming

Clough, Wilson O. *A History of the University of Wyoming, 1887-1937.* n.p., 1937. 199 pp.

--------. *A History of the University of Wyoming, 1887-1964.* Laramie: The Author, 1965. 376 pp.

--------. *The Third Quarter; The University of Wyoming, 1937-1962.* Laramie: University of Wyoming, 1962. 132 pp.

--------. *The University of Wyoming, 1939-1946, a Land-Grant College in War.* n.p., 1951. 89 pp.

Hardy, Deborah. *Wyoming University: The First 100 Years, 1886-1986.* Laramie: University of Wyoming, 1986. 311 pp.

University of Wyoming. *The Seventy-Fifth Anniversary: University of Wyoming; Laramie, 1887-1962.* Laramie: University of Wyoming, 1962. 16 pp.

Veal, Donald L. *University of Wyoming: Our Heritage: Cornerstone for Our Future.* New York: Newcomen Society of the United States, 1986. 24 pp.

Watson, Eddie D. "History of the Organization and Growth of the University of Wyoming with Constitutional Provisions and Legal Enactments." Master's thesis, University of Wyoming, 1935. 83 pp.

URUGUAY

University of the Republic

Montevideo, Universidad. Instituto de Investigaciones Historicas. *Fuentes para la historia de la Universidad. Serie I tomo primero: Actas del Consejo Universitario, 1849-1870.* Montevideo: n.p., 1949. 545 pp.

Oddone, Juan A., and Paris de Oddone, M. Blanca. *La Universidad Uruguaya desde el militarismo a la crisis (1885-1958).* 4 vols.

Montevideo: Departamento de Publicaciones, Universidad de la
Republica, 1971.

Paris de Oddone, M. Blanca. *La Universidad de Montevideo en la
formacion de nuestra conciencia liberal, 1849-1885.* Montevideo:
n.p., 1958. 436 pp.

University of Trabajo

Universidad del Trabajo del Uruguay. *Exposicion Conmemorative del
Centenario, 1878-1978/UTU, Universidad del Trabajo del Uruguay.*
Montevideo: La Universidad, 1978. 32 pp.

VENEZUELA

Central University of Venezuela

Caballero, Manuel. *Sobre autonomia, reforma y politica en la Universidad
Central de Venezuela, 1827-1958.* Caracus: Faculted de Humanidades y
Educacion, Universidad Central de Venezuela, Escuela de Historia, 1974.
113 pp.

Gonzales Bogen, Americo. *Salvar la Universidad.* Caracus: n.p., 1976.
93 pp.

Leal, Ildefonso. *Historia de la Universidad de Caracus, 1721-1827.*
Caracus: Universidad Central de Venezuela, Ediciones de la Biblioteca,
1963. 430 pp.

--------. *250 anos de la fundacion de la Real y Pontificia Universidad de
Caracus, 1721-1971.* Caracus: Rectorado de la U.C.V., 1971. 151 pp.

--------. *La Universidad de Caracus en los anos de Bolivar, 1783-1830.*
2 vols. Caracus: Ediciones de la UCV, 1983.

Universidad Central de Venezuela. *Historia de la Universidad Central
Venezuela, decretada por su rector como contribucion del instituto
a la celebracion del primer centenario de la independencia nacional.*
2 vols. Caracus: Tip. Americana, 1911-

University of the Andes

Chalbaud Cardona, Eloi. *Historia de la Universidad de los Andes.*

8 vols. Merida, Venezuela: Universidad de los Andes, Ediciones del Rectorado, 1966-1978.

University of Zulia

Rincon de M., Imelda; Gameron Leon, Maria; and Ortin de Medina, Nevi. *La Universidad del Zulia en el Proceso Historico de la region zuliana.* 2 vols. Maracibo: Universidad del Zulia, Vice-Rectorado Academico, 1986.

VIET NAM

University of Can-Tho

Vien Dai-hoc, Can Tho. *The University of Can-Tho South Viet Nam; Past, Present, Future.* Can-Tho: Vien Daihoc, 1970. 50 pp.

YUGOSLAVIA

University of Belgrade

Baalic, Dragoljub T. *Zbornik zakona i uredaba o Liceju, velikoj skoli i Univerzitetu u Beogradu Priredio i Uz ovo izdanje [napisao].* Bozidar S. Dordevic: Predgovor. Beograd, "Naucha Knjiga, 1967. 1006 pp.

University of Zagreb

Sveuciliste u Zabrebu. Zagreb: Liber, 1979. 181 pp.

Sveuciliste u Zagrebu. *The Growth of the University of Zagreb.* Zagreb: n.p., 1966. 32 pp.

--------. *University of Zagreb.* Zagreb: SNL, 1979. 178 pp.

Author Index

Aasgaard, John A., 252
Abbott, Maude E. S., 16
Abdul, Ali, 86
Abdullah, Hamid, 88
Abernathy, Thomas P., 399
Adams, Ansel, 153
Adams, Charles K., 247
Adams, Frank, 390
Adams, Harold, 184
Adams, Herbert B., 392
Adams, Myron W., 174
Adams, Rita G., 263
Adams, Virginia, 211
Adamson, Peter G., 81
Addy, George M., 124
Adelskold, Elsie, 127
Aderibigbe, A. B., 111
Adiseshiah, Malcolm S., 87
Africa, Philip A., 289
Agee, Forrest J., 374
Aguilar Pinal, Francisco, 125
Ahern, Patrick H., 166
Ajayi, J. F. Ade, 111
Akeley, Lewis, 360

Akers, Samuel L., 180
Akins, Thomas B., 20
Akintoye, Stephen A., 110
Al-Arif, Shoala I., 89
Albers, James W., 202
Albertini, Virgil, 262
Alberts, Robert C., 349
Albright, Penny, 139
Alcocer y Martinez, Mariano, 126
Aldana Rendon, Mario A., 107
Alexander, John E., 370
Alexander, Samuel D., 275
Alexander, W. H., 19
Alfonso, Oscar M., 115
Alford, Stanley C., 225
Aliu, Y. O., 110
Allchin, William H., 66
Allcott, John V., 309
Allen, Christopher E., 308
Allen, Frederick S., 160
Allen, Ira W., 314
Allen, James E., 299
Allen, Jewel, 388

AUTHOR INDEX

Allen, John E., 332
Allen, Max P., 197
Allen, Paul F., 364
Allen, Peter, C., 152
Alley, Reuben E., 399
Allison, Charles E., 287
Allman, Herbert D., 336
Allom, Vincent M., 52
Almuina Fernandez, Celso, 126
Alsop, Gulielma F., 343
Alstad, Adrien D., 314
Altenhofen, Aurelia, 191
Altomare, George, 102
Alton, Elizabeth B., 278
Alvarez, Lluis X., 124
Alverez Alvarado, Jesus, 109
Alverson, Roy T., 136
Alves, Mariano T., 118
Alvey, Edward, 397
Amadeo, Jaime, 2
Ambrose, Stephen E., 301
Ames, Oakes, 162
Amhurst, Nicholas, 69
Ammer, Thomas, 41
Anamaleze, John, 110
Ancelet, Leroy, 220
Anders, Leslie, 259
Andersen, Niels T., 245
Anderson, Patricia M., 222
Andress, Robert P., 180
Andrews, Israel W., 320
Andrews, Ruth H., 384
Andrews, William L., 234
Angel, Donald E., 160
Angel, Filmon J., 114
Angelo, Mark V., 294
Angerbauer, Wolfram, 42
Ankenbruck, John, 198
Annerstedt, Claes, 127
Anthony, Alfred W., 221
Aoyama, Nao, 102
Aponte-Hernandez, Rafael, 118
Appendini, Guadalupe, 106
Aranda Doncel, Juan, 123
Arellano, Jorge E., 110
Ariail, James M., 354
Ariza S., Alberto E., 31
Armacost, George H., 155
Armstrong, George R., 299

Armstrong, Mary F., 394
Armstrong, Neal A., 138
Armstrong, Samuel C., 394
Arndt, Elmer J. F., 260
Arnett, Benjamin W., 326
Arpee, Edward, 187
Arques, Josep, 122
Arreola Cortes, Raul, 106
Arrington, Michael E., 141
Arrowsmith, H., 51, 77
Arrowsmith, Robert, 284
Arthur, David J., 201
Asbury, Ray, 376
Aschbach, Joseph, Ritter von, 8
Aston, T. H., 69
Atkinson, James H., 142
Atkinson, Thomas D., 56
Atteberry, James L., 140
Attwater, Aubrey L., 56
Atwood, Albert W., 167
Atwood, Wallace W., 232
Auburn, Norman P., 324
Audet, Louis P., 23
Aughey, Samuel, 269
Austen-Leigh, Augustus, 56
Austin, Ben, 369
Avila Martel, Alamiro de, 28
Axen, Richard, 150
Ayers, Ethel S., 394
Ayliffe, John, 69
Azikiwe, Nnamdi, 111

Baalic, Dragoljub T., 416
Babb, Joseph G., 265
Babbidge, Homer D., 347
Bacote, Clarence A., 174
Bail, Hamilton V., 234
Bailey, Alfred G., 22
Bailey, Gemma C., 69
Bailey, Gilbert L., 367
Bailey, John W., 187
Bailey, Kenneth C., 90
Bailyn, Bernard, 234
Bain, Winifred E., 241
Baird, Jesse H., 151
Baird, John A., 338
Bajarias, Dolores O., 114
Baker, Clemon, 257
Baker, Frank S., 197

Baker, John N. L., 69
Baker, Lily, 368
Baker, Raymond P., 293
Baker, Robert A., 380
Baker, Thomas, 56
Baker, Webster B., 257
Bald, Ralph D., Jr., 171
Baldoi Lacomba, Marc, 126
Baldwin, Ebenezer, 164
Baldwin, Theron, 185
Ball, Larry D., 140
Ball, Phyllis, 139
Ball, Walter W. R., 56
Ballantine, W. G., 321
Ballard, Lloyd, 409
Ballard, Robert M., Jr., 385
Balsdon, John P. V. D., 69
Baltra Montaner, Lidia, 28
Bamford, T. W., 65
Banasiewicz, Maria, 115
Banderia, Jose R., 118
Bannon, Michael F., 135
Barahona Jimenez, Luis, 31
Barber, William C., 286
Bardwell, John D., 272
Barff, Henry E., 7
Bargmann, Wolfgang, 41
Barker, W. R., 70
Barnard, John, 321
Barrick, Nolan E., 384
Barringer, Paul B., 399
Barrows, Chester L., 281
Barry, Colman J., 167, 252
Barry, Jay, 351
Barry, John H., Jr., 138
Barth, Eugene H., 334
Bartl, Julius, 32
Bartle, G. F., 51
Bartlett, Willard W., 323, 324
Bartok, Leslie A., 339
Barton, C. B., 185
Barycz, Henryk, 115
Basham, Robert H., 142
Baskin, Henry L., 378
Baskin, Patricia N., 366
Batchelder, Samuel F., 234
Batista del Villar, Guarocuya, 34
Battersby, William J., 361

Battle, Kemp P., 309
Bauernfeind, Ulf, 48
Baughman, Robert T., 167
Baumbart, Peter, 50
Baumer, William H., 301
Bawden, William T., 210
Baxter, Cynthia L., 198
Baxter, Dudley, 69
Baxter, James H., 81
Baynham, Edward G., 349
Beach, Arthur G., 320
Beadle, Muriel, 192
Beaglehole, John C., 109
Beal, Merrill D., 181
Beal, William J., 245
Beardsley, E. T., 109
Beasley, Joan H., 160
Beauregard, Erving E., 326
Bechervaise, John M., 6
Bechtel, Paul M., 194
Becker, Carl L., 286
Beckett, James C., 79
Bedenbaugh, J. Holland, 356
Bedford, Allen G., 27
Bedoire, Fredric, 127
Bedsole, Vergil L., 219
Beebe, Richard T., 281
Beeler, Kent D., 195
Beeman, W. O., 328
Belch, George E., 322
Belden, Exekiel P., 164
Belin, Ferdinand, 37
Belknap, George N., 332
Bell, Sallie M. B., 136
Bellamy, Caroline B., 384
Bellone, Ernesto, 96
Bellot, Hugh H., 66
Belsheim, Osbourne T., 312
Beltran de Heredia, Vicente, 124
Benedict, Harry Y., 386
Benitez, Helena Z., 114
Benitez, Jaime, 118
Benner, Thomas E., 118
Bennet, Jim, 15
Bennett, Hugh F., 277
Bennish, Lee J., 327
Benson, Ann G., 390

Benson, Arthur C., 57
Benson, Mabel G., 146
Benson, William C., 252
Benstead, Charles R., 57
Bentinek-Smith, William, 234
Bentwich, Norman D., 91
Berchtold, Theodore A., 183
Bergendoff, Conrad J. I., 182
Bergera, Gary J., 388
Bergeron, Ronald P., 272
Berkel, A. van, 108
Bern, Paula R., 345, 346
Berquist, David H., 269
Berriat-Saint-Prix, Jacques, 37
Berrol, Selma C., 282
Berry, Margaret C., 386
Berry, Romeyn, 286
Berry, Sidney B., 301
Berte, Neal R., 133
Berti, Giuseppe, 95
Bettenson, Ernest M., 68
Betterworth, John K., 256
Beutler, Albert J., 195
Bevis, Alma M., 234
Beyenka, Barbara, 410
Bezilla, Michael, 345
Bezold, Friedrich, 44
Bezzetti, Dino, 92
Bhatnagar, Shyam K., 85
Bianco, Franz Joseph von, 47
Bibby, Harold E., 53
Bicknell, Thomas W., 352
Bie, Karen N., 112
Biehn, Albert L., 269
Bigelow, Cecil L., 202
Bigler, William H., 344
Bill, Edward G. W., 69
Bilsel, Cemil, 130
Bindon, Kathryn M., 17
Bingham, Caroline, 66
Bini, Vincenzo, 95
Bird, William E., 312
Birdsong, Irene B., 177
Bishop, Morris, 286
Bissell, Claude T., 25
Bixler, Julius S., 222
Black, Hermann D., 6
Black, Malcolm S., 295
Black, Robert E., 362

Blackwell, Jefferson D., 227
Blackwell, Velma L., 136
Blackwood, Robert, 4
Blain, William T., 255
Blainey, Geoffrey, 6
Blair, Ian D., 108, 109
Blair, J. S. G., 81
Blair, John E., 379
Blair, Lyle, 245
Blaisdell, Thomas C., 245
Blake, C. E., 229
Blake, Samuel H., 25
Blakiston, Herbert E. D., 69
Blanchard, Charles, 204
Blankman, Edward J., 295
Blanton, Robert J., 358
Bledsoe, Bennie G., 140
Bledsoe, James M., 373
Blin-Stoyle, Roger J., 77
Blinkenberg, Andreas P. D., 33
Block, Jean F., 192
Blodgett, Geoffrey, 321
Bloxsome, John L., 200
Bode, Coeryne, 327
Bodelsen, Carl A. G., 33
Bodine, William B., 319
Body, Alfred H., 52
Boehm, Laetitia, 48
Bogue, Allan G., 412
Bogue, Lucile, 158
Bohi, Mary J., 413
Bollinger, Donna S., 242
Bollinger, Russell V., 199
Bolt, Doris, 376
Bolton, Geoffrey C., 5
Bond, Horace M., 342
Bond, Oliver J., 354
Bone, Winstead P., 362
Boney, F. N., 179
Bongiovanni, Bruno, 96
Bonicke, Christian, 50
Bonner, Harold G., 183
Bonner, James C., 176
Bonnerot, Jean, 37
Booth, Ethel, 269
Boothby, Neil, 154
Bordin, Ruth B. A., 247
Borgeaud, Charles, 128
Borgmann, Carl W., 391

Borsett Ferranti Bolani, Ferrante, 92
Borst, Otto, 49
Borton, Mark C., 302
Bothne, Gisle C. J., 206
Botsford, Eli H., 241
Boucher, Maurice, 121
Boudard, Rene, 93
Boughter, Isaac F., 407
Bowen, Catherine D., 342
Bower, Alexander, 80
Bowles, Elisabeth A., 311
Bowra, C. M., 69
Boyce, Annabel S., 355
Boyd, Andrew K. H., 81
Boyd, James H., 373
Boyden, Albert G., 232
Boyden, Arthur C., 232
Boylan, Maureen, 77
Bracey, William R., 309
Brackett, Charles H., 142
Brackett, Frank P., 150
Bradbrook, Muriel C., 57
Bradbury, John L., 52
Bradford, Thomas L., 340
Bradley, Mac H., 328
Bradshaw, Herbert C., 394
Brady, Charles A., 283
Brainard, Dudley S., 252
Brandhorst, Carl T., 267
Brando, Mario, 118
Branscomb, Bennett H., 369
Branth, Ellen, 33
Brasfield, Elizabeth B., 133
Bratton, Mary Jo J., 305
Braubach, Max, 44
Braun, H. S., 15
Brawley, Benjamin G., 177
Brawley, James P., 175
Breese, Gerald W., 275
Breidenbaugh, Edward S., 339
Breslin, Richard D., 202
Breuckelman, Fred N., 166
Brewer, Kara P., 156
Bright, John H., 321
Brill, Harry E., 328
Bristol, Lee H., 279
Britt, Samuel S., 399
Brittain, Frederick, 59
Brittain, Marion L., 176
Brockway, Thomas P., 390
Brodrick, George C., 69
Brogdon, Joseph M., 180
Brolander, Glen E., 182
Bronson, Walter C., 351
Bronwell, Arthur B., 241
Brooke, Christopher N. L., 57, 69
Brookes, Edgar H., 121
Brooks, Lyman B., 397
Brooks, Robert P., 179
Brotherton, Hilda, 6
Brower, C. D., 322
Brower, Walter A., Jr., 277
Brown, Alan W., 288
Brown, Algernon L., 57
Brown, Dale W., 212
Brown, Dorothy A., 383
Brown, Francis H., 234
Brown, Olie T., 143
Brown, Revelle W., 349
Brown, Robert A., 195
Brown, Robert T., 240
Brown, Ronald C., 380
Brown, Samuel G., 270
Browne, Archibald D., 57
Browne, George F., 57
Bruce, J. F., 86
Bruce, Philip A., 400
Bruch, Rudiger vom, 48
Bruchmuller, Wilhelm, 39, 40
Bruckner, D. J. R., 193
Brueggemann, Walter A., 260
Bruins, Elton J., 274
Brunelle-Lavoie, Louise, 25
Brush, Carey W., 297, 298
Bruss, Melvin, 254
Bruster, Bill G., 328
Bryan, Enoch A., 405
Bryan, John M., 357
Bryan, Wright, 354
Bryant, Ira B., 383
Bryson, Helen R., 218
Buchan, John, 70
Buchanan, Christine, 211
Buchanan, Tom, 211
Buckley, Louise, 158
Budinszky, Alexander, 37

Buford, Nick, 113
Bugliarello, George, 292
Buhl, Heinrich, 45
Bulloch, John M., 79
Bullock, Henry M., 175, 176
Bunn, Edward B., 168
Bunting, David E., 379
Burchard, John E., 236
Burdick, Charles B., 151
Burgess, John W., 284
Burke, Thomas R., 264
Burleson, David S., 362
Burnett, Howard R., 203
Burnett, J. C., 3
Burnett, Richard G., 70
Burney, Lester, 70, 78
Burns, Cecil D., 66
Burns, Robert E., 157
Burr, Henry L., 228
Burstall, Frederic W., 56
Burton, Cecil G., 56
Burton, David H., 346
Burwash, Nathanael, 25
Bury, John P. T., 57
Busch, Stephen E., 410
Buselmeier, Karin, 45
Bush, George G., 234
Bussey, Charles C., 324
Butler, Addie L. J., 135, 136, 177
Butler, David L., 192
Butler, M. Alene, 297
Butterfield, Consul W., 412
Butterworth, Edwin, 388
Buxton, Alfred G., 379
Buxton, John, 70
Buzza, David E., 389
Byrd, Harry F., 401
Byrne, Muriel S., 70
Byrnes, Lawrence W., 243

Caballero, Manuel, 415
Cabaniss, James A., 258
Cabell, Nicholas F., 400
Cabeza de Leon, Salvador, 125
Cady, John F., 196
Cain, L. Vernon, 185
Caius, John, 57
Callahan, Helen, 174

Caldecott, George H., 228
Calman, Alvin, R., 279
Calvin, Delano D., 17
Cameron, Charles A., 90
Cameron, James R., 233
Cameron, Mary D., 224
Campbell, Clarice T., 257
Campbell, Doak S., 171
Campbell, Marie K., 353
Campbell, Sharon A. C., 248
Campen, Lillian H., 270
Campen, Richard N., 171
Campos, Ernesto de Souza, 12
Canella y Secades, Fermin, 124
Canizales de Urrutia, Dolores, 104
Cannon, Thurlow O., 295
Cant, Ronald G., 81
Cantley, Michael J., 295
Cantor, Leonard M., 53
Cantrell, Roy H., 329
Carbone, Hector R., 352
Cardoso, Irene de Arruda R., 12
Carey, James C., 209
Carleton, Don, 56
Carlson, Alden L., 397
Carlson, Leland H., 189
Carmichael, Leonard, 239
Carneiro, David, 12
Carpenter, Stephen H., 412
Carr, Howard E., 370
Carr, Isaac N., 361
Carr, Jack D., 198
Carr, William, 70
Carranca y Rivas, Raul, 106
Carranza, Niccola, 96
Carreno, Alberto M., 106
Carriere, Gaston, 23
Carroll, Raymond W., 2
Carruthers, Olive, 187
Carson, Arthur L., 114
Carstensen, Vernon, 206
Carter, Albert F., 161
Carter, Edmund, 57
Carter, Edward J., 307
Carter, Hilda R., 411
Carter, T. E., 109
Carter, Wilmoth A., 309
Carus-Wilson, Eleanora, 66

Cary, Harold W., 240
Case, Harold C., 231
Casey, Celestine, 159
Casey, Edgar, 243
Cashin, Edward J., 174
Casimir Gabriel, Brother, 290
Caskey, Gerald C., 266
Cass, Walter J., 239
Casteneda Paganini, Ricardo, 83
Castilla Urbina, Miguel de, 110
Castle, Gladys C., 255
Caswell, Lilley B., 240
Caswell, Render R., 175
Cates, Edwin H., 252
Catto, J. I., 70
Cavanna, Robert C., 413
Caver, Joseph D., 132
Caywood, Elzie R., 328
Cederborg, Hazel P., 190
Cerrato Valenzuela, Armando, 84
Chaffee, Eugene B., 181
Chaffin, Nora C., 305
Chalbaud Cardona, Eloi, 415
Chalmers, Alexander, 70
Chalmers, Gordon K., 319
Chamberlain, John, 244
Chamberlain, Joshua L., 164, 291, 348
Chamberlin, Ralph V., 389
Chambers, Doris M., 197
Chambers, Frederick, 142
Champagne, Roger J., 186
Champlin, James T., 222
Chandler, Douglas R., 170
Chang, Chung-Ping, 129
Chapman, Arthur W., 77
Chapman, Berlin B., 408
Chapman, Oscar J., 224
Charlton, Henry B., 78
Chase, Frederick, 271
Cheesewright, Maurice, 56
Cheeves, Lyndell D., 146
Chessman, G. Wallace, 317, 318
Chester, Ruth M., 29
Cheville, Roy A., 204
Cheyney, Edward P., 348
Chipman, Charles P., 222
Chitty, Arthur B., 368
Chrislock, Carl H., 249

Christenberry, Daniel P., 133
Christensen, Edward L., 388
Christensen, Lawrence O., 265
Christensen, William E., 268
Christiansen, Paige W., 280
Christie, Dudley B., 176
Christie, Octavius F., 52
Christol, Carl, 360
Church, J. E., Jr., 270
Chyet, Stanley F., 318
Citro, Joseph F., 136
Claghorn, George S., 338
Claiborne, Judith H., 402
Clapp, Brian W., 65
Clapp, Thomas, 164
Clark, Andrew, 70
Clark, Burton R., 314, 332, 347
Clark, Calvin M., 221
Clark, G. Gerlaw, 326
Clark, H. A., 236
Clark, James G., 266
Clark, John W., 57
Clark, Thomas D., 198
Clark, Walter L., 221
Clark, William S., 347
Clarke, Jan, 3
Clary, George E., Jr., 178
Clary, William W., 146
Classen, Peter, 45
Cleaveland, Nehemiah, 222
Clees, William J., 337
Cleeton, Glen U., 335
Cleland, Robert G., 148
Clement, Sarah V., 363
Clements, William M., 140
Cleveland, Truman, 387
Clewes, Carolyn M., 241
Cline, Platt, 139
Clippinger, Frank W., 260
Cloer, Bruno, 48
Clough, Wilson O., 414
Clover, Haworth A., 145
Clow, Richmond L., 360
Clutter, Ronald T., 275
Coad, Nola E., 331
Cobb, Alice, 365
Cobb, Berry G., 377
Cobb, Richard, 168
Cobban, Alan B., 57, 58, 70

Coburn, Frances G., 407
Cochran, John P., 401
Cochran, Margaret, 3
Cochrane, John C., 252
Cockerill, Janet, 53
Cockrell, Frank S., 381
Coe, John L., 29
Cofer, David B., 382
Coffee, John M., 233
Coffin, Henry S., 300
Coffin, Seldon J., 341
Cohen, Stan, 267
Cohn, Bernard N., 318
Cole, Arthur C., 237
Coleman, Charles H., 184
Coleman, Francis L., 120
Coleman, Hellen T. W., 350
Coleman, Lena M., 214
Collard, Edgar A., 16
Colles, Henry C., 54
Collins, Varnum L., 275
Collins, Wellyn F., 217
Colman, Gould P., 286
Colvard, Dean W., 256
Colvin, Havard M., 70
Colvin, Lloyd W., 388
Combe, William, 70
Compton, Karl T., 236
Condell, Robert, 360
Conkin, Paul K., 369
Conlin, James W., 201
Connelly, Annie L., 376
Connelly, James F., 346
Connelly, Joel, 201
Connolly, John F. X., 156
Connor, Clarence H., 398
Connor, Donald B., 160
Connor, Robert D. W., 309
Converse, Florence, 240
Conyers, Charline F., 336
Cook, John W., 186
Cooke, Anna L., 363
Coon, Horace, 284
Cooper, Charles H., 58
Cooper, Charles W., 157
Cooper, Frank A., 298
Cooper, Russell M., 173
Cooper, Waller R., 365
Cope, Zachary, 54

Corbett, Charles H., 29, 30
Cordell, Eugene F., 228
Corder, Jimmie W., 382
Corely, Carol W., 384
Corey, Charles H., 402
Corley, Robert G., 133
Cormier, Clement, 22
Cormier, Marie C., 272
Cornelius, Roberta D., 398
Corner, George W., 293
Cornette, James P., 217
Corsi, Michele, 93
Costa, Mario A. N., 118
Costello, Gabriel, 290
Costin, William C., 70
Cotter, D., 7
Cottrill, D. J., 28
Coulter, Ellis M., 179
Coulthard-Clark, Christopher D., 3
Coulton, Thomas E., 283
Couper, William, 401
Coursey, Oscar W., 359
Coutts, James, 80
Covert, James T., 333
Covington, James W., 173
Cox, Dwayne D., 217
Cox, John E., 384
Cox, Kenneth, 17
Cox, Marvin L., 183
Coyle, Darcy C., 237
Cozenza, Mario E., 283
Crabb, Alfred L., 369
Craddock, Bettye, 381
Craft, George S., 145
Craig, Earl L., 370
Craig, Hardin, 213
Craig, Richard H., 387
Craik, Elmer L., 210
Crain, Harry M., 158
Cramer, Clarence H., 315
Crane, John de M. C., 228
Crary, Ryland W., 206
Crawley, Charles, 58
Creek, Mary I., 200
Creigh, Dorothy W., 267
Cremin, Lawrence A., 299
Crenshaw, Ollinger, 402
Crevier, Jean B. L., 37

Crewes, J. Marshall, 311
Crighton, John C., 264
Croft, William, 117
Cronin, Kathleen J., 266
Cronin, Richard J., 278
Cronin, Timothy F., 404
Crooks, George R., 336
Croom, Adlai S., 140
Crosby, Nathan, 271
Cross, George L., 330
Crothers, George E., 152
Crow, Charles L., 172
Crowl, Vaughn D., 225
Crowson, Elmer T., 358
Cruft, John, 54
Crumlish, John M., 227
Cullum, Edward N., 369
Cumberland, William H., 203
Cumbers, Frank H., 66
Cummins, Cedric C., 360
Cunningham, John T., 273
Curl, Carroll A., 370
Curl, Lottie M., 176
Currey, Ronald F., 120
Currie, Thomas W., 371
Curry, Betty L., 180
Curti, Merle, 412
Curtis, Claude D., 364, 394
Curtis, F. Phillar, 148
Custard, Leila R., 273
Cutler, Carroll, 315

Dabney, Virginius, 394, 400, 401
Dahill, Edwin M., 168
Dahl, Orin L., 204
Daley, John M., 168, 214
Dallen, Robert A., 7
Dalrymple, W. H., 219
Dalton, Thomas C., 396
Dalzel, Andrew, 80
Damrosch, Frank H., 289
Dana, Malcolm M., 249
Daniel, Charles H. O., 70
Daniel, Robert N., 355
Dansby, B. Baldwin, 255
Dansereau, Arthur, 20
Dare, Anthony J., 5
Darley, Ward, 160

Davenport, Francis G., 188
Davenport, Walter R., 391
Davies, John L., 66, 78
Davies, Sarah M., 147
Davies, William, 82
Davilla Condemarin, Jose, 113
Davis, Andrew M., 234
Davis, Earl C., 274
Davis, Henry W. C., 71
Davis, Jerry C., 212
Davis, Larry D., 329
Davis, Lenwood G., 307
Davis, Milan, 254
Davis, Phil, 247
Davis, Valentine D., 71
Davis, William E., 160
Dawley, Powel M., 287
Dawson, Edward B., 176
Dawson, John W., 16
Day, Clarence B., 29
Day, H. Summerfield, 205
Dayton, David M., 339
Dean, Arthur L., 180
Dedman, W. Wayne, 297
Dedmond, Francis B., 306
Defferrari, Roy J., 167
DeBlois, Austen K., 191
DeForest, Charlotte B., 99
De Jong, Gerald F., 206
Delaney, Robert W., 159
Delegue, Rene, 37
Delfraisse, Betty D., 330
Delmage, Rutherford E., 295
DeLoney, Willie L., 136
Demarest, William H. S., 277
Demske, James M., 283
Denbo, Philip G., 159
Denis, Valentin, 10
Denman, William F., 184
Denton, Edgar, III, 301
De Remer, Bernard R., 189
Desai, Dhanwant M., 86
Desilets, Andree, 25
Desmaze, Charles A., 38
Despy-Meyer, Andree, 10
Dethloff, Henry C., 382
Deupree, Joseph E., 243
Dew, Lee, A., 140
Dewey, Clifford S., 198

DeWolf, John M, 20
Dexter, Franklin B., 164
Dexter, Nathaniel B., 411
Dhaemers, Margaret P., 143
Diaz Castillo, Roberto, 2
Dick, Everett, 269
Dick, Everett N., 269
Dickey, John S., 271
Dickey, Otis, 209
Dickinson, Elmira J., 184
Dickinson, William C., 371
Dickson, Edward A., 154
Dickson, George, 25
Dietrich, Marietta, 340
Dillard, Walter S., 301
Dillingham, George A., 369
Dingeldine, Raymond C., 396
Di Pietro, Frank S., 272
Di Pietro, Pericle, 93
Dixon, Blase R., 167
Dixon, Brandt V. B., 220
Dixon, William M., 90
Dobbs, Sharron L., 255
Dod, William A., 276
Dodd, William G., 171
Dodge, Bayard, 103
Doherty, William T., 408
Doktor, Guy, 313
Doktor, Hazel, 313
Dolan, Ondrej, 32
Dolenski, Leo M., 334
Donaghy, Thomas J., 342
Donaldson, Gordon, 80
Doney, Carl G., 333
Dongerkery, Sunderkery R., 86
Donnan, Annette W., 254
Donohoe, Patrick A., 151
Donovan, Herman L., 216
Dooley, Howard J., 201
Doran, Micheileen J., 290
Doris, Sebastian, 304
Dornin, May, 153
Dorrance, David B., 316
Dorris, Jonathan T., 213
Doswell, Sallie J., 400
Doten, Samuel B., 270
Doty, Franklin A., 206
Dow, John G., 360
Dowell, George B., 303

Dowell, Spright, 177
Dowie, James I., 268
Dowling, Michael P., 267
Downey, J. Paul, 366
Downs, B. W., 58
Drain, John R., 408
Draughon, Ralph B., 133
Dressel, Paul L., 245
Dreussler, Heinrich G., 40
Dreyfus-Brisac, Edmond, 44
Dryden, Cecil P., 403
Dryer, Edmund H., 136
Dubarle, Eugene, 38
Dubbs, Joseph H., 338
Duberman, Martin B., 304
DuBridge, Lee A., 143
DuFresne, Robert A., 253
Duhn-Schnyder, Emil, 129
Dumas-Rousseau, M., 22
Dumschott, Fred W., 229
Dunaway, Wayland F., 345
Dunbar, Willis F., 245
Duncan, Ivar L. M., 361
Duncan, Virginia C., 377
Duncan, Walter G. K., 5
Dunfee, Walter H., 288
Dunham, Melerson G., 254
Dunigan, David R., 231
Dunkelberger, Harold A., 339
Dunleavy, Jeannette J., 160
Dunn, Georgia, 286
Dunn, William, 378
Dunn, William M., 197
Duran, Miguel A., 35
Durand, Ralph A., 71
Durfee, Calvin, 241
Durham, James G., 212
Durkam, John, 81
Durkin, Joseph T., 168
Durning, Bonnie, 376
Dusenberry, William H., 350
Dyer, George, 58
Dyer, John P., 220
Dyer, Thomas G., 179
Dyker, Mattie M., 262
Dymon, Dorothy, 66
Dysart, Laberta, 335
Dyson Walter, 169

Earnest, G. Brooks, 317
Easby-Smith, James S., 168
Easterby, James H., 354
Eaton, Edward D., 409
Ebel, Wilhelm, 43
Ebert, Roger, 193
Ebright, Homer K., 208
Eckhardt, Carl J., 386
Edel, William W., 337
Edgar, Robert, 276
Edinborough, Arnold, 25
Edward, Austin, Jr., 214
Edwards, Charles W., 133
Edwards, Dorothy L., 216
Edwards, Dwight W., 30
Edwards, Eda B., 334
Edwards, Frederick W., 385
Edwards, Gerald M., 58
Edwards, James B., 356
Edwards, Margaret R., 371
Edwards, Paul M., 204
Eguiguren, Luis A., 113
Eifert, Max, 42
Eisenberg, William E., 398
Elias, Louis, Jr., 255
Eliot, Samuel A., 235
Ell, Carl S., 238
Elliott, Charles, Jr., 157
Elliott, Orrin L., 152
Ellis, Charles C., 341
Ellis, Edward L., 82
Ellis, John, 66
Ellis, John T., 167
Ellis, Roy, 264
Ellis, William A., 391
Ellison, Rhoda C., 134
Emberger, Gudrun, 42
Emden, Alfred B., 71
Emmert, David, 341
Encinas, Jose A., 92, 94
Engelberg, Ernest, 40
England, Joseph W., 345
English, Thomas H., 176
Englizian, H. Crosby, 333
Engram, Irbi D., 174
Engstrand, Iris W., 156
Entrambasaguas y Pena, Joaquin de, 123
Epting, James B., 134

Eriksson, Erik M., 204
Ermini, Giuseppe, 95
Ernst, Harry W., 408
Erpestad, Emil, 358
Eschenbacher, Herman F., 353
Esperabe Arteaga, Enrique, 124
Essen, Leon van der, 10
Estill, Mary S., 379
Eurich, Nell, 53
Evans, Benjamin R., 324
Evans, Jack, 381
Evans, James M., 150
Evans, Mary G., 17
Evans, Robert J. W., 71
Everett, Donald E., 384

Fabroni, Angelo, 96
Facciolati, Jacopo, 94
Faherty, Janette, 51
Faherty, William B., 263
Fairbanks, George R., 368
Fairchild, Edward H., 212, 321
Fairchild, James H., 321
Fancher, Evelyn P., 366
Fanning, James D., 374
Fanning, William H. W., 263
Farley, Joseph P., 301
Farmer, Blake L., 380
Farmer, Ernest K., 264
Farmerie, Samuel A., 336
Farquhar, Catherine B., 211
Farrand, Elizabeth M., 247
Farrell, Harry C., Jr., 382
Fasoli, Gina, 92
Favaro, Antonio, 92, 94
Fawcett, Novice G., 322
Fay, Abbott, 161
Fay, Charles R., 58
Feeler, William, 157
Fennimore, Keith J., 242
Ference, Regina C., 336
Ferguson, James E., 137
Fern, M. Edmond, 159
Fernald, Merritt C., 223
Ferrier, William W., 153
Ferruolo, Stephen C., 38
Ferrus Roig, Francisco, 83
Fick, Virginia G., 312
Fiddes, Edward, 78

Fiegel, Melvin F., 329
Fields, Thomas B., 195
Findlay, Ross P., 389
First, Wesley, 284, 285
Fischer, Edward, 202
Fischer, LeRoy H., 329
Fish, Everett D., 209
Fish, William L., 321
Fisher, Margaret B., 173
Fisher, Michael M., 266
Fisher, Michael P., 211
Fisher, Miles M., 402
Fisher, Rosalind R., 298
Fitts, Dora A., 378
Fitz-Gerald, John D., 140
Fitzpatrick, Edward A., 411
Flahive, Robert F., 409
Flanagan, Frances, 262
Flanders, Bertram H., 176
Fleming, Donald H., 352
Fleming, Thomas J., 301
Fleming, Walter L., 219
Fletcher, Robert S., 321, 322
Flie, George, 20
Flint, Nott W., 192
Flood, Robert G., 189
Florentz, Christopher J., 294
Flower, Olive, 320
Flynn, Jean M., 357
Fogdall, Vergil S., 206
Foley, Patrick J., 153
Folmsbee, Stanley J., 367, 368
Fontaine, Paul, 323
Foray, Cyril P., 120
Forbes, Mansfield, 58
Ford, Guy S., 252
Fordham, Christopher C., 309
Forget, Anastase, 20
Forman, Sidney, 301
Forst, Arthur C., 162
Forsythe, James L., 209
Fortenbaugh, Samuel B., 299
Fortt, Inez L., 332
Foster, David, 54
Foster, Gregory, 66
Foster, R. B., 261
Fowler, Helen, 58
Fowler, Herbert E., 161
Fowler, Joseph T., 64

Fowler, Laurence, 58
Fowler, Thomas, 71
Fowler, William B., 255
Fox, Dixon R., 300
Fox, William L., 226
Fraguas Fraguas, Antonio, 125
Frangopulo, Nicholas J., 52
Frank, Charles E., 185
Franklin, Franklin B., 164
Frantz, Joe B., 386
Fraser, James A., 22
Fraser, William J., 21
Frayling, Christopher, 54
Fraylla, Diego, 125
Fred, Edwin B., 412
Frederick, Antoinette, 238
Freehafer, Ruth W., 199
Freeman, Randall B., 312
Freitag, Alfred J., 267
French, John C., 225
French, Robert D., 164
French, Roger F., 380
French, Stanley, 58
French, William M., 296
Fretag, Alfred J., 184
Frey, Peter W., 340
Friant, John R., 168
Friedberg, Emil A., 40
Friel, Mary E., 233
Fries, Adelaide L., 309
Fromm, Glenn E., 279
Frommer, Harvey, 291
Frost, Jack, 231
Frost, R. W., 16
Frost, Stanley B., 16
Fuess, Claude M., 230
Fugate, Francis L., 387
Fuller, Thomas, 58
Funk, Dorothy R., 406
Funk, Henry D., 251
Furman, Franklin D., 278
Fyfe, Dorthea H., 71

Gabriel, Ralph H., 237
Gagie, Martin R. J., 248
Galbreath, Clarence R., 338
Gall, Franz, 8
Gallalee, John M., 137
Gallaudet, Edward M., 167

Gallot, Mildred B., 218
Galpin, William F., 299
Gambee, Robert, 276
Gamble, Paul, 351
Gamble, Richard D., 412
Gambrell, Herbert P., 371
Gambrill, Mollie D., 108
Gameron Leon, Maria, 416
Gannon, Robert I., 287
Ganss, George E., 263
Gantner, Elliot S. M., 290
Garcia Lasaosa, Jose, 125
Garcia Robles, Alfonso, 38
Gard, Robert E., 412
Garden, Donald S., 4
Gardiner, John H., 235
Gardner, Alice, 58
Gardner, Elva B., 366
Gardner, Robert G., 178
Gardner, W. J., 109
Garland, Martha M., 59
Garrett, Herbert L. O., 112
Garrett, Mitchell B., 134
Garrett, Philip C., 340
Garrett, R. Thomas, 406
Garro, Juan M., 2
Garst, Henry, 324
Gates, Charles M., 404
Gates, Charlynne, 143
Gates, Samuel E., 156
Gatewood, Herman W., 305
Gatke, Robert M., 333
Gaunt, William, 71
Gavin, Donald P., 319
Gay, Roger C., 223
Gbadamosi, T. G. O., 111
Gee, Ruth E., 378
Geer, Curtis M., 162
Geiger, Louis G., 313
Geis, M. Christina, 274
Gendebien, Albert W., 341
George, Arthur A., 307
George, Hereford B., 71
George, Melvin R., 189
Gerber, John C., 207
Gerold, William, 352
Gerrity, Frank, 346
Getz, Gene A., 189
Geurts, Pieter A. M., 107

Gherardi, Alessandro, 93
Gibbons, Harold E., 373
Gibbons, Mary W., 276
Gibbs, Clifford L., 384
Gibbs, Rafe, 170, 182
Gibbs, Warmoth T., 308
Gibson, De Lois, 141
Gibson, Frederick W., 17
Giebel, Arlyn J., 251
Giesendorf, Paul F., 128
Gieysztor, Aleksander, 117
Gilbert, Benjamin F., 151
Gilbert, Dorothy L., 306
Gilbert, William K., 348
Gildart, Robert, 242
Gilfillan, John B., 253
Gilkey, George R., 411
Gillespie, James R., 194
Gillespie, John, 327
Gillis, Ann A., 20
Gillis, Ezra L., 216
Gilman, Daniel C., 225
Gilman, Richard C., 148
Gingrich, Felix W., 334
Gittenger, Roy, 330
Givens, Stuart R., 315
Gladish, Richard R., 333
Glasgow, Edwin, 71
Glasgow, William M., 338
Glassock, Jean, 240
Glatfelter, Charles H., 339
Glazener, Stephen M., 374
Glennan, Thomas K., 316
Gloria, Andrea, 94
Glorieux, Palemon, 38
Gloucester, Richard, 71
Gobbel, Luther L., 306
Godley, Alfred D., 71
Godsey, Helen, 264
Godsey, Townsend, 264
Godson, William F. H., 301
Godwin, George S., 66
Goerig, Violet M., 359
Goggins, Lathardus, 316, 317
Golay, Wasant, H., 88
Goldberg, Barbara L. S., 138
Golden, Floyd D., 280
Goldstein, Israel, 231
Gollancz, Hermann, 67

Gomez, Fausto, 114
Gonzales Bogen, Americo, 415
Gonzalez Cosia Diaz, Arturo, 106
Goodhew, Edna F., 142
Goodrich, Martha H., 331
Goodsell, Charles T., 245
Goodspeed, Thomas W., 192, 193
Goodwin, William A. R., 397
Gordon, Ann D., 336, 348
Gordon, Colin, 77
Gordon, James F., Jr., 254
Gordon, Sheila C., 283
Gorman, Jack, 24
Gosden, P. H. J. H., 65
Gould, George M., 348
Govan, Gilbert E., 368
Graebner, Theodore C., 259
Graham, Roger, 17
Grant, Alexander, 80
Grant, James, 6
Grattan, William J., 232
Grave, W. W., 59
Graver, Lee, 341
Graver, Lee A., 344
Graves, Frank P., 296
Graves, Harold K., 146
Graves, Thomas A., 393
Gray, Alfred O., 406
Gray, Arthur, 59
Gray, David W., 392
Gray, James, 253
Gray, Joseph H., 59
Gray, Leona S., 380
Greason, A. LeRoy, 222
Greathead, Sarah E. H., 151
Green, Edwin L., 357
Green, Elizabeth A., 237
Green, Francis M., 318
Green, Vivian H. H., 71
Greene, Helen F., 239
Greene, Maurice, 26
Greens, Lee S., 368
Greenslade, Thomas B., 319
Gregerson, Edna J., 388
Gregg, James R., 152
Gregg, Robert D., 333
Greiff, Constance M., 276
Gresham, Perry E., 406

Gretschel, Carl C. C., 40
Gretzinger, William C., 334
Grev, Julian R., 251
Griessman, B. Eugene, 176
Griffin, Anne F., 355
Griffin, Clifford S., 211
Griffin, Frances, 309
Griffin, Penny, 72
Griffin, Zebina F., 289
Griffith, Lucille B., 137
Grimsley, James A., 354
Grissom, Preston B., 381
Grohmann, Johann C. A., 40
Gronert, J. I., 203
Groshong, James W., 332
Guardiola, Esteban, 84
GuDni, Jonsson, 85
Guemple, John R., 371
Guild, Reuben A., 352
Gunn, Jack W., 255
Guy-Sheftall, Beverly, 179
Gwynne-Timothy, John R. W., 26

Haag, Edmund V., 403
Hackett, Alice P., 240
Hackett, M. B., 59
Haddock, William J., 207
Haffey, Hugh J., 294
Hageman, Howard G., 275
Haggard, Theodore M., 170
Haglund, Elizabeth, 389
Hahn, Stephen S., 356
Haight, Elizabeth H., 303
Haile, Fisseha, 35
Haines, George L., 275
Hair, William I., 176
Haivala, Paul A., 359
Hajdukiewica, Leszek, 115
Hale, Allean L., 259
Haley, May B., 373
Hall, Christopher W., 253
Hall, Colby D., 382
Hall, Dorothy, 314
Hall, Henry F., 15
Hall, Ida J., 213
Hall, John, 5
Hall, John G., 140
Hall, Morris E., 386
Hall, Reginald W., 132

Hall, William F., 361
Haller, Johannes, 42
Halliburton, Cecil D., 309
Halm, D. Ray, 145
Halm, Dennis R., 145
Halmagrand, Charles N., 38
Halperin Donghi, Tulio, 2
Halperin, Samuel, 248
Halsey, Leroy J., 188
Hambalek, Stephen, 296
Hambrick, Thera O., 180
Hamel, Dana B., 325
Hamelin, Louis-Edmond, 23, 24
Hamilton, Andrew, 154
Hamilton, Herb, 17
Hamilton, Karen E., 97
Hamilton, Mary A., 59
Hamilton, Nancy, 387
Hamilton, Rapheal N., 410
Hamilton, Robert, 16
Hamilton, Sidney G., 72
Hamilton, Thomas H., 180
Hamlin, Griffith A., 189, 266
Hammet, Ben H., 357
Hammon, Walter, 294
Hammond, Brenda H., 365
Hammond, Nathaniel J., 179
Hanawalt, Leslie L., 248
Hancock, Harold B., 324
Handy, Robert T., 300
Hankins, Martha L., 373
Hanley, Francis X., 338
Hanna, Alfred J., 171
Hanna, Glenn A., 313
Hanna, Thomas H., 215
Hanscom, Elizabeth D., 239
Hansen, James E., 158
Hansen, Thorvald, 205
Hanson, Calvin B., 192
Hanson, Richard S., 358
Harcourt, John, 289
Hardesty, Von D., 315
Hardin, John A., 214
Harding, Samuel B., 198
Hardy, Deborah, 414
Hardy, Ernest G., 72
Hardy, Florent, 221
Harlan, John C., 408
Harmon, Geroge M., 256

Harney, Thomas E., 283
Harper, Hoyt H., 174
Harris, Herbert E., 157
Harris, Isidore, 67
Harris, John F., 220
Harris, Ruth M., 260
Harrison, Brian, 84
Harrison, Hale, 141
Harrison, John, 80
Harrison, John F. C., 67, 78
Harrison, Lowell H., 218
Hart, Carolyn G., 330
Hart, Casper P., 228
Hart, Irving H., 207
Harte, Neagley B., 67
Harth, Dietrich, 45
Hartman, William F., 161
Hartog, Philippe J., 78
Harvey, Daniel C., 15
Harvey, McClennon P., 377
Harvey, Robert S., 203
Harvill, Richard A., 140
Haselmayer, Louis A., 205
Haskell, Samuel, 245
Haskins, David G., 369
Hasluck, Nicholas, 7
Hatch, Louis C., 222
Hatch, Richard A., 193
Hatcher, Harlan H., 247
Hatfield, Edwin F., 300
Hatter, Henrietta R., 169
Hauck, Arthur A., 223
Haught, Thomas W., 408
Hautz, Johann F., 45
Havekost, Irene, 382
Havighurst, Walter, 320
Hawkins, Hugh, 225
Haworth, B. Smith, 210
Hayden, Michael, 24
Haydn, Hiram C., 316
Hayes, Donn W., 265
Hayes, J. I., 392
Hayes, Marie T., 289
Hayman, Herbert H., 181
Haynes, William H., 213
Hayter, Earl W., 190
Headlam, Cecil, 72
Headley, Leal A., 249
Healy, Frances P., 273

Healy, John, 89
Hearn, Thomas K., 311
Hearnshaw, Fossey J. C., 67
Hedges, Richard G., 404
Heesom, Alan, 64
Hefelbower, Samuel G., 339
Hegland, Georgiana E. D., 252
Heikel, Ivar A., 36
Heilman, E. Bruce, 399
Heins, Henry H., 288
Heintzen, Erich H., 196
Heirich, Max, 153
Heithaus, Claude H., 263
Helm, Gustav, 45
Helmers, Hermann, 49
Helmreich, Paul C., 241
Hembree, Sillous G., 216
Hemmeter, John C., 228
Henderson, Algo D., 314
Henderson, Archibald, 310
Henderson, Bernard W., 72
Henderson, George D., 79
Hendricks, Marvin L., 201
Hendrickson, Walter B., 188
Henley, William B., 156
Hennessey, Daniel L., 314
Henry, Gordon C., 356
Hepburn, William M., 199
Herlitzka, Adolf, 48
Herman, Beaumont A., 240
Herman, Debra, 302
Heron, Denis C., 90
Herradura, Elma S., 113
Herrick, Clay, 316
Herrscher, Barton R., 163
Herscher, Irenaeus J., 294
Hershey, Charlie B., 158
Hess, Gerhard, 47
Hester, Hubert I., 261, 266, 312, 353
Hester, James M., 291
Hetherington, Martha A., 385
Heulin, Gordon, 67
Hewett, Waterman T., 286
Heywood, James, 59
Hiatt, Dianna B., 145
Hicken, Victor, 194
Hickerson, Frank R., 325
Hickman, Alma, 258

Hickman, Lillian W., 377
Hicks, Arthur C., 405
Higginbotham, Robert L., 386
Higgins, Francis J., 326
Higgs, Elton D., 248
Highfield, Roger, 57, 69
Hill, George B. N., 235
Hill, H. W., 156
Hill, Jack D., 186
Hill, Joseph A., 387
Hill, Ralph N., 271
Hill, Walter H., 263
Hill, William C., 271
Hillegas, Lyle C., 157
Hillerbrand, Bonnie B., 379
Hilliard, Annie P., 169
Hilton, Miriam E., 246
Himes, Charles F., 337
Hind, Henry Y., 20
Hines, Gustavus, 333
Hinkle, Marilyn, 245
Hins, Gerhard, 45
Hinsdale, Burke A., 247
Hinton, David E., 363
Hinton, Edward M., 337
Hinton, Percival, 56
Hinton, William H., 375
Hipps, John B., 30
Hird, Marilyn, 64
Hirschler, E. J., 315
Hitchcock, Edward, 230
Hitt, Bowling M., 375
Hoadley, Grace, 190
Hobbs, Jane E., 350
Hobhouse, Christopher, 72
Hobhouse, Herminie, 71
Hodes, Ursula, 331
Hodgkin, Robert H., 72
Hodson, Paul W., 389
Hoff, Advertus A., 104
Hoffbauer, Johann C., 40
Hoffman, Alexius, 252
Hoffman, Allan M., 295, 296
Hoffman, Philip G., 149
Hoffmann, Mathias M., 205
Hoffmeyer, Oscar, 219
Hogan, Fred P., 144
Hogan, Peter E., 167
Hogue, Harland E., 149

Hoke, George W., 293
Holbing, Franz, 8
Holcomb, Jack B., 179
Holden, Edward S., 301
Holden, Reuben A., 165
Hollingsworth, Virginia N., 195
Hollis, Andrew P., 298
Hollis, Christopher, 72
Hollis, Daniel W., 357
Holmes, Kenneth L., 331
Holmes, Owen G., 21
Holmgren, Philip, 268
Holsten, George H., 277
Holt, Andrew D., 367
Holt, James C., 77
Hone, Ralph E., 155
Hoover, Thomas N., 323
Hope, Arthur J., 202
Hopkins, Ernest J., 138
Hopkins, James F., 217
Hopkins, Lillie A., 174
Hopson, George B., 282
Horlock, John H., 54
Hormann, Arthur, 411
Horn, Calvin, 281
Horn, David B., 80
Horn, Larry, 157
Horn, Thayer S., 153
Hornbeak, Samuel L., 385
Hornell, William W., 84
Horoldt, Dietrich, 44
Horowitz, Murray M., 283
Horton, E. Gene, 363
Hosford, Frances J., 322
Hotz, Joachim, 48
Hough, Franklin B., 296, 300
House, Lloyd L., 139
House, Robert B., 310
Houser, John H., 387
Howard, Lowry S., 148
Howard, Oswald, 17
Howard, Richard B., 25
Howarth, Thomas E. B., 59
Howat, Gerald, 52
Howe, Catherine P., 157
Howells, Dorothy E., 238
Hoyle, Hughes B., Jr., 308
Hoyt, John W., 38
Hubbard, James P., 110

Hubbart, Henry C., 323
Huber, Donald L., 324
Hubers, Dale, 206
Hubley, John E., 346
Huddle, Orlando E., 214
Hudson, James B., 217
Hudspeth, Junia E., 386
Huff, Mary B., 219
Huffman, Harold T., Jr., 150
Hughes, Dorothy, 281
Hughes, Laurie J., 13
Hughes, Mary K., 259
Hughes, Riley, 163
Hulewicz, Jan, 11
Hull, Augustus L., 179
Hulse, James W., 270
Humphrey, David C., 285
Humphrey, Heman, 230
Hunt, Rockwell D., 156, 157
Hunter, Katrina V., 396
Hunter, William C., 313
Hunter, Wilma D., 395
Huntington, Charles A., 391
Huntley, C. William, 300
Hurt, Franklin B., 394
Hussey, Christopher, 72
Hutchins, Francis S., 213
Hutchinson, Melvin F., 139
Hutchinson, William H., 144
Hutchison, Earl E., 376
Hutton, William H., 72
Huttunen, Marja-Leena, 36
Hyamson, Albert M., 67
Hyde, Edmund M., 342

Iguiniz, Juan G., 107
Ike, Chukwuemeka, 111
Ingram, James, 72
Inman, Elmer B., 368
Inman, J. P., 52
Irby, Richard, 398
Irvin, Helen D., 217
Irwin, James R., 248
Isbell, Egbert R., 243
Isham, Charlotte H., 164
Isnardi, Lorenzo, 93

Jaberg, Eugene C., 410
Jabs, Albert E., 358

Jackman, Eugene T., 280
Jackson, John B., 154
Jackson, Sarah E., 176
Jackson, Thomas G., 73
Jacquinot, Adrien, 235
James, Edmund J., 193
James, Eleanor, 384, 385
James, Norris E., 152
Jammaz, Saud I., 35
Jansen, Christian, 45
Janzen, Abraham E., 211
Jarcow, Merrill E., 249
Jauss, Hans R., 47
Jay, Ike W., 374
Jay, John, 285
Jeffrey, Buron, 215
Jeffreys, Richard L., 402
Jenke, James M., 139
Jenkins, Annibel, 176
Jenkins, Clara B., 309
Jenkins, Jerry B., 189
Jennings, Walter W., 216
Jens, Walter, 42
Jensen, Henry W., 311
Jenswold, John R., 411
Jentsch, Christoph, 48
Jeschke, Reuben P., 359
Jessup, Frank, 73
Jewell, Derek, 69
Jewett, Alyce W., 154
Jha, Hetukar, 86
Jha, Jagdish C., 87
Jimenez Catalan, Manuel, 125
John, Walton C., 395
Johns, Walter H., 19
Johnson, Alandus C., 178
Johnson, Charles M., 16
Johnson, David W., 251
Johnson, Eldon L., 272
Johnson, Elwin B., 253
Johnson, Evelyn A., 306
Johnson, Henry C., 193
Johnson, Jesse B., 218
Johnson, Mary L., 308
Johnson, Peter L., 411
Johnson, Richard D., 19
Johnson, Robert G., 363
Johnson, Robert L., 347
Johnson, Roy H., 347

Johnston, Mamie, 261
Jonasson, Jonas A., 331
Jones Anglin, I. Patricia, 224
Jones, Alexander E., 195
Jones, Barbara S., 390
Jones, Clyde C., 215
Jones, Edward A., 177
Jones, Ginny, 15
Jones, Glendell A., 377
Jones, Gwyn, 82
Jones, Ivan L., Jr., 151
Jones, John, 73
Jones, Marjorie F., 292
Jones, Martin D. W., 51
Jones, Maxine D., 135
Jones, Mildred P., 306
Jones, Ralph W., 381
Jones, Richard M., 403
Jones, Rufus M., 340
Jones, T. Mason, 90
Jones, Theodore F., 291
Jones, Thomas E., 362
Jones, Thomas F., 357
Jones, W. Lewis, 82
Jones, Wilfred, 398
Jones, William C., 153
Jones, William H., 375
Jones, William H. S., 59
Jordahl, Donald C., 185
Jordahl, Sivert A., 358
Jordan, Howard, 223
Jordan, Karl, 42
Jorgensen, Arne, 36
Jorgensen, Sharlee C., 148
Jourdain, Charles, 38
Julku, Liisa, 36
Jurriannse, Maria W., 107
Just, Leo, 44

Kaemmel, Otto, 41
Kahn, Ely J., 235
Kaila, Eino, 36
Kale, Wilford, 393
Kane, Robert J., 79
Kanthawongs, Charoen, 129
Karas, Mieczyslaw, 115
Karff, Samuel E., 318
Karimi, Khalid A. M., 119
Karp, Alan, 59, 73

Kartendick, James J., 227
Kasse Acta, Rafael, 34
Kastendieck, Miles M., 292
Kaye, Elaine, 67
Kaylor, Earl C., 341
Kayser, Elmer L., 168
Kayser, Kathryn E., 209
Kearney, Edmund, 183
Keen, William W., 352
Keenan, Edward P., 250
Keep, Rosalind A., 148
Kellam, Nettie L., 382
Keller, Richard A., 46
Kelley, Aloysius P., 162
Kelley, Brooks M., 165
Kelley, Robert L., 155
Kelly, James R., 280
Kelly, Thomas, 66
Kelly, William W., 216
Kelsey, Roger R., 252
Kelter, Weir C., 340
Kelton, Allen, 369
Kempers, Garrett, 208
Kennedy, Walter A., Jr., 355
Kennelly, Edward F., 278
Kenny, James E., 290
Kenny, Michael, 135
Kent, Charles I., 344
Keppel, Alvin R., 305
Keppel, Frederick P., 285
Kern, Richard, 318
Kerr, Alenander, 121
Keynes, Margaret E., 60
Kibler, Lillian A., 355
Kieckhefer, Grace N., 410
Kieley, James F., 228
Killion, Mead W., 247
Kimble, David, 104
King, Carlyle, 24
King, Diane A., 339
King, Horatio C., 337
King, James T., 413
King, Joanne E., 166
King, Stanley, 230
Kingsley, James L., 165
Kingsley, William L., 165
Kink, Rudolf, 8
Kinnear, Duncan L., 401
Kinnison, William A., 322, 326

Kirby, Maurice W., 267
Kirk, James, 81
Kirkconnell, Watson, 13
Kirubi, Gichuhi M. M., 103
Kittelson, David J., 181
Kitzmiller, H. H., 316
Kiyooka, Eiichi, 99
Klages, Alfred D., 383
Klaperman, Gilbert, 304
Klein, Frederick S., 338
Klein, Harry M. J., 335
Klein, Helmut, 39
Kline, Reamer, 282
Kling, Frederick W., 399
Klotsche, J. Martin, 412
Klotz, Richard R., 340
Klotzberger, Edward L., 298
Klupfel, Karl, 42
Knauss, James O., 249
Knepper, George W., 324
Knickerbocker, M. R., 261
Knieriemen, Ruth-Ann D., 390
Knipp, Anna H., 225
Knoll, H. B., 199
Knott, James P., 149
Knust, Edward H., 325
Koelsch, William A., 232
Kolbe, Parker R., 324
Kolde, Theodor von, 43
Kolozsvari, Ivan B., 85
Kolzow, Virden J., 210
Kosanovich, William T., 342
Kosegarten, Johann G. L., 39
Koshman, Lidiia V., 131
Kotzin, Miriam N., 337
Kowalke, Erwin E., 411
Krabbe, Otto C., 41
Krebs, Frank J., 408
Kreher, R. H., 172
Kreis, Georg, 127
Kroeze, Barend H., 312
Krones, Franz von, 7
Kropp, Simon F., 280
Kuehl, John W., 397
Kuhn, Madison, 245
Kujawa, Rose M., 245
Kuntz, Frank A., 167
Kuusi, Sakari, 36

Laberge, Paul A., 21
LaBorde, Maximillian, 357, 358
Lacy, George R., 374
Lahey, William C., 299
Laird, Johanna, 144
Lamb. Robert, 60
Lamberton, Mary, 29
Lamkin, Charles F., 266
LaMotte, Louis C., 175
Landeen, William M., 405
Landolt, George L., 371
Lane, John J., 386
Lane, Ulysses S., 220
Lane, Wheaton J., 276
Lang, Andrew, 73
Langill, Ellen, 409
Langins, Janis, 37
Langley, Nina, 9
Lanier, Raphael O., 383
Lanning, John T., 83
Larkin, Charles W., 224
Larsen, Dale R., 270
Larson, Robert W., 161
Larson, Sexton, 251
Lasley, Jess W., 361
Laub, C. Herbert, 173
Lavallee, Andree, 21
Lavallee, Jean-Guy, 25
Law, Harry, 54
Lawlis, Chelsea L., 203
Lawrence, Evan J., 273
Lawson, Allen L., 148
Lawson, K. C., 120
Leach, Max, 370
Leal, Ildefonso, 415
Lebon, Wilfrid, 21
LeBreton, Marietta M., 219
Leddy, John R., 27
LeDuc, Thomas H. A., 230
Lee, Arthur O., 249
Lee, George R., 260
Lee, John, 80
Lee, Kathryn J., 350
Lee, L. Tennent, 135
Lee, Stephen D., 256
Lee, William S., 390
Legal, Roger D., 21
Leigh, A. A., 60
Leitch, Alexander, 276

Lelon, Thomas C., 191
Lelyveld, David, 85
Lengyel, Emil, 274
Lennox-Short, Alan, 121
Lentz, Harold H., 327, 409
Lenz, Eli G., 191
Lenz, Max, 39
Leon, Edwin, 31
Leonard, Delavan L., 249, 322
Leonard, Edwin S., 190
Leonard, Jacob C., 305
Leonard, Roger A., 5
Le Page, Samuel M., 210
Le-Roy y Galvez, Luis F., 32
Lesesne, Joab M., Jr., 355
Lester, James E., 141, 142
Levensohn, Lotta, 91
Levi, Edward H., 193
Levy, David C., 292
Lewis, Joseph J., 350
Lewis, William D., 166
Liddell, Marilyn N. B., 375
Liflar, Robert A., 141
Light, R. Chambliss, Jr., 400
Lignian, Mildred, 246
Likins, Jeanne M., 224
Lillard, Richard G., 147
Lindquist, Emory K., 208
Lindroth, Sten, 127
Lindsay, Ernest L., 405
Lindsay, Jean O., 60
Lindsay, Julian I., 391
Lindsay, William L., 109
Lindstrom, Andrew, 187
Lingenfelten, Linwood S., 344
Linner, Edward R., 303
Lippincott, Horace M., 348
Little, Bryan D. G., 60
Little, Faye M., 375
Little, Frank J., 134
Littlefield, Henry W., 163
Livingood, James W., 368
Livingstone, Rex D., 108
Llore Mosquera, Victor, 34
Lloyd, Albert H., 60
Lloyd, Garnet C., 194
Lloyd, James B., 258
Lloyd, Ralph W., 364
Lloyd, Raymond G., 366

Locke, Edwin A., 352
Locke, William R., 306
Lockmiller, David A., 308
Lockwood, Theodore D., 163
Loftus, Mary M., 31
Logan, Harry S., 19
Logan, John A., 395
Logan, Rayford W., 169
Loggan, David, 60
Logsdon, Guy W., 330
Long, Charles F., 330
Long, Gordon, 4
Long, Walter E., 386
Long, Watt A., 332
Longenecker, Herbert E., 221
Longfellow, Ernest, 269
Longley, Ronald S., 13
Longworth, Charles, 234
Lopez Cervantes, Gerardo, 105
Lopez Rodriguez, Miguel, 123
Lopez, Salvador P., 115
Lord, Clifford L., 288
Lord, Jerome E., 165
Lorenze, Adolf F., 41
Lossing, Benson J., 303
Lotero Orozco, Gildardo, 30
Lousse, Emile, 10
Love, James L., 310
Lovenstein, Meno, 323
Lovett, Warren P., 178
Lovette, Leland P., 228
Lowe, Walter I., 303
Lowrey, Walter M., 218
Lowry, Mary A., 319
Lowry, Thomas J., 265
Lowry, Vayne A., 359
Lucas, Aubrey D., 258
Luckacs, John, 335
Ludlow, Helen W., 136
Lukac, George J., 277
Lunceford, Charles R., 171
Lund, Doniver A., 251
Lu Pe Win, U., 13
Luthje, Jurgen, 49
Lutman, John H., 26
Lutzeler, Heinrich, 45
Lycan, Gilbert L., 172
Lynch, Kenneth M., 356
Lynch, William O., 197

Lyon, B., 27
Lyon, Elijah W., 150
Lyon, Ralph M., 134
Lyons, Joseph A., 202
Lyte, Henry C. M., 73

McAfee, Joseph E., 262
McArthur, Jackson, 136
McBane, Edith L., 335
McBride, Guy T., 158
McCaffrey, Donna T., 352
McCain, Clara E., 371
Macauley, Irene, 185
McClintock, Marion E., 65
McCollister, John, 170
McCollom, Stewart F., 413
McComas, James D., 256
McConagha, Glenn L., 183
McConica, James, 73
McCord, David T. W., 238
McCormick, Joel, 15
McCormick, Richard P., 277
McCosh, James, 276
McCrady, Edward, 369
McCurdy, Michael, 235
McDevitt, Matthew, 150
McDonald, Cleveland, 316
McDonald, Edward D., 337
McDonald, Emanuel B., 152
MacDonald, George E., 23
MacDonald, John, 19
McDonough, Colleen, 295
McDowell, Robert B., 90
McEniry, Blanche M., 273
McEwen, Mildred M., 308
McFall, Kenneth, 315
McFarlane, William H., 163
McFee, Joseph E., 262
McGaw, Robert A., 370
McGiffert, Arthur C., 183
McGinley, Laurence J., 287
McGinnis, Frederick A., 326
McGlothlin, William J., 355
McGrane, Reginald C., 325
McGrath, Gary L., 253
McGreal, Shirley P., 86
McGregor, Gordon P., 130
McHargue, Robert M., 147
McHugh, James V., 186

McIntire, Stephen W., 296
McIntosh, Clarence F., 144
McIntyre, Donald G., 120
Macintyre, Stuart, 4
McKee, Earl S., 212
McKee, John D., 317
Mackensen, Heina F., 274
Mackenzie, Margaret, 22
McKenzie, Pearle, 357
McKeon, Valarie A., 272
McKevitt, Gerald, 151
McKey, Joseph P., 291
MacKey, Katharine W., 263
Mackie, John D., 81
McKnight, Edgar V., 305
McLaughlin, Marvin L., 376
McLean Albert F., 346
McLean, Celia, 26
MacLean, John, 276
Macleane, Douglas, 73
MacLennan, Hugh, 16
McLemore, Nannie, 256
McLemore, Richard A., 256
McLeod, John A., 307
McMahon, Aileen, 374
McMath, Robert C., Jr., 176
Macmillan, Cyrus, 16
McMillan, Montague, 356
McMullin, William C., 387
McMurtry, William J., 360
McNair, Walter E., 174
McNamee, Mary D., 146
McNeill, William E., 18
McNulty, Helen P., 327
McPheeters, Alphonso A., 175
Madariaga de la Campa, Benito, 122
Maden, Falconer, 73
Magrath, John R., 73
Mahaffy, John P., 90
Mahan, Lessie D. J., 264
Mais, Stuart P. B., 73
Malagola, Carlo, 92
Maldonado, Carlos S., 330
Mallet, Charles E., 73
Mallett, Richard P., 223
Manhart, George B., 196
Manilla, Sundy J., 246
Manley, Louise, 134

Manley, Robert N., 269
Mann, Aubrey E., 280
Mann, Bonita H., 265
Mann, Clair V., 265
Mann, Gordon C., 210
Mansbridge, Albert, 73
Mansfield, Catherine H., 70
Manwaring, Hyrum, 182
Marigold, W. G., 216
Mark, Kenneth L., 239
Markell, Harold K., 16
Marling, Francis H., 16
Marra, Filippo, 97
Marrara, Danilo, 96
Marriner, Ernest C., 222
Marsden, Robert S., 80
Marsh, Alan T., 167
Marsh, Neville, 67
Marshall, Albert P., 261
Marshall, Frank H., 329
Marshall, Helen E., 186
Marshall, Ronald, 79
Marshall, William F., 278
Marston, Everett C., 238
Marti, Hugo, 128
Martin, Claude T., 316
Martin, Dorothy M., 189
Martin, Douglas D., 140
Martin, Eldon H., 391
Martin, James R., 155
Martin, LeRoy A., 366
Martin, Luis, 113
Martinez Albiach, Alfredo, 12
Martinez Rodriguez, Enrique, 125
Martinez, Samuel A., 146
Martzloff, Clement L., 323
Mason, Blanche M., 385
Mason, Edward G., 314
Mason, Frank M., 383
Mason, John F. A., 69
Masters, Robert, 60
Mata Gavidia, Jose, 83
Matheson, James A. L., 4
Mathy, Helmut, 44
Matthews, Alfred W., 404
Matthews, Ben A., 384
Matthews, Geoffrey F., 53
Matthews, James T., 333

Matthews, R. Arthur, 354
Mattingly, Arthur, 264
Matzen, Henning, 33
Mau, Clayton C., 298
Mavrodin, Vladimir V., 131
Maxey, Chester C., 405
Maxie, Earl, 218
Maxwell, Constantia E., 91
May, Arthur J., 302
Mayer, Gerard E., 160
Mayor, John E. B., 60
Mayr-Wallenreiter, Clara, 48
Mead, Gilbert W., 229
Meagher, Walter J., 232
Measells, Dewitt T., Jr., 258
Meek, Vincent L., 3
Megson, Barbara, 60
Mehnert, Klaus, 181
Meigs, Cornelia, 334
Meiners, Fredericka, 378
Meinhardt, Gunther, 43
Meline, Mary M., 226
Mellanby, Kenneth, 111
Mellette, Frank, 354
Mellor, Bernard, 84
Mellown, Robert O., 137
Meltzer, Gilbert W., 286, 287
Melville, Henry, 25
Mendenhall, Thomas C., 239, 322
Mendes, Josue C., 12
Menes Llaguno, Juan M., 104
Menzies, Elizabeth, G. C., 276
Meredith, Howard L., 327
Merrell, Edward H., 411
Merriam, Harold G., 267
Merrill, James G., 362
Merrington, W. R., 67
Merryman, John E., 341
Mertins, Esther N., 155
Metha, J. L., 86
Meyer, Annie N., 282
Meyer, Carl S., 259
Meyer, Leland W., 214
Meyerson, Martin, 348
Meza, Luis A., 105
Michael, Olin B., 312
Michalewicz, Jerzy, 116
Michalewiczowa, Marie, 116
Middleton, Thomas C., 350

Milburn, David, 78
Millar, Graham, 291
Miller, Alice D., 282
Miller, Clara W., 314
Miller, Donald C., 267
Miller, Donald G., 185
Miller, Ed M., 159
Miller, Edward, 60
Miller, Edward A., Jr., 159
Miller, Francis J., 315
Miller, Margaret, 180
Miller, Marilyn, 143
Miller, Mary, 209
Miller, Melvin J., 142
Miller, Russell E., 239
Miller, Stephen S., 169
Millican, Alta, 135
Millis, John S., 316
Millis, William A., 197
Milne, Joseph G., 73
Mims, Edwin, 370
Miner, Nagel T., 147
Mirrielees, Edith R., 152, 153
Miskiewicz, Benon, 115
Mitchell, C. Bradford, 301
Mitchell, John P., 153
Mitchell, Ken, 24
Mitchell, L. G., 75
Mitchell, Samuel T., 326
Mitchell, Yetta G., 385
Mix, Mary D., 299
Moase, Lorne R., 23
Mockler-Ferryman, Augustus F., 55
Moe, Alfred K., 235
Moeder, Monica, 208
Moffat, Charles H., 407
Moffat, James E., 350
Moffatt, Michael, 277
Moffett, McLedge, 397
Mohler, Samuel R., 402
Mohr, Eleanor S., 385
Molen, Clarence T., Jr., 207
Moll, Clarence R., 351
Monahan, Danno R., 261
Monk, Francis F., 87
Montague, Martha F., 331
Montgomery, James R., 367, 368

Montgomery, Thomas H, 348
Monti, Gennaro M., 94
Moody, Theodore W., 79
Mooney, Donald J., 295
Moore, Archibald Y., 197
Moore, Clement C., 285
Moore, Dwain E., 145
Moore, Elif A., 383
Moore, Ernest C., 155
Mooore, Gail E., 144
Moore, George, 55, 285
Moore, Jerome A., 383
Moore, Nathaniel F., 285
Moore, Peter L., 3
Moore, Vivian E., 244
Mor, Carlo G., 93
Moraes, Eduardo R. Affonso de, 11
Morawski, Kazimierz, 116
Moreira, Eidorfe, 12
Morgan Lucy G., 314
Morgan, Alexander, 80
Morgan, Charles C., 177
Morgan, Charles T., 213
Morgan, Chester M., 258
Morgan, D. W., 15
Morgan, James H., 337
Morgan, Xenimer H., 370
Morison, Samuel E., 235
Morow, Peter, 44
Morpurgo, J. E., 393
Morrell, William P., 109
Morris, Don H., 370
Morris, Jan, 74
Morris, Rudolph M., 238
Morrison, Betty L., 220
Morrison, James L., 301
Morrissey, Thomas J., 89
Morton, Albert R., 223
Morton, Arthur S., 24
Morton, William L., 22
Moss, Gerard P., 68
Mountford, James F., 65
Moursund, Walter H., 371
Muck, Steven J., 146
Muelder, Hermann, R., 187
Mueller, William A., 215, 219
Muhlbock, Annemarie, 8
Muir, Gladdys E., 155

Mulder, Arnold, 245
Mulholland, Mary A., 203
Mullaly, Columba, 169
Muller, Herman J., 247
Muller, Rainer A., 48
Muller, Wilhelm, 39
Mullinger, James B., 60
Munro, John M., 103
Munroe, John A., 166
Murdock, Patrick M., 405
Murphy, Ella L., 306
Murphy, Harold L., 91
Murphy, Lawrence R., 35
Murphy, Walter Y., 177
Murphy, William M., 193
Murray-Smith, Stephen, 5
Murray, Bruce K., 121
Murray, Lois S., 371
Myers, Clara A., 341
Myers, Linfield, 194
Myers, Minnie M. P., 106

Nagaraja, K., 85
Nall, Kline A., 384
Nance, W. B., 129
Navarrosa, Optacia I., 114
Navralil, Jan, 33
Naylor, Leonard, 52
Neel, George W., 338
Neelley, Arthur E., 156
Neil, Robert G., 362
Neill, Thomas, 405
Neilson, James W., 313
Nelson, Bernard H., 169
Nelson, C. Hal, 191
Nelson, David T., 206
Nelson, Edward T., 323
Nelson, J. Russell, 138
Nelson, Lawrence E., 143, 155
Nelson, Linnea A., 113
Nelson, Narka, 320
Nelson, William H., 218
Nemoy, Leon, 337
Newcomb, Theodore M., 390
Newcomer, Joe C., 229
Newhall, Nancy, 153
Newman, Jeremiah, 89
Newman, Vernie, 377

Newton, James H., 377
Neyland, Leedell W., 170
Nichols, James D., 140
Nichols, Tom W., 380
Nicholson, Patrick J., 385
Nickerson, Marjorie L., 292
Nickerson, Thomas, 181
Niederer, Frances J., 395
Nielsen, Ida L., 380
Nitzsche, George E., 348
Nobles, Lewis, 256
Noe, Minnie A., 376
Nollen, John S., 205
Norland, Jim, 160
Norris, Clarence W., 379
Norris, Edwin M., 276
Norris, Joan, 171
Norris, Mary H., 303
Norris, Walter B., 228
North, John, 67
Norwood, Frederick A., 184
Norwood, John N., 281
Notestein, Lucy L., 317
Noyes, Gertrude E., 162
Nunley, Joe E., 362
Nurmi, Matti, 36
Nutting, Mary O., 237
Nye, Irene, 162
Nye, Roger H., 302
Nyman, Emil, 389

Obiechina, Emmanuel, 111
O'Brien, Andrew L., 174
Ochsenford, Solomon E., 345
O'Connor, John J., 292
O'Connor, Paul L., 327
O'Connor, Thomas J., 133
Oddone, Juan A., 414
Odegaard, Charles E., 404
Odom, Jane H., 358
O'Donnell, Jim, 278
Oesterley, Georg H., 43
Ogunkoya, T. O., 110
Ohl, Ronald E., 94
Ohles, John F., 297
Ohrnberger, June E., 119
Olbubummo, Adegoke, 112
Oliphant, James O., 334, 403
Oliver, Henry L., 181

Oliver, Mary C., 361
Olmstead, Ralph E., 201
Olpin, Albert R., 389
Olson, Adolf, 249
Olson, James, 265
Olson, Ralph D., 180
Olson, Vera, 265
Olson, Virgil A., 249
O'Mara, Francis L., Jr., 233
O'Neal, William B., 400
O'Neill, Margaret A., 200
O'Rahilly, Ronan, 90
O'Reilly, Edmund P., 155
Orlosky, Elizabeth B., 201
Orr, Bill M., 368
Ortengren, Per I., 126
Ortin de Medina, Nevi, 416
Osborne, Byron L., 319
Osborne, James I., 203
Osborne, Newell Y., 321
Osborne, Ruby O., 393
Osgood, Charles G., 276
Ottersberg, Gerhard S., 207
Ouellette, Vernon A., 153
Overan, Oswald B., 250
Overman, James R., 315
Overturf, Donald S., 281
Oviatt, Edwin, 165
Owen, Derwyn R. G., 25
Owen, William B., 342
Owens, David B., 315
Owens, Hugh M., 263
Owens, James N., 328
Owler, Martha R. T., 282
Oxon, M. A., 74

Pace, Charles N., 251
Paddick, Kenneth L., 201
Padelletti, Guido, 95
Page, Patricia A., 279
Paim, Antonio, 12
Palamountain, Joseph C., 296
Palomeque Torres, Antonio, 122
Pannabecker, Samuel F., 199
Pappas, George S., 302
Paravicini, Frances de, 74
Pardi, Giuseppe, 93
Paris de Oddone, M. Blanca, 414, 415

Park, Bessie L., 297
Park, Julian, 297
Parker, Inez M., 307
Parker, James B., 74
Parker, James M., 19
Parker, Paul C., 97, 118
Parker, Richard, 60
Parkinson, Daniel B., 192
Parks, Joseph H., 133
Parr, James H., 195
Parrish, William E., 266
Parrish, William S., 354
Parrott, Alice A., 201
Parsons, Kermit C., 286
Parsons, Nellie F., 261
Parsons, Willis E., 206
Parton, Hugh N., 109
Parzen, Herbert, 91
Paschal, George W., 311
Patrick, Mary M., 130
Patten, John L., 204
Patterson, Alfred, 77
Patterson, Charles E., 218
Patterson, Franklin, 234
Patterson, George G., 15
Patterson, Samuel W., 289
Patterson, Zella J. B., 327
Patton, John S., 400
Patton, Julia, 294
Patton, William W., 169
Paulovits, Julius G., 85
Pazmino, Robert W., 291
Pe, Josefine L., 115
Peabody, Francis G., 395
Pearce, Brian L., 55
Pearce, J. Winston, 304
Pearson, Jay F. W., 173
Pearson, Karl, 68
Pearson, Willard, 350
Pechell, John, 74
Peck, Elisabeth S., 213
Peckham, Howard H., 247
Pedersen, Robert, 225
Pedio, Tommaso, 92
Pedraza Montes, Jose F., 105
Pedtke, Dorothy A. H., 187
Peebles, James C., 185
Pei-Ching ta hsueh, 28
Peile, John, 61

Peirce, Benjamin, 235
Pelham, Eric C., 53
Pelletier, Lawrence L., 334
Pellman, Hubert R., 394
Pelton, Carol, 409
Penrose, Stephen B., 405
Penrose, Stephen B. L., 103
Pentony, DeVere, 150
Pentzer, Orrin W., 197
Perala, Tauno, 36
Perez Bustamante, Ciriaco, 125
Perl, Larry, 207
Perry, Arthur L., 241
Perry, George S., 382
Perry, Roger N., 241
Perry, Warren, 5
Perry, Wilbur D., 133
Peter, Johanna, 216
Peter, Robert, 216
Peterman, Cy, 345
Peters, David E., 287
Peters, George L., 260
Peters, William E., 323
Petersen, Keith C., 182
Petersen, Peter L., 268
Peterson, Conrad, 251
Peterson, Daniel E., 404
Petit, Judith L., 379
Pettigrew, Larry D., 252
Pettiss, John O., 220
Pfeifer, Hans-Georg, 44
Pfeifer, Helen E., 256
Pfeiffer, Clyde E., 149
Pfister, J. Ralph, 197
Pfouts, Neil E., 294
Phillips, Charles F., 221
Piana, Celestino, 92, 95
Piatt, John J., 319
Pickard, Josiah L., 207
Pickerell, Albert G., 153
Pieper, Anton, 49
Pier, Arthur S., 235
Pierce, Morris A., 161
Pierson, George W., 165
Pieschel, Bridget S., 256
Pieschel, Stephen R., 256
Pihl, Cedric H., 144
Pilkington, Walter, 287
Pillay, Doppappa K., 87

Pine, John B., 285
Ping, Charles J., 323
Pink, Louis H., 295
Piper, L. P. S., 51
Pitsula, James M., 24
Pittard, Homer, 365
Pittman, Samuel P., 362
Plantz, Samuel, 410
Plath, Paul J., 187
Plochmann, George K., 192
Plum, Dorothy A., 303
Plummer, Charles, 74
Plummer, Kenneth M., 408
Pollard, Gerald W., 219
Pollard, James E., 322
Pollins, Harold, 54
Pollitt, Frank C., 381
Polnitz, Gotz, Freiherr von, 49
Pond, Jean S., 231
Poole, Murray E., 286
Pope, Richard M., 214, 260
Pope, Wilbur A., 379
Popejoy, Thomas L., 281
Porter, Earl W., 305
Porter, R. Russell, 161
Posey, Walter B., 137
Potts, John F., 357
Powell, Mae M., 383
Powell, William S., 310
Power, Alacoque, 376
Power, Michael, 27
Powers, William H., 359
Prahl, Marie R., 244
Prantl, Carl, 49
Prentiss, George L., 300
Prescott, Samuel C., 236
Prescott, Thomas B., 215, 374
Preston, Richard A., 18
Preville, Joseph R., 162
Price, Archibald G., 5
Price, Carl F., 163
Price, David T. W., 82
Price, Hugh W., 280
Prickard, Arthur O., 74
Priddis, Ronald, 388
Prieb, Wesley J., 211
Pritchard, Frank C., 78
Probst, Jacob, 8
Proctor, Samuel, 172

Pueyrredon, Alfredo, 2
Purdon, Rowena E., 230
Purington, George C., 223
Purnell, Edward K., 61
Purnell, Henrietta S., 227
Purvine, W. D., 331
Puryear, B. N., 395
Putnam, Daniel, 243
Pyeatt, Margaret F., 267
Pyre, James F. A., 412

Qualls, J. Winfield, 363
Quillen, Herbert N., 378
Quincy, Josiah, 236
Quinn, Bernetta, 250
Quinn, Kevin, 17
Quinn, Michael, 82
Quint, Wilder D., 271
Quiring, Virginia M., 210
Quirino, Carlos, 114

Rabikauskas, Paulus, 132
Rackham, H., 61
Raff, Diether, 46
Ragan, Allen E., 367
Rahim, M. A., 9
Raichle, Donald R., 274, 279
Rait, Robert S., 74
Raleigh, Thomas, 38
Ralson, Hugh E., 379
Rammelkamp, Charles H., 185
Ramsden, Diann, 170
Ramsey, Berkley C., 174
Ramsey, W. M., 340
Rand, Frank P., 240
Rannie, David W., 74
Rashdall, Hastings, 74
Ratjen, Henning, 42
Ratsh, Abraham I., 337
Ratzlaff, Donald, 211
Raven, John H., 275
Rawles, William A., 198
Rawls, Ruth E., 371
Rawlyk, George A., 17
Ray, Joseph M., 387
Ray, Mauldon A., 363
Raymond, Andrew V., 300
Raymond, John H., 303
Raymond, Kenneth, 390

Raymond, William O., 22
Read, Florence M., 179
Read, James C., 258
Read, James M., 326
Reagan, Alice E., 308
Real de la Riva, Cesar, 124
Reale, Miguel, 12
Redmond, Chris, 26
Reed, Germaine M., 219
Reed, Thomas A., 26
Rees, David D., 269
Rees, Frances, 180
Reeve, Frank D., 281
Reeve, Juliet, 209
Regier, Cornelius C., 408
Regnier, Paul R., 22
Reichel, William C., 344
Reid, Alfred S., 355
Reid, J. Juan, 158
Reid, John G., 17
Reilly, Cam, 4
Reitemeyer, Mary, 376
Reiwald, Eugenia D., 385
Rendall, John B., 343
Renfer, Rudolf A., 373
Renger, Christian, 45
Rennie, Thomas P., 227
Retout, Marie T., 130
Reusens, Edmond H. J., 10
Reuter, Frank T., 408
Reynolds, John H., 141
Reynolds, John R., 166
Reynolds, Thomas U., 254
Reznek, Samuel, 293
Rhodes, Jess D., 182
Rhodes, Lelia G., 255
Ribas, Frederic, 122
Ribas i Massana, Albert, 122
Ribhegge, Wilhelm, 49
Ricci, Corrado, 92
Riccoboni, Antonio, 94
Rice, George, 233
Rice, John J., 266
Rice, Kathleen G., 258
Rich, Edwin E., 61
Rich, Ellen M., 207
Richard, Louis, 21
Richards, Bernard A., 71
Richardson, Archie J., 404

Richardson, Frederick, 353
Richardson, Harold, 138
Richardson, Joe M., 135, 362
Richardson, Leon B., 271
Richardson, Rupert N., 374
Ricker, Paul A., 262
Ricketts, Palmer C., 293
Ricks, Joel E., 389
Riddell, Steven G., 143
Riddell, W. A., 24
Rider, Manning C., 171
Ridley, Jack B., 265
Rieke, Robert, 311
Riesman, David, 246, 248
Riley, Arthur J., 238
Riley, Gresham, 158
Riley, John E., 181
Riley, John W., 170
Rincon de M., Imelda, 416
Ringenberg, William C., 200
Riordan, Joseph W., 156
Ritchey, Charles J., 204
Ritchie, W., 121
Rittenhouse, Caroline S., 334
Ritter, Gerhard, 46
Roberts, Clarence N., 189
Roberts, Norene A. D., 253
Roberts, Oral, 329
Roberts, Sydney C., 61
Robertson, Charles G., 74
Robertson, Jenkins M., 401
Robey, Margaret D., 399
Robillard, Jean-Jacques, 15
Robinson, Ivor J., 199
Robinson, Ray E., 226
Robinson, William H., 395
Robson, John W., 285
Rodabaugh, James H., 320
Roddy, Edward G., 237
Rodgers, John A., 3
Rodriguez Cabal, Juan, 83
Rodriguez Cruz, Agueda M., 124
Rodriguez-San Pedro Bezares, Luis E., 124
Roesch, Raymond A., 325
Rogers, Dorothy, 298
Rogers, James L., 386
Rogers, James T., 322
Rogers, John A. R., 213

Rogers, Kenneth C., 278
Rogers, Oscar A., Jr., 257
Rogers, Vance D., 269
Rojas, Pedro, 106
Rolfsrud, Erling N., 250
Rolle, Andrew, 148
Rolph, Rebecca S., 61
Roman, Charles V., 364
Romick, Ann, 144
Roper, James E., 365
Rordam, Holger F., 33
Rosario, Antonio, 34
Rose, Harry E., 215
Rose, Martial, 53
Rosen, Seymour M., 131
Rosenberger, Jesse L., 284, 302
Ross, Alexander M., 20
Ross, Earle D., 205
Ross, Thomas R., 407
Ross, William R., 159
Rossler, Emil F., 43
Roth, Mary A., 206
Roth, Stephen, 391
Roueche, John E., 163. 307
Roulet, Paul, 260
Roundy, Jerry C., 182
Rountree, George W., 178
Roush, Chester A., 314
Rover, Thomas, 168
Rowan, Jonnie, 387
Rowe, Henry K., 230, 270
Rowland, Eugenia, 144
Rowse, Alfred L., 74
Ruane, Joseph W., 227
Rubenstein, Frank J., 337
Rudolph, Frederick, 241
Rudy, Willis, 283
Ruggles, Clyde O., 253
Rulon, Philip R., 329
Rushford, Jerry, 149
Rushing, Jane G., 384
Russ, Anne J., 303, 304
Russell, James E., 299
Russell, James S., 398
Russell, Miriam L., 307
Russell, Phillips, 310
Russell, Ruth W., 238
Rutkoff, Peter M., 290
Rutland, Harold, 55

Rutyna, Richard A., 397
Ryan, Edmund G., 229
Ryan, John J., 226
Ryan, Michael G., 182
Rydjord, John, 212
Ryle, Walter H., 262

Saalfeld, Friedrich, 43
Saarela, Ahti, 36
Sabri, Marie A., 104
Sachar, Abram L., 232
Sackett, Everett B., 272
Sadler, McGruder E., 383
Saelinger, M. Irmina, 216
Saenz, Mercedes, 119
Saenz de Santa Maria, Carmelo, 123
Sagendorph, Kent, 247
Sakuko Yosio, Eto T., 99
Sala Balust, Luis, 124
Salacuse, Donna B., 379
Salinas, Jose M., 11
Salisbury, Albert, 413
Sallander, Hans, 127
Sammartino, Peter, 274
Sampolo, Luigi, 94
Sanchez y Garcia, Juan, 115
Sanchez Hernandez, Antonio, 34
Sanchez Jara, Diego, 123
Sandborn, William C., 364
Sanders, Jane, 404
Sanders, Robert S., 214
Sands, Gene C., 159
Sanford, Edmund C., 232
Sanford, Edward T., 368
Sanford, J. Kenneth, 311
Santavy, Frantisek, 33
Sanz Diaz, Federico, 126
Saraswati, S. Pandit, 86
Sarkar, Jagadish N., 87
Sasaki, Soichi, 100
Satneck, Walter J., 166
Saunderson, Hugh H., 22
Savage, William S., 261
Saville, M. V., 68
Savory, Jerold J., 355
Sawyer, Effie W., 134
Sayah, Edward N., 103
Scanlan, Arthur J., 294

Scanlon, James E., 398
Scarborough, Lee R., 380
Schafer, Daniel L., 173
Schafer, Karl T., 45
Schall, Keith L., 395
Scharff, Alexander, 42
Schauenstein, Adolf, 8
Scheetz, Mary J., 200
Schenck, Janet W., 290
Schianchi, Francesco, 91
Schier, H. Tracy, 200
Schindlbeck, David J., 194
Schisler, Charles H., 279
Schlereth, Thomas J., 202
Schlifke, William H., 289
Schlosser, Ralph W., 338
Schmidt, Charles F., 372
Schmidt, George P., 276. 278
Schmidt, John C., 226
Schmidt, William J., 211
Schmitthenner, John W., 288
Schmuhl, Robert, 202
Schnackenberg, Walter C., 403
Schneider, Franz, 46
Schneider, Lydia E., 144
Schnitzler, Elisabeth, 41
Schoen-Rene, Otto E., 288
Schoenberg, Wilfred P., 403
Schotel, Gilles D. J., 107
Schrader, Wilhelm, 40
Schrey, Helmut, 47
Schroeder, Morton A., 250
Schubert, Ernst, 50
Schulze, Johann D., 40
Schumann, Marguerite E., 410
Schuster, Mary F., 208
Schwager, Sally, 238
Schwarze, William N., 344
Schwenkmeyer, Barry, 53
Scipio, L. Albert, 136
Scofield, Carlton F., 265
Scott, Ernest, 6
Scott, James, 26
Scott, Robert F., 61
Scott, Roderick, 28
Scott, Thomas A., 139
Scott, William B., 290
Scott, Winfield W., 160
Scott-Giles, Charles W., 61

Scovel, Raleigh D., 275
Seale, Lea L., 221
Seaman, Robert D. H., 55
Searle, William G., 61
Sears, L. M., 199
Seay, Elizabeth I., 308
Seelye, Laurenus C., 239
Seib, Kenneth A., 144
Selden, William K., 276
Sell, Edward S., 179
Selle, Erwin S., 253
Selle, Gotz von, 43
Sellers, Charles, 337
Sellers, James B., 137
Selley, George C., 412
Seltman, Charles T., 57
Semple, Anne R., 329
Serinko, Regis J., 335
Serrao, Joaquim V., 117
Servin, Manual P., 156
Sessions, Charles B., 26
Sethi, R. R., 86
Sewell, George A., 177
Sewrey, Charles L., 360
Sexton, John E., 238
Sexton, Kathryn A., 328
Shackelford, Edward M., 136
Shackles, Chrystine I., 375
Shackson, Marian, 244
Shafe, Michael, 79
Shaffer, Lowell D., 349
Shannon, Edgar F., 400
Sharkey, Robert P., 226
Sharpless, Isaac, 340
Shatto, Gloria M., 175
Shaw, Cornelia R., 305
Shaw, Joseph M., 252
Shaw, Wilfred B., 248
Shea, Charlotte K., 237
Shea, John D. G., 168
Shelburne, James C., 132
Sheldon, Henry D., 333
Shepard, William A., 391
Shepardson, Francis W., 318
Shepley, Ethan A. H., 265
Sheppard, Lydia D., 178
Shepperd, Gilbert A., 55
Sheraton, James P., 26
Sherborne, H. W., 56

Sherman, John, 61, 274
Sherratt, Gerald R., 389
Sherwood, Sidney, 296
Shevyrev, Stepan P., 132
Shilov, Lev A., 131
Shimmin, Arnold N., 65
Shirley, Betty L., 199
Shirley, Lawrence, 143
Shively, Roma L., 186
Showers, Renald, 345
Shriver, Philip R., 319
Shrout, Mildred R., 260
Shuckburgh, Evelyn S., 61
Shumacher, Billy G., 372
Shumate, Mildred, 363
Shumway, Arthur L., 322
Shurbutt, Thomas R., 176
Sibley, Carol, 154
Sibley, Marilyn M., 375
Sibley, Robert, 153, 154
Sicca, Cinzia M., 61
Sider, E. Morris, 343
Sieber, Eberhard, 42
Sieber, Marc, 128
Siegenbeek, Matthijs, 107
Sikes, William M., 135
Sills, Kenneth C. M., 222
Silva Andraca, Hector, 105
Silva Herzog, Jesus, 106
Silver, Harold, 68
Simmonds, A., 389
Simmons, George C., 9
Simmons, John S. G., 70
Simmons, Laura, 372
Simmons, Lucy, 262
Simms, T. H., 62
Simon, F. A., 19
Simon, Martin P., 267
Simpson, Ervin P., 406
Sims, Frank K., 356
Sims, Van E., 378
Sinclair, Keith, 108
Singer, Walter E., 9
Sisk, Lorie C., 11
Sitterly, Charles F., 273
Sizemore, Virginia L., 407
Skardon, Alvin W., 327
Skelton, Philip D., 141
Skillman, David B., 342

Skillrud, Harold C., 188
Skinner, Albert T., 282
Skousen, W. Cleon, 388
Slater, John R., 302
Slattery, T. P., 22
Sledd, Andrew, 172
Sliney, Bruce, 321
Sloman, Albert E., 65
Slonaker, Arthur G., 407
Small, Michael W., 14
Smart, James G., 272
Smart, Richard, 51
Smekal, Ferdinand G., 8
Smith, Alic H., 74
Smith, Andrew C., 135
Smith, Andrew T., 350
Smith, Austin W., 366
Smith, Barbara, 74
Smith, Baxter P., 271
Smith, Boyce O., 174
Smith, C. Henry, 315
Smith, Charles B., 136
Smith, Cluster Q., 328
Smith, Cyril E., 39
Smith, David C., 223
Smith, Delazon, 322
Smith, Earle R., 133
Smith, Eric H. F., 74
Smith, Ernest A., 334
Smith, Francis H., 401
Smith, George C. M., 77
Smith, Goldwin, 74
Smith, Henry J., 157
Smith, Jesse G., 372
Smith, Jo Ann, 312
Smith, John E., 332
Smith, Joseph, 350
Smith, Keith L., 388
Smith, Lewis I., 373
Smith, Morris E., 143
Smith, Peter P., 391
Smith, Richard N., 236
Smith, Robert, 150
Smith, Russell T., 393
Smith, Thaddeus T., 212
Smith, Waldo E. L., 13
Smith, Warren H., 288
Smith, William, 349
Smith, Willis L., 379

Smyth, Egbert C., 222
Smyth, John G., 55
Smythe, George F., 319
Sneen, Donald J., 359
Snell, John F., 16
Snyder, Howard A., 247
Snyder, Robert, 214
Solberg, Winton U., 193
Soley, James R., 228
Soltis-Cohen, Solomon, 289
Somerkoski, Pirjo, 36
Sondheimer, Janet, 68
Sonner, Ray V., 396
Sorrels, Carolyn S., 330
Sorrels, William, 364
Souders, Floyd, 209
Souders, Norma, 209
Soulier, Catherine F., 284
Southgate, Donald, 79
Southgate, Wyndham M., 318
Spagnesi, Enrico, 93
Spalding, Phinizy, 177
Spanton, Albert I., 324
Sparks, Robbie S., 133
Speare, Edward R., 231
Spears, George J., 294
Specht, Ellen L., 413
Spence, G. H., 313
Spielman, William C., 409
Spinks, J. W. T., 24
Spooner, Ruth H., 236
Sporl, Johannes, 48
Spring, Leverett W., 241
Springer, Clair G., 332
Stadtman, Verne A., 154
Staehelin, Andreas, 128
Stameshkin, David M., 390
Stanbrough, Amos C., 331
Staniford, Edward F., 145
Stansell, Harold L., 159
Starcher, George W., 313
Starrett, Agnes L., 349
Start, Alaric B., 240
Stathis, John C., 365
Stayer, Samuel N., 133
Stead, Peter, 82
Stee, Agnes M., 313
Steegman, John, 62
Stegenga, Preston J., 244

Steinberg, Allan G., 286
Stemmons, Walter, 163
Stephen, Barbara N., 62
Stephen, Leslie, 62
Stephens, Everett, 83
Stephens, Frank F., 265
Stephens, John V., 362
Stephens, Margaret, 221
Stephens, Mary, 83
Sterling, Wilson, 211
Stevens, Horace W. P., 62
Stevens, Robert, 340
Stevens, William B., 342
Stevens, William H., 403
Stevenson, Dwight, 214
Stevenson, Dwight E., 217
Stevenson, George J., 394
Stevenson, William H., 75
Stewart, Charles J., 359
Stewart, Charles M., 19
Stewart, Edgar I., 360
Stewart, Jo M., 179
Stewart, Noel, 7
Stewart, Richard A., 257
Stine, Leo C., 249
Stock, Amy G., 9
Stockton, Charles H., 168
Stockton, Frank T., 360
Stockwell, Rachel N., 317
Stohlman, Martha L., 399
Stokes, Anson P., 137
Stokes, Durwood T., 306
Stokes, Henry P., 62
Stone, Eugenia W., 179
Stone, Irving, 154
Storr, Richard J., 193
Story, Dale, 327
Story, William E., 232
Stoutenburg, Herbert N., Jr., 246
Stow, Sarah D., 237
Strand, Kenneth, 18
Strange, John G., 410
Stranlund, Kathy, 149
Stride, William K., 75
Strietelmeier, John H., 202
Strode, William, 369
Strother, Martha D., 377
Stryker, Garrett V., 229

Stryker, Mabel K., 211
Strzemienski, Marian, 117
Stubbs, Charles W., 62
Stubbs, John W., 91
Sturtevant, Charles C., 168
Sturzebecker, Russell L., 351
Stybe, Sven E., 33
Suelflow, Roy A., 259
Suellentrop, Joyce, 209
Sulivask, Karl, 131
Sullivan, Jeremiah S., 290
Sullivan, Richard, 202
Summers, Festus P., 408
Summerville, James, 364
Sumner, Charles B., 150
Sumrall, Robbie N., 254
Super, Charles W., 323, 337
Suppiger, Joseph E., 363
Sutherland, Lucy S., 75
Sutliff, Albert, 154
Swain, James E., 345
Swanson, James A., 188
Sweeney, James R., 397
Sweet, William W., 196
Sweetman, Edward, 4
Sweetman, Jack, 228
Swets, Marinus M., 244
Synan, Vinson, 175
Szmczak, Donald R., 191

Taaffe, Thomas G., 287
Taft, Michael, 24
Taft, Robert, 212
Tait, James, 78
Talbert, Charles G., 217
Talbert, Horace, 326
Talbot, Francis X., 346
Talbot, Jean, 253
Taliaferro, Cecil R., 402
Talley, Kate, 372
Talman, James J., 26
Talman, Ruth D., 27
Tamblyn, William F., 27
Tamuno, Tekena N., 111
Tankersley, Allen P., 178
Tappert, Theodore G., 343
Tarbell, Arthur W., 335
Taylor, A. J., 65
Taylor, George R. S., 75

Taylor, Harry T., 273
Taylor, Herbert F., 242
Taylor, James M., 303
Taylor, Katherine A., 153
Taylor, Prince A., Jr., 175
Taylor, R. Hargus, 305
Taylor, Robert, 412
Taylor, Walter C., 356
Taylor, William B. S., 91
Teague, Sydney, J., 68
Tebeau, Charlton W., 173
Tegner, Elof K., 126
Temple, Ella D., 113
Temple, Hilary, 52
Templin, Lucinda D., 261
Tent, James F., 43
Terry, Paul W., 135
Terry, William E., 383
Teufel, Waldemar, 42
Thackrah, John R., 75
Tharpe, Gertrude A., 84
Theiss, Lewis E., 334
Thierry, Adelaide H., 238
Thomas, Alfred, Jr., 138
Thomas, Ben B., 82
Thomas, Charles E., 369
Thomas, Hugh, 55
Thomas, John P., 354
Thomas, Lewis H., 24
Thomas, Mary M. H., 380
Thomas, Thaddeus P., 225
Thomis, Malcolm I., 7
Thommen, Rudolf, 128
Thompson, Alexander H., 62, 63
Thompson, Bertha B., 320
Thompson, Henry L., 75
Thompson, Joseph, 78
Thompson, Joyce, 384
Thompson, Mary M., 226
Thompson, Tommy R., 270
Thompson, Walter P., 24
Thomson, Herbert C., 68
Thomson, James S., 24
Thorbecke, August, 46
Thornburg, Opal, 196
Thornton, John V., 291
Thornton, Richard S., 405
Thostenson, Josephine E., 203
Thourot, Charles, 38

Thrasher, Max B., 137
Thrift, Charles T., 170
Thullberg, Per, 127
Thurman, Frances A., 398
Thurston, Matilda S., 29
Thwaites, Reuben G., 412
Thwing, Charles F., 316
Tice, Margaret B., 353
Tiffen, Gerald C., 149
Tigert, John J., 172
Tikekara, Aruna, 87
Tilghman, Tench F., 227
Tilton, Leon D., 193
Timmerman, John J., 243
Timmins, Geoffrey, 54
Tingley, Donald F., 184
Tinoco, Luis D., 31
Tinsley, Sammy J., 257
Tipton, Elizabeth H., 224
Tisdale, Thomas T., 255
Todorich, Charles, 228
Tola, Pasquale, 96
Toles, Caesar F., 372
Tolson, Billy J., 132
Tomaszewski, Wiktor, 80
Tomlinson, Marie G., 382
Toole, Robert C., 407
Topping, James, 51
Topping, Norman H., 156
Topping, Robert W., 199
Torraca, Francesco, 94
Torre y del Cerro, Antonio de la, 122
Tout, Thomas F., 78
Trares, Thomas F., 192
Treanor, John M., 358
Treudley, Mary B., 319
Trevelyan, George M., 63
Trevor-Roper, Hugh R., 75
Trotter, B., 18
Troup, Cornelius V., 177
Troutman, R. Dwight, 346
Trueman, Albert W., 23
Tucker, Frank C., 259
Tucker, Samuel J., 170
Tuke, Margaret J., 68
Tumbagahan, Tiburcio J., 114
Tunnermann, Bernheim C., 2

Tunnermann Bernheim, Carlos, 123
Turk, Milton H., 288
Turnbach, Catherine R., 343
Turner, Arthur L., 80
Turner, Fred H., 193
Turner, Wallace B., 159
Turner, William L., 349
Tuttle, Joseph F., 203
Tuttlc, Robert E., 244
Twigg, John, 63
Tyler, Frances L., 254
Tyler, Lyon, G., 393, 394
Tyler, William S., 230
Tymeson, Mildred M., 242

Ukariwe, Ukariwe K., 111
Umble, John S., 196
Umeh, John A., 111
Underwood, James L., 363
Underwood, Paul, 323
Unruh, Alice E., 195
Upham, Alfred H., 320
Urata, James H., 145
Urban, William L., 188
Uribe, Angel, 122
Urwick, William, 91
Utt, Richard H., 147
Utt, Walter C., 149
Uyttebrouck, Andre, 10

Vaccari, Pietro, 95
Vachon, Louis A., 21
Vaidyanathan, P. S., 87
Vaille, Frederick O., 236
Valades, Diego, 107
Valcarcel, Carlos D., 113
Valcarcel Esparza, Carlos D., 113
Valentine, Alan C., 302
Vallance, Aymer, 75
Vallance, Harvard F., 314
Vallandingham, Edward N., 166
Van Antwerp, Chiles, 243
Van Derhoff, Jack W., 210
Van Loan, Lillian S., 332
Vance, Russell E., 201, 338
Vande Vere, Emmett K., 242
Varjo, Uuno, 36

Varrentrapp, Conrad, 45
Vaughn, Susan K., 137
Veal, Donald L., 414
Vega Flores, Hector, 105
Venn, John, 63
Verde, Armando F., 93
Vezina, Birgit, 46
Vianelli, Athos, 92
Vickers, James, 310
Vickery, Dorothy S., 396, 399
Vien Dai-hoc, Can Tho, 416
Viles, Jonas, 265
Villa, Antonio M., 125
Vincent, Charles, 220
Vincent, Eric W., 56
Violette, Eugene M., 262
Vischer, Wilhelm, 128
Voigt, Johannes H., 50
Volker, Joseph F., 137
Von Briesen, Martha, 399
Vosper, James M., 268
Vroom, Fenwick W., 20

Wachowicz, Ruy C., 12
Wack, John T., 202
Waddell, Alfred M., 310
Wade, Homer D., 384
Wadell, Joseph A., 396
Wadell, Keith A., 192
Wagner, Charles A., 236
Wagner, Frederick B., Jr., 348
Wagner, Hans, 8
Wagner, Paul A., 172
Wagstaff, Henry M., 310
Wainwright, Frank N., 147
Waite, Frederick C., 231, 316
Wake, Orville W., 396
Walker, Charles A., 334
Walker, Eric A., 121
Walker, Joseph B., 272
Walker, Thomas A., 63
Walker, Thomas T., 386
Walker, Williston, 165
Walkup J. Lawrence, 139
Wallace, David D., 358
Wallace, Francis, 202
Wallace, George R., 277
Wallace, Lydia E., 29
Wallace, Paul A. W., 342

Wallace, Percy E., 371
Wallace, Robert B., 176
Wallace, William S., 26
Walle, Oscar T., 196
Waller, Fred L., 360
Waller, Ross D., 53
Walsh, Benjamin D., 63
Walsh, Walter, 397
Walters, John D., 210
Walters, Raymond, 325
Walton, Richard J., 347
Walton, William C., 188
Warch, Richard, 165
Ward, Bernard N., 75
Ward, Estelle F., 190
Ward, Richard H., 367
Wardale, John R., 63. 64
Warden, James E., 392
Ware, Charles C., 304
Warmington, Eric H., 68
Warner, Mike, 149
Warner, Stephen A., 75
Warnock, Arthur R., 345
Warren, Mame, 228
Warren, Marion E., 228
Warren, Thomas H., 75
Warren, William F., 231
Washington, Walter, 258
Waters, Charles M., 361
Watson, Bert A., 372
Watson, Eddie D., 414
Watson, Elmo S., 186
Watson, Robert J., 347
Watson, Sheppard A., 208
Watters, Mary, 188, 396
Wayland, John W., 392
Weaver, Glenn, 163
Weaver, Oliver C., Jr., 133
Webb, D. A., 90
Webb, Edward, 343
Webster, Lewis G., 389
Webster, Martha F., 187
Wedel, Peter J., 208
Weeks, Stephen B., 310
Wegel, Franz X., 50
Wehrle, William O., 325
Wehtje, Myron F., 230
Weidman, John M., 330
Weigle, Richard D., 227

Weil, Oscar A., Jr., 188
Weinlick, John R., 344
Weisert, Hermann, 46
Welch, Joe B., 376
Wellington, Leah L. N., 222
Wells, D. A., 241
Wells, Herman B., 198
Wells, Joseph, 75, 76
Welsh, David, 121
Wenstell, Egil H., 2
Wentworth, Richard L., 233
Wentz, Abdel R., 339
Werner, Norbert, 44
Wert, Lynette L., 327
Wertenbaker, Thomas J., 277
West, Francis M., 361
West, Thomas W., 355
Westmoreland, Olene, 373
Westover, Janet Y., 139
Wetterling, Horst, 49
Weyer, Frank E., 268
Whalen, Mary G., 199
Wheelock, John, 271
Whetro, R. Kathleen, 325
White, Glen, 195
White, Henry J., 76
White, Homer, 391
White, James F., 380
White, James H., 257
White, Kenneth B., 279
White, Marian C., 282
White, Michael A., 372
White, Raymond J., 150
Whitford, Albert, 410
Whiting, Charles E., 64
Whitney, Henry M., 409
Whitney, Herbert C., 225
Whittemore, Edwin C., 222
Whitworth, Thomas A., 65
Wicha, Barbara, 8
Wichers, Wynand, 244
Wiebe, Jeffrey J., 18
Wiederaenders, Arthur G., 383
Wiggins, David, 204
Wild, Payson, S., 190
Wilde, Arthur H., 190
Wildman, Edward L., 373
Wilkins, James R., 398
Wilkins, Robert P., 313

Wilkinson, Carlton B., 76
Wilkinson, Ernest L., 388
Wilkinson, L. P., 64
Willard, George-Anne, 307
Willbern, Glen D., 381
Willey, Samuel H., 154
Williams, Ann L., 401
Williams, Charles K., 50
Williams, Charles S., 343
Williams, Earl F., 372
Williams, Earl R., 141
Williams, Edward I. F., 318
Williams, Howard D., 284
Williams, J. Gwynn, 82
Williams, John, 327
Williams, John A., 144
Williams, Lawrence H., 215
Williams, Mabel C., 375
Williams, Mary M., 403
Williams, Michael C., 122
Williams, Mima A., 375
Williams, Penry, 70
Williams, Robert, 143
Williams, Wolcott B., 246
Williamson, Glen, 333
Williamson, Harold F., 190
Williard, George W., 318
Williard, Julius T., 210
Williard, Warren W., 194
Willis, Albert H., 6
Willis, H. Warren, 167
Willis, Robert, 64
Wills, George S., 229
Wills, Martee, 171
Wilson, Edward N., 226
Wilson, Goodridge, 396
Wilson, Henry A., 76
Wilson, Joseph, 64
Wilson, Kenneth L., 288
Wilson, Louis R., 310, 311
Wilson, Samuel T., 364
Wilson, Stanley G., 68
Wilson, Wilbert R., 228
Winegrad, Dilys P., 348
Wingard, Kathleen M., 355
Winkelmann, John P., 263
Winn, Evelyn B., 355
Winningham, Geoff, 378
Winship, Frank L., 269

Winslow, Donald J., 236
Winstanley, Denys A., 64
Winters, Richard W., 406
Wise, Henry A., 401
Wise, Jennings C., 401
Wisor, Harold C., 343
Witt, Michael J., 259
Wixom, Nancy C., 317
Wolf, G., 9
Wolfe, Suzanne R., 137
Wolgast, Eike, 45, 46
Wood, Alfred C., 68
Wood, Anthony A., 77
Wood, Edwin K., 330
Wood, George B., 349
Wood, Nathan R., 234
Wood, Susan H., 186
Woodburn, James A., 198
Woodburn, S., 5
Woodcock, George, 19
Woodnick, Michael L., 233
Woods, James R., 292
Woods, Leonard, 230
Woods, Ralph H., 215
Woodward, Carl R., 353
Woodward, Mary T., 383
Woodworth, Frank G., 257
Woolery, William K., 406
Woolfolk, George R., 378
Woolsey, Theodore D., 165
Wooster, Lyman D., 209
Wooten, Rebecca G., 365
Wright, Albert H., 286
Wright, David S., 207
Wright, John D., 216
Wright, Leslie, S., 134

Wright, Melton, 353
Wright, Thomas, 59
Wylie, Francis E., 237
Wylie, Theophilus A., 198
Wyllie, Robert H., 163
Wyman, Walker D., 413
Wynkoop, Mildred B., 366
Wyss, Georg V., 129

Yager, Arthur, 214
Yap, William K., 181
Yardley, Michael, 55
Yates, Bowling C., 178
Yates, Louis A. R., 183
Yeager, Iver F., 185
Yorke, Paul, 54
Yost, Calvin E., 349
Youel, Donald B., 251
Young, Charles V. P., 286
Young, Clarence H., 244
Young, Frank G., 64
Young, M. Norvel, 149
Young, Warren C., 190
Young, William T., 216

Zai, Baqui Y., 1
Zareba, Alfred, 116
Zareba, Maria Z., 116
Zaydon, Jemille A., 341
Zdekauer, Lodovico, 96
Zehmer, George B., 392
Zenz, Emil, 50
Zerby, Lewis, 111
Zerby, Margaret, 111
Ziegler, Gilette G., 38
Zumberge, James H., 156, 24

Subject Index

Abilene Christian University, 370
Academy of the New Church, 333
Acadia University, 13
Adam Mickiewicz University, 115
Addis Ababa University, 35
Adelphi University, 281
Agnes Scott College, 173-174
Adrian College, 242
Agnes Erskine College, 11
Ahmadu Bello University, 110
Air University, 132
Airlangga University, 88
Al. I. Cuza University, 119
Alabama State University, 132
Alaska Pacific University, 138
Albany Medical College, 281
Albany State College, 174
Albert University, 13
Albion College, 242
Albright College, 334
Alcorn State University, 254
Alderson-Broaddus College, 406

Alexander City State Junior College, 132
Alfred Holbrook College, 314
Alfred University, 281
Alice Lloyd College, 212
Aligarh Muslim University, 85
Allegheny College, 334
Alma College, 242
Alma White College, 273
Amarillo College, 370
American International College, 229
American University, 166
American University in Cairo, 35
American University of Beirut, 103
Amherst College, 230
Anambra State University of Technology, 110
Anatolia College, 83
Anderson College, 353
Anderson University, 194

Andover Newton Theological School, 230
Andrew College, 174
Andrews University, 242
Angelo State University, 371
Annamalai University, 85
Anne Arundel Community College, 224
Antioch College, 314
Appalachian Bible College, 406
Arizona State University, 138
Arizona Western College, 138
Arkansas State University, 140
Asbury College, 212
Ascension Seminary, 194
Ashland College, 314
Assumption College, 3
Athabasca University, 13-14
Athenaeum of Ohio, 315
Athens College, 83
Atlanta Junior College, 174
Atlanta University, 174
Atlantic Christian College, 304
Atlantic Union College, 230
Auburn Community College, 282
Auburn University, 132
Augsburg College, 249
Augusta College, 174
Augustana College, IL, 182
Augustana College, SD, 358-359
Austin College, 371
Austin Peay State University, 360
Austin Presbyterian Theological Seminary, 371
Australian National University, 3
Autonomous University of Central America, 31
Autonomous University of Ciudad Juarez, 104
Autonomous University of Hidalgo, 104
Autonomous University of Nuevo Leon, 105
Autonomous University of Puebla, 105
Autonomous University of Luis Potosi, 105

Autonomous University of Sinaloa, 105
Autonomous University of the State of Mexico, 105
Autonomous University of the State of Morelos, 105
Averett College, 392
Azusa Pacific University, 142

Bacone College, 327
Baker University, 208
Ball State University, 195
Bangkok College, 129
Bangor Theological Seminary, 221
Bard College, 282
Barnard College, 282
Bates College, 221
Battersea College of Technology, 51
Baylor College of Medicine, 371
Baylor University, 371-372
Bedford College of Higher Education, 51
Beijing University, 28
Beirut College for Women, 104
Belhaven College, 254
Belleville Area College, 183
Bellevue College, 267
Belmont Abbey College, 304
Belmont College, 361
Beloit College, 409
Bemidji State University, 249
Bendigo College of Advanced Education, 3
Benedict College, 353
Benedictine College, 208
Bennington College, 390
Berea College, 212-213
Bernard M. Baruch College of the City University of New York, 282
Berry College, 175
Bethany College, KS, 208
Bethany College, WV, 406
Bethel College, IN, 195
Bethel College, KS, 208
Bethel College, KY, 213
Bethel College, TN, 361

SUBJECT INDEX / 457

Bethel Theological Seminary, 249
Bhopal University, 86
Biola University, 143
Birmingham-Southern College, 133
Bishop College, 372
Bishop's University, 13
Black Hills State College, 359
Black Mountain College, 304
Blackburn College, 183
Blinn College, 372
Bloomfield College, 273
Bloomsburg University of Pennsylvania, 334
Blue Mountain College, 254
Bluefield State College, 406
Bluffton College, 315
Bob Jones University, 353
Boise State University, 181
Bolivar Pontifical University, 30
Borough Road College, 51
Boston College, 231
Boston University, 231
Bowdoin College, 222
Bowdon College, 175
Bowie State College, 224
Bowling Green State University, 315
Bradford College, 231
Bradley University, 183
Brandeis University, 231
Bridgewater College, 392
Bridgewater State College, 232
Brigham Young University, 388
Brigham Young University-Hawaii Campus, 180
Brighton College of Technology, 51
Brooklyn College of the City University of New York, 283
Brown University, 351-352
Brunel University, 51
Bryan College, 361
Bryn Mawr College, 334
Bucknell University, 334
Buena Vista College, 203
Burleson College, 372

Burritt College, 361
Butler University, 195

California Baptist College, 143
California College of Arts and Crafts, 143
California Institute of Technology, 143
California Polytechnic State University, San Luis Obispo, 143
California State University, Chico, 144
California State University, Fresno, 144
California State University, Hayward, 144
California State University, Northridge, 144
California State University, Sacramento, 145
California State University, San Bernardino, 145
California University of Pennsylvania, 335
Calvin College, 242-243
Calvin Theological Seminary, 243
Cambrone School of Mines, 51
Campbell University, 304
Canisius College, 283
Canterbury College, 195
Capital University, 315
Cardinal Stritch College, 409
Carl Sandburg College, 183
Carleton College, 249
Carnegie-Mellon University, 335
Carr-Burdette College, 372
Carroll College, 409
Carson-Newman College, 361
Carthage College, 409
Case Western Reserve University, 315-316
Casper College, 413
Catawba College, 305
Catholic Institute of Paris, 37
Catholic University of America, 166-167

458 / SUBJECT INDEX

Catholic University of Louvain, 10
Catholic University of the Sacred Heart, 91
Cedar Crest College, 335
Cedarville College, 316
Centenary College, 273
Centenary College of Louisiana, 218
Centennial College of Applied Arts and Technology, 15
Central Connecticut State University, 161
Central Methodist College, 259
Central Missouri State University, 259
Central Philippine University, 113
Central State University, 316-317
Central University, 203
Central University of Venezuela, 415
Central Washington University, 402
Centre College of Kentucky, 213
Chabot College, 145
Chapman College, 145
Charles County Community College, 224
Charlotte Mason College, 52
Chatham College, 335
Chester College, 52
Chestnut Hill College, 335
Cheyney University of Pennsylvania, 336
Chicago College of Osteopathic Medicine, 183
Chicago State University, 183
Chicago Theological Seminary, 183
Chowan College, 305
Christ College, 145
Christian Albrecht University of Kiel, 41-42
Christian Brothers College, Aust, 3
Christian Brothers College, MO, 259

Christian Brothers College, TN, 361
Chuo University, 97
The Citadel, The Military College of South Carolina, 354
City College of the City University of New York, 283
City University of New York, 283
Claremont Colleges, 146
Clarendon College, Aust, 3
Clarendon College, TX, 372
Clarion University of Pennsylvania, 336
Clark College, 175
Clark University, 232
Clarke College, 203
Clarke Memorial College, 254
Clemson University, 354
Cleveland Institute of Art, 317
Cleveland State University, 317
Clifton College, 52
Clinch Valley College, 392
Coastline Community College, 146
Codrington College, 9
Coe College, 204
Coker College, 354
Colby College, 222
Colby-Sawyer College, 270
Coleg Harlech, 82
Colegio Cesar Chavez, 330
Colgate University, 284
College Misericordia, 336
College of Charleston, 354
College of Great Falls, 266
College of Idaho, 181
College of Notre Dame, 146
College of Notre Dame of Maryland, 224
College of Philadelphia, 336
College of Saint Elizabeth, 273
College of Saint Rose, 284
College of Saint Teresa, 250
College of Santa Fe, 280
College of St. Patrick, 89
College of St. Scholastica, 250
College of St. Thomas, 250
College of the Desert, 146

College of the Holy Cross, 232
College of William and Mary, 392-393
College of Wooster, 317
College Sainte-Marie-de-Monnoir, 15
Colorado College, 158
Colorado School of Mines, 158
Colorado State University, 158
Colorado Women's College, 159
Columbia Bible College and Seminary, 354
Columbia College, MO, 259
Columbia College, SC, 354-355
Columbia Theological Seminary, 175
Columbia University, 284-285
Columbus College of Art and Design, 317
Comenius University, 32
Community College of Baltimore, 225
Community College of the Air Force, 133
Concord College, 407
Concordia College, IL, 184
Concordia College, MN, 250
Concordia College, NY, 286
Concordia Seminary, 259
Concordia Teachers College, 267
Concordia Theological Seminary, IL, 184
Concordia Theological Seminary, IN, 195
Concordia University, 15
Concrete College, 373
Connecticut College, 162
Converse College, 355
Copiah-Lincoln Junior College, 254
Corcoran School of Art, 167
Cornell University, 286
Coventry Technical College, 52
Cranbrook Academy of Art, 243
Creighton University, 267, 268
Crozer Theological Seminary, 336
Culham College, 52
Culver-Stockton College, 260

Cumberland College, 213
Cumberland College of Health Sciences, 3
Cumberland University, 362

Daemen College, 286
Dakota State College, 359
Dakota Wesleyan University, 359
Dalhousie University, 15
Dallas College, OR, 331
Dallas College, TX, 373
Dallas Community College, 373
Dallas Theological Seminary, 373
Dana College, 268
Dartmouth College, 270-271
David Lipscomb College, 362
Davidson College, 305
Davis and Elkins College, 407
De La Salle University, 114
Delaware State College, 166
Delaware Valley College of Science and Agriculture, 336
Delta State University, 255
Denison University, 317-318
DePauw University, 196
Des Moines University, 204
Dickinson College, 336
Dickinson State College, 312
Didsburg College of Education, 52
Dillard University, 218
Diocesan College, 120
Diponegora University, 88
Dixie College, 388
Doane College, 268
Doshisha University, 98
Dr. Martin Luther College, 250
Drake University, 204
Drew University, 273
Drexel University, 337
Dropsie University, 337
Drury College, 260
Duke University, 305
Duns Scotus College, 243
Duntroon Royal Military College, 3
Duquesne University, 337-338
Dyke College, 318

Earlham College, 196
East Carolina University, 305
East Central University, 327
East Tennessee State University, 362
East Texas Baptist University, 373
East Texas State University, 373
Eastbourne College of Education, 52
Eastern Arizona College, 139
Eastern College, 338
Eastern Connecticut State University, 162
Eastern Illinois University, 184
Eastern Kentucky University, 213
Eastern Mennonite College, 394
Eastern Michigan University, 243
Eastern Nazarene College, 233
Eastern New Mexico University, 280
Eastern Washington University, 403
Eberhard Karl University of Tubingen, 42
Ecole Polytechnique, 37
Eden Theological Seminary, 260
Edgewood College, 410
Edinboro University of Pennsylvania, 338
Edward Waters College, 170
El Camino College, 146
El Paso Junior College, 374
Elizabeth City State University, 306
Elizabethtown College, 338
Elmhurst College, 184
Elmira College, 286-287
Elon College, 306
Embry-Riddle Aeronautical University, 170
Emerson College, 233
Emmanuel College, GA, 175
Emmanuel College, MA, 233
Emory and Henry College, 394

Emory University, 175-176
Emporia State University, 209
Eotvos Lorand University, 85
Ernst Moritz Arndt University of Greifswald, 39
Erskine College, 355
Eureka College, 184
Evelyn College, 273
Evergreen State College, 403

Fairfield University, 162
Fairleigh Dickinson University, 274
Fairmont State College, 407
Faith Baptist Bible College, 204
Fayetteville State University, 306
Federal University of Minas Gerais, 11
Federal University of Para, 12
Federal University of Parana, 12
Fenn College, 317
Ferris State College, 243
Ferrum College, 394
Findlay College, 318
Fisk University, 362
Fitchburg State College, 233
Flint Community College, 244
Florida Agricultural and Mechanical University, 170
Florida International University, 170
Florida Southern College, 170
Florida State University, 171
Foothill College, 146
Fordham University, 287
Forest Park Junior College Center, 225
Fort Hays State University, 209
Fort Lewis College, 159
Fourah Bay College, 120
Framingham State College, 233-234
Francis Marion College, 355
Franklin and Marshall College, 338
Franklin College, IN, 196

Franklin College, TX, 374
Franklin Pierce College, 272
Free University of Berlin, 42-43
Free University of Brussels, 10
Friedrich Alexander University of Erlangen-Nuremberg, 43
Friedrich Schiller University of Jena, 39
Friends University, 209
Fukien Christian University, 28
Furman University, 355

Gadjah Mada University, 88
Gallaudet University, 167-168
Gardner-Webb College, 306
Garrett-Evangelical Theological Seminary, 184
General Theological Seminary, 287
Genesee Community College, 287
Geneva College, 338
Georg August University of Gottingen, 43
George Fox College, 331
George Washington University, 168
Georgetown College, 214
Georgetown University, 168
Georgia College, 176
Georgia Institute of Technology, 176
Georgia Southern College, 176
Georgia State University, 176
Georgian Court College, 274
Gettysburg College, 339
Gippsland Institute of Advanced Education, 4
GMI Engineering and Management Institute, 244
Goddard College, 390
Golden Gate Baptist Theological, Seminary, 146
Golden Gate University, 147
Gonzaga University, 403
Gonzales College, 374
Goodnight College, 374
Gordon Military College, 177
Gordon Technical College, 4

Gordon-Conwell Theological Seminary, 234
Goshen College, 196
Goucher College, 225
Government College, 112
Graceland College, 204
Graduate Theological Union, 147
Grambling State University, 218
Grand Canyon College, 139
Grand Valley State College, 244
Grand View College, 205
Gratz College, 339
Graylands Teachers College, 4
Green Mountain College, 390
Greensboro College, 306
Greenville College, 185
Greyson College, 374
Grinnell College, 205
Grove City College, 339-340
Guilford College, 306
Gulf Park College, 255
Gustavus Adolphus College, 251

Hagerstown Junior College, 225
Hahnemann University, 340
Hamilton College, 287
Hamline University, 251
Hampden-Sydney College, 394
Hampshire College, 234
Hampton University, 394-395
Hangchow Presbyterian College, 29
Hangchow University, 29
Hangzhou University, 29
Hanover College, 197
Hardin-Simmons University, 374
Harding University, 140
Harris-Stowe State College, 260
Hartford Seminary, 162
Hartwick College, 288
Harvard University, 234-236
Hastings College, 268
Haverford College, 340
Hebrew Union College-Jewish Institute of Religion, NY, 288
Hebrew Union College-Jewish Institute of Religion, OH, 318

Hebrew University of Jerusalem, 91
Heidelberg College, 318
Henderson State University, 140
Hendrix College, 141
Hershey Junior College, 340
Hertfordshire College of Agriculture and Horticulture, 53
Hesston College, 209
High Point College, 306
Hillcroft College, 53
Hillsboro College, 375
Hillsdale College, 244
Hiram College, 318-319
Hitotsubashi University, 98
Hobart and William Smith Colleges, 288
Hofstra University, 288
Hokkaido University, 98
Hollins College, 395, 396
Holly Royde College, 53
Holy Cross College of Calinan, 114
Holy Family College, 340
Hong Kong Baptist College, 84
Hope College, 244
Hosei University, 98
Houghton College, 288
Houston Baptist University, 375
Houston Community College, 375
Howard Payne University, 375
Howard University, 169
Huachung University, 29
Humboldt State University, 147
Humboldt University of Berlin, 39
Hunter College of the City University of New York, 289
Huntingdon College, AL, 133-134
Huntingdon College, IN, 197
Huron College, 359
Huston-Tillotson College, 375
Hwa Nan College, 29

Idaho State University, 181
Illinois College, 185
Illinois Institute of Technology, 185
Illinois State University, 186
Illinois Wesleyan University, 186
Incarnate Word College, 376
Indian River Community College, 171
Indiana State University, 197
Indiana University, 198
Indiana University of Pennsylvania, 341
Indiana University-Purdue University at Fort Wayne, 198
Indiana University-Purdue University at Indianapolis, 198
Institute of Paper Chemistry, 410
Iowa State University, 205
Iowa Wesleyan College, 205
Istanbul Woman's College, 130
Ithaca College, 289

Jackson State University, 255
Jacksonville State University, 134
Jacksonville University, 171
Jagiellonian University, 115-116
James Madison University, 396
Jamestown College, 312
Jamestown Community College, 289
Jana Ev. Purkyne University, 32
Japan Women's University, 98
Jarvis Christian College, 376
Jefferson College, 255
Jersey City State College, 274
Jesuit College of San Pablo, 113
Jewish Theological Seminary of America, 289
Johannes Gutenberg University of Mainz, 44
John A. Logan College, 186
John Brown University, 141
John Carroll University, 319
John Fletcher College, 198

Johns Hopkins University, 225-226
Johnson Bible College, 362
Johnson C. Smith University, 307
Johnson State College, 390
Joliet Junior College, 186
Jones County Junior College, 255
Jordan College, 245
Juanita College, 341
Juarez Autonomous University of Tabasco, 106
Jubilee College, 186
Judson College, 134
The Juilliard School, 289
Justus Liebig University of Giessen, 44

Kabul University, 1
Kalamazoo College, 245
Kansai University, 98
Kansas City College of Osteopathy and Surgery, 261
Kansas Newman College, 209
Kansas State University, 209-210
Kansas Wesleyan University, 210
Karl Marx University of Leipzig, 39-40
Kaskaskia College, 187
Katsina College, 110
Kean College of New Jersey, 274
Kearney State College, 268
Keene State College, 272
Keio University, 98
Kent State University, 319
Kentucky State University, 214
Kenyon College, 319
Keszthely Agricultural University, 85
Keuka College, 289
Kidd-Key College, 376
Kilgore College, 376
King Alfred's College, Winchester, 53
King's College, 130
Kingston Upon Hull Training College, 53

Kirkwood Community College, 205
Knox College, 187
Kobe College, 99
Kobe University, 99
Kogakkan University, 99
Kokushikan University, 100
Konan University, 100
Kumamoto University, 100
Kurume University, 100
Kutztown University, 341
Kyoto University, 100

Lackawanna Junior College, 341
Lafayette College, 341-342
LaGrange College, 177
Lake Forest College, 187
Lakehead University, 15
Lakeland College, 410
Lamar University, 376
Lambuth College, 363
Lane College, 363
Langston University, 327
La Salle University, 342
Lassell Junior College, 236
Lawrence University, 410
Lebanon Valley College, 342
Lee College, 363
Lehigh University, 342
Le Moyne College, 290
LeMoyne-Owen College, 363
Leningrad State University, 131
Lewis and Clark College, 331
Lexington Theological Seminary, 214
Limestone College, 356
Lincoln College, 187
Lincoln Memorial University, 363
Lincoln University, MO, 261
Lincoln University, PA, 342
Lindenwood College, 261
Linfield College, 331
Lingnan University, 29
Lisbon College, 117
Livingston University, 134
Livingstone College, 307
Lock Haven University, 343
Loma Linda University, 147
Lon Morris College, 377

464 / SUBJECT INDEX

Long Island University, 290
Longwood College, 396
Loras College, 205
Loretto Heights College, 159
Los Angeles City College, 147
Los Angeles Pierce College, 147
Los Angeles Southwest College, 147
Los Angeles Trade-Technical College, 148
Loughborough University, 53
Louisburg College, 307
Louisiana College, 219
Louisiana State University and Agricultural and Mechanical College, 219
Louisville Presbyterian Theological Seminary, 214
Loyola College, 226
Loyola University of Chicago, 187
Lund University, 126
Luther College, CAN, 23
Luther College, IA, 206
Lutheran School of Theology at Chicago, 188
Lutheran Theological Seminary of Philadelphia, 343
Lutheran Theological Southern Seminary, 356
Lycoming College, 343
Lynchburg College, 396

Macalester College, 251
McCormick Theological Seminary, 188
McGill University, 15
McKendree College, 188
McMaster University, 16-17
MacMurray College, 188
McMurry College, 377
McPherson College, 210
Madison College, 364
Madonna College, 245
Maharaja Sayajirao University of Baroda, 86
Maine Maritime Academy, 223
Malone College, 319
Manchester College, 199

Manhattan College, 290
Manhattan School of Music, 290
Mankato State University, 251
Marian College, 199
Marietta College, 320
Marillac College, 261
Marion College, 396
Marquette University, 410
Mars Hill College, 307
Marshall University, 407
Martha Washington College, 364
Martin Luther University of Halle-Wittenberg, 40
Martin Methodist College, 364
Marvin College, 377
Mary Baldwin College, 396
Mary Holmes College, 256
Mary Washington College, 397
Marymount College, 290
Marymount University, 397
Maryville College, 364
Marywood College, 343
Massachusetts College of Pharmacy, 236
Massachusetts Institute of Technology, 236-237
Matsuyama University, 100
Mayo College, 86
Mayville State College, 313
Meadville/Lombard Theological Seminary, 188
Medical College of Georgia, 177
Medical College of Pennsylvania, 343
Medical University of South Carolina, 356
Meharry Medical College, 364
Melbourne College of Advanced Education, 4
Memphis State University, 364-365
Menlo College, 148
Mennonite Biblical Seminary, 199
Mercer University, 177
Mercy Teachers College, 4
Meredith College, 308
Merrimack College, 237
Messiah College, 343

Methodist College, 79
Miami University, 320
Michigan State University, 245
Michocan University of Saint Nicholas of Hidalgo, 106
Middle Tennessee State University, 365
Middlebury College, 390
Midland College, 377
Midland Lutheran College, 268
Midwestern Baptist Theological Seminary, 261
Millersville University of Pennsylvania, 344
Mills College, 148
Millsaps College, 256
Milton College, 410
Miner Teachers College, 169
Minot State University, 313
Mira Costa College, 148
Mississippi College, 256
Mississippi State University, 256
Mississippi University for Women, 256
Mississippi Valley State University, 257
Missouri Valley College, 261
Missouri Western State College, 262
Mitchell College, 163
Moberly Junior College, 262
Monash University, 4
Monmouth College, 188
Montclair State College, 274
Montgomery College, 226
Monticello College, 189
Montreal Diocesan Theological College, 17
Moody Bible Institute, 189
Moore College of Art, 344
Moravian College, 344
Morehead State University, 215
Morehouse College, 177
Morgan State University, 226
Morris Brown College, 177
Morris College, 356
Morristown College, 365
Moscow State University, 131

Mount Allison University, 17
Mount Angel Seminary, 331
Mount Holyoke College, 237
Mount Lebanon University, 219
Mount Mary College, 411
Mount Mercy College, 206
Mount Saint Mary's College, 226
Mount Union College, 321
Muhlenberg College, 345
Murdoch University, 5
Murray State University, 215
Muskingum College, 321

Nagasaki University, 100
Nasson College, 223
National Autonomous University of Honduras, 84
National Autonomous University of Mexico, 106-107
National Ginling University, 29
National University, 88
National University of Cordoba, 2
National University of Costa Rica, 31
National University of Ireland, 89
National University of Nicaragua, 109
National University of San Marcos, 113
National University of the Ivory Coast, 97
Navajo Community College, 139
Nebraska Wesleyan University, 269
New Brunswick Theological Seminary, 274-274
New Mexico Highlands University, 280
New Mexico Institute of Mining and Technology, 280
New Mexico Military Institute, 280
New Mexico State University, 280
New Orleans Baptist Theological Seminary, 219

New School for Social Research, 290
New York City Technical College of the City University of New York, 291
New York Law School, 291
New York Theological Seminary, 291
New York University, 291
Newberry College, 356
Niagara County Community College, 291
Niagara University, 291
Nichols College, 237
Nihon University, 100
Niigata University, 101
Norfolk State University, 397
North Carolina Agricultural and Technical State University, 308
North Carolina Central University, 308
North Carolina State University, 308
North Central College, 189
North Central Technical College, 321
North Dakota State University, 313
North Greenville College, 357
North Park College, 189
Northeast Missouri State University, 262
Northeastern Illinois University, 189
Northeastern State University, 328
Northeastern University, 238
Northern Arizona University, 139
Northern Baptist Theological Seminary, 190
Northern Illinois University, 190
Northern Michigan University, 246
Northern Montana College, 266
Northern Oklahoma College, 328
Northland College, 411

Northland Pioneer College, 139
Northwest Bible College, 313
Northwest Christian College, 331
Northwest College of the Assemblies of God, 403
Northwest Missouri State University, 262
Northwest Nazarene College, 181
Northwestern College, IA, 206
Northwestern College, WI, 411
Northwestern State University of Louisiana, 219-220
Northwestern University, 190
Norwich University, 391
Nova Scotia Agricultural College, 17
Oakland City College, 199
Oakland Community College, 246
Oakland University, 246
Obafemi Awolowo University, 110
Oberlin College, 321-322
Occidental College, 148
Ochanomizu University, 101
Oglethorpe University, 178
Ohio Northern University, 322
Ohio State University, 322-323
Ohio University, 323
Ohio Wesleyan University, 323
Oklahoma Baptist University, 328
Oklahoma Christian College, 328
Oklahoma City University, 328
Oklahoma Panhandle State University, 328
Oklahoma Presbyterian College, 329
Oklahoma State University, 329
Okolona College, 257
Old Dominion University, 397
Olivet College, 246
Open University, 53-54
Oral Roberts University, 329
Orange Coast College, 149
Oregon Institute of Technology, 331
Oregon State University, 332
Ormond College, 4
Osaka University, 101

Osmania University, 86
Ottawa University, 210
Otterbein College, 323-324
Ouachita Baptist University, 141
Our Lady of Holy Cross College, 220
Our Lady of the Lake University, 377
Oxford College, 134
Pace University, 292
Pacific Christian College, 149
Pacific Lutheran University, 403
Pacific School of Religion, 149
Pacific Union College, 149
Pacific University, 332
Packer Collegiate Institute, 292
Paine College, 178
Palacky University, 33
Panjab University, 86
Paris Junior College, 377
Park College, 262
Parsons College, 206
Parsons School of Design, 292
Pasadena City College, 149
Patna University, 86
Paul Quinn College, 377
Paul Smiths College of Arts and Science, 292
Peabody Conservatory of Music, 226
Pennsylvania State University, 345
Peoples' Friendship University, 131
Pepperdine University, 149
Peru State College, 269
Philadelphia College of Osteopathic Medicine, 345
Philadelphia College of Pharmacy, 345
Philadelphia College of the Bible, 345
Philander Smith College, 141
Philippine Women's University, 114
Phillips University, 329

Philomath College, 332
Piedmont College, 178
Pillsbury Baptist Bible College, 252
Pine Manor College, 238
Pittsburg State University, 210-211
Point Park College, 345-346
Polytechnic University of New York, 292
Pomona College, 150
Portland State University, 332
Prairie View Agricultural and, Mechanical University, 378
Presbyterian College, CAN, 16
Presbyterian College, SC, 357
Presentation College, 10
Preston Polytechnic, 54
Prince Georges Community College, 227
Princeton Theological Seminary, 275
Princeton University, 275-277
Principia College, 190
Protestant Episcopal Theological Seminary in Virginia, 397
Providence College, 352
Purdue University, 199

Queens College, 308
Queens College of the City University of New York, 293
Queen Margaret College, 108
Queen's Theological College, 17-18
Queen's University at Kingston, 17
Queen's University of Belfast, 79

Radford University, 397
Randolph-Macon College, 398
Randolph-Macon Woman's College, 398
Ranger Junior College, 378
Reed College, 332
Regis College, 159
Reinhardt College, 178

Rensselaer Polytechnic
  Institute, 293
Rhenish Fredrich Wilhelm
  University of Bonn, 44-45
Rhode Island College, 352
Rhodes College, 365
Rhodes University, 120
Rice University, 378
Ricks College, 182
Rider College, 277
Rio Grande College, 324
Rio Hondo College, 150
Ripon College, 411
River Plate College, 2
Rivier College, 272
Riyadh University, 35
Roanoke College, 398
Roberts Wesleyan College, 294
Rochester Institute of
  Technology, 293
Rockefeller University, 293
Rockford College, 190-191
Rockhurst College, 263
Rollins College, 171-172
Roosevelt University, 191
Rosary College, 191
Rose-Hulman Institute of
  Technology, 200
Royal College of Art, 54
Royal College of Music, 54
Royal College of Surgeons in
  Ireland, 90
Royal College of Surgeons of
  England, 54
Royal Melbourne Institute of
  Technology, 5
Royal Military College of
  Canada, 18
Rupert Charles University of
  Heidelberg, 45-46
Rusk Baptist College, 378
Ruskin College, 54
Russell Sage College, 294
Rust College, 257
Rutgers, The State University
  of New Jersey, 277-278

Sacramento Junior College, 150
Sacred Heart Seminary, 246

St. Aidan's College, 120
St. Alban's College, 122
St. Andrew's College, 110
St. Andrew's Presbyterian
  College, NEW ZEA, 108
St. Andrews Presbyterian
  College, NC, 309
Saint Anselm College, 272
Saint Augustine's College, 309
St. Bonaventure University, 294
Saint Charles Borromeo
  Seminary, 346
St. Charles' College, 227
St. Cloud State University, 252
Saint David's University
  College, 82
St. Edward's University, 378
Saint Francis College, IN, 200
St. Francis College, NY, 294
Saint Francis Seminary, School
  of Pastoral Ministry, 411
St. John Fisher College, 294
St. John's College, SOU AFR,
  120
St. John's College, MD, 227
St. John's Seminary, 238
St. John's University, China,
  29-30
Saint John's University, MN,
  252
Saint Joseph College,
  Phillipines, 114
St. Joseph's College, MD, 227
Saint Joseph's Seminary, 294
Saint Joseph's University, 346
St. Lawrence University, 295
Saint Louis College of
  Pharmacy, 263
Saint Louis University, 263
Saint Mary-of-the Woods
  College, 200
Saint Mary's College, ENG, 54
Saint Mary's College, IN, 200
Saint Mary's College, MD, 227
Saint Mary's College, MI, 246
Saint Mary's College of
  California, 150
Saint Olaf College, 252
St. Paul's College, MO, 263

Saint Paul's College, VA, 398
St. Peter's College, ENG, 55
Saint Peter's College, NJ, 278
St. Philip's College, 379
St. Stanlaus College, 5
St. Vladimir's Orthodox Theological Seminary, 295
Salem College, 309
Salem State College, 239
Salisbury State College, 227
Sam Houston State University, 379
Samford University, 134
San Antonio College, 379
San Francisco State University, 150
San Francisco Theological Seminary, 151
San Jose State University, 151
San Luis Obispo Junior College, 151
Sandhurst Royal Military College, 55
Santa Clara University, 151, 152
Sarah Lawrence College, 295
Satya Wacana Christian University, 88
Scarritt Graduate School, 365
School of Mines and Industry, Ballarat, 5
School of the Ozarks, 264
Seattle Pacific University, 404
Seattle University, 404
Seinan Gakuin University, 101
Seisen Women's College, 101
Seminary of the Imaculate Conception, 295
Senshu University, 101
Sequatchie College, 366
Seton Hall University, 278
Seton Hill College, 346
Shantung Christian University, 30
Shaw University, 309
Sheldon Jackson College, 138
Shenandoah College and Conservatory of Music, 398
Shepherd College, 407

Sheridan College, 413
Shippensburg University, 346
Shorter College, 178
Shurtleff College, 191
Siena College, 295
Silliman Junior College, 220
Silliman University, 114
Simmons College, 239
Simmons University, 215
Simon Fraser University, 18
Sinclair Community College, 324
Sioux Falls College, 359
Skidmore College, 295
Slippery Rock University, 347
Smith College, 239
Snead State Junior College, 135
Snow College, 388, 389
Soochow University, 129
South Carolina State College, 357
South Dakota State University, 359-360
Southeast Missouri State University, 264
Southeastern Illinois College, 191
Southeastern Louisiana University, 220
Southeastern Massachusetts University, 239
Southern Arkansas University, 141
Southern Baptist Theological Seminary, 215
Southern California College of Optometry, 152
Southern College of Seventh-Day Adventists, 366
Southern Illinois University at Carbondale, 191-192
Southern Illinois University at Edwardsville, 192
Southern Methodist University, 379-380
Southern Nazarene University, 329
Southern Seminary Junior College, 399

470 / SUBJECT INDEX

Southern Union State Junior College, 135
Southern University and Agricultural and Mechanical College, 220
Southern University of Chile, 28
Southern Utah State College, 389
Southwest Baptist University, 264
Southwest Missouri State University, 264
Southwest Texas Junior College, 380
Southwest Texas State University, 380
Southwestern Assemblies of God College, 380
Southwestern Baptist Theological Seminary, 380
Southwestern Christian College, 381
Southwestern Oklahoma State University, 329
Southwestern University, 381
Spelman College, 179
Spring Arbor College, 247
Spring Hill College, 135
Springfield College in Illinois, 192
Stanford University, 152-153
State University of Ghent, 10
State University of Leiden, 107
State University of Liege, 11
State University of New York at Albany, 296
State University of New York at Binghamton, 296
State University of New York at Buffalo, 297
State University of New York College at Brockport, 297
State University of New York College at Cortland, 297
State University of New York College at Fredonia, 297
State University of New York College at Geneseo, 298

State University of New York College at New Paltz, 298
State University of New York College at Oneonta, 298
State University of New York College at Oswego, 298
State University of New York College at Plattsburgh, 298
State University of New York College at Potsdam, 299
State University of New York College of Environmental Science and Forestry, 299
State University of Utrecht, 108
Stephen F. Austin State University, 381
Stephens College, 264
Sterling College, 211
Stetson University, 172
Stevens Institute of Technology, 278
Stillman College, 135
Stockton State College, 278
Stonewall Jackson College, 399
Sue Bennett College, 215
Sul Ross University, 381
Summerland College, 357
Susquehanna University, 347
Swarthmore College, 347
Sweet Briar College, 399
Swiss Federal Institute of Technology, 127
Syiah Kuala University, 89
Syracuse University, 299

Tabor College, 211
Talladega College, 135
Tallahassee Community College, 172
Tarleton State University, 381
Tartu State University, 131
Taylor University, 200
Teachers College, Columbia University, 299
Technical University of Berlin, 46
Technical University of Cracow, 116

Technical University of Dresden, 40-41
Technical University of Lisbon, 117
Technical University of Poznan, 116
Technical University of Szczecin, 116
Technical University of Warsaw, 116
Temple Junior College, 382
Temple University, 347
Tennessee State University, 366
Tennessee Technological University, 366
Tennessee Wesleyan College, 366
Texas Agricultural and Mechanical University, 382
Texas Christian University, 382-383
Texas Lutheran College, 383
Texas Presbyterian College, 383
Texas Southern University, 383
Texas Tech University, 384
Texas Wesleyan College, 384
Texas Woman's University, 384
Thiel College, 347
Thomas Jefferson University, 348
Thomas More College, 215
Thompson, George E., 109
Three Rivers Community College, 264
Tift College, 179
Tokai University, 102
Tokyo Women's Christian University, 102
Tougaloo College, 257
Transylvania University, 216
Trenton State College, 279
Trevecca Nazarene College, 366
Tri-State University, 201
Trinidad State Junior College, 159

Trinity College, CT, 163
Trinity College, DC, 169
Trinity College, VT, 391
Trinity College of Music, 55
Trinity Evangelical Divinity School, 192
Trinity Lutheran Seminary, 324
Trinity University, 384-385
Trinity Western University, 18
Troy State University, 135-136
Truett McConnell College, 179
Tufts University, 239-240
Tulane University, 220-221
Tunghai University, 129
Tusculum College, 367
Tuskegee University, 136-137
Twickenham College of Technology, 55
Tyler Junior College, 385

Udayana State University, 89
Umm Al-Qura University, 119
Union Christian College, 201
Union College, CAN, 19
Union College, KY, 216
Union College, NE, 269
Union College, NY, 299-300
Union County College, 279
Union Theological Seminary, 300
Union University, 367
United Nations University, 102
United States Air Force Academy, 159-160
United States Coast Guard Academy, 163
United States Merchant Marine Academy, 301
United States Military Academy, 301
United States Naval Academy, 228
Universidad International Menendez Pelayo, 122
Universidad Nacional Pedro Henriquez Urena, 34
University College of Aberystwyth, 82
University College of North Wales, Bangor, 82

472 / SUBJECT INDEX

University College, Cardiff, 82
University College, Cork, 90
University College, Dublin, 90
University of Aarhus, 33
University of Aberdeen, 79
University of Adelaide, 5
University of Aix-Marsielles, 37
University of Akron, 324
University of Alabama, 137
University of Alabama in Huntsville, 137
University of Alberta, 19
University of Alcala de Hernares, 122
University of Amsterdam, 108
University of Arizona, 139
University of Arkansas, 141
University of Arkansas at Little Rock, 142
University of Arkansas at Pine Bluff, 142
University of Auckland, 108
University of Augsburg, 46
University of Baghdad, 89
University of Barcelona, 122
University of Bari, 92
University of Basel, 127
University of Bath, 55
University of Belgrade, 416
University of Berlin, 39
University of Berne, 128
University of Birmingham, 56
University of Bologna, 92
University of Bombay, 86
University of Bonn, 44
University of Bridgeport, 163
University of Bristol, 56
University of British Columbia, 19
University of Bucharest, 119
University of Buenos Aires, 2
University of Caen, 37
University of Calcutta, 87
University of Calgary, 19
University of California, Berkeley, 153-154
University of California, Davis 154

University of California, Irvine, 154
University of California, Los Angeles, 154-155
University of California, Santa Barbara, 155
University of California, Santa Cruz, 155
University of Cambridge, 56-64
University of Can-Tho, 416
University of Canterbury, 108-109
University of Cape Town, 121
University of Charleston, 407
University of Chicago, 192-193
University of Chile, 28
University of Cincinnati, 325
University of Coimbra, 118
University of Cologne, 47
University of Colorado, 160
University of Connecticut, 163
University of Constance, 47
University of Copenhagen, 33
University of Cordoba, 123
University of Costa Rica, 31
University of Cuenca, 34
University of Dacca, 9
University of Dayton, 325
University of Delaware, 166
University of Delhi, 87
University of Denver, 160-161
University of Detroit, 247
University of Deusto, 123
University of Dublin, 90-91
University of Duisburg, 47
University of Dundee, 79
University of Durham, 64-65
University of Edinburgh, 80
University of El Salvador, 35
University of Erlangen-Nuremberg, 43
University of Essex, 65
University of Evansville, 201
University of Exeter, 65
University of Ferrara, 92-93
University of Florence, 93
University of Florida, 172

SUBJECT INDEX / 473

University of Fort Hare, 121
University of Gdansk, 116
University of Geneva, 128
University of Genoa, 93
University of Georgia, 179
University of Ghana, 50
University of Giessen, 44
University of Glasgow, 80-81
University of Gottingen, 43
University of Granada, 123
University of Graz, 7-8
University of Greifswald, 39
University of Grenoble, 37
University of Guadalajara, 107
University of Guanajuato, 107
University of Guelph, 19-20
University of Halifax, 20
University of Halle-Wittenberg, 40
University of Hamburg, 47
University of Hannover, 47
University of Havana, 32
University of Hawaii, 180-181
University of Hawaii at Manoa, 181
University of Heidelberg, 45-46
University of Helsinki, 36
University of Hohenheim, 47
University of Hong Kong, 84
University of Houston, 385
University of Hull, 65
University of Ibadan, 111
University of Iceland, 85
University of Idaho, 182
University of Illinois, 193
University of Ilorin, 111
University of Indianapolis, 201
University of Innsbruck, 8
University of Iowa, 206-207
University of Istanbul, 130
University of Jena, 39
University of Jyvaskyla, 36
University of Kansas, 211-212
University of Karlsruhe, 48
University of Keele, 65
University of Kentucky, 216-217
University of Kiel, 41-42

University of King's College, 20
University of La Verne, 155
University of Lagos, 111
University of Lancaster, 65
University of Las Villas, 32
University of Laval, 20-21
University of Leeds, 65
University of Leipzig, 39-40
University of Lethbridge, 21
University of Liberia, 104
University of Lisbon, 118
University of Liverpool, 66
University of London, 66-68
University of Louisville, 217
University of Macerata, 93
University of Madras, 87
University of Madrid, 123
University of Maine, 223
University of Maine at Farmington, 223
University of Mainz, 44
University of Malawi, 104
University of Manitoba, 21-22
University of Mannheim, 48
University of Marburg, 48
University of Mary Hardin-Baylor, 385-386
University of Maryland, 228
University of Maryland Eastern Shore, 228
University of Massachusetts, 240
University of Melbourne, 6
University of Miami, 173
University of Michigan, 247-248
University of Michigan-Dearborn, 248
University of Michigan-Flint, 248
University of Minnesota, 252-253
University of Minnesota-Morris, 253
University of Mississippi, 258
University of Missouri, 265
University of Missouri-Kansas City, 265

474 / SUBJECT INDEX

University of Missouri-Rolla, 265
University of Modena, 93
University of Moncton, 22
University of Montana, 267
University of Montevello, 137
University of Montreal, 22
University of Moscow, 131-132
University of Munich, 48-49
University of Munster, 49
University of Murcia, 123
University of Nairobi, 103
University of Naples, 94
University of Natal, 121
University of Nebraska, 269
University of Nebraska at Omaha, 270
University of Nevada, 270
University of New Brunswick, 22-23
University of New England, 6
University of New Hampshire, 272
University of New Mexico, 281
University of New South Wales, 6
University of Newcastle Upon Tyne, 68
University of Nigeria, 111
University of North Alabama, 137
University of North Carolina at Chapel Hill, 309-311
University of North Carolina at Charlotte, 311
University of North Carolina at Greensboro, 311
University of North Carolina at Wilmington, 311
University of North Dakota, 313
University of North Florida, 173
University of North Texas, 386
University of Northern Colorado, 161
University of Northern Iowa, 207
University of Notre Dame, 201-202

University of Nottingham, 68
University of Oklahoma, 330
University of Oldenburg, 49
University of Oregon, 332-333
University of Oslo, 112
University of Osnabruck, 49
University of Otago, 109
University of Ottawa, 23
University of Oulu, 36
University of Oviedo, 124
University of Oxford, 69-77
University of Padua, 94
University of Palermo, 94
University of Paris, 37-38
University of Parma, 95
University of Patna, 87
University of Pavia, 95
University of Pennsylvania, 348-349
University of Perugia, 95
University of Peshawar, 112
University of Pisa, 96
University of Pittsburgh, 349
University of Pittsburgh at Johnstown, 349
University of Poitiers, 39
University of Poona, 88
University of Portland, 333
University of Prince Edward Island, 23
University of Puerto Rico, 118-119
University of Puget Sound, 404
University of Quebec, 23
University of Quebec at Trois-Rivieres, 23
University of Queensland, 6-7
University of Rangoon, 13
University of Reading, 77
University of Redlands, 155
University of Regina, 23
University of Rhode Island, 353
University of Richmond, 399
University of Rio de Janeiro, 12
University of Rochester, 302
University of Rostock, 41
University of Salamanca, 124
University of Salford, 77

University of Salzburg, 8
University of St. Andrews, 81
University of San Andres, 11
University of San Carlos, 114
University of San Carlos of Guatemala, 83
University of San Francisco, 156
University of Santiago de Compostela, 125
University of Santo Domingo, 34
University of Santo Tomas, Colombia, 31
University of Santo Tomas, Phillipines, 114-115
University of Sao Paulo, 12
University of Saragosa, 125
University of Saskatchewan, 24
University of Sassari, 96
University of Seville, 125
University of Shanghai, 30
University of Sheffield, 77
University of Sherbrooke, 25
University of Siena, 96
University of Sierra Leone, 120
University of Sofia, 13
University of South Africa, 121
University of South Carolina, 357-358
University of South Dakota, 360
University of South Florida, 173
University of Southampton, 77
University of Southern California, 156
University of Southern Maine, 223
University of Southern Mississippi, 258
University of Southwestern, Louisiana, 221
University of Stellenbosch, 121
University of Stockholm, 127
University of Strathclyde, 81
University of Stuttgart, 49-50
University of Sudbury, 25
University of Surrey, 77
University of Sussex, 77

University of Sydney, 7
University of Tampa, 173
University of Tennessee, 367-368
University of Tennessee at Chattanooga, 368
University of Tennessee at Martin, 368
University of Texas at Arlington, 386
University of Texas at Austin, 386
University of Texas at El Paso, 387
University of Texas Medical, Branch at Galveston, 387
University of the Andes, 415
University of the Azores, 118
University of the District of Columbia, 169
University of the Ozarks, 142
University of the Pacific, 156-157
University of the Philippines, 115
University of the Republic, 414-415
University of the Ryukyus, 102
University of the South, 368-369
University of the West Indies, Antigua and Barbuda, 1
University of the West Indies, Jamaica, 97
University of the West Indies, Trinidad and Tobago, 130
University of Toledo, 325
University of Toronto, 25-26
University of Tottori, 102
University of Toulouse, 39
University of Trabajo, 415
University of Trier, 50
University of Tromso, 112
University of Tsukuba, 102
University of Tubingen, 42
University of Tulsa, 330
University of Turin, 96-97
University of Turku, 36
University of Ulm, 50

University of Urbino, 97
University of Utah, 389
University of Valencia, 126
University of Valladolid, 126
University of Vermont, 391-392
University of Vienna, 8-9
University of Vilnius, 132
University of Virginia, 399-400
University of Wales, 82-83
University of Warsaw, 117
University of Washington, 404
University of Waterloo, 26
University of Western Australia, 7
University of Western Ontario, 26-27
University of Windsor, 27
University of Winnipeg, 27
University of Wisconsin-Eau Claire, 411
University of Wisconsin-La Crosse, 411
University of Wisconsin-Madison, 412
University of Wisconsin-Milwaukee, 412
University of Wisconsin-Platteville, 412-413
University of Wisconsin-River Falls, 413
University of Wisconsin-Stevens Point, 413
University of Wisconsin-Whitewater, 413
University of Witwatersrand, 121-122
University of Wroclaw, 117
University of Wurzburg, 50
University of Wyoming, 414
University of Zagreb, 416
University of Zulia, 416
University of Zurich, 129
Uppsala University, 127
Upsala College, 279
Urbana University, 326
Ursinus College, 349
Ushaw College, 78
Utah State University, 389

Utica Junior College, 258

Valdosta State College, 180
Valley City State College, 313-314
Valley Forge Military Junior College, 350
Valparaiso University, 202
Vanderbilt University, 369-370
Vassar College, 302-303
Ventura College, 157
Victoria College, 28
Victoria University of Manchester, 78
Victoria University of Wellington, 109
Villanova University, IN, 202
Villanova University, PA, 350
Vincennes University, 203
Virginia Commonwealth University, 401
Virginia Military Institute, 401
Virginia Polytechnic Institute and State University, 401
Virginia State University, 402
Virginia Union University, 402
Voorhees College, 358

Wabash College, 203
Wabash Valley College, 194
Wake Forest University, 311
Walla Walla College, 404
Warren Wilson College, 311
Wartburg College, 207
Waseda University, 102
Washington and Jefferson College, 350
Washington and Lee University, 402
Washington College, MD, 229
Washington College, TN, 370
Washington State University, 405
Washington University, 265
Wayne State University, 248
Waynesburg College, 350
Wellesley College, 240
Wells College, 303-304

Wesley College, Nigeria, 112
Wesley College, Sri Lanka, 126
Wesley College, DE, 166
Wesley College, TX, 387
Wesley Theological Seminary, 170
Wesleyan College, 180
Wesleyan University, 163-164
Wessington Springs Junior College, 360
West Chester University, 350
West Coast Christian College, 157
West Liberty State College, 408
West Los Angeles College, 157
West Texas State University, 387
West Virginia State College, 408
West Virginia University, 408
West Virginia Wesleyan College, 408
Western Carolina University, 312
Western Connecticut State University, 164
Western Conservative Baptist Seminary, 333
Western Evangelical Seminary, 333
Western Illinois University, 194
Western Kentucky University, 217-218
Western Maryland College, 229
Western Michigan University, 248-249
Western Montana College, 267
Western New England College, 240
Western New Mexico University, 281
Western State College of Colorado, 161
Western University, 212
Western Washington University, 405
Westfield State College, 240-241

Westmar College, 208
Westminister Choir College, 279
Westminster College, ENG, 78
Westminster College, MO, 266
Westminister College, PA, 351
Westminster College, UT, 389
Westmont College, 157
Wheaton College, IL, 194
Wheaton College, MA, 241
Wheelock College, 241
Whitman College, 405
Whittier College, 157
Whitworth College, MS, 258
Whitworth College, WA, 406
Wichita State University, 212
Widener University, 351
Wilberforce University, 326
Wiley College, 388
Wilfrid Laurier University, 27
Willamette University, 333
William Jewell College, 266
William Paterson College of New Jersey, 279
William Penn College, 208
William Woods College, 266
Williams College, 241
Wilmington College, 326
Wilson College, 351
Wingate College, 312
Winona State University, 253
Winston Churchill College, 194
Winthrop College, 358
Wittenberg University, 326-327
Wofford College, 358
Woodstock College, 229
Worcester Polytechnic Institute, 241-242
Working Men's College, 78
World University, 119

Xavier Pontificia University, 31
Xavier University, 327

Yadkin College, 312
Yale University, 164-165
Yamaguchi University, 103
Yampa Valley College, 158

Yankton College, ND, 314
Yankton College, SD, 360
Yenching University, 30
Yeshiva University, 304
York College, 270
York University, 27

Young Harris College, 180
Youngstown State University 327

Zhongshan (Sun Yat-sen) University, 30

About the Compiler

LINDA SPARKS is Associate Librarian, Education Library, University of Florida at Gainesville. She is the author of *American College Regalia: A Handbook* (Greenwood Press, 1988).